Stanislas Graham Bower St. Clair, Charles A. Brophy

A Residence in Bulgaria

Or, notes on the resources and administration of Turkey, the condition and

character, manners, customs, and language of the Christian and Musselman

populations, with reference to the Easter question

Stanislas Graham Bower St. Clair, Charles A. Brophy

A Residence in Bulgaria

Or, notes on the resources and administration of Turkey, the condition and character, manners, customs, and language of the Christian and Musselman populations, with reference to the Easter question

ISBN/EAN: 9783337299323

Printed in Europe, USA, Canada, Australia, Japan

Cover: Foto ©ninafisch / pixelio.de

More available books at **www.hansebooks.com**

A

RESIDENCE IN BULGARIA;

OR,

NOTES ON THE RESOURCES AND ADMINISTRATION OF TURKEY:

THE CONDITION AND CHARACTER, MANNERS, CUSTOMS, AND LANGUAGE
OF THE CHRISTIAN AND MUSSULMAN POPULATIONS,
WITH REFERENCE TO THE EASTERN QUESTION.

BY

S. G. B. ST. CLAIR, Capt.,
Late 21st Fusiliers.

AND

CHARLES A. BROPHY.

LONDON:
JOHN MURRAY, ALBEMARLE STREET.
1869.

The right of Translation is reserved.

DEDICATION.

WE dedicate this book to J. A. Longworth, Esq., Her British Majesty's Consul-General in Servia, as an expression of respect for the long experience which has enabled him to judge accurately between the different races and creeds of European Turkey, and especially for the courage with which he has expressed (in his Report to the Foreign Office, dated Belgrade, April 7th, 1867) opinions entirely contrary to the general prejudices of Western Europe, but none the less founded on truth and justice.

THE AUTHORS.

PREFACE.

In justification of the Authors' attempt to describe something of a country, which although but five or six days distant from England, is almost as little known as the interior of Africa, it is incumbent upon them to set forth such qualifications as they possess for the task.

One of them has lived in Bulgaria for nearly three years, and, besides many years' experience of Eastern Europe and its peoples, knows Turkish well, and is thoroughly acquainted with all Slavonic languages and dialects, amongst the latter of which Bulgaria is of course classed; the other has spent eighteen months in the same village, and has a fair knowledge of Turkish.

The Authors' head-quarters are a Christian village amongst the hills of the Balkans, where they have learnt to know the Bulgarian Rayah better than if they had resided for twenty years in a town. In the course of many shooting excursions in this and the neighbouring provinces, they have been thrown into close, and in most cases very pleasant, relations with the Mussulman populations — Turks, Tartars, Circassians, and Arnaouts. Not requiring the aid of an interpreter, and trusting to their guns as escort, they have had opportunities of hearing the unvarnished truth from Mussulman and Christian, such as would scarcely fall to the lot of a traveller accompanied by a dragoman or an escort of soldiers.

As an excuse for the many shortcomings and defects of their book, the Authors must state that it was written without the possibility of access to any works of reference, either historical or statistical, and amidst many interruptions from illness and other causes.

When this work was commenced some months since, it was intended to be merely a description of the manners and customs of the people, but as it proceeded, the Authors found themselves irresistibly compelled to allude to the many grievances and defects of organization which distinguish this country above all others, and thus the book has assumed a more political character than they at first intended.

The Authors have certainly no claims to be considered either politicians or political economists, but what they have written is the plain and literal truth, and the inferences drawn therefrom are such as must strike any disinterested person who knows the country districts of Turkey in Europe. In all that they have stated there is not a single instance of mere hearsay, nor have they ever received the allegations of either Mussulman or Christian without inquiring into and satisfying themselves of their accuracy.

The names of individuals which are screened by initials can be given to any one, Philhellene or other, who may be sufficiently interested in the subjects to desire them, as also those of the persons whom the Authors have designated under fictitious names; there is not an anecdote nor an assertion in the book which the Authors are not prepared to prove and substantiate.

What is written about the Eastern Church will probably shock the preconceived ideas of many people in England, but what foundation have these ideas beyond the imaginary tie of a common religion—imaginary, for the Greek religion as practised has nothing in common with our national faith—and sympathy for a people who are falsely supposed to be suffering and oppressed? It is but eighteen months ago that one of the Authors landed in Bulgaria, bringing with him the usual English prejudices in favour of Oriental Christianity and Eastern Christians; how far those opinions have been modified by experience, may be judged from the book itself.

The Rayah has been too much whitewashed by his numerous interested or disinterested admirers, political or sentimental, whilst the Turk has been too much blackwashed by his enemies, or those who know nothing about him, and is very much in the condition of the Scotch minister's client, "Naebody prays for the puir de'il." If the Authors should succeed in convincing their readers that both Christian and Mussulman have been greatly misrepresented in Western Europe, and that the country which they inhabit might and would, if left to a genuine Turkish administration untrammelled by foreign influence, become one of the most flourishing and powerful in the world, the object of this work will have been attained.

DEREKCUI,
  May, 1868.

CONTENTS.

CHAPTER I.

RAYAH VILLAGES OF BULGARIA.

First aspect — The village public — An interior — The gipsy quarter — Habits of the gipsies — "Notice to quit" .. .. Page 1

CHAPTER II.

RAYAH VILLAGES OF BULGARIA.—(*Continued.*)

The traveller's reception — Family meal — Bulgarian features and physique — Ordinary costume — Holyday costume — Gagaous or mixed race — A hard bed — The traveller's reckoning — Bulgarian charges — Hospitality of the Turks 12

CHAPTER III.

ROADS AND MEANS OF COMMUNICATION.

Devious routes — Repair or go round ? — Difficult locomotion — Employés classified — Mithat Pasha's road — Worse than none — A remedy suggested — Varna railroad — Postal irregularities — Telegraph clerks .. 24

CHAPTER IV.

BULGARIAN SUPERSTITIONS.

Paganism and witchcraft tolerated by the Church — Feast of all Nature — Switch day — Dipping day — Bacchantes — A day of mortification for the dogs — All Souls — Feast of Constantine — Miraculous fish — Feast of serpents — Old Mother March — St. George's: why lambs are sacrificed — The Panagia — Feast of pigs — Novel sins — The Vampire — Fountain spirits — Spirit treasure-guardians — Ghosts of the Turks — Our success as exorcists — Notions of a future state 36

CHAPTER V.

BULGARIAN SUPERSTITIONS (*continued*).—MANNERS AND CUSTOMS, ETC.

Witches — Herbalist and poisoner — Prescriptions for a fever — Exorcism sought from the Turkish Hodja — Strictness of morals — Family jars — Birth and infancy — A suitor and his negotiations — The betrothal — The wedding — Dances — The last fashion — Death and burial — mourners .. .. Page 62

CHAPTER VI.

BULGARIAN SONGS.

Spurious literature — Bulgarian language — Deli Marko's match with the Evil One — Philip Junak's boasting — Deli Marko's performance — Joanczo Krym Pehlivanczo — Preparations for the encounter — The Czar's bear overcome — King Marko — Arrival at Philip the Magyar's — A long swim — Combat with a Lomota — The hero's return — Seferina rejected — Legends of other races compared 78

CHAPTER VII.

EASTERN CHRISTIANITY, AND ITS EFFECTS IN BULGARIA.

Feasts and fast-days economically considered — The Bulgarian catechized — The clergy seek union with Rome — Rejected as unworthy — A curacy in Bulgaria — The rector — The parishioners — Fasting — Holy water — Extortion of the priests — Reforms suggested 96

CHAPTER VIII.

BRIGANDAGE IN THE BALKAN.

Ignorance of Consuls accounted for — The Gentleman of the Forest — Generosity — The common Highwayman — Laissez aller — The Outlaw — Justice defeated — A Dogstealer 115

CHAPTER IX.

ORIENTAL COMMERCE.

A dishonesty which defies competition — A good stroke of business — Cent. per cent. for the merchant, but the producer suffers — Privilege of a Greek subject — Country agents — A little usury — Rising in life — Non-Greek foreign merchants — Base is the slave that pays — A swarm of locusts .. .. Page 132

CHAPTER X.

THE REAL POSITION OF THE BULGARIAN RAYAH, HIS SYSTEM OF AGRICULTURE, ETC.

Taxes on Agriculture — Neglect of Manure — Ploughing — "Why grow more?" — Reaping — Six weeks' feast — Grain carried — Threshing — Vintage — Sheep Farming — Who is the injured party? 148

CHAPTER XI.

THE EXEMPTION OF THE RAYAH FROM MILITARY SERVICE, AND ITS EFFECTS UPON THE TURK.

Misconception prevailing in Europe — Original land-tenure — Alteration in consequence of so-called military reforms — Unequal burden imposed on the industry of the Turk by military service — Reform suggested 162

CHAPTER XII.

THE TAXES OF TURKEY.

Taxes, personal and on property — Inequality of property-tax — Dime and its farming — Consequent loss to the revenue — Mode of collection, and injury to the cultivator — Pleas against reform — A land-tax suggested — Already exists in the case of vineyards — Customs — Corvée — Extraordinary contributions 174

CHAPTER XIII.

THE TENURE OF LANDED PROPERTY; THE TAPOU, THE MIRA, THE RIGHT OF FOREIGNERS TO POSSESS LAND.

Registration of occupancy — Sometimes abused to the fraudulent acquisition of title — Undeserved liberality of the Government — Right of pasturage — Leads to loss of production, illegal destruction of timber, and winter starvation of cattle — Probable results of a European immigration — Let the settlers bring their own merchants .. .. Page 186

CHAPTER XIV.

WHAT THE BULGARIANS WISH FOR, AND WHAT THEY DO NOT WISH FOR.

Writers in the pay of Russia — Too much experience of Russian promises — The Bulgarian does not wish what he is supposed to wish — Unambitious minds — Exceptions 205

CHAPTER XV.

TARTAR AND CIRCASSIAN IMMIGRANTS.

Emigration of Crimean Tartars to Turkey — Broken promises, Russian and Turkish — Appearance and manners — Industry and care in agriculture — Circassian immigration — Bad cultivation and poverty — Cattle and horse stealing — Hospitality — Abstinence — Circassian encampment — Unselfishness — May prove useful as warriors 212

CHAPTER XVI.

TURKS OF THE TOWN AND TURKS OF THE COUNTRY.

A Parisian education — Début at Constantinople — A veteran — Town Turks classified — Family life — Rustic integrity — The road sent to Coventry — Confession of fault — Education — The priest and the schoolmaster — Energy — Ballads — Intellectual evenings — A theft rebuked 227

CHAPTER XVII.

RELATIVE POSITIONS OF TOWN AND COUNTRY.

Constantinople and many other towns exempt from taxation — Encouragement to fraudulent commerce — Monomania à la Haussman — Favouritism towards foreigners — Stamp tax licenses and town property tax — "Improvements" at Varna .. .. Page 241

CHAPTER XVIII.

BRITISH CONSULS AND THE CONSULAR REPORTS.

Gammoning a Consul — Harrowing tale — The truth discovered — Consular entourage — Consular dignity — Bullying a Pasha — The reports — Preliminary statements by the authors — Consular complaints from Rustchuk, Smyrna, Kustendje, Salonica, and Prevesa (South Albania) — Trial of Greek autonomy in the Sporades — Vice-Consul Dupuis (Salonica) — Reports from Aleppo, West and East Macedonia, Adrianople, Scutari, Beyrout, Jerusalem, Cyprus, and Janina — Consul-General Longworth (Belgrade) — Reports from Brussa and Trebizonde 252

CHAPTER XIX.

THE CAPITULATIONS.

Prejudice of foreign residents — Origin of the Capitulations — Privilege of a Greek subject — Codes of law innumerable — Justice defeated — Try Turkish tribunals 294

CHAPTER XX.

THE POLICY OF FOREIGN POWERS IN TURKEY, AND ITS EFFECTS.

Russian agents — Russian ecclesiastical intrigue — Mysteries of French policy — No-policy of England — Religious equality — Attacks on the Ulema — Save me from my friends — Colonel Bobrikoff's scientific mission — A thankless task — French civilization — French intervention — The day of retribution — Educate the Rayah — Considerations of expediency — England's true policy 305

CHAPTER XXI.

THE ARMY AND THE MILITARY RESOURCES OF TURKEY.

Born soldiers — Exploits in the last war — English generalship and commissariat at Balaklava — French uniforms — Onerous service of the militia — Organize volunteers — Expense of the militia — Requisites for volunteers and estimated expense — Christian non-combatant corps
Page 336

CHAPTER XXII.

GOVERNMENT AND GOVERNMENT FUNCTIONARIES, ADMINISTRATION OF JUSTICE, ETC. ETC.

Authority of the Sultan — Edict of Gul Hane — The future regenerator — Temporizing policy — Palace of the Porte — Palace of a Pasha — A mixed assemblage — The Cadis and the Medjliss 355

CHAPTER XXIII.

TURKISH REFORMS AND REFORMERS.

Races unfit for liberty — Denationalizing reforms — Despatch of Fuad Pasha — "The tax of blood" — Mussulman troops and Christian officers — Extreme concessions — A village Medjliss or council — The Vilayets 368

CHAPTER XXIV.

MITHAT PASHA.

Mithat Pasha's attempted reforms — Suppression of brigandage — Secularization of education — Inspection of weights and measures — The Agio — Lending banks — Orphanages — Recovery from Philorayahism .. 384

CHAPTER XXV.

THE POLITICAL PARTIES OF TURKEY.

Bulgarian politicians — The project of independence — The project of autonomy — Young Turkey — Old Turkey .. .. Page 394

CHAPTER XXVI.

COMPARISON BETWEEN THE BULGARIAN RAYAH AND THE TURK.

The cause of humanity — Sham civilization — Bad material in the Rayah — Good material in the Turk of the country — Constantinople a school of vice — Discipline for the Rayah — Self-defence 405

APPENDIX.

			Page
APPENDIX	A	..	413
,,	B	..	414
,,	C	..	ib.
,,	D	..	417
,,	E	..	ib.
,,	F	..	420
,,	G	..	ib.
,,	H	..	ib.
,,	I	..	421
,,	K	..	422
,,	L	..	423
,,	M	..	424

MEMORANDA.

TURKISH MONEY, WEIGHTS, AND MEASURES.

40 Paras make 1 Piastre (2d.).
100 Piastres make 1 Lira (about 18s.).

The Oke, as a weight is $2\frac{4}{5}$ of a lb. avoirdupois (2·83).
The Oke as a liquid measure is rather more than an imperial quart.
Two Varna Kilés (or eight Constantinople Kilés) of grain are equal to one Quarter.

The Dulum is $\frac{1}{3}$ of an acre.

BULGARIA.

CHAPTER I.

RAYAH VILLAGES OF BULGARIA.

First aspect — The village public — An interior — The gipsy quarter — Habits of the gipsies — 'Notice to quit.'

A SANDY ravine sloping down to the Lake of Varna between ranges of low hills covered with the remains of once magnificent forests, some three score of mud houses, or rather huts, each surrounded by irregularly shaped enclosures of hurdle-work in every stage of dilapidation, two or three fountains, many wild cherry, plum, apple, and pear trees; buffaloes, pigs, and innumerable cur dogs of every size, wandering about listlessly in search of food. Such is the general appearance of our village, and making the necessary allowance for difference of position, such is the aspect of almost every Rayah (Christian) village in the Bulgarian Balkan.

If the landscape be left out of the question, these villages are not picturesque in themselves, and the prevailing brownish tint of the houses, blending with that of the cleared land around, prevents them being easily seen from a distance; enter one of them, and if you happily succeed in avoiding the bites of all the dogs, whom the arrival of a stranger induces to pause from their usual avocations, you will see a mass of cottages apparently thrown together without order or arrangement, built of mud and rudely thatched with reeds, upon which great stones are sometimes placed (as upon the châlets of Switzerland), to prevent the roof being carried away by the wind. Each of the ruinous fences encloses a structure resembling a child's Noah's Ark immensely magnified and upon raised wooden legs; this is the granary, containing the small amount of wheat or Indian corn reserved by the Bulgarian peasant for the use of his family. A rude plough unaltered in form since the earliest days of agriculture, some equally primitive tools, a heap of logs for firewood, a ladder, an *araba* or springless cart, a few melancholy turkeys, and a brood of famished chickens, trying to pick up their day's meal; these are the invariable appendages of every house.

In the kind of main road which meanders through the village are two or three dwellings distinguished from the rest by their superior size, and by a pergola in front which affords shade from the sun or shelter from the rain: these are the shops of the *Bakals* or public-house keepers, and before the door of each is collected a knot of men, sitting cross-legged on the ground, occupied in drinking, smoking, and discussing their own and their neighbours' affairs, very much as if they were Englishmen in England, except that, as the drugged wine produces its effect, a dispute arises, and they start to their feet abusing one another with all the facile eloquence of Slavonic vituperation, and draw their knives with more than Italian gesticulation. The Italian *coltellata* is, however, seldom given in these public quarrels, for woman, the universal peacemaker, appears upon the scene, armed with persuasive words and a thick stick. But though her verbal or manual arguments may stay the impending strife, she too often shares the proverbial fate of 'those who in quarrels interpose,' for even here the Age of Chivalry is past, and wives are as soundly thrashed in Bulgaria as in Lancashire or Clerkenwell. There is another reason which prevents these drunken quarrels from ending in bloodshed upon the spot; the Rayah, instead of trusting his cause to the *jugement de Dieu* as manifested in a duel with knives, prefers to stab his adversary at an advantage, or to adopt the more silent vengeance of poison, one always safe in a country where the police, seldom seen outside the walls of the towns, is looked upon by the Christian as his natural enemy and therefore rarely appealed to, and where post-mortem examinations have yet to be introduced with the many other civilizing agents from France and England, which are, as the newspapers inform us, soon to raise the standard of Rayah education and morality to a par with that of the Nations of the West.*

This main road is also the favourite resort of those village pigs who are not out on the pasture land, and of dogs, who find a constant supply of food in the enormous heaps of manure which, unused and unvalued, seem to be preserved merely for the purpose of feeding pigs and of breeding fever.

Near the village, or within it, stands the *cheshmeh* or fountain, an erection of stone, or occasionally, though rarely, of marble, seldom showing any architectural taste, or even attempt at decoration. It is usually a piece of wall three

---
* See Appendix A.

or four feet high and as many yards long, with a wooden spout, from which the water flows into a trough and thence trickles away to form a vagrant stream for the wandering ducks and geese. Around this spring are several women and girls, each with a wooden yoke, something like that of a London milkman, supporting a couple of copper pails; and as they wait for their turn at the fountain they indulge in the gossip inseparable from a meeting of the fair sex, whether in the Balkans, or on the chairs of Rotten Row, or the Botanical Gardens.

In the early morning a dozen of arabas drawn by oxen or buffaloes and heavily laden with firewood for sale at Varna, four hours distant, pass slowly through with their drivers. During the daytime the village, if it is not one of the too numerous feast days of the Greek calendar, appears deserted, except by women and children, and the *habitués* of the dram shop; but as evening approaches the men return from the forest or the field, and oxen, pigs, sheep, and goats, arrive from their pasturage under the guardianship of the *chobans*, or herdsmen.

The houses of the Rayahs resemble one another so strongly throughout Bulgaria that to describe one is to give a fair idea of all: few of them rise above the ground floor, the exceptions being perhaps not more than one in each village, although a taste for more pretentious domestic architecture appears to be slowly developing itself; their size of course varies in accordance with the means of the owners, a family of six or eight individuals often living and sleeping together in one small room not above eight feet square and six high; but hardly any houses have more than three rooms, even amongst the wealthiest peasants. There is generally a

verandah in front of the cottage, upon which each apartment
opens separately, instead of communicating with the others.
The principal apartment is used as kitchen, parlour, and
bedroom for the heads of the family, and contains (in a well-
to-do house) an array of tin, copper, and earthenware utensils
for household use, two or three wooden boxes gaudily
painted with impossible flowers, in which repose the gala
costumes of the family, and on a shelf are huge rolls of rush
matting, and coarse woollen rugs for bed and bedclothes.
Plastered into the wall is a little circular mirror two or
three inches in diameter; and huddled away into a corner, or
placed in a conspicuous position, according to the piety
or indifferentism of the family, are the *Eïkones* or pictured
saints of the Greek Church, a roughly-painted wooden
triptych, bought from some travelling Russian pedlar, and
representing a dusky Madonna and child flanked by St.
George and St. Demetrius. In front of this picture is often
placed an oil-lamp, but we have never yet seen it burning.
All about the room are hung on the walls and from the
rafters odds and ends of every kind: dried meat, skins of
fox or badger, waiting for the arrival of the skin merchant,
a rude hand-loom and some bales of wool; the *sofra*, a small
wooden table standing about six inches high and serving
for the family meal; the *tekneh*, a wooden dish shaped like
a butcher's tray without handles and used for making bread;
an old pistol, a gun, some pieces of bacon, a string of onions,
and all the broken crockery of the household. The other
rooms are usually bare, and serve as a sleeping apartment
for the juniors, no separation of the sexes being considered
necessary.

Bedsteads are unknown; a mat is placed upon the

floor, the peasant thrusts his sheepskin cap over his eyes, makes the Greek sign of the cross, covers himself up with a rug or two, and goes to sleep without further preparation.

It is one of the most curious peculiarities of the Rayah homestead, that on a moonless night you may pass within fifty yards of a large village without knowing of its existence, did not the barking of countless dogs warn you of your vicinity to human habitations. Even in the coldest winter no cheerful gleam of fire seen through lighted windows promises shelter and hospitality; all is dark and gloomy as the night, for the Bulgarian cottages are distinguished by the entire absence of windows or of any substitute for them, the only media of light and ventilation being the large chimney and the chinks and crannies of the ill-joined door. The reason assigned for this is the universal dread of brigands who might come at night and fire through the windows (if they existed) at the sleeping peasants. *Abdurrachman* Pasha, a late governor of Varna, recently issued an order that in future no houses should be built without windows; but the villagers, whilst complying with the letter of the law, have artfully contrived to evade its spirit by making the obligatory "window" a mere peephole in the wall, not large enough to pass the hand through, and even this is kept stopped up with rags, in order to prevent the possible intrusion of fresh air or a gun barrel. The simple expedient of strong wooden shutters seems never to have occurred to them, though they might see examples of it in any Turkish village.

The atmosphere produced by these arrangements and by the presence of a dozen persons who do not take off their under-clothing four times during the year, and who are moreover redolent of garlic and *raki*, is not agreeable to the stranger in Bulgaria; for the Rayah, like the negro, diffuses around him a peculiar aromatic odour by no means Sabæan, which makes one feel inclined to apply to the whole race Dante's description of Geryon,

"Ecco colei che tutto il mondo appuzza;"

more especially as this aroma extends itself in some subtle manner even to the cookery, so that it is easy for any one who has eaten food with both Christian and Mussulman to distinguish both by taste and smell the victuals of the one Creed from those of the other.

After what we have just said about the unfrequent changes of clothes and linen, it is not surprising that, as a corollary, parasitic insects of every variety abound in every individual and in every house.

Our village lately possessed a kind of suburb, the *Chinguiné Mahalli* or Gipsy Quarter, which, however, was last June wantonly burned to the ground and its inhabitants turned adrift. These gipsies, following the usual custom of their people in conforming outwardly to the State Religion of the country in which they reside, profess Islamism, though they never enter a mosque, and otherwise observe but few of the precepts enjoined by the Koran: their women (like those of the Tartars) do not even wear the *yashmak*, the veil which should always screen Mahommedan female beauty or ugliness from the gaze of the too curious stranger.

Amongst themselves the gipsies speak Romany, as well as Turkish; their huts differ but little externally from those of the Bulgarian, except that they are usually smaller and have no verandah, but though they are perhaps more squalid in outward appearance, the interior offers a pleasing contrast to that of their Christian fellow subjects by its neatness and cleanliness.

Our *Chinguinés* exercised the universal gipsy trades of begging, basket-making, tinkering, and forging iron, to which the Bulgarians said that they added in an especial degree that of thieving, but this accusation is probably due in a great measure to the fact that two of a trade never agree, as in all our dealings with the gipsies we found them quite as honest (to say the least) as their Rayah neighbours. Every morning the gipsy women, furnished each with a big sack and a long stick to keep off the dogs, who seem to bear them an especial antipathy, start in couples upon an expedition to beg or buy flour and other food amongst the villagers, who occasionally give it to them without payment, not from any motive of charity, but because they are to a certain extent afraid of them, having a deeply-rooted belief in their power to cast spells, cause rain, and other beneficent or maleficent attributes. The men remain at home mending pots and pans, tinning copper vessels, and doing all the iron work required by the village, whilst the children blow the bellows, or accompany the cattle to their pasturage.

Less nomadic than those of Western Europe, the Turkish gipsies seldom, however, settle in one village for more than three or four years, and the voluntary or forced migration of a tribe in search of fresh quarters is one of the most picturesque sights to be seen in Bulgaria. A long string of oxen, buffaloes, and horses (which we will hope have *not* been stolen), transports the tents and cooking utensils of the voyagers, as well as the very old men and young children, the former of whom are often magnificent models for a St. Jerome or St. John in Patmos, the latter, dusky monkey-like little imps naked as when they were born: by their side march the younger men and women clad in rags and tatters of every hue, and carrying in their arms infants, poultry, and new-born calves or colts. The gipsy women when young are often exceedingly beautiful, in the style generally considered in England as 'Eastern,' with dark complexions and black almond-shaped eyes, but their beauty fades rapidly, and at thirty years they are already old, wrinkled, and hideous.

As soon as one of these processions halts in or near a village, tents are pitched, fires lighted, and foraging parties organised, whilst the Bulgarians, at the approach of their unwelcome visitors, keep a close watch upon their poultry, pigs, and other moveable goods, for though the *Chinguiné* may to a certain extent respect the property of the village in which he is settled, no scruples restrain him from profiting by any waifs and strays which may come in his way during a march.

The life of the gipsy in Turkey is very much that of a Pariah: disliked and despised by the Turk, hated by the Christian, he yet earns his living by harder labour than that of the latter, whilst his only crime is petty larceny amongst a people with whom roguery is the rule, honesty the exception, and in villages where you will be calmly told, as an interesting piece of information, that the woman, *Tranitza* or *Kaloushka*, whom you see quietly chatting with her neighbours, poisoned her first husband in order to marry her second. You ask, "But was she not punished?" and the answer is a shrug of the shoulders and "Whose business is it?"

The gipsies are allowed to settle in their villages by Mussulmans and Christians, but are usually much worse off amongst the latter than with the former.

A relation of the way in which the Chinguinés of Derekuoi were treated by the villagers will give a fair sample of the hardships they endure without a chance of redress; they do not complain, for what would be the use of a Mussulman gipsy in Bulgaria complaining to a Turkish Pasha against the immaculate pets of Russia?

The gipsies, in addition to the profits of their handicraft, live in a great measure upon the produce of their scanty herds and the sale of milk and butter in the towns; but having no fields they are compelled to buy from the Rayah flour for themselves and corn for their cattle during the winter; our villagers exacted from them a price far exceeding the value of the articles they sold—threepence for an oke of flour instead of twopence, and one shilling and fourpence for a measure of barley instead of tenpence—and received payment either in money or in labour: in the latter case their profits were easily increased by a judicious abatement of the price asked by the gipsy.

Thus during the winter the *Chinguinés* were a positive pecuniary advantage to the villagers; but when spring came and their herds found fodder in the pasture lands, they had more milk and butter to sell at Varna, realized more money, and were therefore less dependent upon the village. The Rayahs then called an assembly of the notables, in which it was decided that as the gipsies' cattle were then feeding upon *their* grazing land without paying for the privilege,* and as

---

* It must be remembered that the Rayahs themselves *pay nothing* for the enormous acreage of pasture land which they claim and profit by.

they bought but little from the village, it would be well to give them a hint to quit.

This hint was conveyed in the most delicate manner by burning their houses over their heads one night, without any previous notice, and the poor gipsies left; but at the approach of winter many of them returned and asked leave to settle on another spot near the village. As winter is the profitable season to the inhabitants of Derekuoi, this request was kindly granted, and we have again a colony of gipsies, who in the summer will probably be evicted by some process equally summary with that of last year.

Such is an instance of the treatment shown by Christians to Mussulmans, of whom they are not personally afraid; had the Rayahs been the victims of a similar outrage inflicted by Turks, what a glorious theme it would have afforded to the friends of the Oriental Christian or the enemies of Turkey; but who in Europe fights the battles of the Mussulman?

Shortly after the occurrence of this act of arson, the Authors mentioned the fact to the then Governor of Varna: he replied that he could do nothing, having received standing orders from Constantinople to favour the Rayahs in every possible manner.

CHAPTER II.

RAYAH VILLAGES OF BULGARIA.—(*Continued.*)

The traveller's reception — Family meal — Bulgarian features and physique — Ordinary costume — Holyday costume — Gagaous or mixed race — A hard bed — The traveller's reckoning — Bulgarian charges — Hospitality of the Turks.

If you arrive as a traveller at a Rayah village where you have no aquaintances, and you do not wish to put up at the *Khan* or inn (supposing that there be one, for inns are few and far between in the interior country of Bulgaria), your proper course is to send for the *Kyaia*, an official who in some measure unites the duties of town-crier and police magistrate, show him the *firman* or government recommendation with which you are doubtless furnished, and tell him to assign you a lodging for the night. A small *bakshish* will ensure you a billet upon the most comfortable house in the village; you present yourself and are received with the invariable formula of salutation, *Khosh geldin*, 'well come,' to which you answer *Khosh bouldouk*, 'well found,' give your horse to one of the sons of the house to look after, or, better still, see yourself that he is well cared for, and make your way into the chief room.

The place of honour on the mat nearest the fire is offered to you, and your host commences the conversation by asking where you come from, where you are going, why you are going there, whether you will come back the same way, what is your trade or occupation (the mere tourist looms in the future of Bulgaria, but has not yet marked these regions for his own), and a number of similar questions, for the Bulgarian is naturally inquisitive, and Franks are as rare in the interior as fat fowls. Your gun—for of course you are not foolhardy enough to travel without one—is naturally much admired, and its price asked and wondered at, as here no one thinks of giving more than three pounds for the quaint weapon used by the peasant; if it is a breech-loader you may even be requested to make a present of it. Meanwhile the lady of the house has made a big, flat, round loaf of bread, which is put to bake on the hearth and covered up with the hot ashes of the wood fire, and if it is near the hour of the family meal you may, at your choice, order a massacre of skeleton poultry, procure some eggs, possibly even a little milk and butter, and cook your own dinner; or you may dine with the family. If you prefer the latter course, the *sofra* is brought out and placed on the floor, with a mass of sour crout floating in grease and abundantly flavoured with garlic, and before each person is placed a large hunch of the hot half-baked bread; none of the females of the family, with the rare exception of the mother, are allowed to take part in this repast, but wait for their meal until the men have finished.

As a stranger, you will probably be offered the refinement of a wooden spoon to assist you in eating, but the usual custom is to dip your fingers into the dish, extract as large a morsel as possible, throw your head well back, and push the food down your throat as far as you can: if you are very particular, you may wipe your fingers upon your bread between each mouthful, but this excess of delicacy is by no means considered necessary, and may even be taken as a tacit reproach to the rest of the company. A jug of wine is constantly passed round and replenished from one of the large barrels standing in the verandah, and before each draught the sign of the Cross is made, to prevent the devil entering into the drinker with the wine.

A dish of white cheese made from the milk of goats and sheep concludes the repast, and when it is finished you offer your tobacco and cigarette-paper (which even in the country have almost entirely superseded the traditional *chibouque*) to the assembled circle; the villagers who have heard of your arrival drop in, salute you with *Khosh geldin*, and either gaze upon you with mute and awe-struck wonder, or subject you to the same cross-examination which you have previously undergone. The Rayah is always bi-lingual, and if you speak only one of his languages that one will probably be Turkish: if however you understand also Romaic, or the Bulgarian dialect of Slavonic, you will certainly be amused, though perhaps not flattered, by the various remarks made upon and concerning you, which of course are supposed to be unintelligible to their object.

When curiosity is satiated or exhausted a lull takes place in the conversation, which has always been confined to the men present, the women knowing their inferior social position and preserving a discreet silence, at least before strangers; being new to the country you will probably take this opportunity to note the general features of dress and appearance of your entertainers.

Strongly but heavily built, with broad shoulders and round back, a walk like that of a bear, coarse and blunted-looking features, a heavy moustache covering the sensual lips, a beard shaven once a week, and little twinkling eyes, which, whilst always avoiding to meet your own, give a general appearance of animal cunning to the face—you will hardly say, notwithstanding the prejudices in favour of the interesting Christians of the East which you have brought with you from Europe, that this long exiled offshoot is a prepossessing type of the great Slavonic Nationality which All-Mother Russia is so fondly eager to receive into her bosom and mould into one mighty and harmonious whole.

The dress of the men admits of but little variety, being always sombre in colour, a circumstance which has given rise to the epithet of *Kara* (black) *Giaour* occasionally bestowed upon them by the Turks, who are fond of light tints in their costume; it consists of a linen shirt, homespun, a short loose jacket open in front and of dark brown, or black, thick rough cloth, a waistcoat and trousers of the same colour and materials, the latter made excessively full to the knee, from which downwards it fits close to the leg. Round the waist is a red sash of many yards in length, which serves instead of pockets, and contains a knife, flint and steel, tobacco and other necessary articles: the cap, round and brimless, is made from sheepskin dyed black or brown. Boots are a rare but much coveted and expensive luxury, being only worn by the young swells of the village on the occasion of some great feast, when they have particular reasons for appearing to the best advantage in the presence of the assembled damsels: far from the seaport towns they are perhaps entirely unknown, and even in those localities where a pair is possessed by some Bulgarian

Brummel it is regarded more as an ornament than an article to be used whilst walking, for the owner generally walks barefooted, carrying his tasselled boots over his shoulder, to the house where they are to be displayed, where he puts them on with great pride, and when the festivity is over, returns home with them slung in the same manner.

The Bulgarian substitute for boots is the charrek, a species of sandal much resembling the Scotch brogue, or that worn by the Calabrian peasant; it is made of cow-hide or pig-skin, rudely sewn into the shape of a slipper, and worn over rolls of thick flannel in which the foot and ancle are swathed; the strings which fasten it are strips of leather, or a cord made of twisted goat's hair, or from the bark of the elder-tree immersed in water until all but the fibrous parts has decayed. The charrek is warm in winter, cool in summer, and very comfortable for walking, except in muddy weather or snow, when it is impossible to avoid slipping; its great disadvantage is that it takes some minutes to put on, which time is however generally economized by the Bulgarians never taking it off until the sole is worn out, a period of perhaps two months.

The women's dress is usually simple, except on feast days, when they display a perfectly bewildering amount of embroidery; it consists of a linen shirt, a boddice, a cloth jacket, and a skirt of some dark coloured calico or other stuff which descends to within a few inches of the ancle. On the head is worn a little cap of cardboard covered with red cloth, something like a fez in shape, but much smaller, and upon it are sewn coins of silver, gold, or silver gilt, amongst which may sometimes be found rare antiques discovered in ploughing the fields: this cap, being worn from earliest infancy, and fitting very tightly upon the head, gives the skull a peculiar and unsightly conical form, which is however unnoticeable so long as the cap and handkerchief are not removed; this process is just the reverse of that adopted by the North American tribes of Flat-head Indians. Their other ornaments consist of a necklace composed of coins, bracelets of silvered-copper, or glass, and ear-rings of pierced money. If a girl is engaged to be married, she generally wears a girdle of silver, or more often white metal, with a great clasp ornamented with glass rubies or emeralds, which is presented to her by her betrothed, amongst other gifts.

Except when dancing, and not always even then, slippers are scarcely ever worn by the women, who seem to prefer walking barefooted to the fountain or even outside the village.

If the day of your arrival is a feast, you will have the opportunity of seeing all the marriageable young ladies in the full blaze of their toilette. Every spot of their linen which can be seen is embroidered in colours, at the neck, the hem, the boddice, the sleeves; their socks are of open work, and supplemented by knitted or embroidered leggings; their jacket is of cloth, lined with fox-skin, and embroidered with fur; and their necks, heads, and arms covered with the whole contents of their jewel-boxes; their aprons too are woven in bright colours and patterns resembling strongly those of the Japanese, but which produce a picturesque effect; even their handkerchiefs have stripes of colour or of gold and silver tinsel interwoven with them. All this finery is put on for the village dance which on every feast day commences soon after sunrise, and is continued with little interruption till nearly midnight, unless the state of the weather forbids it, as it always takes place in the open air.

The evening dress of the men is by no means so elaborate as that of the ladies; the Rayah exquisite puts an additional, though unnecessary, coat of grease upon the already unctuous masses of his flowing hair, changes his sheepskin *chapka* for a little red cap, in which he sticks, if flowers are procurable, a bunch or two of roses or snow-drops, slips on a kind of flannel legging with a little blue braid upon it over the dirty flannels of his *charreks*, and is ready for the ball.

The costume of the women, as described above, strongly resembles that of the Polish and Russian peasantry, but it is only to be seen in those villages where the inhabitants are of pure Slavonic blood. Along the coast of the Black Sea the Bulgarian is of a very mixed race, partly *Vlach* or Walachian, partly Greek, and partly even Venetian and Genoese; the latter quartering being gained by the long-continued presence of Genoese and Venetian garrisons in that part of the country. They are characterized by the genuine Slav as *Gagaous*, an untranslatable term but involving a great amount of contempt.* They speak besides Turkish, either a corrupt dialect of Bulgarian (which is itself only a dialect) or a very impure Romaic, perhaps even all three languages in a less or greater degree: some of their words are even Italian, and show how firm was the hold once gained upon the East by

---

* The full-blooded Bulgarian, *czisto Bulgar*, has a saying which is not complimentary to the mixed race, it is as follows:—

Nic Syrb, nic Turczyn, nic Bulgar, nic Wlah, nic Ozlak—Gaganz. Neither Serb, nor Turk, nor Bulgarian, nor Wallachian, nor a man; but a Gagaous.

the trading Republics of Italy. Amongst these the traditional Slavonic costume has disappeared as far as concerns the women, who on grand occasions adorn themselves with an utter want of taste, and ignorance of the contrasting effects of colours; but little embroidery is to be seen, their ornaments and head-dress are the same, but their dresses are of silk, and a flaming red skirt is worn with a yellow silk jacket and pink boddice.

When your examination is finished, you will probably find no new topic of conversation, and express a wish to go to bed, upon which the visitors take their leave by degrees; some of the members of the family are turned out, and you find yourself with only some half dozen sleeping companions, male and female, young and old. You select the place nearest the fire, as in winter it is the warmest, and in summer the coolest; take your pillow and a couple of rugs, and retire to rest as best you can, whilst the others just turn in as they are, curl themselves up almost into a circle, and fall asleep in five minutes. Bulgarian habits are matutinal, so you are awakened early in the morning, and probably feel your hip-bones and your head rather sore from the respective hardness of the mud floor and rag-stuffed pillow. A draught or two of wine, and a little bread and crout, prepare you for your onward journey; you order your horse to be brought round, and you ask the head of the family how much there is to pay.

For the first time or so, you make this inquiry with the hope that you will be answered "Nothing at all," and with the intention of giving a sum at least double what you have cost your entertainers, but a few days' experience of travelling amongst the Rayah soon dispels any such fond illusion.

The wine you have drunk, the chickens you have cooked, the bread you have eaten, the corn for your horse—all is counted up with an accuracy of mental arithmetic highly creditable to the financial abilities of the Christian peasant: if your host is not avaricious he only multiplies the sum total of the value by three, and informs you how much your food comes to; for the trouble you have given, and for your bed, you are expected to pay a *bakshish* or present, the amount of which is left to yourself. It is no use, or at least very little, to grumble, so you pay and go to the door. If your *bakshish* has come up to the expectations of your host's wife, you are presented at the door with a stirrup-cup of wine, gratis, your horse is held as you mount, and you ride away amidst a chorus of '*oughourola*,' 'bon voyage,' from the assembled family. If, however, the bill for your food has put you in a bad humour, and sensibly diminished your voluntary offering, you may depart without wine or good wishes or any one to assist your exit. Your host, in the mean time, is rejoicing that he has managed to profit so largely by a guest *billetted* upon him, and by whose advent he will probably escape the lodgment of the next two soldiers who come to the village, who would pay him only the Government allowance, and eat four times as much as the Frank stranger. To explain this, it is necessary to say that a *Bouyortou* or *Firman* from the Government, which authorizes the traveller to claim a lodging for the night from the *Kayaia* (who to his other offices unites that of billet-master), puts the bearer in the position of a Government officer, and therefore he is only obliged to give the regulation tariff for his accommodation, which is about tenpence per diem, and is entitled for that sum to demand any food that is to be had in the house, and to consume as much of it as he likes. The different houses are put on a roster for the billets, and therefore the arrival of a foreigner who pays liberally, instead of a soldier or zaptieh (policeman) who pay next to nothing, is a positive godsend.

The Authors were once charged, in a Christian house of a village in Roumelia, the sum of about 15 shillings for nine pennyworth of flour, a pint of milk, and a half dozen of eggs.

Perhaps you are annoyed by finding the *auri sacra fames* where you had expected patriarchal simplicity—especially in many matters—and you begin to believe that the boasted hospitality of the East is but a mirage which disappears as you approach the spot where it ought to be; next evening, however, you stop at a Turkish village. Here no presentation of your *bouyortou* is necessary, the fact of your being a stranger is sufficient to ensure you food, shelter, and a hearty welcome. You ask your way to the *Mussafir odasi* (guest's apartment), a cottage built for the reception of travellers, whom the Mussulman is of course prevented from receiving into the sacred precincts of his own home. If the village contains any rich men, these will each have a little house within the enclosure of their court, but apart from their own dwelling which contains the inviolable Harem, and to one of these you will be directed; if the village is poor (and Mussulman villages are for good reasons, which will be given hereafter, poorer than those of the Rayah) there is at least a *Mussafir odasi* belonging in common to all the villagers. We will take the latter case; you enter a little room, kept scrupulously clean, and furnished with matting and a few cushions; shortly after your arrival some one comes in with coffee and the apparatus for making it, salutes you, and in a minute or two offers you a tiny cup of coffee made as few but Turks, and Turks of the country, can make it. Then other villagers come in, each with an offering of bread, cheese, cream, buttermilk, lentils, honey, eggs—in short, to use their own words as they excuse the poverty of the meal, 'what God has given to them.' No questions are asked until you have eaten and are satisfied, and are then put in a tone far different from the Prussian-frontier manner of the Bulgarians; no one who has mixed with the true Turks —those of the provinces, uncontaminated by a sojourn at Péra or Paris—can help being struck with their innate tact, refinement, and *gentlemanliness*.

The *Khodja* (schoolmaster) and the *Imam* (priest), the two most respected characters of the village, come in to see you, you begin to ask about the shooting in the neighbourhood, and as the conversation turns upon the favourite topic of arms and weapons, you find that your friends occasionally see a Turkish newspaper, have heard of the Zündnadelgewehr, and have even a very fair idea of its construction. If you touch upon political subjects, you will be surprised at the just appreciation which is shewn of Turkish Home Policy, and you will hear remedial measures suggested by mere peasants, which, if adopted by the Imperial Government, would do more to restore Turkey to the position which her almost boundless internal resources should enable her again to occupy, than a century of the patent nostrums advocated by Occidental Cabinets, whose only knowledge of the East is confined to the foreign quarters of its large towns.

In the morning you are offered a frugal breakfast, and of course coffee; when you leave, no payment will be asked for, and if you offer money in return for the kindness you have received, you will almost insult your entertainers; the only way of compensating them is to give some small sum towards the maintenance of the mosque or the school, and even this may not be accepted if it be given undisguisedly as payment for hospitality.

It is but fair to add, in conclusion, that although the Authors, in a rather extensive series of rambles amongst the villages of Bulgaria, have *never* found a Mussulman who would accept payment from his guests for anything which his house afforded—of course if they *sent* for any luxury which he did not possess, and he was a poor man, he would take back the money he had paid—they have met with *one* instance of a Christian peasant who at first refused money, but even he finally took it without very much pressing.

CHAPTER III.

ROADS AND MEANS OF COMMUNICATION.

Devious routes — Repair or go round ? — Difficult locomotion — Employés classified — Mithat Pasha's road — Worse than none — A remedy suggested — Varna railroad — Postal irregularities — Telegraph clerks.

ROADS, at least as the term is understood in England, are, to use a hackneyed phrase, conspicuous by their absence in Bulgaria. The means of difficult and tardy communication which form their substitutes, appear usually to be but slight enlargements of the tracks through cover made by wandering sheep, buffaloes, and horses: at least such is the only theory which explains their otherwise unaccountable twistings, and turnings, and deviations from the natural line of tracing. Such an obstacle as a fallen tree or projecting branch is even more insurmountable by the Bulgarian than by the buffalo, and to avoid it he drives his araba by a detour of two or three hundred yards through the thinnest part of the adjacent cover, rejoining further on what we must call the main road, until some similar accident forces him again to leave it. That the fallen tree might be removed by the axe, or the projecting branch cut away by the same instrument (one which the peasant here is never without), never occurs to him: superfluous labour, or what he regards as such, is distasteful to him, time is of no importance; his wood or wheat are always sure of a sale at their destination; if he cannot arrive at Varna before sunset, when the gates are closed, he can always bivouac in the

forest, burning down three or four pounds worth of the
Padischah's timber to warm himself; his buffaloes or oxen
will eat leaves if they can get them, dry sticks if nothing
else is to be found, so why should he trouble himself with
twenty minutes' work?

Ten hours' doing nothing is infinitely preferable, and
what matter whether he ploughs or sows his fields
that day or the next?—there is time enough for everything.

The consequences of this system, or want of system, are
that any two miles of the best roads hereabouts would
smash any carriage with springs ever built in western
Europe, and break down the strongest English cart: the
arabas of the country, being moving forests on wheels, suffer
less, and if one of the roughly squared trees which compose
them is broken, the forest is everywhere, and *then* the
Rayah has no alternative but to use his axe. In summer
these paths, from the rapid growth of grass and shrubs, are
hardly to be distinguished from the cover through which
they pass; in winter they are a succession of iron-bound
hillocks and ditches, of treacherous snow-drifts or of
unfathomable mud; when this last is predominant it takes
five hours to accomplish a distance of twelve miles from our
village to Varna, even on horseback: a cart will probably
require an hour more. Araba travelling by these roads is
as may be easily imagined, far from pleasant, one side of
the vehicle being frequently two feet higher than the other:
the Bulgarians, however, will not abandon a favourite path
for such a trifling difference of elevation between the
borders of the road, and as long as they can prevent their
carts tilting over by hanging on to the uppermost side, they

are content: when this is no longer sufficient they strike out a new path. To a stranger in the Balkan who is riding from one village to another by a road new to him, and who is guided merely by his general knowledge of the direction in which his destination lies, it is very puzzling to find some six or seven paths spreading out like a fan, and apparently leading in very different directions: every one of them bears marks of being lately used by horses or waggons, and the choice of one out of the many seems a very haphazard proceeding; but whichever one he selects is tolerably sure to be right, for all of them, after describing innumerable curves, which, however they may take a more or less vitiated line of beauty and grace, are certainly not influenced by any scientific tracing, fall again into the main path, in which the ruts have become a little too deep, or the rain has formed a marsh, or a buffalo has died and left his skeleton, which the dogs and wolves have not yet had time to clear away.

Whilst speaking of the roads in these provinces, it would be unfair not to allude to the Chaussée from Rustchuk to Varna, constructed by Mithat Pasha, the Governor of the Vilayet of the Danube.

Mithat Pasha is an intelligent man, and what is still rarer *amongst the governing class of Turkey*, an honest man; but he has fallen into the common error of mistaking effect for cause, and wishes to introduce into the country under his rule as high a state of civilisation as now exists in France or England, forgetting that Rome was not built in a day, and that, to make a Duke of Wellington out of a South Sea Islander, something more is necessary than a cocked hat and a pair of spurs. The choice of Mithat Pasha by the government of the Sublime Porte is by no means a bad one, and is, indeed, a step in the right direction; but one man alone, especially an Oriental who has only been able to view the surface and effects of the European Institutions which a certain school of Turkish politicians regard as the only panacea for the sufferings of Turkey, can do but little, however excellent his intentions may be. In Turkey, the class of minor officials is of the very worst kind; such is the *entourage* of Mithat Pasha, and such he knows it to be, whilst he is powerless to remedy the evil. These subordinate employés, whether Armenians, Turks, or Greeks, may be divided into three heads :—1st, merely stupid; 2nd, stupid and rapacious; 3rd, cunning and rapacious; to do the Greeks justice, they are seldom wanting in a species of cleverness, and form the majority of the third category. Any foreigner who has enough money to bribe his way to the highest authority, and enough impudence to promise great things for Turkey, is pretty sure of employment, whether as Engineer, Inspector of Mines, or any other self-attributed quality; he is employed on some public work, pockets as much money as he can, on the chance of his incapacity being found out by some miracle; if he is undetected, he gets more work entrusted to him, and speedily makes a handsome fortune, which he of course does not care to spend in Turkey.

But to return to the Rustchuk and Varna Chaussée. This undertaking was commenced about four years ago, and the line traced by a foreign engineer, to whom the contract was given. This gentleman, instead of paying for the necessary work, had it all done by corvée (forced labour of the peasantry), and pocketed the sum intended for the wages of the labourers, in addition to his own handsome salary as engineer. What the road may have been when first completed we are unable to say, but we have a feeling recollection of what it was when we were obliged to travel by it during the early part of 1867. For some six or seven miles out of Rustchuk the road was good and well kept; there were even imbecile trees planted and propped up at regular distances, trying to look as if they were on some high road of France or Belgium; but as we advanced further from the town, the road grew more sickly looking, and after three or four hours' travelling, it apparently disappeared altogether, although the lines of trees were still to be seen at some little distance. This peculiarity was accounted for by the driver of our post-carriage, who told us that the road was so bad that he was obliged to go across country to avoid it, and, as a curve of our track over the fields brought us nearer to what should have been the chaussée, we could see that he had exercised a most wise discretion, for the great artery of communication between the Danube and Black Sea was much in the same condition as the Balkan roads we have already described. Heaps of broken stones for repairs lined the deserted road, but had certainly never been used since its construction, and as certainly will remain unused for the next ten years. The conformation of the country occasionally obliged us to return to the chaussée, a proceeding which we were always aware of by the diminution of speed and increase of jolting, but from Rustchuk to Devna, a distance of about 120 miles, we did not travel over the legitimate road for more than 30 miles, the rest was driven over corn fields, and through thick cover and marshes, anywhere to avoid Mithat Pasha's chaussée. Most probably there is a certain sum allowed in the budget of the Vilayet for the repair of the road. That the authorities knew that a road would need repairs is evident, from the heaps of prepared stone. Who pockets the allowance we do not know; at any rate, it is but a drop in the ocean of peculation by which the finances of Turkey are absorbed.

The remedy for this state of things would be of easy application, but in Turkey no one is responsible. If there existed two communes sufficiently enlightened to construct a good road between their respective villages, and to keep it in repair, no obstacle would be placed in their way by the local government, nor would any assistance be given them. But that two such villages should be found in the Balkan is hopeless. As long as the Rayah is not forced to assist in the work of his own civilisation he will do nothing. If government chooses to make a road for him he will grumble at the work required, even though well paid for it; he will never take the initiative.

If a responsible communal government were substituted for the wretched system of tchorbajes as at present existing, the work of road-making would, by being divided amongst the villages, become comparatively easy. Some of the innumerable Bulgarian feast-days might be devoted to the repair, as well as construction, of the roads necessary, whilst a slight toll would provide funds for the expenses of the former. A great road such as that from Rustchuk to Varna, is, even if kept in repair, of but little use except to those villages lying upon its line, when the lateral roads from the villages, whose commerce should debouch into the main system, are entirely neglected. Taking winter and summer together, the average rate of cart or horse locomotion can hardly exceed two miles per hour, a speed which, however, perfectly satisfies the Bulgarians, and with which they will continue to be contented so long as they are allowed to remain in their present ignorance of the value of time.

The number of idle days (elsewhere given) amongst the peasantry is certainly sufficient to admit of each village making a mile or two of good road, and keeping it in repair every year. Labour being thus found, but little expense is needed. Buffaloes must be fed whether they work or not, and stone is abundant everywhere. If money is required, there are few Christian villages in this Pashalik which could not easily furnish a sufficient sum.

The new railroad from Varna to Rustchuk, in communication with the Danube steamers, is a great advantage to foreigners living in this part of Turkey, as far as the speedy transit of letters is concerned, and is also a great convenience to the grain merchants, but the peasants seldom or never send their corn by it, preferring to carry it in their own carts, even though they start from a village where there is a station. Strategically this line is very badly traced, since, by its running along the north side of the lake of Varna, it is open to be taken by a *coup de main*, in the event of a Russian invasion and march upon Varna, and the communication between that town and Shumla would thus be interrupted. The peasants complain greatly of its being unfenced throughout its whole length, as an immense number of their cattle are destroyed by passing trains. On twelve miles of line more than a hundred head were killed during last year, all of which belonged to poor villages which could ill afford the loss. This railroad has been unfortunately conspicuous by the number of accidents occurring on it since it has been opened: in nine days (Nov. 18th to Nov. 27th, 1867), four trains ran off the lines, and this at a time when there were no quick trains, in consequence of the freezing of the Danube and suspension of the mails by that route.

Contracts have already been made for various railroads in European Turkey, from Constantinople to Adrianople, and from there to Varna, &c., but it will, of course, be some years before these are completed; in the mean time the traveller in the interior has to ride, as the country roads are by no means calculated for carriages, and as carriages are not to be seen outside the large towns; an araba which only goes at a foot's pace, and never has any springs, is by no means a convenient or agreeable mode of locomotion, and in deep snow, or very muddy weather, is often unable to go even a distance of a mile from one village to another.

Turkey, with the logical consistency which distinguishes her system of wasting or neglecting her pecuniary resources, has confided the European postal service to foreign companies, by whom it is carried out in a manner which combines a great deal of apparent method with an entire absence of real order. If you, as a stranger at Constantinople, expect letters from Europe, you must make a round of visits to the various post-offices; those of the Austrian Lloyd and the French Messageries Impériales are in the Rue des Postes, Péra, and reflect a great deal of credit upon their Pérote architect, but you are not at all likely to find your letters on the first inquiry, for there seems to be some bye-law preventing the clerks from giving letters to any one they have not seen three or four times. Probably one of the employés will be polite enough to suggest your trying at the English post-office in Galata, and if you follow his advice you will have a pleasant search of an hour or two amongst the ships' chandlers and potato shops of that fragrant suburb, until you find out a dirty building where your letters are *not*. However, if you have patience to become a regular visitant at the Austrian and French offices, the clerks will in time get accustomed to your face, and hand you over some letters which arrived at Constantinople about ten days before yourself; henceforward you have a fair enough chance of receiving two out of every three missives addressed to you.

Residents in the capital can make special arrangements for letters being delivered at their houses, but even then there is but little certainty of receiving all that arrive at the office. A local post for Stamboul, Péra, and Galata, was organised some time since, but after a little time the company failed, the service was discontinued, and it has not been again started.

If the arrangements at Constantinople are bad, those of the smaller towns are (as far as we can judge by experience) worse; but to do the minor offices justice, they are at least free from the species of hypocrisy which prevails at headquarters, as their exterior is by no means imposing, and they do not make any pretensions to either order or method.

At Varna letters for Europe may be looked for in three post-offices, two Austrian and one French;* between midday and three o'clock these are closed to allow the clerks time for lunch or billiard playing, and even at other hours you are very fortunate if you do not find that the employé you want has gone out, and that the time of his return is uncertain.

---

* There is a third Austrian office, but it seems to have been established more because there is luck in odd numbers than for any other reason, as the clerk is hardly ever visible, and no business of any kind appears to be transacted oftener than once a quarter.

The following dialogue, something very similar to which takes place every time we ride into Varna (and we are tolerably well known on account of our eccentric preference of the dangers of the hills, to the delights of 'society' in the town), gives an idea of the admirable management which pervades the postal arrangements:—

"Est-ce qu'il y a des lettres pour nous?"

"Je ne crois pas, monsieur; je vais voir. Non, il n'y en a point."

"Et cependant il doit y en avoir."

(Looks again over a disorderly pile of documents) "Non, monsieur; vous avez été à l'autre poste autrichienne?"

"Oui."

"Et à la poste française?"

"Oui."

"Vous avez passé à l'Agence anglaise?"

"Oui."

"Alors il n'y en a pas—tiens! c'est vrai, je crois me rappeler qu'il y a quelquechose pour vous quelquepart."

(Looks over several other disorderly piles of documents, at length fishes out a letter, and exclaims, with great complacency), "Voilà! monsieur."

"Mais cette lettre est arrivée ici le mois de Septembre, 1866, et nous sommes dans le mois d'Avril, 1868!"*

(Examines the letter attentively), "C'est fort drôle, ça! nous ne l'avons pas cependant vue!"

A few days afterwards a servant is sent in for letters, and brings back a polite note from the same clerk, informing us that a packet for us has been lying at his office for eighty-

---

* This incident actually occurred to us a short time since.

three days, and suggesting that we should come to claim it! Not having been to Varna since, we are unable to imagine what is the reason that it should not have been given up to us during one of our previous visits.

The new postal route to Europe by the Rustchuk railroad is a very rapid one theoretically; but besides the fact that letters are often mislaid for weeks at the Varna post-office, there is another drawback to their rapid delivery; the clerk at Rustchuk (at least the blame is laid upon him), once a month forgets to separate the Varna letters from those for Constantinople, and they consequently go on to the capital, have to wait for the departure of a Black Sea steamer, and return with an extra charge for postage.

Another peculiarity of the direct route is that although books and small parcels may be forwarded from Europe by the post, they are not permitted to be sent from Turkey.

We wished to send a letter to Adrianople, and fancying that the best way was by sea to Constantinople, and thence onwards, we applied at the Austrian post-office No. 1, which referred us to the French post-office, which referred us to the Austrian post-office No. 2, which referred us back again to the French office, where a grand consultation of charts took place; then we were asked where Adrianople was, and on our saying that to the best of our knowledge it was in European Turkey, we were recommended to try the Turkish steam packet office. The officials there declined to have anything to do with our letter, but pointed out a little sort of hut at the corner of a street, built of planks, and looking just like a Yankee post-office in the back woods; this proved to be filled with a wooden desk, a narghileh, and a Turk, and the latter informed us that letters for Adrianople might be posted (that is, put into an open wooden drawer) there, provided they were legibly addressed in Turkish—so at last we got rid of our letters. But after all we found out that the Austrian and French officers ought, either of them, to have accepted it.

The telegraph works pretty well, but, as far as Varna is concerned, would work better if the clerks were capable of writing any European language correctly, and had a more definite idea of geography. Some time since we had occasion to send a telegram to Frankfurt am Main, but none of the employés had heard of that city, they could not find its name in their books, and there was no map to consult, so, although we described its situation in six different languages (all of which they were supposed to understand), they suggested that we should call next day, and in the mean time they would make enquiries; this proposition we declined, and at length were lucky enough to discover Frankfort on an old tariff-sheet, upon which the *Tel* (according to the Turkish abbreviated form in use) was despatched; but it arrived at its destination in such a mangled form that it was completely unintelligible.

CHAPTER IV.

BULGARIAN SUPERSTITIONS.

Paganism and witchcraft tolerated by the Church — Feast of all Nature — Switch day — Dipping day — Bacchantes — A day of mortification for the dogs — All Souls — Feast of Constantine — Miraculous fish — Feast of serpents — Old Mother March — St. George's: why lambs are sacrificed — The Panagia — Feast of pigs — Novel sins — The Vampire — Fountain spirits — Spirit treasure-guardians — Ghosts of the Turks — Our success as exorcists — Notions of a future state.

As in all Evil there is a substratum of Good, so from the fact that the Greek clergy—interested in their Bulgarian flocks merely as a means of revenue—care but little what may be their morality, and are equally indifferent to what, how much, or how little they believe, so long as their faith or its absence does not diminish the exchequer of the Orthodox Church, it results that the antiquarian in search of ancient Slavonic superstitions, habits, customs, legends, and even rites dating from Pagan times, will find in Bulgaria a rich and untouched field for his investigations.

Unfortunately a total absence of all the books necessary for reference and collation forbids us attempting to make a special study of the subject, and we are forced to content ourselves with a mere catalogue of some of the superstitions prevalent in our immediate neighbourhood; but such is the originality and genuineness of the old Slavonic traditions in these provinces, that even the meagre and imperfect details which we give may not be without interest for the lovers of that folk-lore which is so rapidly disappearing from Europe.

In those Slavonic countries which profess Roman Catholicism, the clergy, with its almost mathematical rigidity of principle, has cast down the images, abolished the feasts, uprooted the superstitions, and even banished the memories, of the ancient gods. Among the Czechs, again, the Croats, the Dalmatians, and others, civilisation and foreign or internal despotism * have produced the same effect, so that the ancient traditions are either entirely effaced, or altered and disfigured by the varnish of a spurious poetry,† whereas in Bulgaria they still flourish and retain intact their original roughness.

A secondary cause of the non-intervention of the Greek clergy in the superstitious beliefs of the peasantry, is the very slight religious faith they themselves possess, an indifferentism which leads them to open encouragement of ignorance. Thus, when the Papas finds that his prayer for rain to St. John the Baptist is utterly ineffectual, whilst the spells of the village witch are followed by a plentiful shower which revives the drooping cabbages, he, being without any belief in the religion which he professes, and yet feeling the necessity of believing in *something*, comes to the conclusion that certain occult forces are really the appanage of the sorceress, and instead of opposing himself to the powers of darkness he thinks it better to make a compact of mutual aid and toleration.

Hence it is, that if the Papas's fields suffer from drought, or his wife or child are ill, he calls in the assistance of

---

* As in Russia, which has been under the successive despotism of Tartars, Lithuanians, and the Emperors.

† It will be seen further on, the legend of the vampire has been poetized in Dalmatia out of all resemblance to its original form.

the village witch,* who performs certain incantations for the benefit of the weather or the sick people, addressed to the Spirit of Evil, and who carries out her part of the treaty by paying the Papas's exactions, and taking her own infant to be sprinkled with holy water every month.

Unchecked by the priest, and unbanished by education, the old Slavonic Pantheism reigns supreme, in fact if not in name, in Bulgaria; and, excluding many doctrines of Christianity with which it cannot assimilate, clothes itself with the garments of the outward observances of the Church, and gives birth to a practical religion of the most extraordinary kind.

Last week a peasant said to us, "The 25th March (o. s.) is the Blagostina; it is only a little Feast of the Church, but it is a great Feast day for all Nature, for then even the swallows and the bees cease from labour: all Nature reposes and makes ready for the birth of Spring; so it is a great festival, for it is that of the new-born Spring and of Serpents."

We find thus certain feasts of pagan origin, and accompanied by rites which are certainly not those of the Church; but owing to the great number of ecclesiastical festivals, heathen and Christian anniversaries often coincide in date and produce a singular mixture of observances taken from the old and the new religion.

On New Year's Day, which is called Chibouque-gunu (Switch-day), everybody procures a little switch of Kizil (cornel wood), and taps with it every one he meets, at the same time wishing him a happy new year; this practice is not of Slavonic origin.

* Fact.

The 19th January (N. S.), the Feast of the Three Kings, is called the Eslama-gunu, or Dipping-day, and every man in the village is carried off to the fountain and thoroughly soused with water unless he ransoms himself by the payment of a certain amount of wine, the forfeits thus collected being drunk by the assembled villagers in the evening. This custom is not Slavonic, but common to all peoples who profess the Greek religion. The day following is observed (though only in those villages which are of pure Slavonic race, and not by the *Gagaous*) as the Babou-dien, Old Woman's Day, when all the married women celebrate a sort of Saturnalia, and wind up by getting very drunk in the evening. This year we arrived at the village of Dervishkivi in Roumelia, on the Babou-dien, and hardly were we seen approaching when a troop of Bacchantes surrounded us, and nearly pulled us off our horses, only consenting to let us pass on the receipt of black mail. In the evening a similar troop, very tipsy, invaded the house where we were staying, and danced about in the most frantic manner, headed by an old lady astride upon a cane, and looking a very impersonation of a witch upon the traditional broomstick. Perhaps it might be possible to trace the origin of the Sabbat of the Brocken to the hills of the Balkans.

On the first day of Lent, all the village dogs are caught, and soundly beaten, to prevent them going mad during the year : this is a very unpleasant day for strangers, as the cries of the men and the howls of the poor brutes are almost deafening, and in a large village the ceremony lasts till nearly evening.

Next comes the Dusz Nitza (Jour des Morts, the All Souls' Day of Western Europe), which with the Bulgarians is on the first day of the second week in Lent; in the evening the women go from house to house with lighted candles, in order "that the souls of the dead may have good appetites, and be well fed in the place where they are."

The Blagostina (which we have already said is on the 25th March) is, according to the.papas, the Feast of Constantine the Great, who is singularly mixed up and confounded with Constantine Palæologus;* on this day, although it occurs during Lent when even fish and oil are forbidden by the Greek Church, the Bulgarians are allowed to eat fish, a dispensation which has its origin in the following strange legend. According to this story, Constantine Palæologus, on the last day of the siege of Constantinople, was busy frying fish in his palace, by the side of a pond, when terrified messengers came running in to announce that the Turks were mounting the breach for the final assault. "Pooh! nonsense!" replied the Emperor, "the Turks will no more take the town than these fried fish will jump into the pond!" As he said this, the fish gave a spring into the water, and, ready cooked as they were, began swimming about merrily. A Bulgarian, lately returned from Constantinople, assures us that he has seen these identical fish in the identical fish-pond, but that of the three who were there formerly one has disappeared (probably having died of old age), and there are now only two remaining; this information may perhaps be useful for the next edition of Mr.

---

* The Bulgarians say "St. Constantine" was the hero of this legend, but as the only saint of that name is Constantine the Great, who is not generally supposed to have been at the taking of Constantinople by the Turks, there must be a mistake somewhere on their part, or that of the priests who taught them this story.

Murray's 'Handbook for Constantinople.' In this tradition, originated by the Greek clergy, may be traced their hatred to the last of the Byzantine Emperors, whom they cannot forgive for having embraced Catholicism, and whom they calumniate by representing one of the bravest defenders of Constantinople as frying fish whilst the assault was raging on the ramparts; perhaps the same authority may describe the traitor Notaras as defending the breach. Still, it seems difficult to understand why all this should permit the Bulgarians to eat fish on the Blagostina.

On that day the peasants do nothing—not even going out shooting—and dare not take off their charreks or sandals, for it is the Feast of Serpents, who then come out of their holes, and any one who thus profaned their Sabbath would be sure to be bitten by them in the course of the year. In the evening large bonfires are lit, and the young people dance round one of them to the sound of the gaida, whilst the married women spin around a second, and the married men get drunk around a third. Taking into consideration these ceremonies and the belief that the Blagostina is the Feast of reviving Nature consecrated by the repose of all animated beings, and remembering that the great Slavonic Festivals of Paganism corresponded in date with the solstices and equinoxes, we see that it is neither Constantine the Great nor the fried fish of Constantine Palæologus that the Bulgarians commemorate, but a tradition of Slavonic Pantheism.

The month of March, which falls in the Spring equinox, is called by the Bulgarians Baba Mart, Old Mother March, and is the only female month of the year, the others being considered as masculine. March in Bulgaria is like April in England, inconstant and capricious, alternating between storms and sunshine; and it is here specially dedicated to the fair sex, who during its continuance enjoy complete idleness, doing no work, and asserting a sort of temporary superiority over their husbands which sometimes even goes to the length of administering a thrashing without fear of reprisal.

In order not to displease Baba Mart, the women do not even smear the floors of their houses with clay (a work which is usually performed every week), wash, weave, or spin; for if they were to do so she would give no rain during the year, and lightning would infallibly strike the house in which she had been thus insulted.

There are certain clever old women who, knowing where Baba Mart resides, pay her a visit, and from her information assign to each of the married women a day of the month on which the weather will be according to the character of the lady whose day it is; thus, if Mrs. Dimitri gets the 1st of March, it will be fine with perhaps a warm and gentle shower or two, for she is an amiable and soft-hearted woman, a little given to shedding unnecessary tears upon any pretext. Mrs. Tanaz is a loud-voiced shrew, so her day will be made up of wind, black clouds, snow, and heavy rain. "Don't go out shooting to-morrow, Chelibi, for it is the day of Kodja Keraz's* wife, and she has such an awful temper that the weather is sure to be horrible."

When a woman is assigned a day for the first time, her character is judged by the state of the weather; fortunately

---

* Kodja Keraz means literally "Old Cherry Tree," a name which reminds one of those fanciful appellations assumed by the North American Indians.

this system is not extended to young ladies on their promotion, or many a match might be broken off by an inopportune storm in the month of March.

On St. George's day (23rd April, N. S.), the Bulgarians make a sacrifice of lambs; the legend which gives rise to it is this:—One day the Creator entered into the house of a very poor man, and asked for something to eat; the man (whose name the Bulgarians say is forgotten) had neither lamb nor kid to offer, so he took his little son, cut his throat, and "pitched" him into the oven. Presently the Creator was hungry, and asked if the food was cooked.

"Directly," answered the man.

"Open the door, and see if it is ready."

The father opened the oven, and saw with astonishment his son, instead of being roasted, sitting down and writing on his knee, Turkish fashion.

The Almighty then told him that in future a lamb was to be sacrificed on every anniversary of that day.

This legend, which we have given exactly as we heard it, seems to be a mixture of the history of Abraham's sacrifice and the story of Shadrach, Meshech, and Abednego; but the peasants relate it as an old tradition amongst themselves, and not as a piece of Biblical history.

About the time of the summer solstice there is another nocturnal feast with bonfires, doubtless that of the Slavonic deity Kupalo (the bathing god); but we have been unable to obtain from the Bulgarians any other reason for its observance than "taki adet," "such is the custom."

On the Feast of the Panagia (the Blessed Virgin) sacrifices of lambs, kids, honey, wine, &c., are offered in order that the children of the house may enjoy good health throughout the year: in order to determine the saint to whom these sacrifices are to be dedicated, the peasants have recourse to a ceremony of divination which savours strongly of pagan origin. Three candles are lit, and behind each is placed a picture of a saint, a little child is brought, and whichever candle he touches first shows that the offering is to be made to the corresponding saint, whose picture probably replaces the images of the heathen divinities; when the saint has been thus chosen the bystanders each drink a cup of wine, saying "Saint So-and-so, to thee is the offering," and cut the throat of the lamb, or smother the bees. In the evening the whole village assembles to eat the various sacrifices, the men of course finishing with the invariable end of all Bulgarian solemnities, drunkenness.

On the Feast of St. Demetrius lighted candles are placed in the stables and the place where fire-wood is chopped, to prevent evil spirits entering into the domestic animals.

In the winter solstice occurs the long feast of the Kolenda, so well known amongst Slavonic nations, which the Bulgarians call Kulada; it is the great time for all kinds of divinatory rites and incantations, especially amongst young girls who are anxious to know who are to be their husbands.

During its whole duration, which includes Christmas (or as the Bulgarians call it Domouz Kirma, the Feast of Pigs, because on that day every family kills one of these animals), all songs which are sung must terminate each verse with the refrain, "Kulada, hy Kulada:" and as it is at this period that the elementary spirits are most powerful and active, the peasants are obliged to take every precaution against them; no carts must be left without at least one log of wood in them, and no water-vessels entirely empty, for fear that some demon should take possession of them, and by his presence render them too heavy to be moved or lifted.

It is easy to see, even from the few instances we have given, that the feasts of the Bulgarians are a strange medley of old Slavonic Paganism and the ill-defined and superstitious Christianity * which exists in the East. The saints of the Greek calendar have taken the place of the heathen idols, but not altogether nor always, for the peasants still offer sacrifices to nature, to the elements, and even to animals; although the oblations of the latter class, as for instance that to the serpent, is really mere Pantheism, the ancient Lithuanians (who probably borrowed the custom from their Slavonic neighbours), having worshipped Spring under the symbols of a serpent, of thunder, and of rain, all of which attributes are connected in Bulgaria with Baba Mart, the mother of vegetation, of summer, of the whole year.

If we now take into consideration those breaches of certain superstitious observances which are considered by the Papas as sins (gunahler), the mixture of extraneous matter with the Greek rite becomes still more easily visible. The confession of a Bulgarian peasant is no easy matter, for in addition to the commandments of Scripture, he has to make a mental review of those ordained by his clergy, of which one of the latest is, that it is a great sin to give alms to a gipsy or an "infidel." Fortunately for him the moral elasticity tolerated in the Oriental Church dispenses him from troubling himself very much about the prohibitions of Scripture, so long as he observes strictly those of the Church

---

* In the following chapter, upon the customs, &c., of the Bulgarians, this connection will be still more clearly made evident.

and especially those of the priests;—of these latter, which to the peasant are sins of the deepest dye, although he can give no further reason for the innate depravity of these actions than the dictum of a Papas, we give an imperfect and abbreviated list, which, however, includes most of those affecting everyday life.*

It is a sin—

1. To give a child a spoon to play with.
2. To give away or sell a loaf of bread without breaking a piece from it.
3. Not to fumigate with incense the flour when it is brought from the mill (particularly if the mill be kept by a Turk), in order to prevent the Devil entering into it.
4. To wash a child before he has come to the (canonical) age of reason, that is to say, seven years.
5. To sell flour before making a loaf from it.
6. To clean a stable, sell milk, or fetch water from the fountain after dusk.
7. To allow a dog to sleep on the roof of the house, as this gravely imperils the soul of any defunct member of the family.
8. Not to throw some water out of every bucket brought from the fountain, as some elementary spirit might otherwise be floating on the surface of the water, and, not being thrown out, take up his abode in the house, or enter into the body of any one who drank from the vessel.

Finally, it is a sin to fail in the observance of any of the hundred superstious practices approved or tolerated by the Papas.

An English Roman Catholic priest of the oratory would be perhaps a little astonished if one of his lady-penitents confessed with tears that she had washed her baby, or that Fido had climbed out on to the roof through the window of the footman's bedroom, and spent the night there; but the Greek Papas treats such backslidings as serious transgressions of morality, flourishes his whip, and imposes probably, for the infant washed, a heavier penance than for the oxen stolen.

By far the most curious superstition in Bulgaria is that of

---

* *See* Appendix B.

the vampire,* a tradition which is common to all countries of Slavonic origin, but is now to be found in its original loathsomeness only in these provinces. In Dalmatia and Albania, whence the knowledge of this superstition was first imported into Europe, and which were consequently, though wrongly, considered as its mother countries, the vampire has been disfigured by poetical embellishments and has become a mere theatrical being—tricked out in all the tinsel of modern fancy. The Dalmatian youth who, after confessing himself and receiving the Holy Communion as if in preparation for death, plunges a consecrated poniard into the heart of the vampire slumbering in his tomb; and the supernaturally beautiful vampire himself, who sucks the life-blood of sleeping maidens, has never been imagined by the people, but fabricated, or at least dressed up, by romancers of the sensational school.

When that factitious poetry born from the ashes of a people whose nationality is extinct, and from which civilisation has reaped its harvest, replaces the harsh, severe, even terrible poetry which is the offspring of the uncultivated courage or fear of a young and vigorous humanity, legendary lore becomes weak, doubtful, and theatrical. Thus, as in a ballad said to be antique we recognise a forgery by the smoothness of its rhythm and the nicety of its rhyme; so, when the superstitions of a people naturally uneducated and savage are distinguished by traits of religion or of sentiment, we trace the defacing hand of the Church or the poet.

---

* The pure Bulgarians call this being by the genuine Slavonic name of *Upior*, the Gagaous (or Bulgarians of mixed race) by that of *Obour*, which is Turkish; in Dalmatia it is known as *Wukodlak*, which appears to be merely a corruption of the Romaic Βρυκόλαξ.

In Dalmatia the vampire is now no more than a shadow in which no one believes, or at best in which people pretend to believe, just as a London Scottish volunteer will assure you of his firm faith in the Kelpie and Brounie of Sir Walter Scott, or will endeavour to convince you that he wears a kilt from choice and not for effect. Between the conventional vampire and the true horror of Slavonic superstition there is as much difference as between the highland chief who kicked away the ball of snow from under his son's head, reproaching him with southron effeminacy in needing the luxury of a pillow, and the kilted cockney sportsman who shoots down tame deer in an enclosure.

In Poland the Roman Catholic clergy have laid hold upon this superstition as a means of making war upon the great enemy of the Church, and there the vampire is merely a corpse possessed by the Evil Spirit, and no longer the true vampire of the ancient Slavonians. In Bulgaria we find the brute in its original and disgusting form; it is no longer a dead body possessed by a demon, but a soul in revolt against the inevitable principle of corporeal death; the Dalmatian poniard, blessed upon the altar, is powerless here, and its substitute is an Ilatch (literally, medicine) administered by the witch or some other wise woman, who detects a vampire by the hole in his tombstone or the earth which covers him, and stuffs it up with human excrement (his favourite food) mixed with poisonous herbs.

We will now give the unadulterated Bulgarian superstition, merely prefacing that we ought to be well acquainted with it, inasmuch as a servant of ours is the son of a noted vampire, and is doing penance during this present Lent by neither smoking, nor drinking wine or spirits, in order to expiate the sins of his father and to prevent himself inheriting the propensity.*

When a man who has vampire blood in his veins—for this condition is not only epidemic and endemic but hereditary—or who is otherwise predisposed to become a vampire,† dies, nine days after his burial he returns to upper earth in an aëriform shape. The presence of the vampire in this his first condition may be easily discerned in the dark by a succession of sparks like those from a flint and steel, in the light, by a shadow projected upon a wall and varying in density according to the age of the vampire in his career. In this stage he is comparatively harmless and is only able to play the practical jokes of the German Kobold and Gnome, of the Irish Phooka, or the English Puck,‡ he roars in a terrible voice, or amuses himself by calling out the inhabitants of a cottage by the most endearing terms and then beating them black and blue.

The father of our servant Theodore was a vampire of this class. One night he seized by the waist (for vampires are capable of exercising considerable physical force) Kodja Keraz, the *Pehlivan* or champion wrestler of Derekuoi, crying out, "Now then, old Cherry Tree, see if you can throw me." The village champion put forth all his strength, but the vampire was so heavy that Kodja Keraz broke his own jaw in throwing the invisible being who was crushing him to death.§

---

* Poor Theodore is head over ears in love with Miss Tuturitza, the young lady next door, who fully reciprocates his affection, but her parents refuse to sanction the marriage on account of the vampire father.

† As when a man is strangled by one of these beings.

‡ He only resembles these spirits in their misdeeds; unlike them, he never does a good turn to anybody.

§ Of course, sceptical persons may be found who would explain this

At the time of this occurrence, five years ago, our village was so infested by vampires that the inhabitants were forced to assemble together in two or three houses, to burn candles all night, and to watch by turns in order to avoid the assaults of the Obours who lit up the streets with their sparkles, and of whom the most enterprising threw their shadows on the walls of the room where the peasants were dying of fear; whilst others howled, shrieked, and swore outside the door, entered the abandoned houses, spat blood into the flour, turned everything topsy-turvy, and smeared the whole place, even the pictures of the saints, with cow-dung. Happily for Dereknoi, Vola's mother, an old lady suspected of a turn for witchcraft, discovered the Ilatch we have already mentioned, laid the troublesome and troubled spirits, and since then the village has been free from these unpleasant supernatural visitations.

When the Bulgarian vampire has finished a forty days' apprenticeship to the realm of shadows,* he rises from his tomb in bodily form and is able to pass himself off as a human being living honestly and naturally. Thirty years since a stranger arrived in this village, established himself,

---

story by the hypothesis of too much wine and a fall over a heap of stones; fortunately our village does not contain any such freethinkers, and Old Cherry Tree will be happy to relate his tale, as we have given it, to any inquirer after truth: to prove its accuracy, he can call many witnesses who will swear to the fact of his jaw having been broken.

* Since commencing this chapter, we have learned that the village of Dervishknoi, six hours from here, is just now haunted by a vampire; he appears with a companion who was suppressed by means of the usual remedy, but this one seems to be proof against poison, and as he will shortly have completed his fortieth day as a shadow, the villagers are in terrible alarm lest he should appear as flesh and blood.

and married a wife with whom he lived on very good terms, she making but one complaint, that her husband absented himself from the conjugal roof every night and all night. It was soon remarked that (although scavengers were, and are, utterly unknown in Bulgaria) a great deal of scavengers' work was done at night by some unseen being, and that when one branch of this industry was exhausted the dead horses and buffaloes which lay about the streets were devoured by invisible teeth, much to the prejudice of the village dogs; then the mysterious mouth drained the blood of all cattle that happened to be in any way sickly. These occurrences and the testimony of the wife caused the stranger to be suspected of Vampirism, he was examined, found to have only one nostril,* and upon this irrefragable evidence was condemned to death. In executing this sentence, our villagers did not think it necessary to send for the priest, to confess themselves, or to take consecrated halters or daggers; they just tied their man hand and foot, led him to a hill a little outside Derekuoi, lit a big fire of wait-a-bit thorns, and burned him alive.

There is yet another method of abolishing a vampire, that of *bottling* him; there are certain persons who make a profession of this, and their mode of procedure is as follows; the sorcerer, armed with a picture of some saint, lies in ambush until he sees the vampire pass, when he pursues him with his *Eikon*; the poor Obour takes refuge in a tree or on the roof of a house, but his persecutor follows him up with the talisman, driving him away from all shelter, in the

---

* A thoroughly Slavonic idea: in Poland the vampire is also supposed to have a sharp point at the end of his tongue, like the sting of a bee.

direction of a bottle specially prepared, in which is placed some of the vampire's favourite food: having no other resource, he enters this prison, and is immediately fastened down with a cork, on the interior of which is a fragment of the Eikon. The bottle is then thrown into the fire, and the vampire disappears for ever. This method is curious as showing the grossly material view of the soul taken by the Bulgarians, who imagine that it is a sort of chemical compound destructible (like sulphuretted hydrogen) by heat, in the same manner that they suppose the souls of the dead to have appetites and to feed after the manner of living beings 'in the place where they are.'

To finish the story of the Bulgarian vampire we have merely to state that here he does not seem to have that peculiar appetite for human blood which is generally supposed to form his distinguishing and most terrible characteristic, only requiring it when his resources of coarser food are exhausted.

Whatever may be the origin of Fountain Spirits,* whether Slavonic or no, they exist in Bulgaria in great numbers, appearing under various forms—of a fair lady, a goose, a cat, &c. The brother of Marynka, our washerwoman, was bitten by one of the Cheshmé cats, and died either from the wound or from fright. Our friend Nicolaki one evening saw a white goose on the top of a fountain, which all at once

---

* The fountains (cheshmé) are nearly always the work of Turks, who regard it as a sacred duty to utilize any spring of water they may find for the benefit of thirsty travellers. They are not usually so graceful in form as the classic drinking fountains of modern London, nor do they display the names of the generous donor in letters of gold; if there is any inscription on them, it is sure to be a verse of the Koran.

changed itself into a cat and commenced rubbing itself against his legs in a most friendly way; Nicolaki suspected that there was something uncanny in the transformation of a goose into a cat, and jumped over a little stream of water which trickled from the fountain, thus placing an insurmountable obstacle between himself and the object of his fear, for it seems that Bulgarian spirits, even those which belong to fountains, have this in common with the witches and warlocks of Scotland,

'A running stream they daurna cross.'

When the Spirits appear as beautiful women they are (perhaps naturally) still more dangerous, the mere sight of them being sometimes sufficient to cause death. Dimitri of Derekuoi was harassed by the persecution of one of these ladies, whom he could never go out of his house without seeing, and after in vain trying to exorcise his tormentor by the aid of the Church, he applied to a Turkish Hodja who prescribed a remedy which we have been unable to learn, but which was perfectly efficacious. For some weeks Dimitri did not see the Lady of the Fountain, but rendered careless by fancied security, he neglected to comply with the Hodja's injunctions, and one evening was seized upon by his supernatural inamorata, who imprinted a fervent kiss upon his lips; a week afterwards Dimitri was dead.

The Bulgarians, from their sordid and avaricious nature, are especially fond of money, and the peasant who would not go to the fountain after nightfall, even to save the lives of his father and mother, for fear of seeing the Spirits which haunt it, will confront all kinds of supernatural dangers on the chance of discovering a treasure; although he will not do two hours' work in order to earn a shilling, or to improve his fields, he will dig for three or four consecutive nights with his hair standing on end and the cold sweat of terror on his brow, in the hope of finding some treasure supposed to have been buried by Delhi Marco or Alexander the Great.

We have been lately invited (probably because it is thought that two Englishmen must be more than a match for all the Spirits of Darkness in Bulgaria) to assist in digging up a famous treasure which is buried somewhere near the river Kamchyk and guarded sometimes by a sudden and violent storm of thunder, wind, and rain, sometimes by a gigantic and frightful negro, whose head reaches to the clouds and whose lower lip hangs down to earth. The man who requested our presence and assistance had tried six weeks before to unearth this treasure, but at the first blow of the pick the storm made its appearance, and as on the second night the negro showed himself, everybody was frightened and judged it better to give up the undertaking for the present, in consideration of the supernatural obstacles encountered.

Besides the well-known method of discovering treasures on the eve of St. John, a curious rite is practised here to propitiate the guardian spirits. When the precise locality has been found, some of the ashes thrown out into the Harman during the Kulada are spread at night over the place. The footmark which is seen imprinted next morning is that of the animal which the genius requires as a propitiatory offering.

In the case of one treasure of which we have been told, the footprint seen the next day was that of a man, showing that a human victim was required before the money could be dug up; for the present this spot has been abandoned, and it is to be hoped that no Bulgarian will be tempted to make his fortune by a preliminary murder.

An hour's journey from Alaja Monastir (a Greek monastery), in the neighbourhood of Baltchik, is a rocky valley called Kourou Dere, in which is a cavern with an iron door, always ajar, through which may be seen an inner cave filled with gold and silver. A Bulgarian Choban entered one day, filled his belt and his pockets with coin, and turned to go out; to his dismay he found the door closed and a hideous negro, armed with pistols and sword, guarding the exit.

The Choban threw away all his gold, but the door remained shut, and the negro drew his sword; then he noticed that a piece of money had stuck in his charrek (sandal), and on flinging this away he was allowed to escape, very glad to have come off so well.

Another time a Turkish Hodja resolved to possess himself of the treasures enclosed in the same enchanted cavern, and set out for Kourou Dere armed with an ancient book of necromancy, and accompanied by seven Bulgarians to carry the spoil and three Turks to guard it. He entered the antechamber and, having strictly forbidden his followers to utter a word whatever they might see or hear, commenced reading aloud from his magic volume; as he read, a side door opened in the rock, disclosing a motionless lady of marvellous beauty. The Hodja continued reading, and the damsel took off her head-dress and laid it upon the ground; the Hodja, without ceasing his reading, removed his turban and laid it on the top of the head-dress: presently the lady took off her jacket and the Hodja his, observing the same ceremony of superimposition, and so it went on till lady and schoolmaster (the latter still reading) appeared in the costume of Adam and Eve before the fall. Then a young Turk forgot the injunction given, and called out, "I say Hodja, what are you doing?" At these words a sudden blast of wind transported the treasure-seeker and his companions to a spot just outside the walls of Alaja Monastir. What became of the Hodja's garments our informant was unable to tell us.

At Pietrych Kaleh, near Gebidjie, the villagers of Evren found a great treasure, but four men (they were Bulgarians) died of terror in digging it up.

Between our village and Varna there is an old choked-up well which the country people say is Genoese.* Nicolaki went there with others to search for treasure, and after a whole day's hard work they found a dead squirrel, which they threw out on the ground. Nicolaki said, "Why I think it's a squirrel!" and the little animal jumped up and climbed up on a tree. When they had dug to a depth of twenty feet they saw a big snake, also dead, and pitched him out too. Next day they resumed their labour and, to their horror, saw the same snake alive in the same hole. This was too much for their nerves, fear conquered cupidity, and they left the place; but in the course of their excavations they sounded a

* In Bulgaria, almost all antiquities are attributed (both by Turks and Rayahs), to the Genoese; at Karamanja, in Roumelia, there are some very perfect remains of a Roman wall (probably that built by Hadrian, from the Danube to the Black Sea), in which may still be traced the gate and flanking towers; these are termed Genoese by the people of the neighbourhood, as are also some ruins in the same vicinity, which, judging from the fragments of pottery and sculptured stone which we saw, appear to belong to the old Macedonian empire.

hole beneath them of about sixty feet, so that they would have had three days' good work to arrive at the bottom of the well, even supposing that they were not impeded by any further supernatural manifestations.

The same Nicolaki was also engaged at night in looking for another supposed treasure not far from this well. The workers heard mysterious voices from the depths of the lake enjoining them to desist; but though they were in a terrible fright they kept on until all at once day broke, and they saw a squadron of Turkish cavalry charging at them through the cover; then the Bulgarians took to their heels and never ceased running till they got to their own village, where, to their astonishment, they found it still black night and that the earliest cock had not yet crowed!

Ghosts, as we understand the term in England, are very rare if not entirely unknown in Bulgaria. There is certainly the white woman of Gebidjie, who haunts a hilly piece of road in the neighbourhood of that village, and without invitation takes a ride in any cart which happens to pass her domain, making the vehicle so heavy that the oxen are often unable to draw it; her costume, as far as we can make out from those who have seen her, is that of an ancient Roman lady, and she is most probably the guardian of a treasure, for the combustible souls of the Bulgarians seem not to reappear under any form but that of a vampire, and bear no resemblance to those spectres whose traditions Europe inherits from the middle ages.

According to a Bulgarian superstition, those Turks who have never eaten of the animal sacred to the Rayahs, the pig, become wild boars after their death. The father of a peasant we know had one day shot a very fine boar in the forest, and invited a lot of friends to partake of it; but when the Kebas were placed on the spit they suddenly and with one accord jumped off it into the fire—a proceeding which a good deal frightened the assembled guests. However, an old man, who had rather a reputation for sorcery, asked the host to bring the head of the boar to look at. In the ears was found a piece of cotton, which the wise man said was a fragment of the turban worn by the Turk who had assumed the porcine shape, so all the meat was thrown away. The Rayahs also pretend that when a Mussulman who has never eaten pork dies, the Turkish women anoint the corpse with pig's lard to prevent his soul entering into the body of the unclean animal.

The action of the priesthood in Bulgaria, we must repeat, has not succeeded (if indeed it has even endeavoured to do so) in eradicating the materialism which characterises the mind of the true Slav, or in producing a thorough belief in one of the great tenets of Christianity, the immortality of the soul. Although the peasantry will tell you that there is a world of spirits beyond this life, they practically deny the fact, for their superstitions, which are more deeply rooted than the doctrines of the Church in their minds, represent the soul, although it may outlast the body, as destructible and subject to the wants of animal life.

The spirits of a more ethereal nature do not seem to be animated by souls of defunct Bulgarians; the guardians of treasures are borrowed from the Turks, who received the idea from the Arabs; the fountain spirits, allowing them to be of Slavonic origin, are mere demons of the elements and not even diabolical; the will o' the wisp is certainly said to be a soul escaped for a night or two from Limbo, but the peasantry have no great faith in him, because he is described as being so only on the authority of the Papas.

In short the Bulgarian mind seems to be capable of conceiving the disembodied soul only as something possessing still grosser appetites than its fleshly covering.

There are other spirits in whom the peasantry believe, but to whom they give no name, describing them "as a kind of invisible beast;" such is the nightmare, which is not the offspring of too much pork and consequent indigestion, but a maleficent being to be exorcised by spells; and a class of spirits (probably connected with the Polish *Chochlik* and the Cossack *Oczeretny-Czort* or reed-devil) who inhabit marshy places or forests, amusing themselves by pouncing upon the unwary passer-by, seizing him by the arm or leg and paralysing the limb by their touch, or knocking him down and beating him. Like most of the supernatural beings in this country they are coarse-feeders, and occasionally leave their sylvan home to banquet upon the plentiful supply of delicacies provided for them in the Rayah villages.

During a recent visit to Dervishkuoi, a young man seeing us reading from a Turkish book, begged that we would do something to cure his knee which had been struck and lamed by one of these nameless spirits whom he had accidentally disturbed in its occupation of feeding upon a heap of manure; at the same time the lady of the house requested that we would 'read,' in order to banish a troublesome being who every night seized and nearly choked her in spite of the presence of various members of the family. Our proceedings in both cases were simple and, as it turned out, efficacious; for each patient we recited some guttural gibberish in an imposing tone, and on the knee of the young man we traced in ink the figure of the fifth proposition of the First Book of Euclid, as the most effectual check to the further progress of any Bulgarian spirit. On our again passing through the village a few days later, we were delighted to hear that the old woman's sleep was no longer disturbed by invisible garotters, and that the young man was already able to walk a little, and going on most favourably. We were here cautioned not to pass a certain stream after nightfall, as it is haunted by a spirit in the form of a white horse, like the Scotch Kelpie or The O'Donoghue's steed of the lakes of Killarney.

Enough has been said upon this subject to show that a comparison between the superstitions of the Bulgarians, and those of any other people (not of Slavonic race), will be much to the disadvantage of the former, who though tracing their origin to the snows of the North, preserve no vestige of that stern beauty found in the traditions of other Northern races; and whose long residence in the East has not enabled them to graft upon their own sordid imaginings any of that fervid and glowing poetry with which Oriental legends describe the Halls of Eblis or the delights of Paradise.

What a difference between the Bulgarian lamed by some foul spirit whom he had knocked up against as it was feeding on the midden, and the Turkish boy who attributes his paralysis to a touch of the pinion of an evil Genie flying too close to the earth!

The Scandinavian Valhalla, with its carousing and feasting under the auspices of All-Father Odin, is material enough, but at least the banquet is the reward of heroes; the Bulgarian does not even distinguish in his own mind between Heaven, Hell, and the Purgatory of the Greek Church, considering the world beyond the grave as a species of chophouse in which the souls of the dead are perhaps but ill fed, and whither he can send contributions of baked meats by the simple process of leaving them upon the tombs of his defunct friends.*

---

* This idea, almost blasphemous as it appears in its enunciation, is but too truly that of the Bulgarians; ask a peasant his idea of Heaven, he will tell you that "it is a place where you are very comfortable, and feed on sugared cakes!"

CHAPTER V.

BULGARIAN SUPERSTITIONS (*continued*).—MANNERS AND CUSTOMS, &C.

Witches — Herbalist and poisoner — Prescriptions for a fever — Exorcism sought from the Turkish Hodja — Strictness of morals — Family jars — Birth and infancy — A suitor and his negotiations — The betrothal — The wedding — Dances — The last fashion — Death and burial — mourners.

IT is a natural consequence of superstitious beliefs so implicit and so well organized as those which amongst the Bulgarians form a second religion, differing from, but more deeply-rooted than, that of the Greek Church, that they should have their professed ministers. Wherever there is a chance of gain some one will present himself to profit by it, and as the most paying investment is the folly and credulity of mankind, quackery of all kinds will continue to flourish so long as there are fools upon the earth; from Egyptian Thaumaturgy to Mr. Hume and the Davenport Brothers, from them to the Witch of Derekuoi, and from her to the Prospectus of an American Land Company, all is but an exemplification of the great truth that cunning will always find an easy prey in superstition and ignorance.

In Bulgaria, where the recognized religion neither affords sufficient food for that craving after the marvellous and supernatural which is innate in the savage or but imperfectly reclaimed mind, nor replaces this appetite by a more legitimate longing, it is not to be wondered at that superstition steps in to supply the want by the means of male sorcerers or female witches, who add to their pretensions to occult power the profession of village doctor.*

In every village there is an old woman learned in all ancient customs, ceremonies of divination, and in the worship of such powers as are anathematized by the Church; able to propitiate or to combat the Kingdom of Darkness, acquainted with the official residence of Baba Mart, on familiar terms with Azrael, and the possessor of an unlimited quantity of marifets or charms, from that which will bring rain to that which will exorcise the demon of fever; able to cast spells which will cause their object to die the lingering death of the spellbound, or cure him of the bite of a cheshmé cat; finally, the High Priestess of every pagan rite, and the first to kiss the hand of the Papas.

Whatever she may have been formerly, the Bulgarian witch of this present day has but little resemblance to her sister of Europe two hundred years ago; she has lost the art of flying through space upon a broomstick, nor does she attend the Sabbat on the Brocken—indeed, probably neither she nor her ghostly superiors (if the latter are genuine Bulgarian spirits) have ever heard of the existence of the Harz mountains—she is not the spouse of the Devil, but the most respected woman of her village; vampires may be poisoned, or bottled and burnt, but the witch receives offerings of fowls, milk, and eggs, from her grateful or timorous fellow-villagers; and in justice to her it must be allowed that she would be almost a greater loss than the Papas; for though like him

---

* In the villages of Bulgaria, no licensed medical practitioners exist; it is easy to imagine that in the case of a dangerous epidemic, plague, typhus, or cholera, this absence of physicians might become a very serious evil to Europe.

she taxes the village, she occasionally renders good service in return by a knowledge of simples (a branch of medicine now too generally neglected) which effects cures apparently little less than marvellous.

We trust to the indulgence of our readers to pardon us a slight digression involving a hypothesis. The Catholic clergy of the West, in their early struggles against classic and barbarian paganism, anathematised the ancient gods, and stigmatizing them as devils, declared that the false divinities whose images still live in marble in the museums of Europe, as well as the elementary spirits of barbarian superstition, were burning in Hell. The Byzantine clergy were not sufficiently powerful thus to crush the heathenism of their new converts, and, probably owing to the troubles caused by the Arabian and Ottoman invasion as well as to their own sophistic origin, were more anxious to put down schisms in their own body than to wage war against the latent memories of paganism. Even now the Greek Church, whilst launching its thunderbolts against the Bulgarian schism with one hand, amicably extends the other to the Bulgarian sorceress; perhaps the Papas, spiritual descendant of feeble Byzantium as the College of Cardinals is the representative of the powerful Roman Senate, hopes to find a rampart against Islamism in the ancient beliefs of the Bulgarians, for whilst he denounces it as a deadly sin for a Christian to be exorcised by a Turkish Hodja, he not only tolerates but approves the spells of the witch.

As the witch is on good terms with the clergy, respected and feared by the people, and stands in no danger of persecution, she has no need to make a secret of a profession which she can exercise openly, and her only point of resemblance to the almost extinct wise women of Europe is her power of doing evil, which she sometimes redeems by 'white witchcraft;' at the festivals of which we have spoken, she is the chairwoman; by the aid of her marifets she assists the Bulgarian in his entry into and exit from the world, and is at once doctor, sorceress, and general reference-book of the village, forming the complement of the Papas, and occasionally even poaching upon his preserves.

Is the Bulgarian ill, he sends for the witch; has he lost some money, he sends for the witch; is he going to give a feast or to die, he sends for the witch; does he require a philtre, he sends for the witch; does he wish to get rid of an enemy, the witch is still his resource; in regard to the last exigency it may be remarked that the herbology of the witch renders her at least as dangerous as she can be useful. In our own village is a woman who is well known (indeed she herself makes no great secret of the matter) to have poisoned her first husband in order to marry a second; the morals of the peasantry are far from stigmatizing this resource of feeble or cowardly wickedness, and in a country where autopsy is unknown, and where even murder by violence often goes unpunished, poison has a fair field and a great deal of favour; the method is simple: the wife goes to the witch, pays a fee, explains the case, and receives an *Ilatch* (literally, medicine) which she administers to her husband, and which is infinitely more effectual than the plan resorted to by more timorous consciences, that of tying a knot in their enemy's hair.

The 'Evil Eye' is believed in by the genuine Bulgarians as well as by the Gagaous, with both of whom, as amongst the negroes of the Gaboon, all illnesses are considered as the effects of spells wrought by human or supernatural maleficence, and their Materia Medica is consequently (also like that of the Africans in question) a mixture of incantations, for the deception of the uninitiated, and the really efficacious use of simples.

When a witch is called in as physician to a case of illness, her first care is to ascertain the gravity of the malady, its nature being of little importance, and this she discovers by the following ceremony: after the preliminary words of incantation she takes a long scarf in which a knot has been tied, and measures it on her arm from the elbow to the finger tips, and if the knot falls near the hand or on the fingers of the patient his illness is entirely imaginary, but if it touches the elbow he is condemned to death beyond the power of the Bulgarian Pharmacopœia.

As she has generally a certain practical knowledge of diseases and a kind of medical experience after her own fashion, she is occasionally able to judge the case correctly, and no doubt can make the knot fall where she chooses; but nevertheless she is often mistaken, a circumstance which by no means lessens her prestige amongst the villagers.

Our late landlord Tancz was given over by the witch and had made up his mind to die; as his illness was merely the effect of accumulated over-doses of wine, a seidlitz powder which we administered very quickly put him on his legs, and we rather gloried over the witch; however, one day we said to him, "Well, Tancz, the witch has made a mistake this time, for you are just as well as ever you were." "No, no; she has said I must die, and so I shall some day, you'll see."

About six months afterwards Tancz kept his word, and the wise woman's prophecy was verified!

Another time the same great authority had told a poor

fellow suffering from aggravated diphtheria that he had nothing the matter with him, and that he must go and work in the fields as usual; with some difficulty we managed to get him to take our prescriptions, and to effect a perfect cure: his thanks were conveyed much after the manner of Tancz, "You see, sir, the witch was right, for I am quite well now."

When the gravity of the case is once decided, then, as every illness is the effect of spells of one kind or another, the patient must be cured by incantations or 'medicines' which banish the demon possessing him; some of these remedies are sufficiently original to be worth giving—for the benefit of the Faculty. Tertian fever is caused by a certain fly having settled upon the sick man, and the two prescriptions most in vogue are as follow:—

1. Take a puppy dog under a month old, the younger the better, wash his hind quarters, and especially his left hind leg, in tepid water, which give as a draught to the patient.

2. Take a snipe, boil it without plucking, and give the broth as a drink.

The dried stomach of a stork is a sovereign cure for the effects of the evil eye, which is a great cause of mortality in Bulgaria.*

Naturally enough, the witches are not disposed to be communicative on the subject of their secrets, and it is

---

* Last year a woman applied to us for part of a stork for this purpose, but it was probably administered too late, as the child died three days afterwards; in this case the "evil eye" exactly resembled the Southern Italian Jettatura, the infant having sickened directly after a neighbour had said, "What a pretty child!" But as far as we have been able to ascertain, the Neapolitan counter charms of spitting in the infant's face, or "facendo le corna," seem to be unknown in Bulgaria.

therefore difficult to discover their pathology, but from what we know of Slavonic witchcraft in Russia, Poland, and this country, we can affirm that their proceedings strongly resemble those of the wise men or women on the West coast of Africa. Here, as there, illness is merely a possession by an evil demon, and madness or idiocy is the result of the presence in or on the body of a more than ordinarily powerful spirit, to exorcise whom it is neccessary to apply to a Turkish Hodja, both Papas and witch being powerless in such a case.

A mad woman was lately taken to the Greek Monastery on Cape Emineh in Roumelia to be exorcised by the monks, who employed in vain a whole arsenal of pious weapons,* and she was finally led to the Hodja of Akindji, who speedily produced a favourable change in her mental health; the relative, Dimitri of Dervishknoi (from whom we heard the particulars), who ventured to give the patient into infidel hands, was punished by the Papas's refusing him the Communion this Easter.

The witch is, however, more liberal than her colleague the Greek Priest, and will occasionally hand over to the Hodja a case which she considers hopeless, but she will not tolerate the competition of any M.R.C.S., and if such a person were to establish himself in a Bulgarian village he would probably fall a victim to the Ilatch of the sorceress.

Bulgarian morality † is tolerably good, for a people with whom religion has no real force, and is so much taken for

---

* Amongst these remedies, an iron cross, heated nearly red-hot, was placed on the woman's breast and back, and a number of similar cruel marifets (which we forbear to mention) were practised.

† This word is here used in a specific, not a generic sense.

granted, that the Papas administers the Communion to young girls without previous confession, a privilege denied to married people; a reason for the comparative purity of morals may perhaps be found in the fact that previous to her marriage a bride goes through an ordeal such as that to which the ancient Queens of France were subjected. Owing to this rule of morality, infanticide is terribly common with those women who form the exception, and is invariably considered by Mrs. Grundy as less culpable than the fault of which it is a consequence.

As for the ties of family, which are so often represented by European tourists as entirely absent amongst the Turks, it is sufficient to say that almost every Bulgarian family rejoices in a general and daily interchange of blows, in which the weakest, the women, naturally go to the wall.

From the cradle to the grave the Bulgarian is haunted by strange customs and observances such as are little known in Europe. When a child is born, the witch, who is present officially, brings a reaping hook into the room, and then proceeds to rub the infant all over with salt, and to fumigate the room in order to drive away all intrusive evil spirits from the mother and child.

With the exception of this bath of salt, a Bulgarian child is never washed until he attains the age of seven years; and for the first years of his life, a piece of garlic (in the case of a girl, one or two coins) is tied upon his head to preserve him from the evil eye. As soon as he is able to work, he is surrounded by superstitions which he is obliged to observe: if he fetches water he must throw away some of it; if he brings flour from the mill he must burn incense under it; in short, he cannot take a step without coming in contact with a superstition or an adet (custom)* which, if not respected, will avenge itself on him, and, without counting the spirits who lie in wait for him in the forest or at the fountain, his life is filled with fears which go far to compensate for its great enjoyments of eating, drinking, and dancing.

When a young man wishes to marry he speaks to his parents, who arrange the matter with those of the lady chosen, and *Swaty* † are sent to propose in due form; the amount of the corbeille is settled, as well as that of the *Baseh Parasi* or head-money presented by the suitor to the mother of his intended, and then the *gody* or betrothal takes place; this is a ceremony of great interest to all Bulgarians, who have the same tastes as those commemorated in the songs about their great heroes, of which the constant chorus is—

> 'Pak jede i pije,'
> 'And he eats and drinks.'

The Gody is usually held at the house of the girl's parents, where the elder guests sit around a cloth spread on the floor and covered with various dishes all strongly flavoured with garlic, whilst the wine-jug circulates freely; in another room the young people indulge in a similar repast, and afterwards dance outside the house, the girls singing songs at intervals. The young man then brings in his presents, which consist of various articles of feminine clothing, several pairs of slippers, bracelets, ear-rings, a head-dress and necklace of gold or

---

* A short list of *Adets* is given in the preceding chapter.

† For this word there is no exact equivalent in English; the Swaty are friends of the young man who act as his proxies in the delicate matter of 'proposing'—to the parents of the lady however, never to herself; the latter ceremony, which is so much thought of in England, not being customary in Bulgaria.

silver coins,* and a silver girdle: the value of these offerings is discussed by the father of the girl, and a fresh bargain ensues, the suitor adding coin by coin to the necklace till his future father-in-law is satisfied, and when this result is attained all the finery is placed in a teknch, a wooden dish used for making bread and for a cradle. Then all the guests set to work again at the banquet,

> 'Jedet i pijet,'
> 'They eat and drink,'

till daylight dawns upon the many tipsy and the very few sober. The next day the young lady puts on all the presents of her fiancé, and is considered as 'engaged.'

This betrothal is in no ways a religious ceremony, and leaves it open to either party to break off the engagement, but such a rupture seldom occurs; the marriage never takes place within six months of the Gody, and is often delayed for two or even three years.

With some rare exceptions these arrangements are by no means love-matches; the young man wishes to establish himself as head of a household, and chooses a wife as he would a yoke of buffaloes, looking upon her as a machine for labour and the probable mother of sons who will in time be able to work for him, and whom he can beat as *his* father beat *him* until he became too strong to permit it,—for a Bulgarian son when he grows up makes no scruple of returning with interest the blows received from his father. Thus the bride is chosen, not for the beauty of her more or less Kalmuck features, but for the muscular strength which will render her valuable as a beast of burden.

---

* The usual amount given is about eight Turkish Liras.

Sometimes you may meet with a Bulgarian Lindoro who translates his passion into the music of the Gaida, or courts some stalwart Rosina by playfully throwing lumps of mud at her as they meet at the fountain, or who buys an enormous pair of boots and spurs to attract the attention of his beloved, and proves the strength of his affection by treading upon her toes.

But Lindoro here, like the true Lindoro everywhere, is poor, and perhaps seeks by a disinterested love to attract into his own purse a few of the zecchini which he needs: at any rate it is no blasphemy to doubt the purity of his motives in a country where a powerfully-built wife is a good investment, instead of being an expensive luxury.

Our servant Theodore sighs for Miss Tuturitza, the daughter of our neighbour Kodja Kostantia, ex-assassin, and landowner of Derekuoi; but who can say that the idea of some buried pots of money, gained on the highroad, does not furnish at least as much fuel to his flame as the personal or mental attractions of his lady-love?

The marriage (Swadba) is prepared for by the bridegroom's installation in his new house, and the purchase of various domestic animals, especially a pair of oxen or buffaloes, without the possession of which the match would be considered a very poor one for the lady, if not entirely out of the question; when all is ready he sends his parents or his *Swaty* to announce that he wishes the ceremony to take place in two or three weeks.

During the week preceding the marriage, which is always celebrated on a Sunday and generally in the dead season,*

---

* The term is not here used in the London sense, but means the time when there is but little work going on in the fields.

the parents of the bride and bridegroom prepare the furniture, &c., of the new ménage, the girls of the village dance before the house of the bride, and the youths pay the same compliment to the bridegroom. On the Friday before the marriage the presents, hung on a cord, are exhibited in the bride's house, and she herself has her hair plaited into innumerable minute tresses; then she takes, *for the first and last time in her life*,* a complete bath, whilst her two bridesmaids, in the same primitive costume as the bather, look on, but without sharing in the ablution.

On the eventful Sunday, when the Papas is ready, the ceremony takes place in the church, if there be one, or otherwise in the bridegroom's house, and after the marriage the happy couple are led in procession to the mansion of the bride's father, where the young girls dance, corn is sprinkled over the husband and wife, and the latter, her face covered with a veil (often scarlet), kisses the hands of all the married women of the village, receiving in return a fig from each of them.

Then all the usual feasting goes on, and all the guests drink more than is good for them,

'Jedet i pijet,'

and the married couple are shut up in their own house for a week, during which time they may neither go out nor receive visits.

---

* Horrible as this statement seems, it is the literal truth; till the age of seven years a child must not be touched by water, and although after that period the face, hands, and feet may be washed, the cleansing of the whole body would be 'chok gunah,' a great sin, and is *never* practised by either male or female Bulgarians, with the solitary exception above mentioned.

When this period of imprisonment is over, the married women fetch the bride, who carries two water buckets, to the fountain, round which she walks three times preceded by the oldest of the women, then the contents of the buckets are thrown over her, she kisses hands all round, and again receives a present of figs.

The same day she pays a visit to her mother, and is henceforward considered as a member of the sisterhood of married women.

The married women are not generally allowed to join in the village dance, although some of the bolder spirits amongst them occasionally do so; this dance which is called in Russian *Bitchok*, is here styled 'Horo' (Χόρος), and strongly resembles the 'Romaika's dull round.' A circle of dancers is formed, the girls and men holding each other by the belt or girdle, and going round and round for hours to the music of the gaida; the motion is slow, monotonous, and ungraceful, but the coup d'œil from a distance is picturesque enough, from the gaudy colours of the female dresses. In our village the feminine taste for ornament has invented a new head-dress, consisting of pieces of the English or French newspapers received by us, which are in great request by the village beauties as 'Bonjouks' or 'jewels;' the portions most sought after are the headings or the advertisements in big capitals, so that the Derekuoi young ladies may often be seen wearing on their foreheads such placards as the following; 'The Times,' 'Mort aux Rats,' 'Pall Mall Gazette,' 'Vente à cause de Faillite,' 'Holloway's Pills,' 'Plus d'huile de foie de Morue,' 'A vendre à grand rabais,' 'Mme. Elise, Marchande de Modes,' and a host of other typographical varieties which are highly prized in the first circles of the Derekuoi fashionables.

At the end of every life, whether one of hardship and labour like the Turks, or feasting and idling like the Bulgarians, comes Death; but just as the latter considers baptism *not* as the admission of the infant into the Church of Christ, but as a mere sprinkling with water for which the Papas receives so much, so he looks upon death as the discharge of a mere animal function.

When he is given over by the witch, he prepares for the passage from life to an unknown world with a *sang froid* strongly resembling courage, but which is merely the result of a fatalism arising from apathy; he bargains with the Papas as to the price of his burial, orders the mortuary feasts, and in short prepares himself very quietly to repose in the grave which is already dug for him. During all this time the room is filled with women, shrieking and groaning in a manner sufficient almost to kill a healthy man.

At the moment of death all pots, kettles, and other utensils are turned upside-down, in order to prevent the soul of the departed taking refuge in one of them and therefrom commencing a system of annoyance against the family; candles or tapers are lit around the body, and the head is dressed with flowers; a great Eikon (picture of a Saint) is placed upon the breast, the body is clothed in its best clothes, or in some specially made for the purpose, and a pair of slippers, whilst all the members of the family run outside and scream a lamentation which is generally after this fashion:—*

"Oh! Tanaz! Bozè! Bozé!
Who will cut wood for us now?
(Shrieks and howls.)

---

* This song is a literal translation of a death-song sung at a house close to ours; they are always on the same model, lamenting the loss of the services of the deceased.

"Who will kill the sheep,
    Or who will take care of the poor buffaloes?
        (Shrieks and howls.)
"Who will carry the corn to the mill?
  Who will beat us as you used to do,
        Oh Tanaz?"
        (Shrieks and howls.)

Five minutes afterwards an araba with a couple of oxen or buffaloes is brought round,* containing a ladder, on which the corpse is placed without either shroud or coffin; but only two men accompany it, one to drive, the other to act as sexton; arrived at the cemetery, the body is thrown into the grave, a few spadefuls of earth thrown upon it, perhaps a stone placed, and all is over. No burial-service is ever said, for although a minimum sum of forty piastres must be paid to the Papas for every burial, he never appears, nor in any way officiates; if the family choose to have masses said for the soul of the dead they must make a new bargain, but in the country it is not much the fashion.

The same evening there is a great Death Feast of relations and friends in the house of mourning, which is repeated in ten days, and again at the expiration of one month, three

---

* Of course if death occur during the night, burial is put off till dawn; but owing to the terribly hasty plan of interring before the body is cold, premature burial must be frightfully common; two instances have occurred, in which we were as sure as (not being medical men) we could well be, that the supposed dead men were merely in a state of trance or lethargy, and did all in our power to stop the burial, but in vain. Some years since a man contrived to rise from his shallow grave, came back to his home, and gave his wife a tremendous beating to prove his identity, and to punish her for being in such a hurry to get rid of him; but a few months afterwards he died again, and that time his disconsolate widow took precautions which prevented him ever re-appearing to trouble her again.

months, six months, a year, and three years; these are called in Bulgarian *Pominki*, commemorations. If the dead man leaves a widow, she goes to his grave every morning for forty days and throws water over it "so that he may not die of thirst." Besides the Pominki, the Bulgarians hold a feast in the cemetery on Palm Sunday, and after much eating and drinking leave the remains upon the graves of their friends, who, they are persuaded, will eat them during the night; on Easter Monday an Easter Egg is placed on each grave.

The Bulgarian mourning, which is worn only by women, consists in wearing every article of clothing inside out; as with us, it varies in duration according to the consanguinity of the relation lost; that of a widow is fixed at one year.

CHAPTER VI.

BULGARIAN SONGS.

Spurious literature — Bulgarian language — Deli Marko's match with the Evil One — Philip Junak's boasting — Deli Marko's performance — Joanczo Krym Pehlivanczo — Preparations for the encounter — The Czar's bear overcome — King Marko — Arrival at Philip the Magyar's — A long swim — Combat with a Lomota — The hero's return — Seferina rejected — Legends of other races compared.

LIKE all people who have neither a literature nor even a perfectly formed language, the Bulgarians have preserved but vague traditions of bygone ages, and if a Bulgarian History founded upon these and their songs were written, it would be a remarkably eccentric one, as may be judged from the specimens of poetry given in this chapter. The Servians and even the Montenegrins, as well as the Bosniacs, in preserving an aristocracy have preserved their history, for in the Court or amongst the followers of the Servian and Montenegrin prince or noble, and of the Bosniac bey, there were always men who, like the Celtic bards, transmitted from generation to generation the deeds of the families to which they were attached, and amongst Slavonic nations the deeds of the nobles formed the history of the people.

The old Bulgarian language was never a written one, and it is only in our own day that a few works have appeared, printed in characters which are a pleasing mixture of the two alphabets respectively used in Russia for lay and ecclesiastical books, and which are self-styled Bulgarian; a critique of these works would probably be of little general interest, and we confine ourselves to stating that the language in which they are written is not understood by the people, even if it be intelligible to the 'literary men' of Bulgaria. They consist for the most part of school-books, in which Russian and Sacred History are inextricably entangled, books of prayer, and a large volume of Bulgarian songs, traditions, manners and customs, printed in Servia; from this last volume we borrow one line:—

'Deli Marko,' 'Mad Marko,'

changed into 'Dimny* Marko,' 'Marko the Magnificent,' which will be sufficient to show the alterations made in the old songs.

Our chief reasons for not troubling our readers with any extracts from this collection are, that there are plenty of original and unadulterated songs amongst the Bulgarians, and that the people themselves deny the authenticity of the Servian versions, saying when they are read to them 'Toi Arnaoutskie Piesni,' 'these are Albanian songs;' and we shall therefore have the honour of introducing some songs 'never before published,' either in England or elsewhere, and which are translated exactly word for word.†

---

* Critics may tell us that 'Dimny' means 'proud,' but according to our knowledge of Slavonic idioms, we fancy that the epithet 'magnificent' is more applicable; 'Dimny' is (to coin a word) a *Cossackism* for 'dumny,' the Cossacks always changing *u* into *i*; still severer critics may possibly derive the word in question from Dym, smoke, in which case they can translate Dimny Marko as Smoked Marko.

† Even for those who thoroughly understand Slavonic languages and idioms there is a great difficulty to be encountered in Bulgarian, for an immense number of Slavonic words, while retaining their original form, have an entirely different signification, e.g.:—

[Bulgarian

A word upon the Bulgarian language and traditions; the language as spoken and sung is by no means that of the books newly invented; it is a strange mixture of Turkish and Persian with Slavonic, and contains many words of Italian and Greek origin, and from other European languages: the most curious peculiarity is that not only Turkish adjectives and substantives are used, but also verbs, and the Turkish inflections of tense, mood, &c., are used with verbs of purely Slavonic origin; those who are acquainted with Oriental and Slavonic tongues may find some instances of this in the song given in Bulgarian in the Appendix: it is constantly done when the singer wishes to render his style peculiarly elegant.

The Bulgarian historical traditions, except in the form of songs, are not numerous; the following is one of the most curious:—

Once upon a time the world was peopled only by heroes and Zmieje (dragons), and of all the former Deli or Kral (King) Marko was by far the stoutest and strongest. One day the Devil was amusing himself with his great mace of wood bound with iron, of the weight of 100 okes (280 lbs.), throwing it up into the air and catching it again with one hand. Deli Marko found him thus employed and wished him good morning very politely.

"Hosh geldin," 'Welcome,' said his Majesty.

"Hosh bouldouk," 'Well found,' replied the hero.

Bulgarian words.	Meaning in Slavonic.	Meaning in Bulgarian.
Dumat	To think	To speak.
Czy	If	And.
Pravit	To say	To do.
Na pravit	To mend	To make.

In Polish however, na prawic is used for 'to mend.'

After these and other necessary compliments, Deli Marko asked the Devil what he was doing there.

"You see, I am practising throwing this mace into the air and catching it: it's for the *Pehlivanlik* (Championship)."

"Let's try together," suggested Deli Marko.

"With all my heart, go and take your place." And the Devil hurled his mace 100 yards, but Deli Marko caught it in the air like a cricket-ball.

"Bravo indeed," cried Satan, clapping his hands, "it's your turn now, throw the mace for me to catch."

But Deli Marko let the Devil's mace lie on the ground and took up his own, which was also of wood and iron and weighed 300 okes; this he pitched with a good swing, and the poor Devil, trying to catch it, was knocked down, and a good deal bruised. Deli Marko took up the mace of his unlucky competitor, threw it up to the sky, where it stuck, and walked quietly away from the Bulgarian Beaufort House, whistling an air.

The Devil went back to his own dominions, very sore from his bruises and his defeat in the Athletic Sports, and set about forging an iron tube, which he loaded with a little dust from the infernal smithy, and a leaden bullet. When these were ready he appeared upon earth again and called upon Deli Marko.

"Good morning, Deli Marko."

"Hosh geldin."

"Hosh bouldouk."

"Come, Deli Marko," quoth the Devil, you beat me the other day, and you caught my mace which weighs 100 okes; do you think you can catch this little ball which weighs two drachms?"

"There's my hand," said Deli Marko, laughing very disdaintfully; "throw your little ball, and let's see whether I can't catch it!"

Then the Devil took his tube, lit the powder (perhaps with a spark from his tail), and the bullet struck Deli Marko in the palm of the hand, perforating it completely; Deli Marko looked sadly at the wound, and sighed out, "Now that guns are invented, this earth is no place for heroes any longer!" and as there was a dragon passing, he called him up, got on his back, and flew away for ever; the same day all the heroes followed his example, and that is the reason that there are now neither dragons nor heroes in the country.

Here we see Deli Marko, the hero *par excellence* of Bulgaria, giving utterance to a sentiment very like that of Bayard and many other preux chevaliers; but we shall see him immediately in his true character, in his affair with Hero Philip.

Many of the Bulgarian songs are translated from the Turkish, and in these the original is much injured and disfigured. Those we have chosen are genuine Slavonic and such as best depict the character of the Bulgarians and their ideas as to the attributes of a hero.

DELI MARKO AND PHILIP JUNAK.*

A Song sung during the Kulada.†

Philip Junak is boasting,
    Hey Kulada moy Kulada!
At the Siedanki ‡ before the maidens,
    Hey Kulada moy Kulada!
At the Bielanki § before the women,
    Hey Kulada moy Kulada!
At the Tukhan || before the young men,
    Hey Kulada moy Kulada!
That he has chained up three monsters. ¶
    Hey, &c.
This Deli Marko learns,
    Hey, &c.
And he seeks for him
    Hey, &c.

---

* *Deli* means mad in Turkish and is not an opprobrious term, being applied to persons of rash and fiery courage. *Junak* is Bulgarian for *hero*.

† The Kulada is the feast of the winter solstice; see Superstitions.

‡ Nocturnal festivals, when the young girls dance around large fires.

§ Where the women sit spinning.

|| The public-house; the men's usual club.

¶ In Bulgarian, three 'Zmieje,' a name wrongly given by the Bulgarians to all dragons; the Zmieja of Polish legends is an enormous and hideous blind serpent which darts fire and smoke but cannot fly like the dragon, who is called 'Smok.' The Bulgarians do not appear to distinguish between the two; but as in all their traditions the dragon is the friend and often the favourite steed of their heroes, it is possible that it was three 'Zmieje' that Philip Junak chained up and not three 'Smoky,' unless he wished to break in some of the latter for riding; or the three monsters may have belonged to the stud of dragons of Deli Marko, which would explain that hero's wrath; but the story seems to negative this hypothesis, and to show that the whole account given by Philip Junak was a vain boast.

At the Siedanki before the maidens,
　　　　　　Hey, &c.
At the Bielanki before the women,
　　　　　　Hey, &c.
In the Tukhan before the young men.
　　　　　　Hey, &c.
What the young men say to him:
　　　　　　Hey, &c.
" Where is Philip Junak ? "
　　　　　　Hey, &c.
" He is staying there on the mountain
　　　　　　Hey, &c.
Towards the setting of the sun (the West)
　　　　　　Hey, &c.
The gates of Dzym Dzyr."*
　　　　　　Hey, &c.
And he goes there, Deli Marko,
　　　　　　Hey, &c.
And the Conac† of Philip Junak
　　　　　　Hey, &c.
Deli Marko finds it.
　　　　　　Hey, &c.
He finds it, and calls,
　　　　　　Hey, &c.
Deli Marko calls him,
　　　　　　Hey, &c.
He calls him and knocks at the gates.
　　　　　　Hey, &c.
Philip Junak his gates of Dzym Dzyr opens not,
　　　　　　Hey, &c.
And he pushes them, Deli Marko, the gates of Dzym Dzyr of Philip Junak,
　　　　　　Hey, &c.
And he gives a kick to the iron‡ gates
　　　　　　Hey, &c.
And he sends them up to the blue sky
　　　　　　Hey, &c.
When he gives them his kick.
　　　　　　Hey, &c.

---

* Dzym Dzyr is a species of wood unknown to us.
† Palace.　　‡ Here demir ('Turkish), iron, is substituted for dzym dzyr.

And into the palace of Philip Junak Deli Marko enters,*
   Hey, &c.
But Philip Junak comes not down,
   Hey, &c.
But the wife of Philip comes down,
   Hey, &c.
Comes down straight towards Deli Marko,
   Hey, &c.
And she wears a plume;
   Hey, &c.
And he snatches it, Deli Marko;
   Hey, &c.
Then Philip Junak comes down
   Hey, &c.
And he claps his hands for the wrestling.†
   Hey, &c.
They seize one another and they wrestle,
   Hey, &c.
With Deli Marko Philip Junak,
   Hey, &c.
And he seizes him (does) Deli Marko, Philip Junak
   Hey, &c.
And ties his hands behind him, Deli Marko,
   Hey, &c.
And brings him to the Siedanki before the maidens:
   Hey, &c.
"Is it thou, Philip, who boastedst
   Hey, &c.
"Before the maidens at the Siedanki,
   Hey, &c.
"Where then hast thou chained up the three monsters?"
   Hey, &c.
And from there he takes him out and brings him
   Hey, &c.
To the Bielanki before the women,
   Hey, &c.
And asks him, "Is it thou, Philip,
   Hey, &c.
"Who boastedst
   Hey, &c.

---

* The literal translation would be "crawls in;" see the original Bulgarian of this song as given in the Appendix C.

† This signal is still used in Bulgarian wrestling.

"Of having chained up three monsters?"
    Hey, &c.
And from there he takes him, Deli Marko, and brings him
    Hey, &c.
To the Tukhan before the young men,
    Hey, &c.
And asks him, "Is it thou, Philip Junak,
    Hey, &c.
"Who boastedst in the Tukhan
    Hey, &c.
"That thou hast chained up tight three monsters?"
    Hey, &c.
Philip Junak begs and prays Deli Marko,
    Hey, &c.
"Let me go, please, O Deli Marko!"
    Hey, &c.
But Deli Marko does not let go Philip Junak,
    Hey, &c.
Did not let him go—hung him!
    Hey Kulada moy Kulada!

We see that the Bulgarian legendary hero is tolerably conceited and cruel by nature, not to mention his unknightly manner of behaviour towards ladies; perhaps he snatched the plume from Mrs. Philip to make her husband fight, but he might have obtained this result in a different manner. We shall see in another song that he is decidedly gluttonous, and not more gallant than in this one; but before that allow us to present to you, our readers, a gentleman who yields in nothing to Deli Marko, and who is even more of a Bulgarian, as he appears to have lived at an earlier period; we beg to present Joanczo Krym Pehlivanczo.

JOANCZO KRYM PEHLIVANCZO.*

Joanczo Krym Pehlivanczo to his mother he says,
"Oh mother, oh my mother, my reputation is declining!
So tell the furrier to make me a Kalpak†
Of nine wolf-skins and the tenth (skin) of a bear."

And she goes, the mother—the mother of Joanczo,
To the furrier that he might make the Kalpak
Of nine wolf-skins and the tenth (the skin) of a bear.

Joanczo Krym Pehlivanczo to his mother he says,
"I am going to the furrier, that he may make me
A pair of trowsers for wrestling ; for a firman from the Czar
Is come to me, and commands me to wrestle with his Pehlivans ;
And I am going to wrestle with the Pehlivans of the Czar,
And the Pehlivans of the Czar are bloodthirsty bears."

The mother says to Joanczo, "Do not go, my son,
Nine Pehlivans have gone to the Czar
And the nine were eaten by the bears!"

Joanczo to his mother he says, "Open the Hungarian trunk
And look there for a handsome suit of clothes,
In order to set out for the Czar's, and to fight his bears;
In order that the bears may not kill me,
And that I may not be ashamed before the Czar."

And Joanczo Krym Pehlivanczo to his mother he says,
"Bake me nine ovenfuls of bread,
And kill me nine fat cows,
And knock me in the heads of nine barrels of wine."

And Joanczo eats the nine ovenfuls of bread,
And he eats the nine fat cows,
And he drinks the nine barrels of wine,
And he will set out for the Czar's to wrestle.

---

* Joanczo is the diminutive of Joan, John; Pehlivan (Turkish) is a champion wrestler, the termination czo being added probably to enable them to pronounce the whole title ore rotundo; how Jack or Johnny became champion of the Crimea is unknown both to us and the Bulgarians.

† A Bulgarian cap, usually made of sheepskin.

And he eat the nine ovenfuls of bread,
And he eat the nine fat cows,
And he drank the nine barrels of wine,
And he set out for the Czar's to wrestle.

Joanczo arrives at the Czar's.
The Czar sends his black Chinguiné* to announce,
By sound of trumpet, the combat.
And he cries and proclaims
Three days and three nights,
" Let great and small assemble
On the fields or the mogila,†
For a great wrestling will take place
Between Joanczo Krym Pehlivanczo
And the bloodthirsty bear of the Czar!"

And great and small they assemble
On the fields and on the mogila,
And the regiment of black gipsies is there.
And nine black men guard (the bear) with the curved steel,
And nine black men with chains of steel
Conduct him, the terrible bear!
And the chains were loosened,
And the bear utters a cry,
At this cry the earth trembles,
And the heavens thunder as he utters it.

Joanczo Krym Pehlivanczo was afraid when he saw this bear,
But he hid his tears from the Czar
That the Czar might not laugh at him.

And they catch hold of one another, the bear of blood
And Joanczo Krym Pehlivanczo.
Three days and three nights they wrestle,
Neither the bear falls, nor Joanczo falls;
Where Joanczo holds the black blood flows,
Where the bear holds the white flesh flies.
Three days and three nights they wrestle,
Neither Joanczo falls, nor the bear falls.

The Czar says to Joanczo, "There you are, then,
Joanczo Krym Pehlivanczo,

---

* Chinguiné, gipsy.

† Mogila, tombs; the tumuli or *barrows* so abundant in European Turkey.

Thou wilt die of thy wounds,
And my bear will not!"

Joanczo Krym Pehlivanczo is very angry.
He catches a good hold of the bear,
Lifts him up to the blue sky,
And dashes him against the earth;
And in four he breaks him,
And the four pieces bury themselves
In four holes in the ground.

Then the Czar was afraid of Joanczo Krym Pehlivanczo.
"In future, Joanczo,
If you kill a man
You are absolved beforehand
From all guilt of murder."
And he commands his regiment of blacks,
"Bring directly to Joanczo Krym Pehlivanczo
Nine heavy mule-loads of gold
As a bakshish for Joanczo."
And directly were brought
The nine heavy mule-loads of gold
As a bakshish to Joanczo,
And were given
To Joanczo Krym Pehlivanczo.

And he goes off, Joanczo Krym Pehlivanczo,
With his nine heavy loads of gold;
And he arrives, Joanczo Krym Pehlivanczo,
At his dearly-loved mother's.
And he calls his mother,
Joanczo Krym Pehlivanczo,
"Come down then, mother, and take
These nine heavy mule-loads of gold."

And the mother of Joanczo Krym Pehlivanczo comes down,
And she sees the nine heavy mule-loads of gold.
"Bré!* Joanczo Krym Pehlivanczo!
Thou hast not been to the Czar's to wrestle,
But thou hast been at some Haydutluk,†
And thou hast robbed the Czar
Of these nine heavy mule-loads of gold!"

---

* Bré, a Turkish exclamation of astonishment.
† Haydutluk (Turkish), brigandage, highway robbery.

"The Czar gave them to me," says Joanczo Krym Pehlivanczo,
" And more than that, he has allowed me
To kill any man
That I choose.
Such is the permission he has given to Joanczo Krym Pehlivanczo,
That is to say, to me."

The Czar in this song is probably some Cæsar of Byzantium, and Joanczo is doubtless some big barbarian Bulgarian who really existed; as for his enormous appetite, those who know the Slavs will agree that their bards have not much need to exaggerate this point, to make it seem monstrous or heroic. After all, poor Joanczo is a very *material* hero.

KING MARKO AND THE DAUGHTER OF PHILIP THE MAGYAR.—(*Hungarian.*)

King Marko the foreigner
Throws up his grey falcon
In the Palace of Philip the Magyar.

It perches on the knee of Philip the Magyar
And sees seventy-seven Kings
Who are eating and drinking.

And King Marko stops on the threshold
And whistles his grey falcon from the knee of Philip the Magyar.
It perches on the knee of King Marko,
And says to King Marko,
" In the Palace of Philip the Magyar
There are seventy-seven Kings eating and drinking."

King Marko stays on the threshold
And says, " Give me the grey horse."
And he mounts the grey horse.
The King Marko gives a battle horse.

(There are evidently some verses wanting about here, but no one in this neighbourhood knows of their existence.)

  * * * * *
Let us go to the Palace of Philip the Magyar,
And the fair Seferina, daughter of Philip the Magyar, we will take.

The King Marko says to his comrade,
" We will go to the Palace of Philip the Magyar,
And we will take of Philip Magyarina
The lovely daughter Seferina.*
  * * * * *

(Here again verses appear to be missing.)

> King Marko goes to the Castle of Philip Magyar;
> Philip Magyar says to the seventy-seven Kings,
> " When King Marko arrives
> And dismounts, stand on the threshold
> And take his horse from him, but do
> Not salute him, King Marko;
> You do nothing but eat and drink,
> You are only a set of blackguards! "†
> King Marko arrives at the gates of Philip Magyar;
> King Marko calls aloud at the gates of Philip Magyar;
> Seventy-seven heroes are eating and drinking,
> And do not allow King Marko to pass.
> King Marko gives a kick to the gates of Dzym Dzyr,
> Breaks them, and enters.
> The seventy-seven Kings place themselves on the threshold,
> And say to him 'Bouyour,'‡ and take his horse, and walk it up
>   and down.
> King Marko sits down near the Sofra (table)
> And he eats and drinks.
> King Marko sees the fair maid Seferina,
> She comes, but she does not give him wine.§
> Philip Magyar from his Palace he says,
> " When you go, King Marko, across

---

 * This is the only rhyme in the song, and seems to be much admired, for it is repeated on every possible occasion.

 † It seems difficult to account for this sudden burst of unparliamentary language on the part of Philip, unless the seventy-seven kings were all Bulgarians, in which case he probably found he was being eaten out of house and home.

 ‡ 'Bouyour,' a Turkish expression of politeness, 'pray enter.'

 § A girl's giving wine to a suitor is a sign that he pleases her.

The sea three hundred hours, and you
Disembark in the island of Kierspiczensk,
And you take from the tree of Kierspiczensk
Three apples, and bring them
And place them on the table for dessert,
Then you will have done.*
If you wish to have my daughter Seferina,
Mount your horse and let us see if you arrive
At the island of Kierspiczensk."
This hero, King Marko, springs upon his horse
And he swims the three hundred hours of sea
And lands in the island of Kierspiczensk.
A Lomota† attacks him, and swallows
The half of his horse.
The horse says to him, to the King Marko,
"If, O King Marko!
Thou hast any wit, thou wilt hit
The Lomota on the head."
King Marko hits the Lomota on the head,
And chains him with a chain behind the horse,
And drags the Lomota behind him.
Then he tears up the tree by the roots,
Puts it under his arm, and swims
The three hundred hours of sea,
And arrives at the Castle of Philip Magyar.
Philip Magyar from his Castle
Looks over the boundless plain
Through the mist, and he says,
"Will King Marko be drowned
In swimming the three hundred hours of sea?"
But behold! he is not drowned,
And behold! he brings the tree under his arm,
And the Lomota he drags behind him.
Philip the Magyar then says, "Go to meet King Marko
And tell him not to bring the Lomota here,
In order that fear may not seize upon the seventy-seven Queens,
And that the seventy-seven little Kings may not die."
But King Marko does not listen to them,
Does not listen to them, and drags the Lomota.
"Let King Marko tie the Lomota to the gates,
That the seventy-seven Queens may not be afraid."

---

* "Then you will have done' something worth talking about.
† The Lomota is a kind of monster half dragon and half whirlwind.

But King Marko does not hear what is said to him,
And drags the Lomota into the court.
And the seventy-seven Queens are afraid,
And the seventy-seven little Kings die.
King Marko sits down by the sofra,
And he eats and drinks;
He looks for the maiden Seferina,
And she comes to the sofra and gives him wine
And dessert; she gives wine to all,
But the Queens drank no wine—they were afraid—
And they refused the dessert.
King Marko says to them,
" Why do you not drink,
And why do you not eat? "
The Queens answer King Marko
" We have been frightened."
" Haida !* take the fair maid Seferina ! "
Philip Magyar says, " Bring the carriage of gold
And harness two good horses to it,
And put the fair maid Seferina into the carriage,
And let him take her, King Marko."
They bring the carriage of gold
And they put into it the fair maid Seferina with King Marko.
Philip Magyar remains in the Palace of Philip Magyar,†
And they went away, King Marko and the fair maid Seferina,
And King Marko brings her to his Palace,
And ninety-nine Kings are assembled,
And a splendid marriage is prepared.
Then Philip Magyar arrives with nothing on but his shirt,
" You know it and you remember it, King Marko!—"
King Marko sees him, but leaves him on the threshold,
But the fair maid Seferina
Goes towards Philip Magyarina.
" You go towards him to the threshold!
I am angry ! "
And he gave back, and he (Philip) took back,
The fair maid Seferina.

---

* Haida! (Turkish), all right! off with you! Who makes this remark it is not easy to conjecture.

† The simple but poetic beauty of this line must strike even the most prosaic reader.

In these three heroic poems of the Bulgarians we see the great deeds of two of their heroes; one is a formidable wrestler, but he eats, drinks and dresses in (or rather out of) proportion —in short he is but an enormous animal, and even his mother has no great opinion of his morals, since she says

"Thou hast been at some Haydutluk."

Kral Marko, by far the most famous hero of Bulgaria, is but little better; he too has an immense appetite and immense strength, but he is, to say the least, most impolite to ladies.

What strikes us most is the entire absence of anything like poetry; there is no *sentiment*, except that of chronic hunger. Kral Marko obtains the fair Seferina (probably Seraphina) after an exploit of which the success is chiefly due to his horse, who has certainly more presence of mind than his rider, since, though "half swallowed," he advises him to strike at the head of the monster. But there is neither love nor any other sentiment of the heart or soul in anything which Kral Marko does; nor has he the least spark of generosity, for he hangs poor Philip Junak simply because he boasted falsely of having enchained three monsters. All that is sung of is merely animal prowess, and well fed bears would have done as much.

These remarks are worth noting, for in heroic songs we generally find the ideal of the perfect man which is formed by the nation; the Bulgarian people of the present day greatly admire Deli Marko and Joanczo, and in doing so they pass judgment on themselves.

In the traditions, legends and songs of all half savage peoples (except the Bulgarians) there is a great deal of poetry and generosity of feeling; an Indian chief would not have killed Philip Junak, nor have sent away the fair Seferina for behaving dutifully to her father. The heroes of Walhalla are dark and terrible, their feast is gigantic almost as the dinner of Joanczo; but they are giants, and their deeds, their vices, and their virtues are proportionate to their stature.

What a difference between these legends and songs and the poetry of the Turks! Needless to take the written works of Arabian or Persian, or even Turkish authors, but listen to the first peasant you meet who pours forth some "unpremeditated lay;" what vivacity in its sentiments, what poetic colour in its imagery, what simplicity, and yet what strength!

No doubt the education of the people does much; but since Christianity, grafted on the Norse and Teutonic Deli Markos and Joanczos, has produced a noble literature, why has it failed with the Bulgarians? Perhaps its Spiritualism cannot penetrate the gross hide of the Bulgarian, or perhaps *Oriental* Christianity has caused a reaction.

In any case it is not oppression nor slavery which is the cause, for the Polish and Lithuanian peasants possess songs which find an echo in the heart, because they come from the heart, the source of all true poetry: the source of the ballads of Bulgaria seems to be, alas!—the stomach.

CHAPTER VII.

EASTERN CHRISTIANITY, AND ITS EFFECTS IN BULGARIA.

Feasts and fast-days economically considered — The Bulgarian catechized — The clergy seek union with Rome — Rejected as unworthy — A curacy in Bulgaria — The rector — The parishioners — Fasting — Holy water — Extortion of the priests — Reforms suggested.

IT is not our intention to enter upon a discussion of the dogmas or doctrine of the Greek religion, which we shall consider merely in its effects upon the morality and education of the Christians of the East, in short, as a school of civilization. When we find that a religion as preached and practised by its clergy has no beneficial action whatever, it must be regarded, economically, only as a method by which a parasitic class enriches itself at the expense of public credulity: but if the fruits which it produces are idleness, ignorance, drunkenness, and an utter absence of morality, *then* such a religion deserves to be placed under the ban of public opinion. All these evils, which exist to a terrible extent in Bulgaria, can be traced to the influence of the Greek clergy.

The Fetichism of the Gaboon would never be tolerated in England—not because its exercise would shock the religious feelings of a nation whose troops not long ago presented arms to the statue of Buddha in the procession of Juggernaut, —but because Cannibalism, the murders committed by the priest-sorcerers, and the constant terror inspired by the fear of White Devils, render Fetichism incompatible with our civilization.

And is a religion which absolutely prohibits labour during 183 days of the year, and during the other 182 weakens its professors by such fasts as are unknown in Europe, except perhaps in a Trappist monastery, likely to encourage civilization to any great extent?

Such precepts are, no doubt, more honoured in the breach than the observance by those whom a superior education has rendered free thinkers, or placed above the necessity of conforming to popular prejudices. Aristides had no false scruples to prevent his profaning the Sabbath of St. Mitrophanes by altering the address on the ownerless box which he found at the Custom House,* and a chicken may appear on a fast day at the table of Monsignor Benedictos,† under the name of a vegetable marrow: but what is inevitable is, that the corn will remain ungarnered upon the fields for at least fifteen days,‡ during which it pays tithe to the pigeons and turtle doves, or is spoilt by the rain,—for these fifteen days are days of feast, when labour is forbidden by the Greek priest, though no interdict is laid upon the peasant's consumption of wine or spirits; and that, during a Lent of sixty days, the scrupulous peasant-mother will refuse her sick infant any other nourishment than bread, onions, or garlic and cabbage-water; the child may die, but the fast has been observed.

"I know all that," said Miltiades to us one day, " but, with us, it is only the lower classes who believe in that nonsense;

---

* *Vide* 'Eastern Commerce.'

† Metropolitan of Monastir; a prelate concerning whom information is given in later pages of this chapter.

‡ This feast varies in duration from fifteen to forty days.

every educated Hellene is an atheist, for our religion has one grand advantage, it leads to Atheism sooner than any other." *

Strange apology for a Christian religion!

Though abstaining, as we have said, from all criticism of dogmas, we must point out some of the effects produced upon the Rayahs by the doctrine of his Church as the Papas interprets it to him.

A short time since a peasant of our village remarked, whilst drinking a cup of wine in our house,

"After next Sunday I shan't drink any more of your wine."

This resolution, a very strange one for a Bulgarian to take, astonished us not a little, especially as our friend N—— is rather a hard-drinker, and we began to wonder whether any Apostles of Teetotalism had arrived in our neighbourhood; however, we congratulated him upon his proposed abstinence from fermented liquors.

"No, no, not at all; I am not going to give up wine or raki, but I say I shall not drink any more of *your* wine after next Sunday."

"Why not? is it too strong for you?"

"Oh no! your wine is very good indeed, but the Easter Lent begins next Sunday, and your wine is *yaghli.*" (*Yaghli* here means *gras*, technically used as opposed to *maigre*, and applies to everything which may not be eaten during a Fast).

"But how is it *yaghli?*"

---

* This was said as we have quoted; another Greek, holding a high official position, who was present at this conversation, added: "As for me, I only believe in Jupiter," and he was speaking seriously without any arrière pensée of sarcasm.

"Because you put eggs into it."

Then we remembered that as on its arrival the barrel of wine was very muddy, we had put in half-a-dozen whites of egg to clear it.

N—— continued, "If I drink your wine, when I go to confession the Papas will refuse me the *Koumka* (Communion), and I shall be ashamed, because there are always a lot of people looking on."

The conversation then turned upon Papasses and religion, and N—— was much astonished to learn that the clergy of Europe are not in the habit of lending out money to their flocks at sixty per cent. interest.

The greatest sin which can be committed by an orthodox Christian of Bulgaria (as well as by his brother of St. Petersburg) is to break a Fast day by eating forbidden food, any act of theft being nothing in comparison with this. We asked N——, which the Papas would consider the greater crime, to drink our wine during Lent, or to steal a goose; and the answer was, "Well, to steal a goose is certainly a sin, but to drink your wine would be a *much* greater one."

"How fortunate you are," concluded he, as he drank off his *yaghli* wine, "to have priests who don't walk off with your last fowl!"

The ignorance of the Bulgarians with regard to all the precepts and maxims of the Gospels, and even of everything that concerns their religion, with the exception of its outward forms is, even to those who know their clergy, most astonishing; and even with these outward observances are mixed various curious relics of the old Slavonic Pantheism, a mixture which is tolerated by the priests either from ignorance of the presence of the Pagan element, or from reasons already mentioned.*

It would be useless to ask a peasant to quote any passage from the Bible, for there are few Papasses who are capable of doing so; they being frequently unable to write or read, and holding a book in their hands during the performance of Divine Service only to give themselves a greater air of dignity; the prayers, &c., they learn off by heart.

Put the simplest questions to a peasant, such questions as a Sunday School child of six years old will answer with ease, and you will receive the strangest replies. We give a specimen of such a catechism, from which some part has been omitted, as the answers, though given in ignorance, appear too blasphemous to write down :—

Q. " How many Gods are there? "

A. " Kto znaje? " (who knows?) the invariable reply at first, but on pressing the question we were told—

"Probably many, for there is one for the Turks, and another for us, and no doubt the English and French have another—a rich one, too—for there are only Chinguinés (gipsies) who have no God." †

Q. " Who is Jesus Christ? "

A. " Do you mean Christos? "

Q. " Yes; who is he? "

---

* *See* Chapters IV. and V.

† There is a Turkish and Bulgarian tradition that when religions were given out to the different nations of the earth, the recipients cut their several creeds upon stone, engraved them upon wood or metal, or printed them in books (the Franks, for instance) ; the gipsies however wrote their canons upon the leaves of a cabbage, which was shortly afterwards seen and eaten by a Turkish donkey; this is the reason that the Chinguinés have neither religion nor God of their own.

A. "Kto znaje?"
Q. "Is he not the Son of God?"
A. "Don't laugh at a poor peasant, Chelibi (Sir)."
Q. "What is the Koumka (Communion)?"
A. "It is bread and wine which the Papas gives you to eat: it costs ten piastres."
Q. "Is it not the body of Jesus Christ?"*
A. "Now you are laughing at me again, Chelibi!"
Q. "What is a sin?"
A. "It is a bad thing, for which you have to pay the Papas."
Q. "Mention some sins."
A. "Oh, there are a great many; for instance, to clean a stable or to buy or sell milk after sunset, to sell a loaf of bread without breaking a piece off it, not to fumigate flour with incense if it has been ground in a mill belonging to a Turk, to give a spoon as a plaything to a child, not to sweep the place where an unbeliever has sat down in your house, to let a dog get up upon your roof, and ever so many others—and quite lately it has become a sin to give alms to a gipsy."

Crimes against property, false witness, and many such acts as are not only against the precepts of every Christian religion, but also punishable by law, are mere peccadillos for which absolution may be purchased from the priest at the rate of an egg apiece.

Such is the impression made upon the conscience of the Rayah by the religious and moral instructions of the Papas.

If the Rayah is not ten times richer than the Turk, if

---

* The Greek Church holds the doctrine of the Real Presence.

he is totally and pitiably uneducated, if he professes a religion swarming with Fetiches and which eradicates none of the thousand superstitions which embitter his life, if his morality is of the lowest possible standard, if he is a disloyal subject and a dangerous neighbour,*—for all this he may thank, *not* the Turkish Government, but the Greek Hierarchy which distant England so much admires.

Not very long ago the Ultramontane party in France was congratulating itself upon the reported union of the Bulgarians with the Papal See, and about the same time England was occupied with the project of a fusion between the Anglican and Greek Churches.

The report had never much foundation, and the union of Bulgaria with Rome was never carried out: how far it would have been possible may be learnt from the words of the Chief of the Roman Catholic Mission at Varna, a Cappucino monk of exemplary life and character :—

"Some time since several Bulgarian (not-Greeks, though of the Greek Church) Papasses called on me with questions as to the possibility of a union with the Holy See—but I can assure you, Signore, that such a thing is quite out of the question."

"Why so, Padre? on account of the marriage of the clergy?"

"Not that, for the United Greek Church has a dispensation; but there is one insurmountable religious obstacle to admitting this clergy into union with our Church, and as

---

* To our knowledge the following maxims are inculcated by the Greek clergy: that the authority of the Wladyka (Bishop or Metropolitan) is in all cases, civil as well as ecclesiastical, paramount to that of the Padischah, and that it is no sin to rob or cheat a Mussulman.

to the people, it would be a very toilsome mission that of endeavouring to instil into their minds any kind of morality whatever, and I think few of them would accept the severe maxims of our religion upon this point. Just imagine,—all these Papasses, without exception, who came to consult me, were so totally ignorant of all that relates to even the first principles and simplest doctrines of Christianity, and their ideas of morality, even of social morality, were so vague or so loose, that it would not only be utterly impossible to admit them into our Church as priests, but I doubt whether, without previously preparing them by a course of study, I should be justified in accepting them as catechumens." *

Such was the opinion of a member of that Church which is supposed to be only too ready to make any proselytes by any means; and though it may startle some of those who have fancied the Greek Church to be everything that is perfect, it is probable that it is not strong enough to change the opinion of the many who persist in thinking the Greek Church to be a sister of the Anglican. Let us draw a picture, not altogether fanciful, of what might take place if these two Churches were amalgamated.

An English gentleman, just ordained, and fresh from Oxford, accepts a curacy in Bulgaria under an incumbent of the Greek Church; he has prepared himself by attending a series of lectures at the Taylorian upon "The Bulgarian dialect of Slavonic as connected with Mœso-Gothic," and starts upon his journey with the expectation of finding the "rector" of his future parish a specimen of sublimed humanity attired in a patriarchal beard, and flowing robes

* See Appendix D.

whose severely graceful folds give to his figure a dignity like that of the Moses of Michael Angelo, whilst he unites in his single person the lofty affability of all the heads of houses, the learning of a whole Common Room, and the mild justice of a dozen deans or sub-rectors, with the simplicity of manners and purity of heart of a bishop of the early centuries of Christianity.

He arrives at the scene of his labours; he finds the beard and the flowing robes, but both are undeniably greasy, and their owner, a portly personage who diffuses around him a perfume of garlic and raki, salutes him with a humble bow, and addresses him as 'Chelibi'; when he is informed of the respective positions of himself and the new-comer, he takes a slightly higher tone, and demands—

"Have you any money?"

"Yes, Sir, a little."

"Very good; but don't call me 'Sir,' only plain 'Dimitri,' since you have money and I have none,—for these wretched villagers no longer pay as they used to do, thanks to the Schism; and as the Papadika* pockets everything, you shall pay for us both, and we will go to the Tukhan."

The curate assents, and follows his rector, fancying that he is going to make a round of visits in the parish: after a minute's walk along a muddy road an old woman stops them, saying,

"Papas, my husband Tanaz is dying, and he implores you for the love of Heaven to come and see him."

"Have you got the seventy piastres?" is the reply of the priest.

"We are poor; very, very poor, Papas."

---

* The Papas's wife.

"That's a lie, Tranitza, you are quite rich enough to pay me."

"But the funeral only costs forty piastres!"

"That's what I have to pay to the Wladyka, but do you suppose I have bought this parish in order to make nothing out of it? Pay me the seventy piastres or ——"

"Then I will sell the cow and pay you ——"

"Not a bit of it, I shan't give credit."

"Bozé, Bozé!* my husband is dying!"

"Let him die, then, if you are not going to pay me!"

The curate offers to go and console the dying man, for, thanks to Professor Max Müller's lectures, he has understood something of this dialogue, though he is rather astonished at the absence of the Mœso-Gothic element; but the Papas stops him with "What! you'd go and rob me of my seventy piastres? these people will never pay unless we get it out of them in advance."

The woman goes away sobbing, and the sensitive heart of the Oxonian is so touched that he ventures to offer the sum in question to his rector, who accepts it with the greatest possible condescension, and calls back Tranitza.

"This young gentleman has advanced some of the money for you, so I'll come and see your husband for you presently, but get ready for me two dozen of eggs, six fowls, and five *sahans*† of flour."

The Tukhan is reached, and they enter, slightly to the surprise of the curate when he finds himself in a very dingy

---

* A Bulgarian exclamation as frequently used as the French "Mon Dieu," and with the same literal meaning.

† The *sahan*, literally "bowl," is a measure devoted to the use of the priest, and averages about an oke.

and disreputable-looking pot-house; but as all the villagers rise and kiss his hands as well as those of the Papas, he fancies that he is being presented to his parishioners. Time passes rapidly with the Papas, who calls for innumerable small glasses of raki varied by numberless big tumblers of wine. About 4 o'clock he begins to sing unclerical songs, and by 5 he cannot stand upright. At this stage enters the son of Tanaz, asking him to visit his father, who is at death's door. "Get along with you," says the Papas, whom his potations have rendered ill-tempered, adding a strong-flavoured Turkish oath much in use amongst the Rayahs. The young man has also been drinking, probably to drown his grief, and he answers so rudely that the Papas raises his arm to strike him; a scuffle ensues, in the course of which the sacerdotal garments are torn to rags, and half of Dimitri's beard remains in the hands of his adversary, whilst his cap is thrown down, trodden under foot, and loses all trace of its former peculiar shape; his co-adjutor tries to interfere, but all the bystanders rush upon him, and he extricates himself only by putting in practice certain athletic exercises which he has learnt at Maclaren's; and finds himself in the open air again with a much modified opinion of the Greek clergy.

Though he leaves the Papas to his fate, his first thought is to hasten to the house of Tanaz, saying to himself, "The clergy may be illiterate and even worse, but for all that I must not abandon my poor people." With this charitable reflection he arrives at the door of the miserable hut in which Tanaz is dying, but stays a moment on the threshold, almost fancying that he is at the gate of Pandemonium, so loud, so guttural, and so shrill are the shouts, screams, and wailings which proceed from the sick-room. For a moment the sight of a foreigner stops the uproar, and a hideous old woman, whom the scarf bound round her arm shows to be the village witch on duty,* places herself, arms akimbo, in front of the stranger, saying,

"I suppose you are the doctor; be off with you! I have tried with the scarf, and Tanaz will die."

"I am a priest."

"You a priest! where's your Bakar,† and your Kalpak?‡ You're nothing but an impostor, get along with you!"

But a silver key gains admission to the room, and the curate makes his way through the throng of 'keening' relatives and friends to the bedside of the dying man, to whom he whispers words of hope and consolation.

But Tanaz rejects them; "It is no use, there is no hope for me, none! and so, Chelibi, give me back the seventy piastres, for it is only so much money wasted."

The curate tells him not to despair of the Divine mercy if he truly repents.

"But I know there is no mercy for me, I must go to Hell, for a dog slept upon the roof of the house to-day; § so please give me back the seventy piastres!"

"But your wife did not give the money, it was I who gave it to the Papas."

"Yes, but your honour ‖ gave it for my wife, so it belongs to us, and we don't want to give it to the Papas, because we know he can do nothing for me; he won't give back the

---

* *See* the Chapter on Superstitions.
† Holy water pot.   ‡ Cap.
§ *See again* Chapter on Superstitions.
‖ *Vasza milost,* literally "your love," a Bulgarian term of respect.

piastres, but you, Chelibi, are too much of a gentleman not to do so."

After a year spent in charity and zealous labour amongst his peasant parishioners, helping them with money, healing their bodies as well as their souls, defending them against unjust extortion from the tax-collector and advocating their cause through his Consulate, the curate finds that he has sown his seed in a barren soil, and reaped neither gratitude, nor moral nor religious progress: so he leaves the country with much the same opinion of it as that of the Authors of this book.

The foregoing sketch will appear to many people exaggerated, if not impossible; yet even the existence of an English clergyman in Bulgaria is not quite fictitious, for the peasants of this neighbourhood have told us of English missionaries who settled in the Balkans, and after some years of devotion to the poor, the sick, and the ignorant, were at last driven away by those who owed the most to their kindness and Christian charity. As for the dialogues and scenes,—the Papas in the Tukhan fighting with his parishioner, the deathbed of Tanaz, and the others,—they are unhappily no fictions, but relations of events.

Returning to the Greek Church, and leaving the question of its union with that of England, we find that the monks are often better educated than the country Papas, and it is from their ranks chiefly that the bishops and archbishops are chosen, as they furnish men who are more clever, if not more scrupulous, than the secular clergy of the country districts. The position of archbishop (or metropolitan) is a prize not to be disdained, the revenues sometimes amounting to 700,000 piastres, about 6000*l.* per annum.

As for the morals of these ecclesiastical dignitaries, it is to be feared that their superior education is, in too many instances, only employed to do on a large scale what the Papas does on a small one,—to extort money from the people. The recent dissensions between the clergy and their Bulgarian flock have had the effect of bringing to light many instances of ill-conduct on the part of the spiritual chiefs of the Greek Church, but we will only cite, from these many, one case, as alluded to in a letter (one of a series on the same subject) to the 'Courrier d'Orient,' which will give a slight idea of the moral and financial state of the Eastern Church, and even of its internal discipline.

As the censorship of the press in Constantinople is one of those imported French institutions which flourish most vigorously, the grave charges brought forward, in this and other letters, against Monsignor Benedictos would certainly have drawn an "avertissement" upon the newspaper in which they were published, if their truth could have been in any way impugned.*

We have thus traced the action of the Orthodox Church and its clergy upon the Bulgarians,† and the résumé of its effects is as follows :—

That there are 183 Feast Days during the year, on every one of which labour is absolutely forbidden, and the other 182 days are strict Fasts which weaken the peasant by their

---

* *See* Appendix E.

† We have not alluded to the Armenians, as the only members of that race to be found in Bulgaria are all either Government employés, or merchants in the towns; we have, however, very good reason for believing the Armenian clergy to be not much better educated than those of the Greek Church, and quite as rapacious.

extreme rigour (particularly as they occur on the only days when he may labour), as his diet is reduced to bread, onions, garlic, or one of the few kinds of vegetables which he cultivates. Fish is as strictly forbidden as meat, and no exception is made even for sickness, infancy, or old age.

That it encourages gross superstition whilst it fails to civilize, educate, or improve the morals of the people; and finally

That the average Papas is hardly less ignorant than his flock, and in point of morality is even inferior to them.

Let us now calculate how much the Eastern Christians pay for these benefits.

In every village you may see, at least once a month, a Papas, accompanied by the Kiaya (nearly always a Mussulman gipsy), who carries a large copper vessel filled with holy water, a brush, and a big sack. The Papas enters every house, and sprinkles the walls and floor with the holy water, and throws a little over the people themselves, who in return pay him a sum whose minimum is fixed at one piastre, the money being thrown into the *bénitier* carried by the Kiaya. This payment is obligatory and cannot be evaded; moreover custom demands the addition of at least one oke of flour, which we will value at only one piastre, and this must be contributed even by the poorest families.

The Papas dines at the expense of some rich villager, and perhaps puts up for the night, if his church is too distant to admit of his returning the same day.

Many villages have no church nor resident Papas. This is not the fault of the Turkish Government but the choice of the villagers, who argue that it comes cheaper to have a Papas amongst them occasionally than one who would reside with them all the year round.*

As the priest has usually bought his parish from the *Wladyka*, he is obliged to make as much out of it as he can, and therefore though the *aiasmas* (sprinklings with holy water) are fixed at one per month, he takes the opportunity of renewing them as often as he is sent for to a christening, marriage, burial, or other ceremony.

The other taxes levied by the Papas are: from each married couple two *sheniks* of corn, which are equal to one Constantinople kilé, or a fourth of a Varna kilé, and average in value thirty-two piastres (1867-1868).† There is besides a tax for the metropolitan, which varies in different districts, being fixed here at sixteen piastres. The so-called voluntary contributions, such as eggs, butter, cheese, wine, grapes, lambs, fowls, flour, wool, &c., &c., amount to at least twenty piastres per house. Adding these sums to the twenty-four piastres annually paid for the *aiasma*, we find that the Papas receives from each family seventy-six piastres for himself, and sixteen for the metropolitan.‡

Further, as every baptism is charged at five piastres, every marriage thirty, and every burial forty piastres, there is a very large sum annually paid in from these sources to the ecclesiastical coffers. Taking the deaths at thirty per

---

* Our village, which is a rich one, has neither church nor school, and there is not one of the peasants who can either read or write; lately a *Chorbadji* proposed the erection of a church, and offered to contribute ten pounds in money, all the timber necessary, and fifty cartloads of stone; this proposal was negatived in the village council on the ground that they paid enough to the priest already, and that if he were to live in the village always, they would be quite ruined.

† *See* Appendix F. ‡ *See* Appendix G.

thousand annually, the births at the same rate, and the marriages only at ten per thousand, we find that the twelve millions of Eastern Christians* pay an annual sum of nearly twenty millions of piastres for these three charges alone; and adding to this sum the seventy-six piastres of the Papas and the sixteen of the Wladyka paid by every family, we arrive at the grand total of 240 millions of piastres, or more than two millions of pounds sterling paid every year to the Eastern Churches. And we have omitted in this calculation the sums paid by communicants, collections at churches, the revenues of the monasteries and of land possessed by the Rayah clergy, &c., &c., which would probably nearly double this amount.

The monasteries especially bring in a large income to the Greek Church; numberless gifts are presented at their shrines and frequent pilgrimages made to them, when the pilgrim is made to pay pretty heavily for his board and lodging. The monks, however, make very good landlords, and if they are well paid are as polite as can be desired.

These pilgrimages are generally the result of confession, for when the penitent finds himself face to face with a white-bearded priest armed with a whip,† he is glad to escape unhurt, and promises to do penance in any monastery which the Papas chooses for him.

The study of the action and effects of Eastern Christianity is a very painful one to the Christian of the West, as he sees a parasitical clergy preying upon the credulity, the ignor-

---

* We believe that we are doing no injustice to the Armenian clergy in supposing them to be at least as well paid as those of the Greek Church.

† One of the customs (at confession) of the Greek Church in Turkey as well as in Russia.

ance, and the misery of an entire people; and that the Christian Church in Turkey is now what that of Europe was during the darkest ages of its profligacy and venality, with the same unbounded immorality in all those of its acts which ought to tend to the greater glory and advantage of true religion.

Painful too is the contrast between the morals of the Mussulman Hodja or Imam and those of the Christian Papas,* between the education and honesty of the two peoples,— Turks and Rayahs,—and even between the revenues of the Ulema and those of the Church; the former serving to disseminate learning and afford a gratuitous education to the people, the latter being dedicated to keeping Papasses in luxury, and to corrupting Exarchs.

A remedy is possible; but Turkey is so unwilling to interfere in the ecclesiastical affairs of the Christians, that it would be necessary for the Western Powers to urge her, in the name of humanity, to compel a radical reform, not of doctrine, but in the morals and social position of the Greek clergy. Such a change would do more to benefit the Rayah than a century of the concessions which are now so liberally bestowed upon him.

It would be but reasonable that a Government, which carries religious toleration to such an extent as is practised by Turkey, should be permitted to exact from the Christian clergy some such conditions as the following:—

1. An amount of education sufficient to enable the priest to teach the people.

---

* The priest of the largest church in an important town upon the Black Sea kept for years, unnoticed and unrebuked by his superiors, a house of ill fame; we could give many other nearly similar instances.

2. That this teaching shall not be contrary to the interests of the State, nor to the tenure of property. (See note, p. 102).

3. That the clergy shall not be permitted to ruin the subjects of the Government by oppressive exactions.

4. That the clergy shall, for offences not ecclesiastical, be subject to the civil tribunals.

It would be thus necessary that every candidate for holy orders should be compelled to pass an examination before a civil board of education, as well as to produce unexceptionable certificates of morality; and if any candidate failed in these points and afterwards succeeded in being ordained priest, both he and the metropolitan who ordained him should be liable to punishment.*

The tribunals and the police should be allowed to take cognizance of the civil offences committed by the priests; sermons and pastoral letters should be subjected to the same censorship as the press, whilst a Papas convicted of robbing or cheating his parishioners should go to Widin as surely as would Moustapha the Hodja, or Ali the Imam.

Perhaps such a reform as this might introduce honesty and education among the Eastern Christians, who would have to thank the Padischah for the boon, and not the Wladyka or the Patriarch: but neither education nor honesty will take any hold amongst them so long as the clergy remain in their present ignorant and vicious condition.

---

* Under the present system no examination of candidates is fairly practised; the person who wishes to become a priest, usually pays the Wladyka for ordaining him, and perhaps has to bribe against two or three competitors; after he becomes a priest he has to buy a parish from the Wladyka, of course, and to make what profit he can by the transaction.

CHAPTER VIII.

BRIGANDAGE IN THE BALKAN.

Ignorance of consuls accounted for — The Gentleman of the Forest — Generosity — The common Highwayman — Laissez aller — The Outlaw — Justice defeated — A Dogstealer.

THIS prominent feature of the Bulgarian Provinces is passed over in silence, or but slightly alluded to, by the authors of the 'Reports received from Her Majesty's Ambassador and Consuls relating to the condition of Christians in Turkey' in 1867.

For this partial or entire reticence there are two good valid reasons: 1st, That if a British Consul happens to be animated by the laudable desire to see something of the country districts of his consulate, his personal dignity and consular precedents equally require that he should travel with his interpreter, his cavasses, and even with an additional escort of *Zaptiehs*: being thus accompanied, his quality of Western Foreigner, well guarded and well armed, is soon known to any brigands who may be exercising their vocation in the forests through which he passes, and as a matter of course he rides unmolested by roads on which no Greek or Armenian merchant dare show himself. Too often however the Foreign Consul does not take the trouble to extend his search after knowledge beyond the walls or limits of the town in which he resides; his motto is, "Take care of the towns, the country will take care of itself;" and consequently he knows as little of the plague of brigandage as he knows of everything else relating to the status of the genuine Turkish peasant, Mussulman, or Christian. 2nd, The peasants, especially Christians, who may have been robbed, dare not complain to the authorities, preferring rather to put up with their losses, than to bear the consequences of making accusations which may bring down misfortune upon themselves and their families: the wisdom of their choice will be seen from a later portion of this chapter.

The Pashas and Governors of Provinces will of course reply, if questioned as to the amount of brigandage existing in their governments, that it has entirely disappeared, or at least is rapidly decreasing; and this answer often expresses their genuine belief, although the fact may be just the reverse. So long as no complaints are made by the sufferers, the *Zaptiehs* prefer their coffee and cigarettes at their guard-house or their billet to scouring the country in search of brigands, of whose existence they are perfectly aware, but whom they have no reason or inducement to arrest. Thus, as no brigands are captured and lodged in the town prison, the Governor takes it for granted that "brigandage is extinct," and flatters himself that his Pashalik is a model for the rest of the Sultan's dominions.

Brigandage nevertheless not only exists but flourishes in Bulgaria: its members may be classified under three distinct heads, of which each division differs from the others *toto cœlo:* if the English language offered any one word which would not convey a sense of opprobrium, it would be but fair to distinguish by such a term the first class from the others;—as it is, we must be content to qualify all the genus as brigands, and to separate their species as follows:—

1st, The *Balkan Chelibi*, or "gentlemen of the forest."
2nd, The *Khersis*, or common highway robber.
3rd, The *Haydut*, or outlawed murderer.

The "gentleman of the forest" claims a distinct classification, although he is numerically far inferior to the other two classes. He is generally the descendant of a family of *Balkan Beys* who, like the *Dere Beys* (or lords of the valleys) in Anatolia, were as practically independent of the Turkish Padischah as the English Barons of the end of the 12th century were of King John. His ancestors, before they were despoiled of their property, for the benefit of the conquered Christians who were added to the number of their fellow-subjects, enjoyed certain rights which their descendant has not forgotten. That the Beys of *Akindji* paid no taxes in money, but that they offered their blood for their country, and that the Rayah for whom they fought paid them in return a tenth of his produce, is an historical fact which *Said* of *Akindji* has not forgotten: but he does not enter upon his career of *Balkan Chelibi* without a reason—he has a dispute with the Zaptiehs about a certain immemorial right of cutting wood upon ground which the latter, being bribed accordingly, maintain to belong to the Rayahs of *Derekuoi*. The Zaptiehs threaten to take him to Varna, and Said thereupon takes to the forest, where he is well aware that the Zaptiehs will never find him. His life as "a banished man" is not a disagreeable one, for no Turk will betray one of his class, and the Rayah is too timorous to do so: Said's game, however, is not from the preserves of the Rayah villages; he prefers to wait for some fat Armenian or sharp-eyed Greek who has ventured to travel with a sum of money from Varna to Adrianople, and as *Agriochoiros* or, *Odian Effendi* emerges from the gorge upon a path which is the only road for a hundred yards, he is confronted by Said pistol in hand, and hears the ominous words, "*Dour ver para,*" "Stand, and give up your money." Neither *Agriochoiros* nor *Odian* requires much pressing, for valour is not their strong point, and life is preferable even to gold, and they know that Turkey is large, and that the Goddess of Eastern Commerce soon enriches her devout votaries: so they surrender their money, not without regret indeed, but still without a thought of resistance. If there is an escort in the shape of a Zaptieh, that functionary fires his muskets in the air, and retires leisurely, returning to Varna to report that he has been attacked by ten brigands, of whom he shot three, and with difficulty escaped from the remaining seven: he is a cousin's cousin of Said, or, his own brother is a "Balkan Chelibi" in another part of the province, so why should he embroil himself with Said or Said's friends for the sake of a Greek or an Armenian? Meanwhile the victim pursues his way or returns, lighter in purse but unharmed in person, and makes no complaint to the authorities; for he knows that Turkish provincial justice is tardy and expensive, and that Said will have had plenty of time to retire into another Pashalik until pursuit has ceased.

But it must not be thought that Said is an ordinary highwayman, even of the Claude Duval species: he has many qualities in common with the long extinct knight errant of chivalry, and, when he hears a tale of injustice wrought by the strong upon the weak, he is ready to redress it if within his power, and to distribute a wild kind of justice without appeal to any other tribunal than his own arms and his own courage. *Achmed* of *Hassanare* has been cheated out of 500 piastres by the *Beylikji*, or officer appointed to collect the tithes of his village: Said waits for the culprit, takes the 500 piastres from him and gives them back to Achmed, without putting a penny into his own pocket, although he may perhaps gratify his sense of justice by bestowing a couple of dozen blows with the flat of his knife as a receipt in full for the amount taken. All things considered, the *Balkan Chelibi* has many fine points in his character, and no comparison can be made between him and any species of robber existing in Europe: to find his parallel we must go back to the days of Roderick Dhu, of Rob Roy, of Robin Hood, or of the Golden Farmer;—he takes no advantages of numbers, for the gentleman of the forest is generally alone, or at best with but one companion, while no traveller with money ventures himself without a servant or armed escort amidst the Balkan; he comes forward boldly and risks his life against that of the man whom he stops; he never fires first, but with something of the spirit which animated the English and French lines at Fontenoy, waits until he is fired at. He is not bloodthirsty, and few instances of homicide can be laid to his account: if he stops you, and you are armed, shoot him if you can; if you miss, so much the worse for you.

In a small way, the *Balkan Chelibi* even applies a remedy to one of the great curses of Turkey, for every pound which he takes by main force from the trader, Greek or Armenian, has been wrung by legal cheatery from Turkish subjects, Osmanli or Christian, and if it did not fall into his hands would certainly not be spent in the country where it has been gained: the foreign merchant in Turkey robs, and shelters himself behind the Capitulations; the *Balkan Chelibi* robs, and having no Capitulations, takes shelter in the forest.

But in time Said wearies of his nomad life, and, when years have cast a veil over his misdeeds, returns to his village and becomes an ordinary hard-working member of society; his former life has left no taint upon his morals or character, and he is as scrupulously honest as are the vast majority of the Mussulman peasants. We know personally many Turks who have been *Balkan Chelibiler*, as well as some who are still exercising the profession, and any one of them may be trusted implicitly, and with no other guarantee than his word, with a sum of money which to him would be wealth. If any one likes to try the same experiment with a Greek merchant or a Christian villager he is welcome to do so, but we, who have had some experience of this part of Turkey, should decline.

It may seem curious that we should speak of robbers in tones of apology, perhaps almost of eulogy, but when the *Balkan Chelibi* is compared with the other classes of brigands, his faults will appear almost as virtues.

The second class, that of the *Khersis*, or highway robber, is by far the most numerous, and is one of the permanent sores of this country. As a rule it is composed of Rayahs who, abandoning their baptismal names of *Vola, Michal*, or *Triantaphyl*, call themselves *Mahmoud, Mazim*, or *Hussein*, put on big turbans in place of their sheepskin caps, and pass for Turks. The harvest has been bad, or the taxes heavy, and so they set off on a tour of the forest, furnished with recommendations to the different Christian villages which they purpose to visit. They steal horses, sheep and cattle, stop travellers, carry off the young men of a village, and demand a ransom for their prisoners. But their attacks upon travellers are carried out in a different way from that adopted by the *Balkan Chelibi*. When notice is given that some one is approaching, the *Khersis* rests his gun in the fork of a tree, carefully covers with his weapon a certain portion of the road, and as the unsuspicious voyager passes this point, fires, without giving him the chance of preserving his life by a voluntary surrender of his property.

If the aim is correct, the robber takes all the money and valuables from his victim, whose body he buries in some remote spot of the forest, and goes off with his companion to the *Tukhan* or public-house of some Rayah village, where a portion of the spoil is spent in wine or spirits. Perhaps the murdered man may be from the very village in which his murderers are carousing, and the fact of the crime be known as well as the names and persons of the brigands, but the criminals remain unmolested and depart unharmed. The reason for this is that there is not a Rayah village in Bulgaria of which some of the inhabitants have not been lately robbers, or will not be such again, and they are very naturally afraid of counter-denunciations which will affect their own people. If *Gebidjie* arrests *Janko* of *Evren*, of course Janko will turn Sultan's evidence, and tell all about *Vassili* of Gebidjie, and that will compromise some of the most respected families of the latter village; therefore Janko is let alone.

At first these bands of *Khersis* content themselves with stealing cattle, &c., but an unlucky stab, given to some herdsman, who is imprudent or courageous enough to defend his charge, puts them under the ban of the police, and they extend their operations from cattle-stealing to murder.

In the present state of these provinces, the repression of

this class of brigandage is a work of great difficulty, inasmuch as every Rayah village is their accomplice, as well as the receiver of their stolen goods.

"What can we do?" said an officer of Zaptiehs to us, "we cannot catch the brigands, because the villagers give them information of all our movements. Why, Vassili took bread and meat to them again yesterday."

"Why don't you arrest Vassili?"

"Of course I could arrest him, and he would be sent to *Widdin* for ten years; but what's the good of that?"

"At any rate it would prevent others doing the same."

"Not at all: if Vassili goes to *Widdin*, *Janaki*, and *Dimitri* will still carry food to the brigands."

"Then arrest Janaki and Dimitri."

"I might arrest all the men in the village, the women would take the provisions."

"Then what *can* you do?"

"Just what I am doing—I eat and drink, and make my men eat and drink at the expense of the village."

"I don't see the good of that."

"It's very easy to understand. After a week or two the villagers will get tired of us, and will beg their friends the brigands to leave this part of the country, which will thus be quiet till they come back here again."

Another conversation between the Authors and *Nicolaki* the *Chorbaji* (or head man) of this village, will still better explain the immunity enjoyed by the *Khersis*. Nicolaki is a long-headed but honest man, uneducated like the rest of the villagers; but, unlike them, he sees that things are not going on as well as they might do, and would be sincerely glad if a change could be effected.

We had been talking of this evil, and suggested to Nicolaki that, as having some influence in Derekuoi, he might be able, if only in a small degree, to put a stop to it.

"Now, Nicolaki, it is very well known that there is a man in this village who is a receiver of stolen goods from the brigands: I suppose you know whom we mean?"

"Perfectly."

"And you know the names of those who carried food to that band of brigands who were about here last year?"

"Yes; I know them."

"Then why don't you have these people arrested and taken to Varna; that would give a good lesson to the other villagers."

"I couldn't do that; I am afraid."

"What are you afraid of?"

"Well, you see, I am a man without grown-up sons to protect me, and I have no one here to fall back upon; the people I arrested, and their families, would owe me a grudge, and I have no protection against them."

"But if you did as we suggest, you would have the protection and approval of *Mithat* Pasha, who is a just and honest man."

"What is the use of his protection? He is at *Rustchuk*, and I am at *Derekuoi*, and some fine day I should get a bullet from behind a tree or a rock, and then where's Nicolaki? No, if there were any organization in this village which could protect me, I would do these things; as it is, I am afraid, I am afraid!"

Of the class of *Khersis* there are many who are merely apprentices, and confine their depredations to stealing horses, oxen, and sheep, without risking any attack upon the person of travellers. It would be very difficult to mention any family of Rayahs of whom at least one member has not stolen cattle, and the explanation of this fact is simple. There is even a sort of logic in the reasoning of the Bulgarian upon this subject. He says to himself, "Some one has stolen my oxen, I can't get any redress, so I will go and steal from some one else;" but, like a wise man, he provides against eventualities, and if he has lost *two* cows, he goes to the pasturage of a neighbouring village and steals *four*. Thus in a Bulgarian Rayah village at least half of the oxen, horses and buffaloes have changed hands three times or more, and it would be almost as difficult to find their original owners as to discover the author of the 'Letters of Junius.'

The *Haydut*, or outlaw, differs from the two preceding classes by having *no* friends except amongst his own band; but he has two chances of safety—the inefficiency of the Turkish system of *Zaptiehs*, and the fear which he inspires. He seldom merely robs, he murders from sheer lust of blood; a year or two's successful career of crime secures him a sort of prestige of invulnerability, and the peasants, who would willingly deliver him up, are deterred by the remembrance of the vengeance he has taken for such attempts as were unsuccessfully made. A noted character of this class was *Kara Kostia*, a native of the Greek village of Akdere in Roumelia, near Cape *Emineh*. For years this man was the terror of the province, his band consisting of three men and a woman, but most often he worked alone. By an organized system of relays of good horses, he accomplished long distances in a space of time which to the slow-travelling peasant seemed little short of miraculous. On Monday a traveller would be found murdered near Varna, and on

Tuesday morning, a horribly mutilated corpse within a mile of *Burgas* showed the presence of *Kara Kostia*. Not content with merely taking life, he committed such atrocities as are hardly to be paralleled even by the brigands of Southern Italy. The Government set a heavy price upon his head, but in vain; he was hunted by the police, who might as well have pursued a will-o'-the-wisp as *Kara Kostia*, whose very flight was marked by fresh crimes.

One man, a Turk, *Hassan* of *Ayvajik*, resolved to rid the country of Kara Kostia. Hassan had been a *Balkan Chelibi* in his youth, and perhaps for this very reason felt more contempt and hatred for the outlaw than others. He took his long knife and his single-barrelled rifle, went out into the forest, and for days stalked *Kara Kostia* with the same perseverance which he would have shown in following a deer or a wild boar; but for some days no favourable opportunity presented itself. At last, however, the time came, and Hassan saw *Kara Kostia* riding down a road in company with his three male companions. What followed is best described in Hassan's own words to us:—

"I waited till *Kara Kostia* and another were well in line, brought down the two with one bullet, drew my knife, and after a fight I killed the two others."

This event happened about four years ago, when Hassan was over sixty years old. From others, not from him, we learned that he had refused the reward offered by Government to the slayer of *Kara Kostia*, saying that he "had only done his duty."*

Another story of a famous *Haydut* was related to us a few

---

* *See* Appendix H.

days ago by an inhabitant of *Yasabasch*, who said that he had been an eye-witness of the tragedy. The fact of our informant being a Rayah would make us distrust his testimony, were not the details too picturesque and romantic to have been imagined by an uneducated Bulgarian. At any rate we tell the story as we heard it.

A certain *Stirion*, a Bulgarian-Greek, and like Kara Kostia a native of *Akdere* (which village was till lately a mere nest of brigands), was the head of a band of thirty or forty brigands, and had distinguished himself by his success in escaping capture, and by his cold-blooded ferocity. He is said to have committed with his own hands seventeen murders.

At last, however, a quarrel with one of his accomplices destroyed him. The negro *Abdoullah* had been one of his oldest friends, but, from some real or fancied insult, avenged himself by delivering up Stirion and his band to the troops of the Pasha. The robbers were encircled by a cordon of soldiers at the village of *Kouroukuoi*, near Akdere, then a den of outlaws, and now a peaceful and industrious colony of Tartar immigrants. They fought with the courage of desperation, but were at last shot or cut down to a man. Stirion was the last survivor, and though wounded stood at bay near the fountain of Kouroukuoi. His betrayer, Abdoullah, marched up to him, and presented a pistol at his head.

"Fire!" said Stirion.

"I cannot," replied the negro, as his arm dropped to his side, "we have been friends."

"No matter; I will kill myself, but wait a moment, and before I die let me sing a song."

And with the soldiers, a silent chorus, standing round motionless from curiosity or fear, Stirion began to sing;

the song he chose was one which he and his betrayer had often sung together in happier if not more innocent days, and as he sang, the negro covered his face with his hands and wept like a child. When the song was ended the primo tenor cut his throat with his knife, and Abdoullah, the basso profondo, blew out his own brains with the pistol which he had aimed at his former friend.

The whole story is sufficiently poetical to form a theme for a new 'Masnadieri' or a 'Fra Diavolo dei Balkan'; if true, it is at least curious as offering one of the few historical instances where a moribund hero or ruffian of real life sings a song before he dies, and as redeeming the Italian opera from the charge of being untrue to nature.

An idea of the difference between the Balkan Chelibi and the Haydut may be gathered from a conversation with *Khalil*, a Mussulman and a member of the former class: he had been dining with us, and we asked him after dinner if he knew anything of Stirion.

"Yes, I remember about him."

"How long since was it that he killed himself?"

"Eight years ago."

"Did you ever see him?"

"Not I, he kept out of the way of us Turks, for he knew that any one of us would have shot him like a dog."

"You don't consider him as a Balkan Chelibi, then?"

"A Balkan Chelibi! Why, he robbed people even of their clothes and murdered women and children!"

And Khalil shrugged his shoulders with a gesture of disdain and contempt untranslatable by words.

A couple of instances will show how justice is evaded, and how robbers escape punishment in Turkey.

One morning, two years ago, a crowd assembled in front of our hut, shouting, talking, screaming, and disputing, with the usual volubility of the Slavonic race.

"What do you want? what's the matter?" said St. Clair. "Don't all speak at once, but tell me what you have come for."

A deputation of *Chorbadjis* (head men of the village) entered the house.

"You see, Sir, *Said* of *Akindji* has just captured a horse-stealer in the very act, he has brought him here, and we don't know what to do with him; *Dimitri* wants to let him go if he promises to bring back twice the number of horses he has stolen from our village."

"Of course I do," said Dimitri, "for you want one of us to take him off into the forest, and what will happen then? He'll just give a good thrashing to the man who's with him, as soon as he is out of sight of the village!"

"Very well, four of us will go with him."

"And he'll thrash the whole four! he's a brigand!"

All the villagers, *Chorbadjis* and *Medjliss* (village council) included, suggested a hundred different ways of getting rid of the culprit, but no one thought of delivering him up to the constituted authorities.

Unfortunately, St. Clair thought he knew better; having a personal acquaintance with *Abdurrachman Pasha*, then Governor of Varna, and considering him as an honest and well-meaning man, he imagined that to give up the prisoner, with conclusive evidence of his crime, was to ensure his punishment: so he had the thief, his captor, and the heads of the village, brought into the house.

The examination of the horse-stealer was interesting

enough, for he denounced not only the members of the band to which he was affiliated, but also the receivers of the property stolen by them; amongst the latter was a rich and highly-respected Greek merchant of *Bazardjik*, a small town in the Pashalik of Varna.

The prisoner's confession was taken down in writing, and re-translated into Turkish for the benefit of the *Medjliss*, who testified to the accuracy of the document. The culprit was then sent to Varna under the escort of Said, who being a Turk was not afraid of being thrashed by a Rayah, together with a letter addressed to the Governor and containing the details of the affair and the confession of the thief. But St. Clair was not able to write in Turkish, and, as *Abdurrachman Pasha* does not understand French, the letter naturally passed through the hands of the Pasha's dragoman, or interpreter, *M. Commiano*, a Greek by birth.

No official answer was vouchsafed to St. Clair's letter, but a few days after this occurrence, when out shooting in the forest, he met the stealer of horses, who saluted him with a courteous and perhaps slightly sarcastic "*Oughour ola*," "*bon voyage.*"

The explanation of this failure of justice is simple: on enquiry, St. Clair learned that the Greek merchant of *Bazardjik*, who was compromised by the disclosures of the robber, is a near relation of M. Commiano, and that the letter never reached the Pasha's hands.

In Turkey the Pasha's residence is always paved with good intentions, but this pavement is trodden by so many Greeks, and other Oriental Christians, that the only result is dirt and mud.

Another instance of a slightly different kind: Some months

K

since a Greek, *Hassan* of Varna, sold us a hound, which a few weeks afterwards he stole from us whilst we were out shooting, and re-sold in a village thirty miles distant.

We found out Mussulman witnesses of the theft who were ready to give their evidence when required, and we complained personally to the Pasha of Varna, who told us "that he was very sorry, but the Capitulations required that in a case of an affair between Englishmen and a Turkish subject, in which the latter if guilty would be liable to punishment, the British Consul should take official cognizance of the matter."

So we went to H.B.M.'s (present) Vice-Consul at Varna, and that gentleman at first informed us that we could get the matter settled without his interference by merely applying to the Pasha; when we stated that this could not be done without infringing the Capitulations, we were told, with a good deal of hesitation, that "it was scarcely consistent with the dignity of a British Consul to interfere officially in a case of dog-stealing."

During the reign of the Bourbons, there was an organization in Sicily which had a certain effect in checking brigandage in that island. Companies of the farmers and their labourers were formed under the name of *Compagni d'armi*, they enjoyed a rate of pay higher than that of the ordinary gensdarme, but from it they were required to put aside a certain portion into the chest of the Company; their duties were to patrol the roads and to apprehend brigands, and if any unpunished act of brigandage was committed within their district, the sufferer was indemnified from their reserve fund. This system, however incomplete, worked well, because there was somebody who was responsible. In Bulgaria no one but the Pasha or *Kaimakam* (Lieutenant-Governor) is responsible, and he is virtually unapproachable, for to reach him the peasant has to wade through a mire of corrupt subordinates, whose demands equally exhaust his patience and his purse.

CHAPTER IX.

ORIENTAL COMMERCE.

A dishonesty which defies competition — A good stroke of business — Cent. per cent. for the merchant, but the producer suffers — Privilege of a Greek subject — Country agents — A little usury — Rising in life — Non-Greek foreign merchants — Base is the slave that pays — A swarm of locusts.

"PROFIT" is the primary motive of the existence of commerce in all its branches, but if profit is not kept in check by competition it ceases to be legitimate, and soon attains such monstrous proportions as finally to ruin both producer and consumer. Where there is no competition there is monopoly, and the disastrous effects produced by this system upon the country which tolerates or employs it are too well known to need repetition; in Turkey, however, monopoly flourishes in a degree happily unmatched elsewhere. In other lands it usually is but a last resource of the tottering finances of a Government, and even then is extended only to articles of luxury, such as tobacco; in the East it is the special property of a foreign nationality, the bitter and declared enemy of Turkey, and is not confined to a few articles of consumption but embraces every species of trade; all gradations of commerce or business in Turkey are in the hands of Greeks.

The reason of this is easily explained.

For competition to be possible it is necessary that the competitors should be able to use the same arms; competition against Greek merchants is impossible, for no other trader is able to employ the same weapons so skilfully wielded by the Greek merchant in Turkey :

"None but himself can be his parallel."

The Turk is put out of the field by his innate honesty, and the European by his laws, which provide a punishment for fraud and for crimes against property.

No code, but that of modern Greece, carries its patriotism so far as to shelter its subjects and protégés from the penal consequences which ought to follow such a career as that of the Eastern merchant who transacts business upon the Greek system.

Entry into the guild of Oriental commerce is far from difficult, a few foolish scruples of conscience may require silencing if by some strange chance they should exist, but little capital is necessary: the only indispensable qualification is that the aspirant should be a Greek, for without this he will encounter nothing but hostility amongst his new brethren. The commencement of the commercial career, is as follows:—Aristides arrives fresh from Greece at some port of Turkey, with a few piastres in his pocket, and a good "knowledge of business" in his head. For a day or two he walks about the town in search of an opening, and as he who seeks very frequently finds, provided he be not too particular as to the object of his search, the Chapter of Accidents soon puts him in a position to mount the first step of the ladder of commerce. A case of goods has arrived at the Custom-house with an illegible address: a little paint, and a fee to the *Gumrukji* (Custom-house officer) soon remedy this; to be sure there is no bill of lading, but another is easily manufactured, and passes muster with officials who cannot read a European language: the case belongs to Aristides, as the first fruits of his applied "knowledge of business."

Just after this lucky stroke, Aristides sees a train of carts laden with grain approaching the town, he goes out to meet them, represents himself as the emissary of Pisistratus the great corn merchant, and offers them a price thirty per cent. under the last quotation. The peasants hesitate, but they are accustomed to the capricious falls in the price of wheat, they see that the streets of the town are blocked up with *arabas* of grain, and finally a hundred piastres of earnest-money conclude the bargain, and make Aristides the owner of their corn. He runs into the office of Pisistratus, is directed to the café where that gentleman is playing billiards, calls him aside, and says, " I have just bought so many *kilés* of grain for you at fifteen per cent. under the market price, send out one of your men with me to take them." Of course Pisistratus is delighted with his portion of the spoil, and Aristides pockets his fifteen per cent.* Next day the thing is talked over at the Merchants' Club, and Aristides wins golden opinions from all the members present; Pisistratus relates the history of the clever bargain,

---

* It may be well to explain, for the benefit of country gentlemen, how Aristides succeeds so easily in buying wheat at 30 per cent. under the quoted price; it is a common trick of Eastern grain merchants to send round into the country districts announcing a certain price per *kilé*, say 100 piastres, and when some hundreds of peasants are assembled in or outside the town with their corn, a messenger is sent to say that no more than 70 piastres per *kilé* will be given. The peasants have come long distances, often three or four days' journey, and sooner than return home again with their laden carts, they accept the depreciated price offered.

No fall has really taken place in the price of grain, but the Greek merchants, acting together, see their way to "a good thing," and don't mind the road being rather dirty.

and Brasides adds, "Yes, and I found out this morning that the case of goods he sold me, (certainly I bought it cheap enough), cost him only thirty paras (three halfpence) for black paint, and five piastres *bakshish* at the Custom-house; decidedly, Aristides is a clever fellow who will make his way in the world, and I hope we shall soon see him amongst us here." So henceforth Aristides' reputation is established, and he has no difficulty in borrowing a small capital at 100 per cent. without further security than his proved commercial ability. He sets up for himself, and as his affairs prosper, that is, as he makes 200 or 300 per cent. profit, he is soon able to pay back the money borrowed, and even to commence lending to others at the same rate, whilst he launches out into the grander enterprises of Eastern commerce, which afford him still larger profits, and a wider scope for the exercise of his business talents.

Should things turn out badly, Aristides converts every thing he can into money, leaves his office for the benefit of his creditors, and withdraws to another field of action where he recommences business: in the East this proceeding is called "failing"—it is regarded as an "inseparable accident," and in no way damages the reputation of the merchant, for what trader in the East of five years' standing has not thus "failed"?

Such is a fair sample of the ordinary career of the Greek merchant. We will endeavour to sketch the progress of the Turkish subject in the same road; but, before studying individuals, let us glance at the general effects of Eastern commerce upon this country.

It is a remarkable fact that Turkey, whilst its exports are enormous, imports but very little, for the imports can hardly amount to four per cent. of the exports: the natural deduction would appear to be that the country must be excessively rich in specie, and yet in truth it is miserably poor: this is a sad economical anomaly, but nevertheless a fact. Yet it is not taxation which ruins the country, for, as may be seen in the chapters which treat of "The True Position of the Rayah" and "The Taxes of Turkey," this is fixed, all things considered, at the lowest possible rate. If we seek for the causes of this permanent pauperism of Turkey, we shall find one of them in Oriental commerce.

Eastern commerce is an illegitimate commerce, even leaving out of sight its prominent feature of dishonesty, for it is based not upon capital but upon credit, and upon credit purchased at an interest of sixty per cent. The profits accruing from it must therefore evidently surpass this percentage before they can benefit the merchant, and by supposing that they only amount to cent. per cent. we are understating the question.

In England or France, where the rate of six per cent. is rarely exceeded, and where temptations to usury are checked by the existence of large capitalists and of equitable laws, commerce taxes the country only to the amount of ten per cent. or one-tenth of the black mail levied by Greek commerce in Turkey.

Yet if the fortunes, or more correctly speaking the *capitals in specie*, acquired in the country were spent in the country, as in France or England, or if these capitals were used to encourage industry, these immense profits would be but a minor evil, the effects of which would be felt only by the producers and, *par contre-coup*, by the labourers, as is the case in England, where nevertheless the gross capital annually increases or at least is not diminished. But as in this country commerce is almost exclusively in the hands of foreigners, the gross capital does not increase, and leaves Turkey, to benefit other nations, whilst the land in which it has been gained is left equally destitute of specie and of produce. Such is, in our opinion, one of the greatest economical sores of Turkey.

Again, were this commerce legitimately based upon capital, and subject to the compensating law of competition, the percentage of its profits would not exceed ten or fifteen, and the evil would be mitigated in so much as the country would lose but fifteen per cent. instead of 100; but to prevent this the Capitulations step in, and, thanks to them, the competition even of capital against the absence of honesty and justice becomes impossible.

No man more honest than a Greek can live by commerce in Turkey, and a curious proof of this is that the Jews, who in other countries subsist upon the scraps of trade, cannot here compete with the Eastern merchant, whose morality is such that Turkey is perhaps the only country in the world where the Jew is, as it were, compelled to become a labourer or an artizan.

It may be objected, "Since you allow that large fortunes are made in the East, how can you say that its commerce is not based upon capital?"

We answer: first, because really large fortunes are rare, owing to a circumstance which acts as a counterpoise to the large profits made, namely, the absence of security; thus, the merchant who has realized a large sum of money well knows that, should he continue to speculate with it, it may be lost by the exercise of the same talent (in others) which gained it, and consequently he invests his earnings in some country where they will be beyond the reach of others like himself. Occasionally, one of these millionaires will embark some thousands in an affair which will double his stake in a few months; but this affair is not one with other merchants, his debtor is the easily duped Turkish Government, and as soon as he has pocketed the winnings of his final coup, he betakes himself to Europe with his booty.

Small fortunes made in Turkey are numerous: but for them what would become of Greece, whose soil is a desert— to the people of the West a desert, but peopled with the memories of great deeds and great men long since passed away, and leaving no legitimate descendants; but to the Hellene a desert which he abandons because there is no money to be made from it. But for them how would the Cretan insurrection have been kept up? Whose money purchased the Panhellenion, the Arcadi, and the Hellenos? Without these fortunes, how would the swarm of parasites in black frock-coats and varnished boots, who abound in every Turkish town, manage to exist?

Are they grateful to the authors of their fortune? ask one of them his opinion of the Turkish Government or the Turkish peasant, and from his answer judge for yourself.

Thus far we have shewn the general action of Eastern commerce upon the state of Turkey, we will now turn to the tenacula of the great *pieuvre* that drains the life-blood of this unhappy country, and, having traced its vital principle, we will glance at its many arteries.

This vital principle is to be found in the Capitulations; if these did not exist there would still remain a certain amount of corruption in the Turkish tribunals which might allow this commerce to drag on its existence during a period, but corruption might be punished or even eradicated, and then the great monopoly would be at an end.

Such corruption would even act in some degree as a palliative of the disease by which it profited, as the bribes would at least be spent in Turkey: it may seem strange to say this, but what must Eastern commerce be when corruption itself is preferable?

Let us suppose that the Capitulations are abolished, or have never existed, and take the imaginary case of an Englishman who has been cheated by a Greek, and whose cause is brought before a Mussulman court of law: the *Cadi* (Judge) influenced by bribes gives judgment against him, contrary to the evidence.

The Englishman writes to the 'Times,' the British Consul storms, and the Cadi is deprived of his post as a lesson to those who may come after him. Unhappily, however, the Capitulations *do* exist in a very lively state; let us see what chance our Englishman has in fighting against those granted to Greece, and the better to show it, let us take not an imaginary but an actual case, one of the many which occur, and which are not known outside the consular and mercantile circles of Eastern towns.

The English firm of K. Brothers, of Birmingham, had a business connection with the Varna railroad then in course of construction by an English company: at Varna there lived a merchant who enjoyed the reputation of being one of the most honest and straightforward men in the town (every Greek gives himself this character, finding it useful in his transactions with Europe), and who was moreover the possessor of an English Foreign Office passport, and registered at the British Consulate as a British subject. He being thus subject to British jurisdiction, Messrs. K. Brothers believed that they might trust him as their agent for certain articles of merchandise, paying him a handsome percentage on the sales effected.

Mr. M., the merchant in question, opened a "store" or shop in which he sold the articles sent out by K. Brothers, with whom he was guaranteed by a declaration of agency legalized at the British Consulate. He certainly sold at twice the rate of profit prescribed by the English house, but as the other shops which dealt in similar imported wares of English manufacture were not content with a gain of less than 200 per cent., his business was very large.

In a short time K. Brothers sent out a further supply of goods, directing their English agent with the railway company, Mr. G., to examine the books of Mr. M.; these were found to be perfectly well kept, and showed a balance of 1800*l.* in favour of Messrs. K. At the end of the year the English house asked that their balance should be handed over to them, and in consequence Mr. G. called upon Mr. M. with this request; he was answered that his authorization to receive the money for Messrs. K. Brothers was not sufficiently formal. Mr. S. of *Kustendji* (an Englishman) was then sent, and received the same reply.

At last the affair was put into the office of the British Consulate, and Mr. M. was sued for the whole sum, nearly 3000*l.*, owing to Messrs. K. Brothers—but in vain, for a barrier insurmountable by justice was encountered: the fraudulent merchant had become a Greek subject. On learning this, the Birmingham firm gave up all chance of recovering their money, and knowing something of the peculiarities of modern Greek law, forbade their agent to commence any proceedings in the Hellenic Consulate, preferring to put up with their loss rather than to lose their suit and be saddled with the costs in addition. *Immediately* after this affair Mr. M. was elected a member of the Merchants' Club of Varna: he is still living and trading, and still enjoys his old reputation as an honest man.*

Returning to the general features of Eastern commerce we find that not content with levying its percentage upon exports and imports, it even takes possession of the Government taxes: it buys, sells and resells the tithes, seizes upon such produce of the country as embraces articles of luxury (*e. g.* wine and tobacco) and whilst it has in no way contributed to the cultivation of the fields, it nevertheless raises the price of their produce by a system of action peculiar to itself.

This system consists in spreading over the whole country a network of agents who little by little absorb the small amount of specie distributed by commerce amongst the peasants, buying up their remaining produce at a reduction of fifty per cent. upon its value. But, as in Turkey the European dress does not confer upon its Oriental wearer the courage and pluck of the European, the former would find himself utterly powerless in presence of the courage of the natives: he is therefore compelled to employ Rayah

---

* A Greek Consul admitted to one of the Authors that in a case such as the one related above, the English firm would have had *no chance* of obtaining redress from a Greek tribunal, and he added that "he was sorry to say that in any trial for fraud, no matter how gross, committed by a Greek upon a foreigner, the former was always sure of an acquittal at the hands of his patriotic countrymen."

agents, whose cunning is more than a match for that of their customers, and whose known poverty *in specie* ensures them against the attacks of brigands. The civilized Greek does not dare to risk himself amongst the dangers of the mountains, nor indeed will he venture five miles outside a walled town: the Greek who is not yet civilized becomes a *Bakal*, and the village Bakal is the last, but by no means the least noxious, link in the chain of Eastern commerce.

Any Christian Rayah may attain to the dignity of this position, provided he can count upon his fingers, and that he have a clear idea of profit and percentage.

The village Bakal is usually a Greek, sometimes a Bulgarian, but invariably a Rayah: his stock in trade when he commences business need be no more than a pair of trowsers, or rather knickerbockers, cut after the Greek fashion, and an entire absence of anything resembling a conscience.

. He buys a barrel of wine at 30 *paras* an oke, with money borrowed at 100 per cent., obtains a stock of *mastica* (the common spirits of the country) on credit at 150 per cent. interest from some merchant in the nearest town, purchases a dozen tallow candles and a few salted fish, rents a hut, and opens his establishment.

Let us examine his mode of carrying on his business: the Rayah is returning from the neighbouring town where he has sold his wheat at 50 per cent. under its real value, that is, he brings back 50 per cent. of the value of his produce; he stops at the door of the *Tukhan*, or Bakal's shop, and calls for wine; he is served from the very same barrel which he made, and sold at 30 paras the oke, but he now pays for it 60 paras: the money received for his grain therefore suffers a reduction of 50 per cent., or to put it in another way, 75 per cent. of the produce of his labour has already passed into the capacious pockets of Eastern commerce! If he purchases cotton or calico from the stock of the *Bazergan* (travelling pedlar), he loses still more; or if he buys an English (?) knife at one of the town stores, he is cheated to at least the same extent.

Happily for the Mussulmans, Mahomet appears to have foreseen and provided against the village Bakal, and by prohibiting the use of wine to his followers has prevented the Turkish race from becoming completely extinct in Europe.

The Bakal has sold his barrels of wine and mastica, but as the villagers do not pay ready money, he can securely indulge in a little usury, and obtains from each of his debtors a signature (in the shape of a cross) to an I.O.U. payable at the time of *Harman*, or thrashing of the grain; this I.O.U. is marketable; the Bakal sells it, at a discount of course, to a merchant who pays him in mastica, and he continues his trade. He has paid 50 per cent. more than its value for his mastica, so he cannot sell it to the peasant under a profit of cent. per cent., in addition to which he charges an interest of 50 or 60; so he realizes clear profit of 100 to 110 per cent., which reduces the sum remaining in the hands of the peasant to 5 or 10 per cent. upon the value of his produce; Eastern commerce has absorbed 90 per cent., leaving the Rayah 10 per cent. in return for his labour and the produce of the fields bestowed upon him by the munificence of the Turkish Government.

These are the effects produced upon the country by the Bakal. We will now follow him in his upward career. In a short time he has amassed a small capital invested in loans at 60 per cent. upon the only reliable security in Turkey—that of the peasant. He has bought a pair of varnished boots, and indulges the ambition of becoming a *bonâ fide* merchant.*

With this view he calls in his debts, and realizes. Shortly afterwards he strikes out boldly into the sea of commerce, in which he occasionally encounters a shark or two; for whatever harmony a Turkish proverb supposes (perhaps erroneously) to exist among wolves, the genuine Greek shark has no scruples which prevent him preying upon his smaller and less audacious Rayah congeners. Very frequently, however, the Bakal succeeds in his new sphere, cheats the town with the same facility with which he taxed the country, and is soon able to buy the tithes of a village. His shop deals in contraband articles, such as gunpowder; his gains from these and similar speculations enable him to farm the taxes of an entire district, and before he is an old man he is a millionaire—in piastres not in pounds—but even this is not bad considering the easy manner in which his money has been made.

His reputation for wealth secures his election as *Chorbadji*, or mayor, of the town in which he trades. He still wears the Rayah fez (different in shape from that peculiar to the genuine Hellenes) but his Hellenic patriotism finds a vent in Greek breeches and white stockings. He is to be seen any day at the *Conac* (Pasha's official residence) seated modestly on the very edge of a chair, and approving with humble salaams every word that falls from the sententious lips of the Governor.

---

* The Authors mean to say a member of the higher branches of commerce; *bonâ fide* is a term singularly inapplicable to anything connected with trade in the East.

The Bakal's son, being destined for still greater things,

"Per correr miglior acqua alza le vele,"

wears clothes of the latest European fashion (as translated by the indigenous tailor), and is vehement in his orations against Ottoman tyranny. Miltiades has studied political oratory, amongst many other arts and sciences, at the university of Athens. More fortunate than his father, he is a Greek subject, and Eastern commerce in full uniform throws open the gilded portals of her temple, and invites Miltiades to enter even into the sanctum sanctorum.

His fez changes its shape, for he is no longer a Rayah, he need not tremble before a Pasha, nor conceal the means by which he earns his money. He is a Greek gentleman, and can even speak Greek-French; he speculates in the funds and upon the rate of exchange; he "fails" and makes a fortune by his failure. Whilst he cheats you he grasps your hand cordially and calls you " cher ami." Miltiades will some day be one of the " leading merchants " and " most honest men " of Constantinople.

There is yet another species of foreign merchant in Turkey—the *European merchant* as we will call him, to distinguish his class from that of the Greek. He is usually a consul, vice-consul, or consular agent, or at the least a brother, nephew, or cousin of the consul of some nation to which Turkey has granted Capitulations. He is by no means so clever as his Greek competitor, and his business does not flourish with the same bean-stalk rapidity, but his quality of consul, or relation to a consul, stands him well in stead. This dignity makes him a power in the eyes of the local government, and though he wisely avoids litigation with a

Greek subject, he can generally gain his suit against a Rayah, and always against a Mussulman.

Turks form but an infinitesimal fraction of the merchants of the East. They are occasionally to be found as grocers in a town, but this branch of trade is more usually engrossed by Persians, who show a greater aptitude than the Turk for the petty details of commerce. The Turk is rarely anything but a shopkeeper on a very small scale, with a little band of friends whose custom is always to be depended upon. He manages to exist upon his small profits, but he never makes a fortune.

We know of no Mussulman merchants in these districts. The reason may perhaps be found in the Report of Mr. Consul-General Longworth to the Foreign Office, dated Belgrade, April 10, 1867, and numbered 22 in the collection of Consular Reports on the condition of Christians in Turkey, presented to the House of Lords by command of Her Majesty.

"In a mixed commission for the settlement of debts between Turks and Christians, and the proceedings of which have been brought to my notice, some 300 or 400 claims have been respectively brought forward on both sides. On the part of the Turks they were without exception, whether substantiated by written receipts or by oral testimony, at once admitted. Of those preferred in the same manner against the Christians, how many will it be supposed were in the first instance acknowledged by the parties themselves? Not one."

How could a commercial firm of Mussulmans exist amongst the Christians of the East, if it were to adopt the novel and ruinous principle of admitting its just debts?

The Mussulman of the towns is then usually an artizan or manufacturer. He is a baker, gunsmith, blacksmith, carpet-maker, or shoemaker. He prefers gaining his bread by honest hard work, and hard work is repugnant to the finer susceptibilities of the Eastern Christian. A Mussulman tutunji (tobacconist) or kavehji (coffee-shop keeper) is occasionally to be found, but he is usually a "civilized Turk," and *ipso facto* a bad representative of his nationality.

Mussulman and European traders are but the few exceptions to the general rule that all commerce in the East is monopolized by the Hellene, or by the Greek or Armenian Rayah, but more especially by the first. Every year a swarm of individuals, whose only capital is a tall hat, varnished boots, and a "knowledge of business," which is born with the Hellene, alight upon the shores of Turkey. Of these every individual locust may not make his fortune, but at least he consumes enough of the produce of the land to enable him to live well, to wear a black frock coat and even gloves—luxuries paid for of course by the poor Turk or Rayah peasant. Add to the number of these comparatively insignificant parasites the greater "pieuvres," and the legions of the Bakal tribe and of the Rayah trader. When you have done this you will have some idea of the extent to which Turkey is drained of the produce of her labour, and you may even see how great must be her vitality since she feeds all these blood-suckers and yet exists.

CHAPTER X.

THE REAL POSITION OF THE BULGARIAN RAYAH, HIS SYSTEM OF AGRICULTURE, ETC.

Taxes on Agriculture — Neglect of Manure — Ploughing — " Why grow more ?" — Reaping — Six weeks' feast — Grain carried — Threshing — Vintage — Sheep Farming — Who is the injured party?

THE great mistake committed by most writers who attempt to estimate the position of the Rayah peasant, and especially by the authors of the British Consular Reports from Turkey in 1867, is that he is always looked upon merely in the light· of a tax-payer, and *not* of a farmer of Government lands, although it is this latter condition which more especially affects his politico-economical status.

In some districts the Rayahs rent land from the Beys—the Mussulman landed gentlemen of Turkey—and are taxed at the same rate as those who are tenants of the Government, but it is a financial mistake by which the Beys suffer more than their tenants. In most parts of Turkey and throughout Bulgaria, the Rayah peasants hold lands directly from the Crown. We shall therefore take this case as the rule, and by analysis divide the taxes paid by the Christian subject to the Turkish Government into two distinct classes:—

1st. Taxes paid by him as subject of the Sultan.

2nd. Taxes paid by him as a farmer of Government lands.

In the first category are

	Piastres.
A. The *Bedel Askerie* or tax paid by every adult Christian as exemption from military service; it varies from 20 to 30 piastres; the average may be taken as	25
B. The income tax upon the head of the family (*chorbaji*), which like that of Russia, varies according to the quantity of land sown, &c., &c., and averages	30
	55

In the second category are
    a. The tithe on produce.
    b. The *Beylik*, which includes the taxes upon sheep, pigs, vineyards, &c.

Thus it will be seen that in reality the Rayah is very lightly taxed; for roughly he pays no more than eighty piastres per house, *i. e.* fifty piastres for two * exemption taxes, and thirty piastres of income tax, or in English money at the present rate of exchange about fourteen shillings and sixpence, and even this calculation is a little exaggerated.

He pays nothing for the land he occupies except the *tapou*, or registration tax of thirty paras per dulum, about four pence an acre. This sum is only once exacted, and is not an annual imposition; upon its payment the Rayah is considered as bonâ fide proprietor of his lands. Taking this into account, the rent-taxes, as he may term the tithes, Beylik, &c., will be seen to be very small.

To understand this better, let us take the case of any average Bulgarian peasant. He " owns " (that is, he has appropriated and paid for at the rate above mentioned of thirty paras per dulum, which amounts to the gross sum of 2*l.* 10*s.*) 150 acres of land. Of this he cultivates in grain fifty acres yearly, and pays as a rent-tax one-tenth of the produce; potatoes and other vegetables pay no tithe, and

---

* Assuming an average of two adult males to the family.

are generally grown only by the *Bakchavan*, or professional market-gardener. Thus for the 150 acres he farms from Government he pays only one-tenth of the produce of fifty acres; the rest is rent free.

Again, he has 1000 acres or more of pasture land, for which he pays at the rate of three piastres (6d.) per sheep, and four piastres (8d.) per pig; cows, horses, and buffaloes paying no tax. This is not a very large sum in itself, and as the Rayah claims and exercises the right of cutting as much wood as he chooses from this land, a few cartloads sold at the nearest town soon pay the tax to which he is liable for his sheep and pigs. Thus he in reality enjoys an almost unlimited amount of grazing land from the Crown gratis.

Surely no farmer in the world is placed in a more favourable position, and if the Rayah is not rich, it is the fault of his own innate laziness, and of the 185 feast days of the Greek calendar. Let him and his friends then blame the Patriarch and not the Padischah, for the only really heavy imposition from which he suffers is that laid upon him by the *Papas* and the Metropolitan.

The Turkish villages are taxed in the same degree, except that they often possess lands as grants for distinguished military services, or by genuine purchase. We shall allude hereafter to their position when speaking of the great revolution effected by Sultan Mahmoud, and of the spoliation of the Osmanli by his own Government for the benefit of the Rayah. But by his military service the Turk is deprived of more than half a year's labour for each year of his adult life.* Fortunately for the Mussulmans, and in the Authors'

---

* Vide Chapter XI. on the Military Service of the Turk.

opinion for the world, he works harder and better than the Rayah, or his race would have been long since effaced from the ethnological map of Europe.

The Rayah system of agriculture is perhaps unique. The plough, as has been already mentioned, is of the rudest and simplest kind that can be imagined. The team consists of four or six oxen or buffaloes, according to the quality of the land to be ploughed. In the selection of the fields he intends to till, the Bulgarian farmer appears to trust himself very much to chance, or to be influenced by the convenience of the moment. He will not plough the ground from which he obtained last year's crop, and he will not plough fields which though once put under culture, have remained fallow for ten years; perhaps he has a fancy for a piece of ground yet uncleared, and in such a case he burns down the big trees, and digs up the thorn bushes till he considers the field fit for cultivation. Manure is to be found in great heaps everywhere in his village, merely waiting to be carted, but he disdains such adventitious aids to nature, either because he never heard that manure did any good, or because he thinks that it "burns the ground;" an idea which we have proved here, on a small scale, to be utterly fallacious, though unfortunately our experiment failed to convince the agriculturists of Derekuoi, who are all content to raise grain as it was raised by their grandfathers, and who look with distrust upon all new-fangled appliances, calling them "*marifetler*," a word susceptible of many different translations, but in this case most aptly rendered by the slang term "dodges."

At last, however, our farmer determines to plough a field in preference to any other, and he sets out with his plough, his buffaloes, and four human aides-de-camp. Arrived at the scene of action, the buffaloes start, not without a painful effort. One man guides the devious ploughshare, a second walks at the head of the leaders, a third surveys the wheelers knowingly from a little distance, a fourth pulls out his bagpipes and lightens the labour by playing the air appropriate to the favourite Bulgarian ballad of *Deli Marco*, whilst the fifth relates in a plaintive falsetto how King Marco kicked in with his feet the iron gates of Adrianople, took the city, and was finally slain by the infidel Mussulmans. Not far off sits an old woman with her distaff, who has come out apparently to see that everything is done properly, or to hear "King Marco," for it would not be easy otherwise to explain the necessity of her presence. She is always busy, however, as indeed are the females of most civilized or semi-civilized countries, and she works with a perseverance and rapidity which the male labourers are far from emulating.

One of the effects of the misgovernment of this country is that every Rayah is the owner of more land than he knows what to do with, and therefore it is not to be expected that he should make the most of every acre. When he has turned one furrow, he ploughs on the other side of the ridge, so that his field is turned with just half the labour which an Englishman would give to the same surface. But even of this work, as of every other, Rayah human nature will not stand more than an hour at a time. King Marco is not yet killed, for the Slavonic ballads are almost endless in the mouth of a chanter gifted with a memory which embraces the whole of their innumerable stanzas, and his tragical death is left unsung, whilst the exhausted musician and tired labourers gather strength for new efforts by repose and application to their wooden flasks of wine.

In an adjoining field is another gang of toilers, who are easily induced to cease from their labour and join our lotus eaters. The females of each party draw near and help to enliven the conversation, but *they* do not leave off their work.

After half an hour's rest the ploughing is resumed, King Marco is slain, and is resuscitated and again before the walls of Edirna by the time that another interval of *dolce far niente* is considered necessary.

The amount of grain sown by the Bulgarian per acre is nearly three times that employed for the same purpose by the English farmer, and the amount of produce reaped equals the average of a good year in England: but, besides the smaller surface of land actually ploughed by the former, we must remember that his furrows are mere scratches about four inches deep, that the harrow is an instrument unknown, and that the seed is devoured by a countless flock of crows, pigeons, and other birds, which he never takes the trouble to drive off or keep away even by the simple expedient of a scare-crow.

The bounteous crops with which these provinces are blessed are the results of a most fertile soil and a most favourable climate: little is due to the labour of the Rayah: * a little

---

* If it were possible to kill all the pigeons who feed upon an acre of sown land in Bulgaria, to take out the grain from their crops, to throw it out hap-hazard upon any piece of ground which has once been in cultivation, even if it have lain fallow for years, and to prevent other birds from coming to it, the produce in corn would be at least as great, acre for acre, as that of any land tilled by the Rayahs; this may seem an absurd way of stating a question, but it is very near the truth.

more work and a little more intelligence would treble his produce, but if you try to explain this to a Rayah he will answer you, " Why should he trouble himself? if he wants to sow more grain he has plenty of land: what he sows is enough for himself, his family, the taxes, and to sell at the town, and if he raised more grain he would have to pay more Beylik!" As you can seldom get beyond this last piece of logic with a Bulgarian, it is perhaps best to leave him alone until his calculating powers are developed by some system of education other than that at present in force.

The culture of Indian corn requires rather more trouble and attention than that of wheat, and for this reason it is commonly left by the Rayah to the women: for the same cause and from its being less certain of success but little of it is grown by the Christians, and the Mussulman villagers are by far the larger producers of this cereal.

The cutting of the grain is the occasion of a general pic-nic of the villagers; the whole family, from the grand-parents down to the two-months-old lady, turn out and encamp under the shade of some spreading tree near the cornfields: wine, bread, and sour crout are in abundance, and neither King Marco nor the bag-pipes are absent. After an interval of recreation, the women, girls, and children take up their sickles and begin to work, whilst the men and youths smoke their cigarettes in the shade, with that pleasant feeling enjoyed by a lazy man who sees others perspiring under a hot June sun, whilst he is stretched at full length in some cool place with plenty of tobacco and light wine within reach.

In about a week the corn is reaped and the sheaves bound up, but it would be *gunah*, a sin, to carry the grain immediately, and so it is left upon the fields for six weeks. These six weeks are employed by the peasants in dancing, feasting, and drinking; and to set about any work, except perhaps that of cutting down the Sultan's forests for the benefit of town or village hearths, would be wrong in the eyes of the Papas. In the mean time however the sheaves are not left untouched, for millions, literally millions, of turtle doves, apparently attracted by the unlimited supply of food placed within their reach, congregate in every field: what the farmer loses by their meals is not easily calculated, but to gastronomic epicures we can heartily recommend the Bulgarian grain-fed turtle-dove as an excellent though little known dish.

At last the six weeks' feasting is ended, the tax-collectors have taken their tenth, and the grain is brought home from the fields: then begins the work of threshing; the earth of the hurdle-fenced inclosures before each house is beaten and stamped down until it acquires the solidity necessary for a threshing-floor, and the herds of half-wild horses which during the rest of the year roam loose in the forest are driven into the village, which for some ten days is almost unapproachable, the air being filled with flying chaff and dust, and the ears ringing with the guttural cries of the peasants urging their team of twelve or fifteen reeking horses round and round the enclosures.

The sifting of the grain is entirely the work of the unmarried girls, and when this final operation is finished, it is housed in the queer wooden granaries constructed for the purpose. Then comes the calculation of how much is to be kept for household use, how much must go to the merchant who lent 4*l*. in November to be repaid 10*l*. in July, how much to the *Bakal* to pay the house-father's account for wine, tobacco, and *mastica*, during the past year, and finally how much will remain for sale to the corn merchants of the town.

When the *Harman* is over, the Bulgarian has little to do except to enjoy himself in his manner during another three weeks' feast and to wait until his grapes are ripe, or rather till he supposes they ought to be ripe, for he seldom waits till they are properly matured, not being particular as to the quality of his wine, so that it be sufficiently heady to afford him the luxury of getting drunk upon it.

The vintage occupies only two or three days and is another universal pic-nic, which takes place in the *Baghla* or vineyard: this vineyard, which also contains the peaches, melons, and apricots of the village, is generally situated at some little distance, and guarded by a *Bekji* or watcher. Even in the Rayah villages the *Bekji* is invariably a Mussulman, as the Christians themselves allow that they could not trust one of their own faith, who would certainly allow himself to be bribed by the inhabitants of the neighbouring villages, and suffer them to come with carts during the night to carry off the grapes and other fruits: the Turk or Arnaout, however, is incorruptible, even in the opinion of the Rayah.

The average pay of a Bekji for his eight or ten weeks' guard is five *kilés* of grain, in value about 4*l*. 5*s*., a small proportion of the grapes, and his food gratis: his duty is to stay in the vineyard night and day, to watch the vines and shoot all foxes, village dogs, or other thieves and trespassers, who may come into the enclosure. If the vineyard is very large, the Bekji constructs a sort of perch eight or ten feet high from which he looks out for intruders; his sleeping apartment is a lean-to of thatch, in shape like a French *tente d'abri*.

The process of making wine is simple: the press is the primitive one of men's feet; and in our neighbourhood white and purple grapes are mixed indiscriminately in all stages of greenness, ripeness, or rottenness: excellent wine might be made if the peasants knew anything about the proper method of manufacture, but like all the other resources of Turkey this branch of industry is extremely neglected. As the Rayah is not even aware of any other way to prevent wine turning acid, he puts into it a bitter herb when the fermentation has ceased, and of course thereby utterly destroys any claims to excellence which under other treatment it might have acquired. The Bakal, to suit the taste of his customers, adds another herb which has the effect of making the wine more heady and more rapidly inebriating, for drunkenness is too often the only object of the Rayah who drinks; he might say with the Negro, "Me drinkee for drunkee, me no drinkee for dry."

Sheep farming is carried on extensively in Bulgaria, the system adopted being equally primitive with that of ploughing. The sheep are turned out upon the pasture-land of the village under the superintendence of a herdsman (the *Choban*) whose duty it is to look after them just as much or as little as he likes. The vocation of a *Choban* is one much affected by the Rayah youths and men, as he has nothing to do but to saunter lazily after his sheep, leaving to his dogs the care of collecting stragglers, and he has consequently unlimited time at his disposal for the concoction of variations upon the air of Deli Marco; the choban is never to be found without a bagpipe or a flute, with which he solaces his lonely hours and scares away eagles and wolves from his flock.

The male lambs are sold, and the females kept, as the latter pay no tax until they have lambed: the milk of the ewes is mixed with that of goats, and a very indifferent sort of cheese and *yaourt* (a kind of curds and whey) is made from it. The wool is used for household purposes or sold; in either case it is not cleaned, as the Rayah cleverly argues that the dirt in it will make the weight heavier: he does not however proceed so far with his reasoning as to reflect that the price he receives per oke is much less than that paid for the cleaned wool of the Turkish villages.

The only animal to which the Bulgarian pays any real attention is his buffalo, which in winter occasionally enjoys the luxury of a little straw to eat, a gift denied to his cattle and sheep; but little hay is made, and that little is usually sold in the towns; turnips are utterly unknown, and it is hardly too much to say that if snow were to lie on the ground for two consecutive months there would probably not be 500 cattle or sheep left alive in the whole of Bulgaria.

We have now seen the Rayah "at work" passing the small portion of the year not given up to unmitigated idleness in a lazy imitation of labour; his working days are pic-nics enlivened by music and wine, and he exerts himself just enough to return to his hut with a good appetite.

Let us compare this Rayah, as we know him to be, with the idealized Eastern Christian for whom Europe is almost ready to enter upon a nineteenth-century crusade.

Everywhere, but above all in this country which is only known to the West by the pictures of Hellenic magic lanterns and Russian phantasmagoria, the romantic becomes in the highest degree absurd when viewed as it really is, and not as it appears when seen by the deceptive light of sentiment or of political interest.

Observe the Rayah in his fields, in his cottage built of mud and plastered over with cow-dung, or lying drunk at the door of the *Bakal;* how different is this animal from the pensive Christian, oppressed by the infidel, enduring martyr-torments with a martyr's courage, and secretly brooding over the glorious memories of his obscured nationality, whilst he breathes a patriot prayer, such as that by which the people of Poland made Russia tremble and almost raised a feeling of sympathy in the heart of the Governments of the West, despite the triple shield of indifference which guards them from all pity save for "the sufferings of the Rayah."

Yet such is the light in which the Rayah is presented to the eyes of Europe by travellers who pass through the country as quickly as—as the state of the roads will permit them— and whose only remembrance of it is a vague souvenir of picturesque costumes, of songs sung in a language which they did not understand, and some pamphlets written or profound remarks suggested by a Greek or Russian Consul. To those who have studied the Rayah question deeply, seriously, and impartially, a very grave social question presents itself: Is it right to give too much to a man? Too much time, too much liberty, too much land, too much of everything? And especially is this right, when such a man abuses the gift and employs the resources confided to him merely to keep himself in idleness?

Such is the question which in spite of the early prejudices of education and ignorance must strike any one who has conscientiously studied a Rayah village. In our opinion one of the gravest economical faults, or perhaps even crimes, of the Turkish Government is the unbounded license which its mistaken generosity has granted to its Christian subjects. Work is the law of humanity: yet the twelve millions of Christian subjects of the Sultan escape this elsewhere universal necessity by the lenity of a Government which Europe has been taught to consider tyrannical and oppressive.

The English or French labourer must work six days in the week, or 313 days in the year, in order that England and France may "live": the Rayah works one day in three or 120 days in the year; is this fair to the labourer of France and England?

European Turkey occupies perhaps a fifth of the wheat-producing surface of Europe, and is by Nature intended to be the granary of the world: thanks to the idleness of the Rayah it produces less than one-third, or even but one-fourth of the amount of grain which should be grown upon it: thus, $\frac{3}{4}$ of $\frac{1}{5}$, or $\frac{3}{20}$, that is 15 per cent. of the entire produce of Europe, are lost by the nullity of the Rayah considered as a labourer, and with the consent of the Turkish Government. One of the consequences of this loss is that the French and English labourer pays 15 per cent. more for his loaf of bread than he ought to do.

The non-value of the Rayah as producer affects then the price of bread in Europe to the extent of 15 per cent., but as we see from the last chapter, Oriental Commerce, the plague of Europe, raises this percentage to 20 or even 25. The Eastern grain trade is chiefly dependent upon the Rayah, and we may therefore consider him not only as a social non-value, but as an active instrument of evil to Europe.

If the Rayah worked as he ought to work, England and France would buy their bread 20 per cent. cheaper, which means that the labouring classes in these countries *would live one day more in six;* and this 20 per cent. might perhaps even do much in checking pauperism; this aspect of the Rayah is probably a novel one, but surely it merits serious consideration.*

The résumé of this chapter is easily made: we say that the Rayah, far from being oppressed by his Government, is in reality the oppressor of Europe. Let those who can not merely deny, but disprove the exactness of our data, draw a different conclusion.

---

* If the fall of prices were checked at a certain point by diminished production in other regions following as its consequence, and if the labourer were prevented from receiving the full benefit of the fall even to this point by a fall in wages also following from it, he would even then, we maintain, be considerably a gainer, and is by comparison at present a sufferer to a very appreciable extent.

CHAPTER XI.

THE EXEMPTION OF THE RAYAH FROM MILITARY SERVICE,
AND ITS EFFECTS UPON THE TURK.

Misconception prevailing in Europe — Original land-tenure — Alteration in consequence of so-called military reforms — Unequal burden imposed on the industry of the Turk by military service — Reform suggested.

GREATEST among the anomalies of Turkey is one which by its inordinate injustice astonishes even those who through long experience of the country have ceased to be astonished at anything else. The Mussulman alone pays the tax of blood, the Rayah is wholly exempt from military service.

Europe makes a note of the fact, and thereupon proceeds to draw from it the most extraordinary conclusions. According to her idea it is the Christian in vain aspiring to the honour of bearing arms in the service of his country, who painfully feels the inequality of the situation, and is for ever seeking redress from rulers who shrink from conceding a privilege which may one day be used in the vindication of rights ignored and trampled upon.

Sentiments such as these may indeed be seen every day in the foreign newspapers of Constantinople. Trace them to their authors, ask whose are these longings for instruction in military discipline and strategy, and you will find that they are the excercitations of some learned Armenian, who certainly undertakes a great deal in answering for the martial tendencies of his compatriots, or else that a Bulgarian of comparatively advanced education has availed himself of his skill in penmanship to sign his name to an article which some European politician has written for him.

As for ourselves, whilst complaining of the injustice as loudly as any of the friends of the Rayah, we assert that it is not *he* but the Turk who suffers—and suffers terribly— from the anomaly of which we are about to treat, and for clearer understanding of which a brief historical sketch is necessary.

When Orchan, the son of Osman, organized his system of conquest and his troops (who formed the first regular army known in Europe), he created a motive for territorial aggrandisement, and a desire to retain the country conquered, by granting the lands of the vanquished to his victorious soldiers, who held them on the condition of military service, and were bound to follow the Sultan in his wars.

The foot soldier (piade) received a grant of land free from all taxes, and even obtained the right of levying certain imposts upon the *Rayahs* or conquered nations who continued to live upon the territory thus conceded to him ; the *Timars*, *Ziamets*, and *Beys*, thus acquired considerably larger portions of the soil as well as a greater number of vassals, the Timars holding from 300 to 500 acres, the Ziamets from 500 to 2000, and the Beys still more extensive estates.

These military colonists or fief-holders were personally, as well as their lands, exempted from all taxes, and authorised to exact from the Rayah a tithe of his produce, a tax which was named Beylik, or impost of the Bey, a title which it still retains, although it is no longer the Bey who profits by it.

Formerly the Turk, though bound to take up arms in time of war and to serve without pay, during peace remained in his own home, and received in compensation for his service lands free of tax, and a revenue regularly paid to him by the Rayah: but even then the Rayah was not entirely exempt from military service notwithstanding the *Kharatch* paid by him, as besides the annual quota of a thousand Christian children who were enrolled in the ranks of the Janissaries, he was forced to follow the army in a non-combatant capacity in the army works corps, military train, &c., such auxiliaries being known as *Woinaks*. In the good old times, when money was worth ten or twelve times its present value, the *Kharatch* was probably sufficient to warrant his exemption from the dangers of war, considering the services rendered in camp and barracks by the Rayah, and at any rate in time of peace the Mussulman had the best of it, but things are much changed in our day.

The illogical revolution effected by Sultan Mahmoud in the Government destroyed the political, social, and economical organization of Turkey, only to replace it by a state of affairs which is best described by the Turkish word *Kalabalik*.* The reforms inaugurated by the late Sultan Abdul Medjid, the famous edict of Gul Hane, and the Hatti Sheriff of 1856, only made things worse, whilst Europe looked on and clapped her hands with the delight of a street boy at a "good fire." In reality, these concessions, which were to be so many steps in the upward path of progress, have proved an almost insurmountable obstacle in the way of civilization—an apple of discord thrown between the two races, a negation or rather

---

* Confusion worse confounded, more chaotic than chaos itself.

annihilation of undeniable rights, an infinite injustice, and one of the causes of the weakness of Turkey.

We are far from disapproving Article IX. of the Treaty of Paris. What we wish to see is its stipulations *literally* carried out, and an amelioration of the condition of the subjects of His Majesty the Sultan, *without distinction of religion or of race*, and *not* a monopoly of this amelioration in favour of the Rayah alone.

It is not our intention to examine the details of these concessions and reforms, but to study the effect produced by them upon the respective positions of the Mussulman and Christian from the point of view of military service.

The Turks, as we have seen, enjoyed numerous privileges in return for their service as soldiers, before the period of the sweeping reforms "alla Turca" of Sultan Mahmoud. The summary abolition of the Janissaries brought about a radical but ill-considered change in the organization of the army. The old and powerful system of levées en masse from the various sandjaks (military provinces) was replaced by a conscription, and the formation of a regular army which is certainly the worst organized in Europe; in short, French institutions were copied by Turkey with much the same success as would attend the efforts of a Parisian to make a cup of good Turkish coffee in the Turkish fashion.

By the new system, every Turk was, as formerly, obliged to serve in the army of the Padischah, not as before for the campaign only, but for a period of years fixed by the Government, as in the case of the French conscript. Then, as the Government bestowed upon the soldier an infinitesimal * rate

---

* See Appendix I.

of pay, always in arrear and sometimes never paid at all, as it clothed him in "shoddy" cloth, and armed him with a gun dangerous only to himself, it considered itself justified in depriving him of the Beylik which he received from the Rayah, and appropriating the sum thus obtained to its own use, as an equivalent for his pay and equipment. Had the Government stopped here, there would have been a semblance of justice in its proceedings; it went further, however, and yielding to the current of "Reform," not only deprived the military colonist of the taxes he had raised from the Rayah, but in its pursuit of "Equality" thought it necessary to make *him* pay imposts similar to all those exacted from time immemorial from the Rayah. By a clemency incomprehensible in such zealous re-organizers, they did not force him to pay the *Kharatch*, and though he has since been saddled with a tax upon income and property, he is (in common with the Rayah who has served in the Christian regiments, the Cossacks of the Guard of the Sultan) exempted from the "Bedel Askerie," a sum paid by the Rayah in lieu of military service, and amounting on the average to twenty-five piastres.

The concessions thus granted to the Rayah have produced two effects, differing apparently, but both tending to the same end of weakening the Turkish Government. The Rayah who sees himself suddenly placed in a position not only equal with, but in many points superior to, that of the Turk, is by no means grateful to the Sublime Porte, for he notices the coincidence of time between these concessions and disastrous or indecisive wars;* and by the foreign secret

---

* That of the Crimea, for instance.

agents, and by the Greek clergy, he is confirmed in the idea that it is to Russia he owes this amelioration of his condition. When a boon is considered as granted only by the influence of extraneous pressure, and not from good will or magnanimity, the donor can expect but little gratitude, and it is not to be wondered at that the recipient should despise a Government suspected of subserviency to foreign influence.

This reasoning is the one universally adopted by the Rayahs, and it easily explains their continual agitation, especially that of Crete, seeing they have arrived at the conclusion that Turkey is nothing, and Russia everything; so that in spite of their habitual apathy, their idleness, and their ignorance of politics, they would perhaps break out into open rebellion at the bidding of those agents whose unceasing efforts tend always to this end, were they not as cowardly as they are ungrateful; the Rayah despises the Government of the Sultan, but he trembles at the sight of a Mussulman turban.

The Turk, on the other hand, finding himself deprived of his ancient privileges, not only ruined by the new laws, but insulted (which to a Turk is harder to bear), and being no longer the *Master* but the *Rayah* of the Rayahs—he too reflects, and accuses his Government of a cowardice worse than criminal.

Such are the effects of the new institutions in this country: whilst in Europe they are regarded merely as having opened a door to those foreign intrigues which they almost legitimate, and whose object is the dismemberment of the Turkish Empire.

But it is the injustice of those so-called Reforms that

makes them still more injurious to the country: the Turk, deprived of his privileges and taxed equally with the Rayah, is moreover forced to serve in the army—true, it is an honour, but an honour which costs him dear.

The present regulations compel every adult Turk to serve in the army for a period of five years (in the navy of seven), after the expiration of which term he is placed in the Rediflik or Reserve for seven years more, and as this latter force is, consequent upon the continually harassed state of the country, almost always under arms, his active service cannot well be computed under a minimum of ten years.*

The Turk however has the option of paying his exemption by a sum of 8000 piastres, rather more than 70*l.*; the price paid by the Rayah is an average of 25 piastres, or 4*s*. 6*d*. for every year of his adult age.

The difference between these sums plainly proves our assertion of injustice, but to illustrate it still further we will cite an example, giving the real names.

Mehmed Agha of Ayvajik, in Roumelia, possesses land which requires for sowing 300 kilés of grain, and he has two pairs of buffaloes; he pays a property tax of 300 Turkish lire annually, besides the tithe and other imposts.

Anastaz of the neighbouring village of Akdere, a Rayah, owns fields which require 500 kilés for sowing, and has eight pairs of buffaloes; he too pays 300 lire per annum.

Thus far the Christian starts with an advantage.

But Mehmed Agha has six sons, of whom five are serving in the army, and the eldest of whom he has exempted by the

---

* We have not taken into account the Bashi Bozouklouk, a force which is called out in time of need from those who have completed their service in the Rediff.

payment of 8000 piastres, and he is forced to replace their labour by hired servants, to whom he pays 3000 piastres (about 28l.) a year; whilst the four sons of Anastaz work, or get drunk at one of the numerous Tukhans of Akdere, and pay for the license of either employment only 25 piastres per annum.

If now we submit this question of the non-service of the Rayah to an arithmetical analysis, its proportions become still more grave.

Taking the average duration of life here, after twenty years, at twenty years more, that is from twenty to forty,* twenty years of the vigour and endurance necessary for constant and sustained labour, we know that the Turk is forced to serve from the age of twenty years, and that the Rayah then begins to pay his Bedel Askerie or Exemption Tax of 25 piastres; thus the Mussulman gives to his country ten years of his adult age, or one-half of his most profitable age, whilst the Rayah exempts himself for these twenty years by the payment, in minute instalments, of 500 piastres.

There is another way of looking at this; since one-half of the Mussulman's adult age is taken from him by the Government, he has but 182 days in the year at his own disposal,

---

* We do not profess to be actuaries, and if the amount of life we have given to every adult (we do not take into consideration the deaths of infants, which might reduce the general average of life to 33 or 35) seems too little, we beg the curious reader to find out how many 10 years' men there are in the ranks of an English company, and thence to evolve how many 20 years' men there might be. Of course this calculation only applies to the Turks, but to the Bulgarians drunkenness is as fatal as the Russian bullets, starvation, or the diseases incident to camp and quarters.

In our village of 350 souls, 11 men between 20 and 37 years died within the year, most of them from drink.

whilst the Rayah has the whole 365, paying only 4s. 6d. for the privilege; the Christian should then produce, in a corresponding proportion, more than the Turk, but this is by no means the case, and if there is a difference in the amount of corn, &c., raised by the two, it is in favour of the latter: for this strange fact a reason is easily found in the innate idleness of the Rayah, and in the peculiarities of the Greek Calendar; for the Rayah profits by the gift of half the year, which the Ottoman Government makes him, to idle during the 183 days of Feast ordained by the Greek Church; whilst the Turk marches and fights, the Rayah dances and drinks, and his exemption from military service is only a more or less direct encouragement of a gigantic parasitism and an authorized debauch.*

Another phase of this question involves a point which touches Europe more nearly than all the rest, the state of the Turkish finances.

The Mussulman subject of the Sultan pays as personal taxes (we omit those dependent upon produce and the possession of immovable property) a capitation tax upon his presumed income which averages 30 piastres, and he also pays to Government 182 days of labour, which the Government itself values at 400 piastres,† making a total of 430 piastres.

The Rayah pays the same 30 piastres, and a further sum of 25 piastres for exemption from military service; in all, 55 piastres.

Thus the Mussulman pays in personal taxes in the pro-

---

* See Appendix K.
† Taken at the exemption price, 8000 piastres for 20 years equal 400 per annum.

portion of 130 to 55, or eight-times as much as the Rayah,* whence the latter may in justice be said to owe to the Imperial treasury a sum of 375 piastres every year, an addition which would be very welcome to the budget of Turkey, since, taking the number of adult Rayahs at only one-fifth of the whole population of twelve millions, it would amount to the enormous sum of 900 millions of piastres, between eight and nine millions sterling; to us it seems that it would be only just to exact this sum, since it can hardly be denied that if the Ottoman Government taxes its Mussulman populations to this extent, it has the right to demand an equivalent sum from the Christians.

More than this, in the interest of Justice and of equality of all Turkish subjects before the law, as promised and guaranteed by the Treaty of Paris, it is the sacred duty of the Government to do so, and thus to increase its own prosperity and gladden the hearts of the holders of Turkish Government Stock.

An objection might be raised against such an act, on the plea that to tax the Rayah 400 piastres instead of the 25 he pays at present would be to deal unjustly with *him*, since the

---

* There are various other ways of calculating this difference, each of which tells strongly in favour of the Rayah; for instance, a day's work in Turkey is always worth *at least* five piastres, and counting the working days of the Mussulman year, the year is worth 1500 piastres instead of 400 piastres. Again the Mussulman paying for exemption 8000 piastres, whilst the Rayah pays 25 per annum, buys his liberty at 320 years' purchase, without entering into the calculation of the respective value of the sum paid down and of that paid by instalments. It may be said that the Government feeds and clothes the soldier, but the labourer hired at five piastres a day is also fed by his employer, and the risks of war are certainly worth more than the very indifferent clothing given to the Turkish troops.

Turk has the option of exempting himself or of serving, and because such heavy tax could not be paid by a poor man.

This last objection is easily refuted, for, as we have seen, the poorest Rayah has 182 days in the year more than the Mussulman, and 182 days of labour are worth, even in Turkey, more than 400 piastres, so that the poor Rayah would only find himself obliged to work for 100 or 120 days in the year more than is his custom, and to spend less time and money in drinking. Furthermore we by no means advocate denying the Rayah the option of exemption, and we even suggest a great concession in his favour, viz., that he should be allowed to choose between the combatant and non-combatant branches of the service, and either to enter the Christian regiments of the Sultan or a corps of Forest Rangers, army works, army train, or any other such civil branch as shall be militarily organized.

Although the friends of the Rayah may deny his obligation to fight for the Crescent, they can hardly maintain that it is not his duty to contribute towards the material improvement of the country in which he lives, an improvement by which he will be the first to benefit.

It would be easy to write at great length upon the details of this question, and to propose, for instance, that the exemption tax should be proportioned to the means and social position of the person exempted, since it is unjust that the *Hamal* (street porter) should pay as much as the Rayah trader, who with a capital of 250*l.* realizes an income of 300*l.* by the mysterious proceedings of Eastern commerce: in time of war too the exemption tax should (in our opinion) be largely increased. But it is not our duty to point out remedial measures; if the Turkish Government some day throws off its apathy and seeks to cure the wound it has inflicted, it will find salves enough and to spare.

In conclusion we repeat that such a service as we have proposed would not be absolutely new to the Rayah; we have mentioned the organization of the *Woinaks*, which proves the fact of the Christians having formerly served, and Von Hammer attributes the rapid successes of Bajazet to an excellent system of Rayah camp servants and workmen.

At that time, when the Turk was in the full enjoyment of all his privileges, and the Rayah had neither civil nor political rights, this forced service might have been a hardship; but in the present day when the Turk is placed exactly on the same footing with the Christian as regards everything except military service (an exception which threatens the Osmanli race with extinction and ruin), when the Rayah can attain to the highest positions and the most lucrative posts, when all Government schools and colleges are open to him, there is no possible or even plausible excuse for exempting him from the tax of labour, whilst the Mussulman pays the tax of blood: as an old Turk said to us the other day, " Since they make Giaour Pashas, why don't they make Giaour *nefers ?* Decidedly our Government is *deli* or *korkak*." *

---

* Nefers, private soldiers. Deli, mad. Korkak, cowardly.

CHAPTER XII.

THE TAXES OF TURKEY.

Taxes, personal and on property — Inequality of property-tax — Dime and its farming — Consequent loss to the revenue — Mode of collection, and injury to the cultivator — Pleas against reform — A land-tax suggested — Already exists in the case of vineyards — Customs — Corvée — Extraordinary contributions.

IN the preceding chapter we have stigmatized the gross injustice of the arrangement whereby the severest of imposts, that paid by the youth and available labour of Turkey, is distributed so as to affect but one Creed and one Nationality.

This anomaly, which has never been appreciated in Europe, may perhaps have astonished our readers; and the contents of the present chapter will furnish them with equal matter for reflection, if they take any interest in the welfare of Turkey, and have formed definite ideas upon the subject of those economical truths which are in our day recognized as the bond between Government and people.

The authorized and regular taxes which are levied upon the subjects of the Sultan are of two classes:—

I. Those which may be called personal.

	Piastres.
A. The *Virghu* or tax upon the person and supposed property, which may be fairly averaged at	30
B. The tax of blood, or of military service, which as we have seen costs the Mussulman	400
And the Rayah (as Kharatch)	25
By these the Mussulman peasant or soldier is taxed annually	430
Whilst the Rayah proletarian pays only	55

II. Taxes upon the produce of lands granted and held

under a *Tapou*;* these vary according to locality, but in Bulgaria consist of

C. The tax of the *Ashar*, 'Dime,' or tithe of the produce of cereals.
D. The *Beylik* or capitation tax upon various domestic animals.
E. A tax upon orchards, vineyards, and market gardens.

There are also indirect taxes upon various home or foreign products, which are paid to the *Gumruk* or customs.

We have already sufficiently proved the hardship inflicted by the unequal partition of the exemption tax between Mussulman and Christian, the former paying in proportion to the latter as 400 to 25, or 16 times more than his favoured fellow subject.

As for the *Virghu* or property tax, we have given one instance out of a thousand, the case of Mehmet Agha and Anastaz, in which the Turk pays the same sum as the Rayah for an estate which is only about one third as large: it follows that there must be either a very faulty and unjust system of classification or, what is possible but not probable, venality or peculation on the part of the collectors of this tax; this last hypothesis we qualify as improbable, not from any high opinion of the character of the tax-gatherers as a body, but because the details of extent of property, sum paid, &c., &c., in each case are set forth in the official *Teskeres* or receipts for taxes, and this would act as a check upon fraud; rejecting then this supposition, we conclude that the system of valuation is excessively imperfect.

As regards the tax upon produce, or dime, it will be seen from the brief historical sketch given in the last chapter (and without the aid of arguments which we reserve for

---

* This system of tenure will be explained in the following Chapter.

another place), that a great injustice is committed upon the Turk, who, from being the receiver of a certain tax, has been reduced to pay it himself; at any rate he should be considered as bonâ fide proprietor of the land he cultivates, and consequently the taxes paid by him upon his produce are really *taxes*, whilst the Rayah, whose tenure of land (if not illegal) is not on the same footing with that of the Mussulman, is in reality merely a farmer of Government lands, and the tithe paid by him is no longer a *tax*, but a rent paid for the ground he holds.

Without further remark upon the unequal manner in which these taxes press upon the two populations of Turkey, we will pass to a detailed examination of their general effects upon the state of the country.

The most important of these taxes is the dime of produce, which (putting aside for the moment the bad economy it leads to) is raised in a manner equally disadvantageous to the treasury and the country, for it is not collected by Government officials but sold to tax farmers—what this sale involves will be understood when we remember that the buyers are speculators to whom 50 per cent. is a despicable profit.

The tithes of the Vilayat are sold by auction, and if bought by a single person are resold, privately, by Pashaliks or districts, which are again sold in small lots, so that the final proprietor of the tithes of a village has obtained them at fourth or fifth hand and consequently three or four different profits have already been made, each of which, to take a very low average, reaches 30 per cent., the whole forming a loss to the Government of 120*l*. to 185*l*. for every 100*l*. it receives.

He does not, however, lose by the bargain, for any commercial transaction with the Turkish Government is sure to put money into the pockets of everybody who has to do with it, even to the last link in the chain of the tithe-farmers, and if the Beylikji* of a village does not contrive to gain at least 100 per cent. upon his purchase, he is either less skilful or more scrupulous than most of his fellows.

Those whose trade it is to whitewash ruinous or tottering institutions so as to give them an appearance of strength and solidity have not forgotten to daub over the laws which regulate the farming of the tithes, and have even invented new regulations concerning the manner in which payment is to be made and the method in which the sale is to be conducted, as well as the qualifications necessary in a purchaser; for Turkish reformers have yet to learn that mere palliatives will not cure a disease which requires the knife of the surgeon.

There is no doubt that these new laws, which forbid an employé of the Government to become a purchaser of the tithes, which compel the auction to be held in public, and which even permit a village to buy its own tithes, are but so many evasions which can be recognized as valuable reforms only by the facile good nature of Europe; in Turkey *all* laws are easily eluded, and these perhaps more easily than any others.

Even if we admit that these checks have extirpated or at least thrown obstacles in the way of abuses in the collection of the tithes (which *may* be the case under the jurisdiction of a man like Mithat Pasha), and that by their aid some millions of piastres have been rescued from the illegal pecu-

---

* Acquirer of the tithe or beylik.

lations of a few employés, still the ruinous absurdity remains, in the fact that the country pays three or four times more than is received by the Imperial treasury: in other terms, the collection of the tax costs the Government from $\frac{2}{3}$ to $\frac{3}{4}$ of what is really paid by the people, and Eastern commerce, or rather Eastern speculation, which we have shown to be a monopoly of the Greeks, taxes the Ottoman Budget to the extent of $\frac{2}{3}$ or $\frac{3}{4}$ of its principal source of revenue—and it is hardly necessary to say more in proof of the absurdity, in a financial point of view, of the present system of tax farming.

In the collection of the tithe upon grain the tax-farmer has not very many opportunities of abusing his power, as he can do little more than choose the finest sheaves for himself, but in localities where this tithe is taken from olives, cocoons of silk, and other produce which cannot be estimated in the same manner as sheaves of corn, the farmer does not forget to bring with him his falsified weights and measures, whilst his natural ingenuity will suggest other means of getting as much as he can out of the poor peasant.*

---

* To give an idea of the profits realized by the tax farmer; the dime and beylik of our village was sold in 1867 for 400 Turkish lire, and the purchaser made, by the grain alone, 950 lire, a clear profit of 137½ per cent., and in this instance the farmer was a Turk, and therefore probably less "business-like" than a Greek would have been. The farmer of the taxes of Baltchik cleared more than 4000*l*. in the same year, but we are unable to state the sum he paid for his bargain. Counting the gains of the tax farmer of a village in a grain-producing district (other localities being still more advantageous to him) at only cent. per cent., and those of the respective purchasers of the Pashalik and district at 50 per cent. each, we obtain the gross sum of 200 per cent., which reduces the sum paid to Government to one-third of that paid by the peasants; startling as this calculation may be, it is to our knowledge not exaggerated, but might be raised still higher without exaggeration.

The manner in which the tax-farmers collect the tithe is generally as follows: a little before harvest time they send to view the standing corn and estimate its value; if the harvest is likely to be a bad one and promises but small profits, they besiege the residence of the local Governor, and by the intervention of the original purchaser either procure a remission of some part of the sum paid to Government, or leave to take a smaller or larger percentage from the peasant, the difference to be made up the next year.*

The day of harvest arrives and the grain is cut, but not a sheaf may be carried home until the tax-farmer or his delegate comes to take his share: to the Rayahs this is no great hardship, as their feast of 15 days occurring at this period prevents their working; but the Turk suffers much by it, as the Beylikji frequently appears two or three weeks after the corn has been cut, during the whole of which time it remains at the mercy of the weather, or of the pigeons who never fail to exact *their* tithe from it. In looking at the sheaves thus left upon the fields we have frequently noticed that from the heat of the sun and other causes much of the grain falls out, and that instead of sixty or seventy grains in the ear we could rarely find more than a third of that number, whilst every day the loss became greater and greater.

The loss thus occasioned cannot be estimated at less than six or eight per cent., and the tithe costs the peasants sixteen or eighteen instead of ten per cent., through the negligence

---

* It is not often that the Government gives up any part of the money it has received, but permission is easily granted to take either 5 or 15 per cent. of the produce instead of 10. As the harvest of 1867 was a very plenteous one, the tax was raised from 10 to 15 for the benefit of the farmers, and next year it will only be 5 or 7½.

of the tax-farmer, who, though he must be aware that he loses in proportion, probably regards such an infinitesimal percentage as of no account, being occupied during this time with other affairs which bring him in from 100 to 150 per cent., and which enable him to disregard the loss of a few hundred piastres in the village whilst he is making some hundreds of pounds in the town.

When the sheaves of wheat are counted, the tax-farmer has his corn carted to the village, and placed in a spot reserved for it, before the peasants are allowed to carry their own grain: they are also forced to thrash and clean it, and finally to transport it to the nearest town, for which last service they are entitled to a certain payment per cartload. From Derekuoi to Varna, a distance of four hours by cart, they are paid two piastres, but unless compelled they would not do it under fifteen. Even this reduced price is not paid in money by the tax-farmer, who merely gives the peasant *saman*—chopped straw—for the amount due to him.

We have seen that this tax costs the country three times the amount it brings in to the Treasury, and occasions great loss to the taxpayers. But even these are minor evils when compared with the economical falsity of its principle, since it has the effect of rendering all agricultural enterprise almost impossible: in fact, can there be a worse-devised tax than one which affects produce and labour, instead of consumption?

In spite of the generally light taxation of Turkey, the tithe has the effect of discouraging intelligent labour, and driving the peasant to his present ruinous system of agriculture. It cannot be otherwise so long as an enterprising man who, by a new method of cultivation, has succeeded in doubling or tripling the produce of the soil, shall have to pay the tithe in proportion, and thus submit to a not inconsiderable deduction from the profit he had hoped to clear. As it is his talent and industry which have increased his produce, it is these qualities and not the land which are taxed by Government. Can any system be more injurious to agriculturists, or tend more to discourage labour and offer a premium to idleness?

The peasant who cultivates his land with intelligence and industry is heavily taxed, whilst he who leaves hundreds or even thousands of acres uncleared, pays nothing at all for them. It is to the Dime that Turkey owes the system of Mira (right of pasturage) of which we shall speak in the next chapter, and which is one of the numerous causes of her financial ruin.

Some time ago even Turkey appeared to realize the fact that if the Dime was not a means of destroying her prosperity, it was at any rate a very unprofitable tax to the Government. The political economists of Constantinople cudgelled their brains to solve the great problem of converting the tithe paid in kind into a fixed tax payable in money, and after much thought excogitated the following scheme: to calculate the sums paid to the tax-farmers during a period of five years, to strike an average from this amount, and exact the payment of such an annual sum from the provinces, villages, &c.

This experiment failed, for the peasant (who is not gifted with too much intelligence) preferred to pay in kind; and all those who were interested in the lucrative speculation of tax-farming agitated so successfully, that the authorities were obliged to return to the good old system.

The arguments employed in favour of the present farming of the tithes by its defenders—amongst whom are ranged all the Government employés, a fact which induces us to fancy that in spite of the new restrictions this class still manages to profit by the tax—are as follows:—

1st. That as the country possesses no roads, it is consequently impossible for the peasant to sell his produce and pay the Dime in money.

2nd. That the collection of the tax would cost more to Government than the loss occasioned by the sale to the farmers.

3rd. There having been no survey of the lands (*cadastre*), it would be impossible to tax the land instead of its produce.

4th. That to abolish this system would be to the disadvantage of commerce, and of those who live by farming the Dime.

Such pleas hardly require refutation. As to the cost of collection, it could surely never equal two-thirds of the revenue; a statistical record of lands granted and held *does* exist in the Tapou or Official Register, and if every commune were forced to mark out the limits of their lands, forest and pasturage included, a very approximative idea would be arrived at of the superficies of its possessions, and the tax could be easily and justly levied.

There are few new schemes or projects in which there are no difficulties to be encountered, but a little difficulty ought not to stop a Government when the welfare of its finances is at stake, and when the country has to be rescued from misery and placed in the path of prosperity and progress.

It seems to us that to change the Dime into a fixed tax,

keeping in view the great object of encouraging industry and rendering idleness and parasitism ruinous if not impossible, is in itself sufficiently easy. To effect this it is only necessary to tax the land in place of its produce, an alteration by which the prohibitive tax which now oppresses labour will fall upon the idler instead.

The simplest plan would be to levy a fixed sum, say of five piastres, upon every dulum of land, whether cleared, arable pasturage, or forest, belonging to or in any way used by the commune to be taxed.

Taking an example in this neighbourhood, we find that the municipality of Varna possesses *de facto*, on the south side of the lake alone, a tract of land whose superficies is twenty-three square miles, or 37,500 dulums, for which it pays something less than 100*l.* per annum as Beylik for the sheep, cattle, &c., which pasture in the forest. Supposing this land to be taxed at five piastres per dulum—that is, from one-quarter to one-sixth of the sum raised by the Dime from land sown in grain*—the town of Varna would have to pay a sum of 187,500 piastres, or 1875 Turkish lire, eighteen times more than at present. The natural consequence would be that the municipality would farm out this tract, cultivate it for itself, or give it up altogether, in which latter case it would revert to Government, and plenty of persons would be willing to take it even at ten piastres per dulum.

This tax might be received in kind from districts where there are no roads, and where specie is consequently rare,

---

* Five dulums require one Varna kilé of grain as seed, and produce at least 12 to 15 kilés of corn, of which the tenth will be from 1·2 to 1·5 kilé; valuing the kilé at an average of 100 piastres, the five dulums pay from 120 to 150 p., and each dulum 24 to 30 p.

always holding to the system of taxing the acreage possessed, without reference to the amount of produce raised.

Such a change would have the effect of forcing the peasant to cultivate his land properly, whilst the idler would soon be ruined or compelled to hire himself out as a day labourer, and the poor sheep or cattle would no longer, during a severe winter, wander half dead in the forest, for their owners would either feed them at home or sell them. The corn, too, would be thrashed by flails instead of being trodden out by miserable horses kept for that sole purpose.

We have thus dilated upon the Dime because it is the most ruinous tax both to Government and people, and in comparison with it such others as three piastres for every fullgrown pig, four piastres for every ewe which has lambed, and three piastres for every hive of bees, are entirely inoffensive and innocuous.

The tax upon market gardens of one Turkish lire (100 piastres) per labourer is not a very reasonable one, but is not of sufficient importance to discuss.

Vineyards pay a tax, similar to that which we advocate in place of the Dime, of ten piastres for every dulum, and the vines are comparatively well cultivated, not an inch of ground being wasted, as the peasant knows that in this case he has to pay for the ground occupied, and not according to its produce. There is also an octroi duty of four paras per oke upon wine, and twelve piastres per oke upon tobacco.

The customs dues are eight per cent. *ad valorem* on exports and on imports, a tax which, however foolishly imposed, does not do much harm to the country; as, though it may displease the merchants, it hardly touches the people, the dues received by the Government being as nothing when compared with the enormous percentage levied by Eastern commerce.

Besides the regular taxes which we have enumerated, there is another species of impost, irregular and arbitrary, which being in itself an authorized abuse, produces other abuses in the course of its execution, and much well-founded discontent among the peasantry. We allude to the tax of Corvée, or forced labour and extraordinary contributions. The Corvée, has always been a bad system, for a man just taken off his own labour is sure to work badly, and this forced labour in Turkey is sometimes a very heavy burden. By its aid the one or two roads which exist are kept in a state of dilapidated repair, the baggage of troops is transported, wood for gun-carriages is cut, &c., &c. The only merit which the Corvée can claim is that of impartiality, for it presses upon the Mussulman as heavily as upon the Rayah.

Extraordinary contributions are levied by the Pashas and Mudirs, often without the knowledge and nearly always without the consent of the Supreme Government at Constantinople; for it is not to be expected that a Pasha should inform the Sublime Porte that he has exacted from every house a bushel of corn to feed his horses, or that he has given permission to his friend the tax-farmer to have eleven sheaves instead of ten from each hundred because the harvest is bad.

Both corvées and extraordinary contributions are abuses, and the sooner an abuse is extirpated the better for the country.

CHAPTER XIII.

THE TENURE OF LANDED PROPERTY; THE TAPOU, THE MIRA, THE RIGHT OF FOREIGNERS TO POSSESS LAND.

Registration of occupancy — Sometimes abused to the fraudulent acquisition of title — Undeserved liberality of the Government — Right of pasturage — Leads to loss of production, illegal destruction of timber, and winter starvation of cattle — Probable results of a European immigration — Let the settlers bring their own merchants.

It would be taking up too much of our time and space to enumerate all the petty abuses, small anomalies, and insignificant faults of legislation to be found in Turkey, such as the law of mortmain relating to the Vakoufs, which has been magnified into a grievance because it affects in some measure the inhabitants of Péra, the householders of the Sixth Circle * willingly forgetting that all property they possess is held only by an evasion of the law of the land, and wishing for nothing more than that this property may be as far beyond the reach of Justice as are their persons, thanks to the Capitulations.

We have enough to do in pointing out those graver fundamental blunders and errors which exercise a decisive influence upon the progress of Turkey, without losing time in the discussion of minor local questions affecting only a small clique of petty foreign traders, who, after eluding the law, have contrived to suggest an impression in Europe that they are the advanced guards of civilization in the East, and that consequently the Reforms of Turkey must be modelled

---

* Péra is the Sixth Municipal Circle of Constantinople.

for their especial benefit and in the manner which it pleases them to dictate.

Setting aside this and similar questions, we turn to the two great principles which affect landed property in Turkey. 1st. Its tenure by Tapou, and the dependent corollary, the system of Mira, or pasturage; 2nd. The permission accorded to foreigners to possess land in this country.

All writers upon the Reforms necessary to the growth of civilization in Turkey fall into the serious error of measuring things by an European standard. In this country there exist two widely differing elements: the Mussulmans, who are susceptible of a civilization adapted to their nationality, and in accordance with the precepts of the Koran, a civilization other than that of England, but which amongst them might not only be easily introduced, but would take root and flourish; and the Christians, who are degraded not by Turkish rule, but by their own vices and those of their priesthood, as well as by those traditions of the Lower Empire which form the basis of their morals, institutions, and religious prejudices: this latter race is as yet unprepared for any well-grounded civilization, being, like all the peoples who profess the Greek rite, capable of receiving only a thin surface polish, under which the barbarian of the East still remains visible.

The laws which regulate the tenure of land by Tapou,* at least for the Vilayet of the Danube, or Bulgaria proper, are as follows:—

Any subject of the Sultan may occupy any Government land uncultivated at the time, may build a house and

---

* The Tapou is a species of certificate of registration of land, which guarantees the tenure.

cultivate as he chooses, on condition of paying the tithe and other taxes established by law; for this land he must take out a Tapou, that is, register his land with the proper authorities, a proceeding which costs from 60 to 100 paras per dulum, or from 9*d.* to 1*s.* 3*d.* per acre. From this land he cannot be turned out on any pretext whatsoever, and having paid the tithe during twenty years he becomes its legal proprietor.

An instant's reflection will show the absurdity, in all ways, of this law, of which the inevitable corollary, the system of Mira, acquires by custom the force of law, and is in itself sufficient to ruin the country and to exclude all progress and civilization more thoroughly than the wildest schemes of the most rabid Communist.

In fact, this law of property annihilates all property.

According to its rules, a man occupies land for the possession of which he pays, once for all, from 9*d.* to 1*s.* 3*d.* per acre, but only becomes its actual proprietor after having paid the tithe during twenty years—and when the land is actually his own, what further advantage does he derive from the fact? He has still to pay the tithe, and the only difference in his position is that he has the right of sale; but who in Bulgaria waits the twenty years if he wishes to sell his land? or who will buy it if the owner is forced to leave that part of the country? As soon as he is gone the land is taken possession of by some one else, or at any rate Turkey is large enough, and contains land enough to satisfy any man who is not over particular about his title deeds.

Moustapha Agha dies, his four sons have been killed in battle, his nephew is a soldier at Bagdad, whence he will not return for eight years; the lands of the dead man ought by law to become Vakoufs until his nephew, Ali Agha, returns to claim his inheritance. In the mean time Anastaz and Dimitri seize upon the estate, cultivate it and pay the tithe, and when Ali Agha comes back he finds that he cannot regain his property, for the two Rayahs pay the taxes and shelter themselves from all legal pursuit in the shadow of the Consul of the North.

In twenty years Anastaz and Dimitri would become legal proprietors of the estate of Moustapha Agha (for which they have had no difficulty in obtaining a Tapou on their simple statement that the land was not occupied), but they do not choose to wait for this period; and they sell their respective Tapous to Kako Effendi, a Greek Rayah who has every inducement to become a landed proprietor, as he is exempted from all taxes by his position as Member of the Medjliss of the neighbouring town of Bulgaropolis, of which he is also Mayor, a dignity which gives him the command of the market for vegetables, &c.

What chance has Ali Agha against such an opponent?

By comparing the rights of Ali Agha with those of Anastaz and Dimitri, who have ceded their title by sale to Kako Effendi, the absurdity of the law of Tapou becomes plainly manifest.

The estate of Djenkdere was conceded to Moustapha Agha's ancestors by the Sultan Amurath II. for services rendered to the State, at the same time as certain rights of Beylik,* &c., over the neighbouring village of Giaour-dere, of which Anastaz and Dimitri are natives, which latter privileges were taken away by the changes of Mahmoud II. Although Djenkdere at that time was rendered liable to the taxes

---

* The origin of the Peylik is explained in the preceding Chapter.

formerly paid by the Rayahs alone, it was still valued by the family as a souvenir of the munificence of Amurath and the valour of their ancestors. Now the estate exists no longer, and Ali Agha, who has gained his rank of lieutenant by his own courage, and not by the favour of a Pasha, starves upon his meagre pension, whilst Kako Effendi cultivated the lands of the Turkish Timors of Djenkdere, pays no taxes, uses or rather abuses his position in the Medjliss to corrupt the Government employés, and laughs at the incontestable rights of Ali Agha, the descendant of the Osmanli lords of the soil.

The village in which we live has a somewhat similar history, but here murder was added to robbery, and extinguished the claims of the Turkish owners.

If our readers recollect the sketch given in another chapter of the origin of landed property (rightfully held), and of the taxes, they can hardly help seeing the great hardship and injustice with which the present law affects the Turk,[*] rendering all legal tenure ruinous to the holders, and consequently destroying all hope of civilization, of which justice is the very foundation. By the existing laws a legal proprietor whose estate has descended to him through many generations, or who has acquired it by a bonâ fide purchase, is placed on precisely the same footing with the squatter upon Government lands, and even with the man who has stolen the estate of another. This is in

---

[*] The Rayahs were dispossessed of their property by conquest, which is in itself a right, and consequently the only legitimate proprietors in Turkey are the Turks, to whom estates were granted by the Sultans; the existing laws permitting the Rayah to possess land do so to the prejudice of all justice, and consequently they do not alter the question.

itself an absurd anomaly, but is only one in a long series of mistakes; let us examine the effects of this law upon the financial and economical state of the country.

The first result obtained by the promulgation of this law is that Government lands are worth nothing, for it cannot be considered that the price paid for the Tapou is an equivalent to their value, or is anything more than a fee paid for registration.

The political economists of the East will answer that this law was passed with the object of promoting the clearing of forest land, as an inducement to cultivation, and for the development of agriculture; the weakness of this argument will be shown immediately in an economical point of view: as for the financial absurdity, Turkey surely has not the right to waste her most valuable resources in order to bestow a doubtful boon upon an ungrateful race, or to act like a madman who throws his gold into the river. Indeed, it is little less than a financial suicide to tolerate such a law, and, since the Sublime Porte has insured its life with those European capitalists who have subscribed to the Turkish loans, it is high time that the insurance office composed by the creditors of Turkey should issue a Commission *de lunatico inquirendo,* and demand that the physicians, or rather the quacks, who are poisoning the patient should be dismissed, and replaced by doctors who have a direct interest in the preservation of his life and his restoration to reason. Such physicians can only be found amongst the Turks of the country,* but unfortunately they are a class

---

* For the Turk of the country as distinguished from the Turk of the town, see Chap. xvi.

whose opinion will never be consulted, and not one amongst them would be found either sufficiently imbecile or sufficiently corrupt to aspire to rank amongst the present Reformers or political economists of this country, which, after all, owes its continued existence, precarious as it is, to the courage and loyalty of these same village Turks, as well as to the dread which they inspire in the Rayah.

Whatever may be said, the fact is that the Ottoman Government grants its lands gratis to any one who chooses to take them; *gratis*, because if the tithe be considered as rent, it should not be exacted from those who are the rightful proprietors of their estates by such titles as are recognized everywhere; but since the tithe *does* fall upon such proprietors, it, as well as the Beylik, &c., is in reality a genuine tax and not rent, and as the Government receives from those who take its land no other payment, these lands are in reality granted *gratis*.

In a country only six days' journey from London, with the finest soil and climate possible, land is to be had at the maximum price of 1s. 3d. per acre, less than is paid in the wilds of Australia or at the foot of the Rocky Mountains; surely thousands of colonists flock to this new Eldorado? Not so, for there is an obstacle; the Rayah who wastes the land can have as much of it as he chooses, but there is not an inch for enterprising and intelligent foreigners, and this in a country of whose total superficies a tenth, or, more correctly speaking, a sixteenth only is cultivated, and that imperfectly, every year, although two-thirds of the whole is susceptible of utilization. This fact is the result of the Government's bestowing lands for nothing upon a people who do not deserve the gift; of these laws of property which we have already described, and of an abuse which springs from them, the system of Mira, to which we now pass.

We have already mentioned, in the preceding chapter, that the municipality of Varna possesses on the south side of the lakes of Devna * (without counting its possessions to the north), an extent of land amounting to twenty-three square miles, and that for this immense tract it pays only about 100*l.* a year to Government, whilst of the whole surface only about thirty acres are cultivated (chiefly as vineyards), the rest serving as pasturage for miserable sheep, cattle, and half-wild horses.

Seeing the wretched state of the land and the animals you would feel tempted to exclaim, " Is it possible that this good soil should be left thus uncultivated, and that these poor beasts should be left to die a lingering death of inanition!" But you would be still more astonished to be told that the land is left so for this express purpose, that the cattle may pass their lives in a state of perpetual starvation: yet this is actually the case.

This species of agricultural economy is to be met with only in Turkey, where it flourishes over the whole empire.

These twenty-three miles, voluntarily left desert, form part of the Mira of Varna, being land which that town claims a right to as pasturage; by what right they belong to the town it would be hard to say, we do not believe that they were purchased, and yet Varna *has* an incontestable right to all this territory, and chooses it as a place of torture for its

---

* Thus named in the maps, but the real Lake of Devna is separated from that which washes the walls of Varna, from which town it is more than 15 miles distant.

cattle. Anybody who attempted to take any of this land, and bring it under cultivation, would soon learn who are its owners.

The Mira is then a right of pasturage, and on the other hand a right of property, claimed by every municipality, commune, or even owner of a chiftlik (or farm) in Turkey, without giving themselves even the trouble of taking out a Tapou for its registration, and without paying to Government the tithe of the produce which should nominally render them proprietors of it in twenty years.

The theory enunciated by the political economists of Constantinople about the encouragement of agriculture does not appear in a very favourable light when viewed in connection with the enormous non-value of the Miras of the whole of the empire : the extent of land thus rendered unproductive in European Turkey being at least nine-tenths of its superficies.

But it is argued that pasturage for cattle is absolutely necessary, that the forests must be preserved, since for this latter purpose a "Corps Forestier" has been instituted at Constantinople — (by-the-bye, these gentlemen never leave the capital, and for all the good they do there or anywhere else, might just as well be employed in planting fir-trees on the roof of the Grand Vizier's palace, or cedars on the Tower of Galata)—which will cost the Government a heavy sum, whilst the forests are none the less left to be burnt down for the benefit of the Bulgarian, or bought up for the benefit of some Greek speculator. One man of common sense would be worth the whole of the scientific instruction of all the Turkish re-organizers put together.

If there were a financier, an economist, or even a Pasha,

who not only pretended to see beyond the lighted end of his cigarette, but really was capable of doing so, he would never rest if he felt the least love for his country, so long as the absurd system of Mira existed. This system, or rather the right based upon the abuse of it, is ruining Turkey, for to this it is owing that, even with the faulty method of taxation in force, the Dime does not amount to five times the sum it reaches at present; since the country produces five or six times less than it ought to do, did not the Mira leave nine-tenths of the forest land uncleared, and were the actual state of agriculture in Turkey improved.*

Not only, as we have said, do all municipalities, communes, and owners of farms monopolize large tracts of land over which they pretend to have the right of pasturage; not only do they think and say that they are the lawful owners of this ground; but they also arrogate to themselves the right of cutting down for their own use or for sale as much timber as they choose,† set fire to the forest trees for the benefit of the grass, and exercise other and equally intelligent seigneurial rights.

This is doubtless a terrible waste of resources, but the true economical evil lies in the fact which we have pointed out—that nine-tenths of European Turkey bring nothing to the Government, and cannot be disposed of to foreign

---

* We have calculated, in the Chapter treating of the Taxes, that the revenue of Government suffers a diminution of two-thirds; and it therefore follows from the above statement, that if the Mira were abolished and the produce of the Dime paid intact into the Treasury, this revenue would amount to at least fifteen times as much as it does now.

† The village of Derekuoi has destroyed within the last three years timber belonging to Government of the value of about 20,000*l.*

colonists, because this portion is Mira, and the owners would sooner sell their wives than an acre of it.

To explain this love for land which is of little real value to its proprietors, we must take into consideration the character of the Bulgarian peasant, who fancies that by keeping his Mira he is cheating the revenue, and who argues with himself much in the following manner: "I have 300 dulums of arable land on which I sow every year sixty kilés of grain and pay the Dime; Aman!* how heavy that Dime is! To be sure I only pay for a third of my land, because I leave the rest fallow or grow produce which isn't taxable, but still it's very hard, and I don't see why I should pay any tax at all. However, as I am obliged to pay, I must make it up somehow, so I take 2000 dulums of forest belonging to Government, and I have a right to this Mira because my buffaloes strayed all over it once last winter; for this I only pay a Beylik of 400 piastres for the 100 ewes I own to—(I should like to find a Beylikji who could make out how many I really have; *I* don't know to within fifty!)—and thirty piastres for ten sows, which make 430 piastres altogether; but then I cut down, one year with another, 3000 piastres' worth of wood to sell at the town, and my horses and buffaloes feed in the forest—though it is true that the horses are more good to the wolves than they are to me; so I manage to *do* the Government in return for the Dime it makes me pay, besides preventing it selling or letting a single dulum of my Mira."

The Turkish peasant values his Mira, because, owing to the amount of time taken from him by his military service, he

---

* A Turkish expression of grief or dismay; literally, Pity!

is forced to devote his attention to cattle-farming as well as agriculture ; the Rayah, without the same compulsion, is very fond of keeping cattle, and adores the profession of choban (herdsman), because his dogs can look after his charge, and he has nothing to do but to saunter about and improve his knowledge of the bagpipes. This idle occupation is disliked by the Turks, and the chobans of a Mussulman village are nearly always Bulgarians or gipsies.

If the system of Mira had the effect of making Turkey a great centre for the production of cattle, wool, &c., &c., this feeble excuse might be urged as a palliation of the economical error of employing arable land as pasturage —the Dobrudscha, for instance, might plead thus ; the Mira, however, has not this result, for instead of producing fat cattle it turns out only living skeletons.

The Bulgarians have large herds of cattle, but they never take the pains to mow a single acre of grass to feed them with during the winter, and carrots, turnips, or clover, are as much unknown to them as oilcake and Thorley's food; the poor brutes are left during the winter to chance, hunger, and the wolves,* those who survive the care of their triad of guardians finding a little nourishment in the young spring grass; but hardly do they begin to lose their hibernal translucence, when the grass is burned by the peasants, and the second bovine Lent commences, and it is only after harvest that they pick up sufficient food

---

* The wolves, which are increasing in number every year in our part of the country, do a good deal of damage (to-day we heard of seven horses and oxen killed within the last two nights), but not so much as might be expected ; possibly they are gourmets, and prefer a fat deer to a skinny cow or sheep.

in the stubble of the cornfields and the abundant wild fruits of the forest to enable them to support their winter torments, and to prevent them being carried away bodily by the first breath of the North wind. From this system arises the present degeneracy of the cattle of this country; the horses not having a single good point about them, and the horned beasts being mere frameworks of skin and bone, about the size of a very small Shetland pony.

If you give a property to an idiot, it does not make him a proprietor in the true sense of the word, and a child will throw a bank note out of the window; so it is with the Bulgarian. To create real *proprietors* in this country it is necessary to create real *property*, and to allow labour capitalized to represent a title to the land; there is no use or object in working to obtain possession of the soil, when an equally legal possession and title may be secured without the trouble of work. So long as legal and illegal possession are on the same footing, and capitalized labour, which is property, valueless and a dead letter, it is impossible to hope that labour will be held in esteem, or to dream of progress.

There is one mode of escape from these evils, by applying a remedy which we have mentioned in the preceding chapter. Do not tax the producer, but the consumer of the raw material, for the producer represents labour and agricultural enterprise; in short the producer is Turkey, and the consumer Europe, and it is unjust to tax the former whilst exempting the latter. Tax the soil, but not labour, and the bad farmer will give up what he does not want of his land to the good farmer, who will never have too much. This is what another system of taxation might effect; but in order to do justice and to render such property as is the result of labour no longer valueless but valuable, distinguish between the legal and illegal proprietor; let him who has no better title deed than a Tapou pay five piastres extra rent per dulum in addition to the five he will pay as land tax, grant a right of Mira to the old soldier who has faithfully served his country, but scrutinize the title of him who keeps his pasturage merely to keep himself in idleness, and let him pay rent for such land, or buy it at a price fixed according to the locality. If such laws were in force, it is probable that the greater part of the seven-tenths of the country now uncleared would be again in the hands of Government, who might let them, not *sell* them, to foreign speculators.

But to this last scheme there is a drawback; for to grant lands, if only for ten years, to foreigners enjoying all the privileges guaranteed them by the Capitulations, would be (in spite of that clause of the new law permitting aliens to possess land in Turkey, which decrees that landowners of foreign nationality shall be subject as regards their landed property to such laws as in Turkey regulate the possession of land), to give up the country entirely to foreign influence, to denationalize the Turk even more than is done at present, and to give a still wider range to foreign intrigue.

Even here there is an amendment possible, in spite of our own conviction that the possession of land in Turkey by foreigners is an absurdity so long as the Capitulations are not abolished, or at least radically modified.

Turkey is here on the horns of a dilemma; for whilst on the one hand it would be financially advantageous to the Government, as well as economically and materially to the country, to let the unoccupied lands to foreign enterprise, on the other it would be an ever germinating seed of troubles and petty warfare, and a certain method of still further weakening the prestige of the Government.

Between this good and this evil it is difficult to choose, but we will examine the question of the right of possession granted to foreigners, and endeavour to solve this difficult problem as well as we can.

If foreigners are permitted to buy land, it is certain that in a short time their intelligent labour, backed as it will be by capital, will enable them to extend their properties, and little by little to become owners of the greater part of the soil of Turkey by legal dispossession of the Rayahs. The Turks, at least the peasants (though the rich Bey with his European semi-civilization may not care much for his patrimony except as a source of income), are deeply attached to the land which has been paid for by the blood of their fathers; they are hard working and sober, and the only race in Turkey who are really fond of agriculture :* these qualities may enable them to make head for a time against the foreign colonists; but the Rayah, with his habit of idling 183 days in the year, his love of drink, and his contempt for all modern improvements,† will soon become poor in spite of the fact that his land is double that of his new neighbours; and when he is offered for his property a sum greater than its real value to him, he will be only too glad to sell it, and

---

* The Rayah, especially when of Greek race, cultivates land only for want of a more congenial employment, the towns and his own system of commerce possessing an irresistible attraction for him.

† Many well-to-do Turks in this neighbourhood are introducing European improvements in their farms, such as machinery, &c. &c.; of the Rayahs not one has done so.

settle in some town; there, his smaller means being placed in competition with larger capitals, he will soon be ruined and driven back upon the country; but a new order of things will be established, and he will find no more land to be had for nothing, and no more gratis timber to be cut for firewood; and as the new immigration will necessitate a new and effective system of police, the laws will no longer be violated with impunity—the Rayah's last resource, that of turning thief or highwayman, will be closed to him—and his only choice will be between mendicancy and becoming a day-labourer.

Such an expropriation of the Rayah by the consequences of his own vices, is the natural and inevitable result of the settlement of foreign farmers in Turkey.

The Turk, as we have said, may hold out longer, but he will have the disadvantage of being obliged to copy the improvements introduced by the settlers, without having the capital necessary to make them profitable to him, whilst the heavy burden of military service falls upon him alone, leaving his antagonist untouched. The struggle will be a hard one, and the Mussulman will be forced to employ all the resources of his character—all the energy, patience, sobriety, and courage with which he is gifted—to avoid the fate which has overtaken the Rayah.

Under these circumstances the position of the Government becomes very difficult, as it will be placed between the Turkish people and a rich and consequently influential class of landed proprietors, whose territorial possessions are indeed subject to Ottoman laws, but whose other property, as well as their persons, can be affected only by foreign jurisdiction; whilst the Rayah element is becoming gradually extinct, like the savages of North America, by the influence of its own idleness and passions.

To help the Turks, the Government must protect them in such a manner as will rise to an apparent injustice, and cause loud complaints on the part of the colonists, whilst the Rayah pauperism will be a continual source of embarrassment.

The substitution of a hard-working class, in place of the parasitic and hostile Rayah, will be an undoubted gain economically, but its political effect is not so easily defined.

In our opinion, the way to obviate these difficulties would be to give the colonists an interest in their adopted country by permitting them to participate in the local and even the general government under certain conditions, which should be as follows: that all foreign settlers in Turkey should be subject to all the laws and burdens imposed upon the subjects of the Sultan, as well in their persons as in their property, so that, for instance, they should be liable to military service, or to pay an exemption tax proportioned to their means; when the colonists left Turkey, they would take their passport from their Consul, and enjoy all the privileges conferred by their original nationality. Such colonists as did not choose to agree to these terms should be allowed no share in the Government, and should be treated as foreigners, that is, as entitled to none of the rights of a Turkish subject.

This amendment would urge the settlers to inscribe themselves under the laws of the country by the inducement of the brilliant careers which would be opened to them, in entering upon which they would find themselves in precisely the same position as those foreigners at present in the service of the Sultan.

If it is asked, What would attract European farmers to Turkey under such conditions? we answer by a question: Where in Europe can you find such land to be let at 1s. 3d. per acre, the total taxes only amounting to 2s. 6d. more, and arable fields to be bought at 42s. per acre—recollecting that this soil will produce, without manure, two or three times more than the soil of Europe with it?

We believe that the Turkish Government would do well to grant uncleared land to foreign companies for a term not exceeding fifty years, at a rent of 8 or 10 piastres per dulum per annum (4s. to 5s. per acre), and no doubt many companies would be glad to avail themselves of such an offer.

As sincere friends of Turkey, we should be glad to see foreign companies established in the country under such conditions; and we should prefer this speculation to be undertaken by companies rather than by individual colonization, because in the first place the former would offer better guarantees of solvability, and, secondly, because they would be forced to defend their property by making war upon Eastern commerce. For the benefit of these possible associations, we suggest a plan which would render success in this war certain; the companies who farm the soil of Turkey should establish large commercial houses in the towns of the coast, for the purpose of buying up the cereal and other produce of the country at (even) 25 per cent. profit, and importing the manufactures of Europe to sell at the same rate: such an enterprise would, besides realizing enormous profits, benefit Turkey by rendering Eastern commerce impossible to its present followers. There is one necessary principle to be observed, and never to be deviated from, namely, that no Greek and no Armenian or other Rayah

be admitted into these houses in any capacity whatsoever—
even that of Hamal (porter)—or they will have the same
fate which has hitherto attended every enterprise of the
kind which has been attempted in the East.

In conclusion we venture to express a hope that what we
have written on this subject, though it would probably possess
no interest for the present officials of Turkey, may at least
afford matter for reflection to our readers in England.

CHAPTER XIV.

WHAT THE BULGARIANS WISH FOR, AND WHAT THEY DO NOT WISH FOR.

Writers in the pay of Russia — Too much experience of Russian promises — The Bulgarian does not wish what he is supposed to wish — Unambitious minds — Exceptions.

IT is very difficult to say what changes in their political or social government are really desired by the mass of the Rayahs, of whom most are too apathetic and ignorant to imagine for themselves any remedy against the oppression from which the emissaries of a party endeavour to make them think they suffer. In Turkey, as elsewhere, the loudest talkers attract the greatest attention, and to judge by articles written in some of the journals of Constantinople and Athens, the dearest wish of the Bulgarians is to be united to Russia. These articles are, however, even when written by genuine Bulgarians, only the exponents of the feelings of a very small party, who imagine that in the event of this union taking place, their services will be gratefully remembered and rewarded by their new masters. But as the number of Bulgarians in Turkey who are capable of expressing their wishes in writing is excessively limited, those pathetic letters bearing the signature of 'Un Bulgare' or 'Βούλγαρος,' are usually composed by some of the innumerable foreign agents who earn their roubles or their drachmas by unceasing attempts to sow the seeds of discord and separation between the Government of the Porte and its Christian subjects; and yet these epistles, if read in France and England, are probably considered as the wail of an "oppressed nationality" groaning under the fetters of their Ottoman tyrants.

Although Russian agents may have succeeded formerly, when the Rayahs had some fair grounds of complaints against their rulers, in persuading them that the mild government of the Czar was preferable to the cruelties of the Padischah, this species of propaganda has now become almost hopeless since the Bulgarians have learnt wisdom by their sad experience. Russia committed the folly of inviting emigrants from these provinces to settle in her territories, with fair promises of many special advantages to the new settlers; the Porte was wise enough to profit by this false move of its adversary, and placed no obstacles in the way of the intending emigrants. In some instances whole villages left their native land for the promised Canaan, whilst in others one or two families only went out to spy the land: their immovable property was converted into money, much to the advantage of the purchasers, who of course profited as much as possible by the enforced sale. And with this small stock of cash they landed in Russia with the expectation of making rapid fortunes. A few years elapsed, and those of the exiles who were able to escape from the paternal care of the Muscovite returned to their villages, wiser and poorer than when they had left them, to advise their families and friends not to change bad for worse, and to relate over-true tales of the scorpion scourge of Russia for which they had exchanged the iron rod of Turkey. The sufferings of their fathers are still too fresh in the memory of the present generation of peasants for the Russian agent to have much chance of recommencing his played out game; and though he is still frequently to be met with in the Balkan, under the disguise of a travelling pedlar, a collector of old coins, or a seller of Greek Calendars for the few who can read, and of Russian saints painted on wood, he generally confines himself to endeavouring to make the Bulgarians discontented with their Government, and to assuring them that in the event of their endeavouring to cast off the yoke and become a great and independent nation, Russia will disinterestedly assist them, and that France and England will never again appear in arms for the rescue of an effete oligarchy. Even these attempts produce no great fruits, for the Bulgarian has learnt to distrust Russia, and has perhaps even heard of her fondness for fishing in troubled waters.

The meteor of Panslavism, however it may dazzle the eyes of the guests of Moscow, has no attractions for the Rayah of the Balkan, to whom ethnological questions are of little importance compared with the price of wheat or pigs at Varna, Burgass, or Adrianople, and who would receive with equal stolidity and belief the information that he was allied to the great Slavonic family of Europe or to the North American tribe of Tête-de-Boule Indians.

Independence such as that of the Principalities, union with Servia, annexation to Greece even—such are the political cries of the small band of agitators who represent themselves to Europe as the organs of Bulgaria, knowing well that even if their representations should reach the ears of their supposed constituents, these latter are two apathetic as well as too illiterate to contradict them.

All such changes are what the Rayah does *not* wish for, and are questions which interest him no more than the history of the Prussian campaign of '66 would do if it were related to him. What he *does* wish for is, as we have said, difficult to determine.

He has a general idea that he is in some way an ill-used being, for the rumours from the outer world penetrate, however slowly, even into the ravines and gorges of the Hæmus; and Janaki the schoolmaster (if there is a school in the village), or Dimitri the Papas (if he can read), has somehow got hold of an old copy of some Greek newspaper, and one evening at the Bakal's has, by the light of a solitary tallow candle stuck upon a wine barrel, *précisé* its news, and informed those present that the Russian Ambassador at Stamboul has spoken seriously to the Porte upon the subject of the infamous treatment of its Christian subjects; that the French Ambassador has presented with the same intention a collective note from the representatives of Italy, Prussia, Greece, and the Emperor Theodore; and that even England has ordered her Consul to report to the Foreign Office upon the manner in which Turkey has carried out the stipulations of the Hatti Humayoun. Janaki, who completed his studies at Athens, enlarges upon the topic, and says that it is a shame that the Bulgarians should not have their interests cared for by a Chamber of Representatives chosen by and from amongst themselves; and this idea, from its grandeur and because no one but Janaki has the least idea of what it means, meets with general approbation, and the assembly finally separates with the unanimous conviction that something ought to be done by some one towards the formation of such a desirable institution. Tanaz, as he goes home, thinks that the Chamber of Representatives might perhaps be able to tell him where he buried his crock of money last year, as he has never been able to recollect the spot, having been far from sober when he hid it. Michal thinks that being a Chorbadji he would have a fair chance of being one of the Representatives, and that if the work was not hard, the pay good, and mastica near at hand during the deliberations, he would not dislike the employment. However, as thinking, especially upon political questions, is hard work, Michal and Tanaz forget all about the Chamber of Representatives by next day, and retain merely the impression that perhaps some day the somebody will be found to do the something, and that they will be immensely benefited by the operation. Not having any great hardship to complain of, they do not exactly know what ameliorations to hope for, unless it be that the farmers of the beylik may get the worst of the mutual attempt to cheat each other between them and the peasant; or that the Zaptieh should not be allowed, when he spends the night at their village, to pry about the houses and seize upon the concealed horde of eggs and butter which were promised to the Papas.

Perhaps some amongst them hope that the Government will remit all taxes, and send Turks to cultivate the fields of the village, giving all the produce to the Rayah, and then buying the grain from him at double the market value. Schemes more practical than these seldom enter the head of the peasant, who is contented with his lot, so long as he has little work to do and plenty to drink. The Rayah in general has no ambition to become rich, so long as he has enough to eat and drink: if he makes money, he hides it;

he does not employ it in buying more land, or better ploughs, because he has enough of the former to give him and his sons as much work as they care for, and to produce grain which will pay for his year's expenses: as to the latter, he does not see the good of these new inventions, the old plough does well enough, and he is satisfied.

The question of the schism in the Greek Church which will probably lead to the formation of an independent Bulgarian hierarchy, is one which exclusively interests the priests: the peasant does not care whether his Papas owns allegiance to a Greek metropolitan, or Bulgarian bishop, or patriarch: although he is too superstitious to refuse compliance with arbitrary exactions of the priests (which are spoken of at length in another chapter), he undoubtedly feels that the continual abstraction of his lambs, eggs, fowls, pigs, &c., is a grievance; but if he knows of the proposed ecclesiastical change, he has sense enough to see that the priest will not want less mutton or fewer eggs because there is a new Bulgarian Church, and therefore he does not care about the result of the movement.

The wishes of the Rayah, when he takes the trouble of wishing, are confined to the removal of a few petty grievances which equally affect his Mussulman fellow-subjects: what his "friends" wish for him is sufficiently well known in England from the newspapers of Russia and one or two other countries, and diplomatic reports. Of course if he is told that such and such a change will improve his condition, he is willing to put his mark to a petition to that effect, and the next day he would do the same for another petition which might be perfectly contrary to and incompatible with the first. He, however, has sense enough to know that he is well off, and excepting when he is told that he is not so much so as he deserves to be, he is contented.

These remarks apply only to the genuine peasant, and not to the Bulgarian who has deserted the peaceful and humble occupation of ploughman or herdsman for the luxuries of a town, and whom the prospects of clothes *alla Franca* and varnished boots have induced to turn shopboy to some Greek trader, with the hopes of becoming later one of the pillars of Eastern commerce.

CHAPTER XV.

TARTAR AND CIRCASSIAN IMMIGRANTS.

Emigration of Crimean Tartars to Turkey — Broken promises, Russian and Turkish — Appearance and manners — Industry and care in agriculture — Circassian immigration — Bad cultivation and poverty — Cattle and horse stealing — Hospitality — Abstinence — Circassian encampment — Unselfishness — May prove useful as warriors.

AT the end of the last Russian War many thousand families of Tartars received permission from the Russian Government to leave the Crimea and settle in Turkey: the fields and other immovable property of the emigrants, their houses, herds, &c., were to be paid for by the Russians according to their valuation by a commission specially appointed for the purpose.

There is a Russian adage which does no great honour to the reputation of the Government Commissions; it runs as follows :—

"Kto Tiebie z-voroval?
Chynovnek.
Kto Tiebie zruinoval?
Komissia."

"Who has robbed you?" "The employé." "Who has ruined you?" "The Government Commission."

So it is probable that the value set upon the goods of the Tartars promised at least a good bargain to the Government; but even this depreciated amount was never paid, and the answer to all remonstrances on the part of the peasants was simply "Russia will owe you the money," and to this day Russia does still owe the money, and her former subjects have lost all hope of the debt ever being discharged.

In consequence of this want of faith, and breach of one of the stipulations of a treaty guaranteed by France and England, the Crimean Tartars landed in Turkey with a very small capital, and families which in their own country had been comparatively rich, found themselves obliged to begin life anew in the land of their adoption.

The Porte had promised to its new colonists houses, land, a couple of oxen or buffaloes, for each family, and seed for the first year's sowing, as well as exemption from certain taxes and from military service for a fixed period.

These were fair promises, but they were never fulfilled, and all that the Tartars really received was limited to a few sheds in which an English dog would hardly sleep, a pair of buffaloes *per village*, for each family the very insufficient amount of twenty-five okes of grain, and a few scraps of uncleared land; in some cases, as in the instance of the village of *Karamanja* in Roumelia, no land at all was given.

In all the cottages of the Tartars there are some relics of past prosperity which contrast touchingly with the present poverty of their owners; mirrors, dishes of copper or even of silver, different in form from those used by Turk or Rayah, quaint old-fashioned chests—all speak of better days now past. Poor people! they have been plundered by their former masters and cheated by the subordinates of their present Government; yet after all they make their way to comfort if not wealth, for they possess both industry and intelligence.

Unlike the Turk, the Tartar will receive you into his own

house, and you may even gaze upon the unveiled faces of his wife and daughters, but in many respects he is even a more scrupulous observer of the Canons of the Koran than the Turk himself. In England, and indeed throughout western Europe, the general idea of a Tartar is of a flat-nosed, thick-lipped savage, who gets drunk upon a mixture of mare's milk and blood, whose only pleasure is war, and who loves war only for the sake of pillage; in short the Tartar is too often confounded with the Cossack. "Grattez le Russe, vous trouverez le Tartare" is a *mot* which has long been accepted as a truth, but unfortunately it is the Kalmuck and not the Crimean Tartar who lies hid under the Muscovite epiderm : were it the latter, the more Russians are well "grattés" the better would it be for Europe.

The Tartar is not generally ugly, and many of his race are even strikingly handsome, whilst his dignified manners contrast most favourably with the servility or surliness of the Rayah. Enter a Tartar house, and you feel that your entertainer is your host, whilst in that of the Bulgarian you merely see a landlord who is calculating how much he can make you pay for the "hospitality" you receive from him.

The Tartar villages, moreover, are making progress year by year, and it is easy to guess the reason, for whenever you come across a field really well cultivated, or some grafted fruit trees, or a field of potatoes, you need not go far to find a colony of Tartars. They are also frequently traders as well as farmers, they buy tobacco, corn, butter, and sheep, and sell them at a profit; they are generally honest, and this rare quality secures them a connection sufficiently numerous to enable them to compete even with the *Bakal* as far as the amount of their profits, though they do not exact the same iniquitous percentage. They never, however, suffer the allurements of commerce to make them forget that the true source of riches in Turkey lies *in the earth;* their gains are devoted to the purchasing, clearing, ploughing, and sowing of more fields, and are not, like the savings of the Rayah, buried in an earthern pot, or employed to fan the dying embers of an insurrection in Crete. The Tartar's money is spent in the country, his son goes to school, his daughters are decked in Turkish finery, and not in English calicoes bought at five times their real value; his garden produces even the rare luxury of potatoes; and if you are particular in the choice of tobacco or honey, you will find the best and purest of each in a Tartar village.

The Rayah leaves everything to Nature, and gets more than enough for his wants; the Tartar assists Nature, and his crops are treble those of the Christian.

Intelligence is by no means wanting to the race, although it may be somewhat deficient in the sharpness and cunning peculiar to the Greek, or Rayah with Greek blood in his veins. A Tartar boy of fifteen years old has lately constructed a marine steam engine out of some bits of old iron, and a kettle as boiler; and a tiny craft worked by this machinery is at present conveying passengers on the Black Sea, between Varna and the Monastery of St. George, a distance of about eight miles.

By the efforts of these colonists the forests are being gradually converted into arable land—gradually, because their system is different from that of the Rayah, and they only clear as much land as can be properly brought under cultivation, whilst the other burns down fifty acres of timber to make one field of five acres, which after the first year's ploughing and sowing is probably neglected for the next quarter of a century.

Perhaps it will be asked by some of those who believe that from Islam no good can come, "Is not this comparative civilization and superior intelligence of the Tartar due to the effects of the Russian rule?"

Let those who know what Russian rule really is answer this question; *our* space will merely permit us to reply that the Tartars are honest and intelligent *in spite of* Russian government, and we shall find supporters amongst all those who have lived in Russia sufficiently long to have acquired the entrée behind the scenes of the theatre, in which so many brilliant operatic spectacles of happy peasants and kindly landlords are advertised for the admiration of the West.

Russia's gift of the Crimean Tartars to the Sultan, though coming from an enemy, is nevertheless a valuable one; but it is a pity that the latter was not advised to return the present in kind, and as an exchange for hard-working Mussulmans to present the Czar with as many thousands of hard-drinking Christians from Bulgaria. The gift would have been a graceful one, and it would have left the donor still richer than before.

At a short distance from the Tartar village you may find another assemblage of huts, inhabited not by the colonist, but by the exile; not by the agriculturist, but by the soldier; the Circassian's sword has not yet been (and perhaps never will be) converted into the ploughshare, and his memories of his lost home in the Caucasus, with its snow-capped mountain peaks, its raids, its skirmishes, its battles, its defeats, its victories, are still too fresh and too deeply rooted to allow him to change his warlike nature, and to become a peaceful tiller of the soil.

His fields are almost worse cultivated than those of the Rayah, and bring him in no more than the little he requires for the bare subsistence of himself and his family; he has no aptitude for trade, produces nothing for sale, and seems to have no wish to enrich himself; he has not adopted Turkey as a permanent home, but regards himself as a sojourner only, whom some happy turn of events is destined, sooner or later, to restore to his native country.

The Circassians are consequently always poor, and, whilst wanting many necessaries, have but one luxury; their weapons, rifles, swords, and knives are inlaid with that peculiar silver-work for which they are famous, which is their only industry in the Caucasus, and which they no longer exercise in their exile, perhaps because they have no longer the opportunity of taking off the boots of a Russian soldier, or the sash of a Russian officer.*

In their village you will find no coffee, and they are often unable even to offer tobacco to their guest. We lately visited a Circassian village in Roumelia, and were escorted into the *Mussafir Odasi* (guests' room) of the village; our foreign costume soon brought nearly all the men of the village to gaze upon the strangers, and we found ourselves surrounded by some thirty or forty Circassians, whose type, both physically and morally, differed widely from that of Turk or Tartar. Small, delicate hands and feet, and slender figures, at first sight gave them almost an appearance of

---

* The Russian soldiers generally conceal their money in their boots or in the knee of their trousers; the officers in their waistbelt.

effeminacy; but as we examined more closely, the clear, resolute eyes, broad shoulders, and the whole "setting up" of the men proved to us that neither strength nor courage was wanting, and that their almost too "elegant" build is but a characteristic of race.

Poor and warlike, the Circassians in Turkey are usually freebooters, and they are themselves well aware of the reputation they enjoy amongst their neighbours. At the village of *Abdikuoi* we had been talking to the assembled company for some time, and had handed round our breech-loaders for the inevitable examination and admiration; suddenly a young man, who had previously been silent, said to us:—

"You have plenty of courage."*

We asked, "Why?" not at first seeing that we had displayed any great amount of pluck.

"Because you come here alone, and let us handle your guns; haven't you heard that we are all brigands?"

"Yes; but this is not the first time we have been amongst Circassians; we trust you, and we are not in the least afraid of you."

"Of course, and we *are* good friends; but all the same you have plenty of courage."

And this last complimentary phrase was repeated several times to us.

Certainly the reputation of the Circassians here is none of the best, and they are avoided, if not feared, by their Turkish neighbours; whilst if a Rayah sees at a distance the tall white sheepskin cap of the *Cherkess* he leaves his cart or his flock to look after themselves, and runs off till he

---

* "Siz chok erkek adam," literally, "You are very manly men."

reaches his village, though even there he can hardly persuade himself that he is out of danger until two or three glasses of spirits have convinced him that he is under the friendly protection of the *Tukhan.*

Yet the Circassian can hardly be classed with any of the thieves or brigands whom we have already described; poverty, and even absolute hunger, are the mainsprings of the robberies he commits, and if he finds a strayed sheep in the forest he cuts its throat with his knife, skins it, and carries it home to his village, where it is roasted and divided amongst the poorest family; but it never enters into his head to *sell* even the skin. If the cattle of another village wander upon the Circassian pasturage, they are immediately impounded, and notice sent to the owners that they may be redeemed for a certain sum. As this plan is constantly pursued by the Turks when Rayah cattle (and more especially pigs) are found upon their limits, and as the Rayahs, though not daring to retaliate upon the Mussulman, do the same for their co-religionists, it cannot be considered as a very great crime in a country where no law regarding property is impartially administered, and where the peasant who pays the ransom to a Mussulman one day, exacts the same sum from a Christian the next.

A horse is undeniably the most tempting booty to the Circassian, who has a great objection to travelling on foot when there is a possibility of riding, so if he has a long journey to make he begins it by a détour, which brings him to a *herguilé,* or troop of half-wild horses, turned out to graze in the forest; he catches one of them, and being an excellent horseman, the absence of a saddle is no great inconvenience, whilst a strap or a rope forms an improvised bridle. The horses of Bulgaria, though vicious, are small, and usually weak, from the want of proper feeding, so that it is an easy matter for the new proprietor to break in the one he has chosen, and perhaps before he has proceeded far he may have the luck to meet a Greek or Rayah *Bakal* riding along; in that case if the steed of the latter is better than his own an exchange is effected, and the Circassian gains a saddle and bridle by the operation; if, however, his eye for horseflesh tells him that the Rayah's steed is worse than his own, he contents himself with demanding merely the saddle and bridle, which are of course given up in the fullest spirit of resignation to unavoidable misfortune.

When at his journey's end, the Circassian does not sell his horse as a common *Khersis* would do, he merely turns it loose into the forest, being tolerably sure of always getting the loan of another mount on similar terms.

Pillage in Circassia, like theft in ancient Sparta, or fraud in modern Greece, has always been considered rather as a merit than a crime; the raids of the mountaineers are like those of the Scotch upon the fertile lowlands of England, and the Circassian who carries away the most booty from his natural enemy, the Russian, is esteemed second only to the one who has killed most Muscovite soldiers. True, our Circassians are no longer in the Caucasus, but in Turkey, amongst a friendly Mussulman population; but still it is but a few years since they left their homes, the effects of early habit and education are hard to eradicate, and the Bulgarian language sounds so much like Russian that they may perhaps even imagine, whilst despoiling a Rayah, that they are stripping one of their hereditary foes. As for the occasional loan of a mount, which they take without asking leave, it is no great loss to the owners of the *herguilé*, for they can never tell the exact number of their horses within half a dozen, and practically (putting the morality of the affair out of the question) a man is not robbed who never discovers his loss.

Poor as he is, the *Cherkess*, like all genuinely oriental races, is very hospitable. During our visit to *Abdikuoi* constant apologies were made for being able to give no coffee, and for the absence of anything to eat; of course we said that we had not come for the sake of eating and drinking, but to make acquaintance with the village, and after staying more than an hour we rose to take our leave, when a cake, hot from the fire, baked especially for us and made of boiled Indian corn cooked in the ashes of a wood fire, was brought in, and we were begged to sit down again and partake of it. When at last we left, a young man accompanied us for more than a mile, to show us a short cut through the snow-covered forest to the village where we intended to sleep, and we were cordially pressed to pay the village another visit whenever we were in the neighbourhood.

One of the causes of the spareness and delicacy of Circassian figures and features is to be found in their extreme temperance as regards both food and drink. When the Circassian enters upon a campaign he takes with him a month's provisions on his back, and this food is prepared in the following manner: a kind of millet, resembling the Couscoussou of the Arabs, is thrown, handful by handful, into a large pot containing boiling mutton fat, and as the grain acquires a brownish tint it is taken out and put into a bag of sheepskin or deerskin, which contains enough for thirty days' consumption, at the moderate rate of feeding of the Circassian, who contents himself with a mere taste of it once, or at most twice, during the day, whilst his only beverage is water.

How very simple the commissariat of an army composed of Circassians would be, and what a weapon their inextinguishable hatred of Russia would furnish to Turkey, were she not too loyal to avail herself of it!

The Ottoman Government has committed the error of trying to convert a race, essentially warlike and by no means industrious, into ploughmen; the experiment has failed, and will fail again. Some eight years since the Circassians, to the number of several thousands, asked the Porte, instead of granting them lands, to give them each a horse, a good rifle, and ammunition, and to let them go where they liked, promising not to touch a hair of the head of any Turkish subject, and saying that by adopting this plan "Turkey would be rid of the Circassians, and the world of some thousands of Moscovs."

The Government refused, actuated by a feeling of honesty, or rather honour, which has been but ill repaid by the conduct of Russia during the Cretan Insurrection; perhaps in some future exigency Turkey may not disdain the assistance of a guerrilla army ready made to her hands.

As the genuine songs of an uncivilized people are the best exponents of their nature, a Circassian ballad, which has been translated into Polish by M. Brzozowski, may serve to show the intensity of the hatred entertained by the Circassians for the Russians; its subject is as follows:—

A young Circassian warrior is deeply in love with a maiden, whom her father has sold to an Armenian merchant in exchange for powder and ball, and who is destined by her owner for a Turkish harem. The Armenian has of course cheated the father in the transaction, but the word of old *Hassan* has been given, and though cheated, he still holds to his bargain in spite of the prayers and entreaties of *Ali*, who at last, in despair, carries off Nedjbé from the slave merchant. Ali is, however, captured, accused before the *Sheikh* of having made Hassan, a Circassian, false to his word, though it was only pledged to a Giaour, and he is condemned to death.

"His life belongs to thee, Hassan," says the *Sheikh*.

Ali tries to buy back his life, and offers his horse with four white feet,* whose pace is even fleeter than that of the flying Moscov who has seen the Circassian *Kinjal*† glitter before his eyes.

Hassan says nothing, and smokes on in disdainful silence.

Ali then offers him his rifle with the stock of satinwood.

"Take it, Hassan," he says; "see'st thou yon eagle, who is soaring so high in the blue heaven that he seems no larger than a bullet? Take my rifle, thou hast but to wish, and that eagle will fall at thy feet like a Cossack who sees thee too near."

But Hassan is still silent.

"Then at least accept this as my ransom!" says Ali, and he flings at the feet of Hassan a bag filled with Russian ears and noses.

Hassan rises, throws his arms round Ali, and exclaims,

---

* The Circassians, like the Arabs, differ from the popular English saying about white-stockinged horses, and consider this mark as an infallible sign of excellence.   † Dagger.

"Take thy life, and my daughter; to the merchant I will give gold for his bullets—there is gold on the mountings of my dagger."

And Ali replies, "He wants no payment; he has eaten lead."*

Another Circassian picture; but from life, not from poetry—in Bulgaria, and not in the Caucasus:—

In the month of June last we were returning from Constantinople by sea, had landed at Varna, and taken the opportunity to change some gold into the copper piastres indispensable in country villages, where it is frequently impossible to convert a Turkish lira into small coin; we had noticed an unusual number of Circassians in the town, and were informed that some days previously two ship-loads of them had arrived from the opposite coast, and were then encamped outside the walls.

As we left Varna we saw on the great marsh between the lake and sea (a very hotbed of fever, and which even the wild-fowl shooter can hardly tread), some hundred of these poor exiles, sheltered under coverings of green branches; their sunken cheeks and hungry-looking eyes sufficiently showed the misery they were suffering from want of food, the Government ration of bread served out to them not being enough for half their number.

But none of them begged; the men in their ragged but picturesque costume looking the very incarnation of pride and poverty, though the general absence of weapons proved the extremities to which they were reduced, for in war a

---

* *i. e.* been killed by a rifle ball.

Circassian parts with his life before his arms; and in peace he regards them next to his life.

We stopped our cart, called up a wretched-looking woman with a child in her arms, and put a few coppers into the baby's hand; on seeing this, other mothers with their infants crowded round us, and our bag of coppers was speedily exhausted; one of the women, to whom we had by mistake offered money twice, refused it the second time, and beckoned to another to take her place. The men stood by and looked on, not one putting out his hand; we offered some coins to a very old man, who spoke a few words of broken Turkish, but he put them back, saying, "Give them to that poor lad; he is a cripple."

Before we drove on, some of the women had baked us a tiny cake of coarse black bread, and offered it to us, with some salt, as the only thanks in their power.

For more than a fortnight these Circassians were left upon the pestilential marsh with as little regard to their health as to that of the town of Varna; happily no epidemic was engendered, but the experiment was a very hazardous one, and perhaps its next repetition may be attended with serious consequences.

Finally, the railroad conveyed them to different parts of the interior, where they were "settled," utterly destitute of resources, and ignorant even of the language spoken in their new country. Considering the trials of these unhappy immigrants, it is not difficult to find charity enough to excuse even the lawless acts which they undoubtedly commit.

To conclude this chapter, we need only remark that in our short sketch of these two gifts of Russia to Turkey, it may be seen that that of the Tartars is the only one which the Porte has at present profited by; but perhaps the time is not very far distant when the warrior will be more valuable than the farmer; and judging from this point of view, it may be no bad policy on the part of Turkey to plant Circassian villages amongst the passes and mountains of the Balkans.

CHAPTER XVI.

TURKS OF THE TOWN AND TURKS OF THE COUNTRY.

A Parisian education — Début at Constantinople — A veteran — Town Turks classified — Family life — Rustic integrity — The roué sent to Coventry — Confession of fault — Education — The priest and the schoolmaster — Energy — Ballads — Intellectual evenings — A theft rebuked.

ANY one who has been at an embassy ball at Paris must have noticed the young gentleman with a red fez, who appears to be concentrating all his attention on his feet, which are enclosed in the shiniest of varnished boots, in which they exhibit, either by the fault of Nature or the taste of the wearer, a miniature resemblance to the hoof of an ox; this personage is the *ne plus ultra* of Turkish elegance, young Turkey in its brightest blossom.

His future destiny is to be a Pasha, to govern, to re-organize the old state of Turkish affairs—in short, to patch the political small clothes of his country; and to fit himself for this task he is sent to study in Paris, which he does by assiduously attending a course of lectures at the Café Anglais and the Bal Valentino.*

In Paris he is only ridiculous, at Constantinople he is

---

* Thanks to the present influence of France in this country, twenty young Turks are to be found undergoing a process of civilization in Paris, for one who is in England; those who come to our country usually acquire a more useful and solid education, but their number is so small that they produce but little effect upon the state of Turkey.

unbearable; point out to him the architectural beauties of the Ottoman capital, and he shrugs his shoulders, twists up the ends of an invisible moustache, glances with a satisfied air at the gorgeous pattern of his trousers, looks at his habitual confidants, his boots, and answers with that languid drawl affected by Turks and Russians who have seen the world, "Do you think so? As for me, I hate Constantinople, it is such a barbarian city."

He admires above everything Regent Street or the Boulevards, and if you ask him to look at the Soulimanié, he goes into extasies over the Bourse.

If he has the luck to be the son of a Pasha in favour, he is to be found every day in the anti-chamber of some great personage, where he is much looked up to for his knowledge and correct imitation of French life and manners; if he is not so fortunate in the accident of birth, he nevertheless manages to pass his days in the anti-chamber of somebody or other of influence, for this is the only system in Turkey which opens the official career, and a steady six months of it in the Conac of a great man is worth more than half-a-dozen campaigns and a score of wounds.

Any day in passing through the dirty but picturesque streets of Stamboul, you may see some grey old veteran whose face is seamed with scars; it was he who defended the ditch of Varna in '28, it was he who was first to swim the Danube to obtain the boats necessary for the passage of the river opposite Oltenitza; he has served his country and his sovereign loyally and bravely, but he has been seen in no anti-chambers save the battle-fields which lead to the presence of the Minister Death, and so when he passes our young friend he salutes respectfully. The boy of nineteen has gained the rank of Colonel by the favour of a Vizier, and the soldier has gained by his campaigns some wounds, a medal, and a captain's pension, about five pounds a year.

We have described this *jeunesse dorée* of Turkey because it unfortunately exercises a baneful influence upon the country: whilst the young men of birth become governors, pashas, aides-de-camp, or secretaries, those of less distinguished family accept inferior employments in the household of some official of rank as clerk, boot-cleaner, pipe-bearer, &c., and from this eagerness for this kind of life arises one of Turkey's great misfortunes, for every high functionary is surrounded by a dense cloud of underlings who form a fog penetrable by the humble suitor only with the aid of that key of the East, Bakshish, and who are a part of the parasitism whose rust clogs the wheels of the governmental machinery of Turkey.

When we treat of political parties, we shall devote greater space to those gentlemen who are either in power, or aspire to it; at present we confine ourselves to comparing the town Turk with the country Turk, or peasant.

Besides the underlings, or servants of the Pasha (and of these perhaps the larger proportion are Rayahs, who are by their nature better fitted for submission than the Turk), the inhabitants of the towns are generally Beys, Pashas out of office, and a few Turks whose property chiefly consists in houses; then come the shopkeepers and retired officers, and finally the labourers and artizans, the latter class being of course the most numerous; among the two first, with the exception of the Turks of the old school (as those are called who have not given up the turban for the fez), reigns that demoralization and looseness of conduct which Europe has inconsiderately learnt to couple with the generic name of Turk.

In all lands, towns are the birthplace of vice, but in Turkey the distinction between town and country in this respect is more strongly marked than elsewhere, and for this fact a reason may perhaps be found in the almost universally Greek origin of the towns, and the consequent inheritance of those traditions of immorality bequeathed by the Lower Empire.

The Turk of the towns, from his contact with Greek and other quasi-Europeans, is usually slightly infected with such Western civilization as is to be met with in the East; he may occasionally be seen in varnished boots at the theatre, and drinks wine and spirits freely; but this specimen of the Orient must not be mistaken for one of its pearls.

But it is not the fault of the Turks as a nation that such exceptions exist; if you, an Osmanli, send your son to acquire European polish and civilization amongst the moral sewers of Paris, what can you expect? No doubt there are young Englishmen and Frenchmen who have run the same race, and who have yet turned out worthy members of society; but with the Turkish youth it is different; on his return to his country he does not re-enter the family he has quitted, but is sent off to govern and re-organize a province, where, forgetting the homely morals of his native land, he remembers only the brilliant "life" he led abroad, begins to believe that the mire which he loved was really the pure spring of civilization, and sneers at the embassy ball which bored him, while he thinks with delight of the Closerie des Lilas or the Château des Fleurs. Well would it be for

Turkey if the journey to Paris cost fourteen hundred instead of fourteen pounds!

Such imperfect and debased fragments of an imported civilization, and the stain of a contact with Greek morality, distinguish all classes of the Turks of the towns, even including the labourers, from those of the country; even yet, however, there is a wide difference between them and the Christians, for you may still trust to the word of the former (though they are not the best of the Osmanli race), to that of the latter but seldom, unless indeed it be to his advantage to keep it.

To understand the Turks you must have lived with and amongst them, a thing which is impossible in towns, where Turkish inner life—with the exception of that led by the "civilized" among them, with whom you may easily fraternize by the aid of a glass of spirits, and who in your company are less Turkish than you are yourself—is invisible and inappreciable by the European tourist, the greater part of it being passed within the precincts of the harem or home, and their social meetings (of men only) being almost impossible of access to the unturbaned stranger, although they will otherwise extend to him the fullest measure of hospitality.

In the country, especially where the peasants are poor and their village remote from a town, little by little you may succeed in gaining their confidence, and seeing them as they really are; and gradually you begin to understand their manners, their customs, and their family affection; from all of which you may evolve an idea, more or less correct, of the inner life of the Turks of the towns.

To make a sketch of these manners and customs in this

chapter is superfluous, but we must say once for all that the morals of the Turks as a race are as pure as those of any class in Europe; the harem is not what you imagine it to be from steel engravings and chromo-lithographs, but is just as much a "home" as your own. It is only wealthy tax-farmers, and Pashas who have made their fortunes, who people their harems with Odalisques; that of a genuine Turk encloses a family as much loved, and sentiments of relationship as strong and as well developed, as will be found in any English mansion or cottage, notwithstanding that the enemies of Turkey never cease repeating that this country can never have a great future because family ties are unknown—an assertion which is not an error, but a wilful calumny. We are by no means going to advocate polygamy,* but we must repeat that the purest family love exists in the harem as much as in any household of Europe.

Another common mistake is to represent Turkish women as obese beings, whose beauty is estimated by the number of stones of fat which compose it, whose occupation of stuffing themselves with sweetmeats from morning till night is interrupted only by the torture of a Nubian slave or two, and whose sole education is a love of jewels, dress, and luxury.

The Turkish girl, till her fifteenth year, goes to the village school (Mekteb), and though it may be that the Hodja cannot teach her many accomplishments, and that she is

---

* For arguments in favour of this system, we refer the curious reader to those of Napoleon, as quoted in Montholon's Memoirs; not having the book here we are unable to specify the page where they may be found, but as far as we recollect, it is in the Chapter upon the War in Egypt.

ignorant of the favourite air from Offenbach's latest opera as given by the French Dramatic Company at Constantinople, she at least learns to read and write; and in the same school where the boys are taught to become honest men, she learns to be an honest woman and a good mother of a family.

The Turk has far more respect for his wife than the Rayah shows to the female of his species, whom he constantly thrashes and forces to do work only fitted for men; the Turk acts with a certain feeling of delicacy, and does not compel his wife either to labour in the fields or to do the hard work of the household, and she is consequently generally occupied in the care of her family and such other essentially feminine employments as embroidery and cookery, in both of which arts she excels.

It is amongst the mountains and the forests that we find the true Turk, of pure morals, simple habits, and upright character; the corruption of the towns may have soiled some of the Turks who inhabit them, rendering even the most honest suspicious, and in a manner denationalizing the Osmanli exposed to its influence, but its pestilential breath does not infest the pure air of the Turkish villages. Perhaps the voice of the Imam from the white minaret, as five times a day he summons the faithful to prayer, drives away the Evil Spirit to seek refuge in a Rayah village amongst the Tukhans, those shrines dedicated to him.

If a young Turk going to the town meets there a friend who belongs to the civilized class, he may perhaps be led astray by bad example; but as he returns to his quiet hamlet its very tranquillity and repose seems to rebuke his fault, and to cause a profound disgust for those pleasures of the town which degrade body and soul by an indulgence in liquors forbidden by the Prophet; even were it not so, the stern regard of the Imam and the Hodja are mute reproaches which act as a check upon those who are inclined to develope tastes, which, though tolerated in the towns, are stigmatized in the forest.

A Turk of the towns who has acquired the vice of drinking, or upon whose character there is a stain, is no longer received as a brother by the Turks of the villages; they give him the hospitality he claims, for shelter, fire, bread, and water may be denied to none; but their hearts are not open to him: "There is bread, eat; there is fire, warm thyself; there is a rug, sleep." But on his arrival the old men are silent, the young men quit the oda,* the children do not group around the stranger, and as soon as the civilized Turk is served he remains alone in a sort of moral quarantine. This hospitality is irksome to him, and he soon learns to make his halting-places in the Rayah villages, where he is sure of finding congenial boon-companions to drink with him, and to listen to stories which would shock the ears of the country Turk but are the delight of the Papas and the Tukhanji.

The country Turks are sober in the extreme, and alcoholic liquors are not allowed to be sold in their villages; we have *never* seen a Turk of this class tipsy, and it is probably to this abstinence as well as their extreme personal cleanliness that they owe their great longevity; a Mussulman of eighty years old is much more frequently met with than a Rayah of fifty-five, and is infinitely more vigorous and active:

---

* The mussafir odasi, or guests' apartment.

within a circumference of a few leagues, in this neighbourhood alone we know of nearly a dozen centenarians.

The peasants are usually, and with very rare exceptions, of unimpeachable honesty, their word is sacredly observed, their manners are simple and patriarchal, and from a tolerably wide experience we believe them to be far superior, in point of general morality, to the corresponding class of any part of Europe.

This great superiority is chiefly owing to the presence in their villages of the two deputies of the Ulema, the Hodja, and Imam,* to the respect felt for them by the people, and to the religious and moral instruction which they bestow upon the young, as well as the censorship which they exercise over the morality of the adults.

History and tradition have also their salutary effects; one Turk will say to another, "Thy ancestor Kara Hassan would not have acted thus," and as Said has none of that false shame so common in the West, which makes a man ashamed of confessing that he is in the wrong, he says, "Thou art right, Mechmet; I have acted badly, forgive me;" and by this frank apology he does not lose either the esteem or respect of his friends and acquaintances—on the contrary, they say of him, "Said is a *doghrou adam* (a straightforward, upright man) who is ashamed of having done wrong, and admits his fault bravely and openly."

This is a kind of courage which is very rare in Europe.

Duelling is unknown amongst the Turks, perhaps because they are all brave, and in their opinion mere courage does not make wrong, right; but another cause of its absence

---

* These two offices are sometimes united in the same person.

is undoubtedly the extreme and delicate sense of justice which reigns amongst them:—Mourad offends Hassan, who tells him of it openly, and Mourad asks pardon and endeavours to make reparation; should he refuse to do so it is he, and not Hassan, who is dishonoured, for the whole village gives its verdict, and if he persists in refusing reparation he is put under the ban of public censure, and his life becomes so unbearable that he is forced to give in or to quit the village.

A point little known in England is the good education possessed by the Turkish peasants in general; thanks to the excellent schools which exist in *all* their villages, at least half of the population are able both to read and to write a language which requires five or six times more study than any one of the European family of tongues; in Turkish there are fourteen different kinds of writing, and if a man wishes to put his knowledge to a profitable use he must be able to decipher at least four or five out of the number— a fact which proves that the primary education of the Turk is not a very easy matter. There are few Turks who cannot read the Koran, and many are well acquainted with arithmetic as far as the rule of three, besides having a fair knowledge of geography and the history of their country; they are often familiar with the writings of the Ottoman poets, historians, and philosophers, their greatest pleasure being to read aloud or to listen to tales of old times.

The greatest benefit conferred by the Hodja is the religious instruction in the precepts of the Koran, which inculcates a severe practical morality, and renders the Turk susceptible of a civilisation, which, though it might differ in some points from our own, would be based upon the same foundation of social morality and absolute respect for the rights of property.

It must not be thought from what we have said that the Mussulmans are in any way priest-ridden: the Imam, in spite of his office as interpreter of the Koran, is not considered as a sacred personage; both he and the Hodja are respected for their superior learning, and the example of good conduct which they set, rather than as ministers of religion, and an Imam of bad character would be speedily expelled from his village. These two functionaries, of whom the one represents religion and the other education, are usually poor, as they do not tax their villages after the manner of the Greek Papas; their respective offices do not prevent them labouring in the fields or elsewhere, but they exact no forced help from their neighbours, and though sometimes a young man will help an old Imam to plough or sow his fields, it is old age that he assists, not the priesthood.

It is to this influence that Turkey owes the high moral character of her Osmanli population, and from it she may hope one day to introduce a reasonable civilization into the country. This adaptability of the Turk for civilization is discussed elsewhere, but we take this opportunity of remarking that the extreme religious fanaticism, which is so inseparably connected in the ideas of Europe with the Mussulman race, does not exist at all, at least in those provinces which we have studied. If the Turk despises the Rayahs, it is not because they are Christians, for he considers the religion of Christ as next best to his own, but on account of their character and morals; and in this he is right, for the most sensitive Rayahphile, after a year's residence amongst the professors of the Greek rite, will hardly be able to deny that in all points, *even that of Christianity*, the Eastern Christian is far inferior to the follower of Mahomet. The Turk, far from refusing, asks for civilization, but he demands that it shall not be created by sapping the foundations of his creed and his nationality, and will not accept such a system as begins by informing him that he is an ignorant brute, that his religion is infamous, that his nationality is a delusion, and which urges him to renounce his belief, his traditions, and his memories of the past, that he may the better copy the Greek merchant or the young Turk with his fresh coating of bad French polish. Such a mockery of civilization, such a whited sepulchre as this, the Turk rejects with horror, and it is for this reason that the reformers of the present day have as yet done nothing but entangle and destroy all they touch, and that, whilst they follow the system on which they seem bent, they will attain to no other result so long as the heart of the noble Turkish peasant is in the right place.

The Turk works hard, and, contrary to the general idea, is extremely active and supple as well as powerful; the conventional Turk, stretched upon a divan and yawning between innumerable cups of coffee and countless chibouques, is as unknown in the Balkan as the conventional Rayah, passive, pious, and patriotic. The Turk of eighty years labours to make up for the time taken from him by his military service; whilst the Rayah, morally and physically degraded and idle, lies dead drunk upon a dung-heap in front of the Tukhan. Such is the photograph of the two races, as opposed to the fancy sketches of Europe.

To see a Turk work is a real pleasure, for he seems as

if he liked his labour, and as he walks at the tail of his plough he sings an "Aman,"* which relates the deeds of Selim II. or some other Ottoman hero; as he wields with his brown but delicately shaped hands a huge axe, heavy as the mace of Cœur-de-Lion, you almost fancy that you see Roland cleaving the black cow down to the chine; what a difference between him and the Rayah, who scratches up his fields like a hen, and handles his axe as if all his fingers were blistered!

Even the amusements of the Turk are hard work, for they generally consist in shooting, and he reposes from his labour by a walk of forty miles over mountain and ravine in search of game. When evening comes on, the young men sit around the elders, who read aloud, relate the history and deeds of by-gone heroes, or discuss the questions of the day, political or social, in a manner far more profound than the occupants of an English country tap-room, whilst by listening to them the youths form their minds and their opinions. Sometimes athletic games and gymnastics (of which they are very fond), occupy their leisure hours, but there is no drinking and no quarrelling; what a difference between these sober and quiet recreations and the drunken orgies and obscene dances by which the 183 days and 365 evenings of idleness of the Rayah are occupied!

The Turk has his faults, but who has not? He is honest, sober, industrious, would recoil with disgust from a fraud or a cheat, and would never *steal* a sum of money or an ox; but he will in his youth become a Balkan Chelibi, and

---

* The generic name of most Turkish songs: "Aman, Aman!" is the general refrain of their ballads, like the old Spanish "Aydemi," with which it is identical in meaning.

he cannot resist the temptation to possess himself of his neighbour's hound.

His natural activity and courage urge him to the adventurous life of a gentleman of the forest, but, like the Scotch freebooter of old, never will the Turkish brigand stain his conscience by an act of cowardly violence or by a crime which he considers dishonourable; he robs, but he retains his sentiment of honour intact. Although a sportsman by nature, or perhaps because he is so, he does not consider that he is doing a dishonourable thing by taking a hound belonging to some one else, but the older Turks are not of the same opinion, as the following anecdote will show.

Some time since a young Turk stole a hound from us in the forest and in broad daylight: we had an idea as to the identity of the robber, and sent a servant to his village to complain to the elders; they summoned the offender, and told him that he had dishonoured the village; he replied, "I took the dog in broad daylight;" but the old men answered him, "You *stole* it." The young man, with tears in his eyes, gave up the hound, and his shame at being thus reproached was so great that he enlisted in order to leave the village.

CHAPTER XVII.

RELATIVE POSITIONS OF TOWN AND COUNTRY.

Constantinople and many other towns exempt from taxation — Encouragement to fraudulent commerce — Monomania à la Haussman — Favouritism towards foreigners — Stamp tax licenses and town property tax — "Improvements" at Varna.

WHEN Mahomet II. had conquered the capital of the last of the Cæsars he found the town almost deserted, and in order to induce the inhabitants to remain, as well as to attract others, he exempted from all taxes the dwellers in Constantinople.

In a time when Turkey was but one vast camp, the resources of the country districts of but little importance compared with the welfare of Stamboul, and the science of political economy completely unknown, such an idea of creating a vast and splendid capital was consistent with the reasoning of the period; but in our days when every statesman, worthy of the name, seeks for means of dividing as equitably as possible amongst the people the burdens rendered necessary by the expenses of the State, when every sensible Government calls in the aid of political economy to assist in developing the resources and utilizing the dormant wealth of the country, when it encourages all industry which tends to increase the riches of the nation, and in every possible way diminishes the parasitism which would mar its prosperity, such an infatuation in favour of the

R

towns on the part of the present rulers of Turkey is more than illogical, it is inexplicable.

According to some old statistics, unfortunately the only ones we have, the inhabitants of the towns number nearly two millions, of which Constantinople absorbs about half, and the total population of European Turkey is given as eleven millions; thus if the capital alone were exempted from taxes, there would still be one-eleventh of the entire population thus favoured, but this privilege is shared by many other towns, and forms a still more sensible burden upon the country, and a great diminution of the revenues of the state. When we proceed to compare the position of the dwellers in the towns with that of the inhabitants of the country, the evil becomes still more apparent.

Besides the Pashas in office, or looking out for office, with their households and the crowds which fill their anti-chambers—besides these parasites who fatten upon the blood of the State—the population of the towns is composed (with numerically few exceptions, consisting of artizans, labourers, &c.), of the members of the great Affiliated Society of Eastern Commerce, their servants and their subordinates, in short, of all the horse-leeches of Turkey.

To exempt the towns from all taxes is to multiply *ad infinitum* these leeches, whose application has weakened the country almost beyond the power of remedy; it is a folly or a crime.

When we remember that of the two million inhabitants of the towns, at least fifteen hundred thousand are engaged in this commerce that we have described, that they are people who live and grow rich without working, that every morsel of bread they eat, and every penny they put into their pockets, has, by means of proceedings, which in England would come under the ban of the law, been robbed from the poor peasant who had earned them by honest labour; when we remember that the country, the producer, is crushed down by the burden of taxation, whilst the self-styled banker, who makes 800*l.* a year out of a fictitious capital of 400*l.* by clipping gold coins, by inventing or speculating upon an Agio as fictitious as his capital, by the use of false weights and measures, or by any other of the thousand and one tricks of Eastern commerce, pays not a farthing of taxes for his house and shop, for the stamp which he puts upon his fraudulent invoices, or even for the license to ruin the country by his trade—recollecting all this, we no longer wonder at the statesmen of Stamboul, but we despair of them!

"The encouragement of commerce" is the plea usually advanced; we admit that there are evils which it is necessary to *tolerate*, but we deny the right of a Government to *protect* them, and the commerce of the East is an evil, not a good—a curse, not a blessing. The conduct of the Government might perhaps be explained on the theory that it is unwilling to sully the purity of its treasure-chests by the contact of such ill-gotten gains; but it must not be forgotten that when Eastern commerce is exonerated from all taxation, the country districts are in a manner forced to pay tribute to it, and it thus acquires a legalized right to levy another indirect tax upon the producers in addition to those other direct and illegal ones which it exacts on its own authority; such is in fact the effect of a measure which in reality only encourages parasitism while it discourages production.

The greatest, if not the only real riches of Turkey, consist in the extent and fertility of her soil, and it is therefore in agriculture that the capital and energy of the nation should be employed, it is agriculture which the Government should encourage by all the means, direct, or indirect, in its power.

Unfortunately Government does just the contrary.

We have already shewn in the preceding chapter that landed property can scarcely be considered as property, that by the abuse of the system of Mira bad tillage is authorized and protected, and that, thanks to the manner in which the taxes are at present made to press upon the produce, intelligent farming would be simply ruin to the intelligent farmer; in all these cases the Government sins, by omission or negligence, against agriculture, for not to extirpate abuses which crush and check all progress is as bad as actual oppression.

The Turkish Government is either too short-sighted to see, or does not give itself the trouble to look at these causes of ruin to the country, and in our opinion it is the latter of these two reasons which accounts for the laws at present in force in the country districts; for from the smallest Pasha to the greatest Vizier one sole idea fills the mind of the Turkish authorities, that of embellishing, enriching, and developing the towns.

There is not a petty Kaimakam* whose heart is not set upon boulevards, an exchange, public walks, and gardens, for the rickety assemblage of wooden sheds overlooking rivers of mud,† from the centre of which rises his yellow-

* Lieutenant-Governor.
† It is a remarkable fact that the urban improvements of Turkey, however tasteful and European they may be in other respects, *never* include

fronted Conac with its green or red roof. What matters to him the state of the interior country, that people are robbed in broad daylight within two miles of the newly-painted walls of his beloved town, that the peasants are dying of disease or hunger, that the Beylikji ruins the country, whilst the locusts devour the crops; what is the importance of all this compared with a yard and a half of macadamized boulevard, or the zoological gardens he dreams of so fondly? In the time of misery and disease he will send neither food nor physicians to the peasants; but he will order a corvée for the laying out of his gardens, and the making of a bit of road planted with trees on either side—not to open the country, but that he may drive along it in his new carriage, and fancy himself in Paris again. Yet this Pasha, instead of being sent to finish his days in an asylum for criminal lunatics, will be decorated and promoted to some wider field for his talents of civilization and re-organization, so strongly has this monomania *à la* Haussman taken possession of all those connected with the Government of Turkey. Perhaps it may have a political cause, and the secret thoughts of the governor of a Turkish town may be thus put into words: " So long as I keep my position or obtain promotion, what does it matter what becomes of the villages, or whether the country makes any progress or no." He knows that the arbiters of his destiny are Europe and those high functionaries of Constantinople who pay such persevering court to her, so he continues his reflections: " Either foreigners or

---

the removal of the ubiquitous streams of mud; the man who first invents mud carts and scavengers in this country will certainly deserve, and probably receive, a handsome pension from the Sublime Porte.

my official superiors will decide my fate; but as neither of these will risk themselves in the country districts, it is in the town and its immediate neighbourhood that my capacity will be judged, so let me beautify the town, and let the country look after itself as best it can."

Such is a sketch of the probable arguments of these reformers, and alas! of their actual organization. The authorities forget that it is the country and not the town which pays them; but to forget benefits and benefactor is not a vice exclusively Turkish.

The exemption of towns from taxation naturally tends to draw to them, and from the country, the well-to-do classes, and thus acts as a check upon agriculture; it is a grave economical error to discourage the only industry profitable to the nation, and to encourage that which is its ruin.

An objection may be raised, that unless commerce be encouraged produce becomes worthless, as no market will exist. We answer that a market will always be found, for Europe every year requires more and more raw produce, and consequently commerce will find its way to Turkey at any hazard; and from the day when it shall be impossible for a fictitious capital to profit by the position of middleman between producer and consumer, when the law shall punish usury, fraud, and the other companions of commerce as it exists in the East, legitimate commerce based upon capital, and acting according to the precepts of justice and integrity, will be able to compete with the present parasitism, and even to drive it from the field. Encourage honest commerce in every possible way, but do not protect roguery disguised in the mantle of trade.

It is to commerce at least, as much as to industry, that

England owes her prosperity, and yet English commerce is heavily taxed, more heavily perhaps than any branch of industry, and certainly a merchant after the fashion of the East could not do business in England, not merely on account of the police, but because *there* commerce demands capital, and is taxed according to its profits; but then England is a far-sighted country, whose statesmen think before acting, and are patriotic enough to act even against their own private interests for the benefit of the nation; in England, too, there are mad-houses for madmen, in Turkey their occasional asylum is office.

It appears just and reasonable, since the rule seems to be to tax the profits, and as the labourer pays the tithe of the produce of the soil in which he has invested a certain capital of labour and seed, that the trader, who generally puts into his business neither labour nor capital, should be liable to a similar tax upon his raw produce. But the Capitulations are there to guard the monopoly of commerce for foreigners; if Turkey is not mistress in her own house whose fault is it? It is a false calculation to dread the expense and risk of a war, which after all might be a successful one for Turkey, and prefer a state of things which is ruining the country, and leading surely to the political death of the Ottoman Empire.

This protection of foreign commerce is also detrimental to native enterprise, since the native trader, except in towns, pays certain taxes, whilst the foreign merchant pockets his gains without any such drawbacks.

The Turkish Government is so weak that it dare not decree that every foreign trader shall be subject to the laws of the country; why then does it impose upon the foreign landed proprietor obligations from which it exempts the foreign trader?

Being avowed enemies of the present system of taxation, we do not advocate even a tax upon the produce of the merchants, though an income tax (which is unjust to the producer, especially if it fall upon the gross produce), might fairly be paid by them; such a tax as this last would, however, be too easily evaded by such ingenious gentlemen, and therefore it might be more advisable to levy a stamp tax, since the merchant is always obliged to take a *Teskere* to load or unload his goods, whilst he could easily falsify the return of his income.

It will be necessary, however, to prevent this tax falling, like that of the exports and imports, upon the peasant instead of the trader; a method of securing this result would be the establishment by Government of houses of commerce in connection with the Ottoman Bank, which should be bound to content themselves with a profit of (say) 10 per cent. upon their exports and imports. Not only would these do good by ridding the country of the present traders, and offering better prices to the agriculturists, whilst supplying them with foreign wares at a cheap rate, but they would also have the financial and economical advantage of causing a part of the profits, at present pocketed by Greeks, to come into the coffers of the National Bank, and of keeping the money in the country.

In order to equalize in some measure the respective positions of town and country, it is necessary to proceed logically, and to tax each in the same proportion.

A peasant who sows one Varna kilé of grain, of the average value of 100 piastres, reaps (as a minimum) ten

Varna kilés, value 1000 piastres, of which he pays, besides personal taxes, &c., one-tenth, or 100 piastres, as dime; in other words, a tax of ten per cent. on the whole revenue of his agricultural speculation.

The owner of land in a town, of the superficies of 400 square mètres, lets his ground for at least 1600 piastres per annum, or four piastres per square mètre, whilst the average income of the peasant from four times the same extent of cultivated land is 200 piastres, or one-eighth of a piastre per square mètre, out of which he has to pay a tax of twenty piastres, whilst the inhabitant of the town pays nothing ; to put each on the same level, the latter should be taxed four-tenths of a piastre for every square mètre of ground owned by him.

Besides a stamp tax, a license to buy or sell, and a rate fixed upon land owned in towns according to its position and their importance, it might be only just to impose another sort of trade license of so much, say ten piastres, upon every square mètre of ground upon which is any building destined for commercial purposes, and to punish by confiscation, and even by imprisonment, any evasion of this tax. Thus, the Eastern trader who stores his goods in an unlicensed house should be liable to have them forfeited, as well as to a heavy fine; if he signs a contract, or does business in an unlicensed house, the sum affected by the contract should be paid as a fine by the two contracting parties.

If contracts upon unstamped paper were invalid, and their amount liable to forfeiture, this law would be very difficult to evade.

We shall be told that such absurd exactions would have

the effect of destroying Eastern commerce entirely; to annihilate the commerce of Turkey as it at present exists, and to see it replaced by a sound and healthy system of trade, is exactly what we should most desire, and in our opinion it is always better to kill a venomous snake than to "scotch" it.

The towns would not suffer, but benefit, by such a land tax as we have proposed, for the proprietor, finding himself obliged to pay, would naturally try to get as much for his ground as possible, and build respectable and solid houses instead of the flimsy structures which now exist in all Oriental towns. Take the example of Péra, where the municipality have taxed pretty heavily, and see the improvement which has taken place in domestic architecture.

One word upon the municipalities; they are a quite recent creation, but with the exception of the Sixth Circle of Constantinople—that is, Péra—they exist only in name. Municipal guards, a sort of *sergents de ville*, have been established, and French institutions are copied in other ways; but all this does not prevent people from selling with fraudulent weights and measures under the very eyes of the new police, or the streets from being fathomless mud-holes, and the towns themselves a collection of sheds, compared with which the huts of Little Kamiesch or Balaklava would have appeared palaces. If it is necessary to reform and embellish the towns, some other and more practical plan must be struck out; as for the country, it would perhaps be better for its welfare that the Turkish reformers of the present day should forget its existence and leave it to itself.

Last year, however, they recollected it sufficiently to raise the dime from 10 to 15 per cent., whilst they whitened the tumble-down walls of Varna, planted a few trees, and pulled down a street of huts painted blue, to replace it by a street of huts painted yellow.

CHAPTER XVIII.

BRITISH CONSULS AND THE CONSULAR REPORTS.

Gammoning a Consul — Harrowing tale — The truth discovered — Consular entourage — Consular dignity — Bullying a Pasha — The reports — Preliminary statements by the authors — Consular complaints from Rustchuk, Smyrna, Kustendje, Salonica, and Prevesa (South Albania) — Trial of Greek autonomy in the Sporades — Vice-Consul Dupuis (Salonica) — Reports from Aleppo, West and East Macedonia, Adrianople, Scutari, Beyrout, Jerusalem, Cyprus, and Janina — Consul-General Longworth (Belgrade) — Reports from Brussa and Trebizonde.

It is not without a certain degree of wonder at our own temerity that we approach this subject, with the knowledge of the general impression prevailing in England, that nobody can be better qualified to speak upon the Eastern Question in all its branches than those gentlemen who have spent years in Turkey, with the advantage of an official position, and with the two objects of protecting the interests of British subjects and of reporting from the store of their vast and varied experience upon the true condition of the Christian subjects of the Sultan; the latter being the one point which possesses any interest for the general public, who, except as a matter of balance of power, do not much care whether Russia swallows up the Ottoman empire this year or a hundred years hence.

A British Consul home on leave from his Turkish consulate is, naturally enough, regarded everywhere (outside the Foreign Office) as an infallible oracle upon Eastern affairs, and his dicta are listened to by his friends with admiring acquiescence and without a thought of contradiction, except perhaps from some gentleman, whom a month's stay at Missori's Hotel, or a winter on the Nile, has endowed with an individual opinion on the *vexata quæstio.*

"Mr. Consul Blank must know all about these things, he has spent ten years in the East."

Very true, so he has; but let us see how he has spent them, and whether he is likely to have amassed any very reliable information during these ten years.

The British Consul in Turkey,* although officially resident in a town, reigns over a very large extent of country: on his appointment to a new post he is generally animated by a laudable desire to see something of "the interior," and "to judge for himself," of the real state of affairs.

In most cases he is unfortunately ignorant of Turkish or Bulgarian, though he may perhaps have a sufficient knowledge of the former to order tobacco and coffee at a country *Khan,* and therefore convenience, as well as consular precedents, requires that he should be accompanied by his dragoman or interpreter, invariably a Greek or Armenian; the roads are not very safe, and for this reason as much as for that of keeping up the consular dignity in the eyes of the natives he thinks it better to be escorted by his two Cavasses, Greeks or Arnaouts.

Of course the dragoman advises him not to put up at Mussulman villages, "the inhabitants are all more or less brigands," or "it's better to avoid any possibility of being rudely received;" so the Consul consequently passes every

---

* We must remind our readers that we only pretend to speak authoritatively of Bulgaria, but at the same time we fancy that our remarks will not be much less applicable to the Consuls of Anatolia and other parts of the Sultan's dominions.

night of his tour amongst Rayahs, who are sufficiently humble to satisfy even his own notion of his own importance and to impress him in favour of a people who show such a proper and becoming respect for their superiors.*

Mr. Consul Blank is naturally and officially anxious to learn whether the Rayahs have any well founded complaints to make of tyrannous acts committed by Mussulmans, and intimates this wish to his dragoman Spiro, who goes out, and after a short absence returns in company with an old man, who kisses the feet and hands of the "Consular Effendi," and pours forth his tale of woe in Turkish, which, as translated by Spiro, runs as follows:—

Some months previously a few soldiers, commanded by a sub-lieutenant, *Osman Agha*, were quartered in the village: Osman Agha fell in love with the fair face of old Dimitri's daughter Frushi, the belle of the village; the Christian maiden rejected all the advances of her Mussulman admirer, who, despairing of success in any other manner, carried her off by force, after murdering her father and mother who had endeavoured to oppose the abduction.

These facts, adds Spiro, are already known to the other foreign Consuls of Mr. Blank's residence, and will be reported to the Turkish authorities.

Mr. Blank thinks it is a very dreadful case, and makes a note of it in his pocket-book, as learnt from the uncle of the unhappy girl.

Thus he proceeds from one village of Christians to another, gleaning everywhere the most harrowing details of Turkish

---

* He has not yet learned the truth, that the obsequiousness of his hosts is due less to himself than to the ornamented pistols and overbearing demeanour of his Cavasses.

oppression (always through the medium of Spiro), and flattering himself that his first despatch to the British Embassy or the Foreign Office will prove that his salary has been well earned by his tour in the country, during which he has been a horrified ear-witness of so many painful facts proving the reality of Turkish license and oppression.

A few days after his return to town, Mr. Consul Blank is invited by the rest of his colleagues to join in a collective despatch to the Porte relating and complaining of the murders and abduction committed by Osman Agha.

But in spite of the notes taken in the pocket-book, and much to the surprise of his official brethren, he refuses to do so: by a fortunate chance he happens to have received ulterior and more reliable information from a relative of his own who is travelling in the country, and the collective despatch is therefore sent without his signature.

The British Embassy hears of the affair, and telegraphs to Mr. Consul Blank for information: his answer is a telegram to the effect that the whole thing is a mare's nest, and next day he writes a despatch relating the true version:—
Osman Agha was a very handsome fellow, and Miss Frushi fell violently in love with him, her passion being moderately reciprocated by the gallant officer; finally, the young lady carried off her prize, and landed him safely at Constantinople; these particulars were learned from the murdered father and mother, who were only anxious (just as if they had been parties to a civil action in England) to obtain some pecuniary compensation for the loss of their daughter's services.

Osman Agha is, however, accused by so many Consuls that he is arrested, and, the British Embassy not interfering, is punished for the murders he had never tried to commit by several years' imprisonment.*

The whole business was got up by the Greek dragomans of the various foreign consulates, who, if their masters required hoodwinking, were able to blind them by judicious mistranslations and garbling of evidence; here Mr. Blank was saved by a fortunate accident from aiding a gross act of injustice—but how many Consular Mr. Blanks hear similar stories, do *not* find out their falsehood, and report what is simply a lie invented by Greek ingenuity to injure Turkey?

In the town Mr. Consul Blank is by his official rank placed amongst the heads of society, and is therefore still more open to the influences which have already abused his credulity in the country, for in the provincial towns of Turkey society is composed of Greek (and perhaps a few Armenian) merchants and the foreign Consuls, who are also (the English representative of course being excepted) traders: from these, many tales of Turkish oppression are poured into the unsuspecting consular ear, for of the Greeks any one would almost sooner lend money to his best friend under 60 per cent. than say anything but evil of the Turks; and of the other Consuls it is the duty of one or two to use all means in their power to injure the Ottoman Government in the eyes of Europe; whilst the rest, who may be really very well-meaning persons, are quite as liable to be imposed upon as their British colleague.

---

* This story, like most of the apparently fanciful instances we cite, is perfectly true; the scene was a village in the Dobrudsha, the time between two and three years since.

Lord Lyons in his despatch to the Secretary of State for Foreign Affairs, dated Constantinople, May 6, 1867, fully recognizes the fact of the over-credulity to be found amongst foreign Consuls: "The Christians constantly bring complaints to him (the foreign agent), whilst the Mussulman is not equally in the habit of seeking foreign aid and sympathy." It is no small credit to his Excellency to have discovered a circumstance which, if borne in mind, will materially aid a truer appreciation of the foreign official statements concerning the Christians in Turkey, and we are especially glad to have on our side the opinion of an ambassador, since it may perhaps relieve us* from dilating on the important point, which we should otherwise have to prove by other instances than the one (of Mr. Consul Blank) already given, that foreign Consuls usually hear but one side of the question; this common error is, however, so chronic that it vitiates the testimony of a great part of the Consular Reports of 1867, and in criticizing them it is essential to remember it.

Another little weakness, though of a different kind, which is very often to be discovered in Mr. Consul Blank, is that he is not contented with being the protector of oppressed Christians as well as of travelling Cives Romani: he likewise fancies that his own dignity requires to be asserted at the expense of that of the Turkish Pasha, and he occasionally takes rather questionable means, which he calls "upholding his position" to accomplish this desirable end. As an in-

---

* Instances could be easily given by the half-dozen, but a short residence in Turkey soon exhausts one's stock of good paper and good pens, and as an extra copy of one's MS. is indispensable, thanks to the insecurity of all the postal services, any saving of the manual labour of transcription is a decided boon.

stance, we will give an episode in the jurisdiction of a gentleman, whom we will call Mr. English to distinguish him from the generic Consul Blank.

Young Mr. English was appointed to the consulate of the town of Triantaphyl in European Turkey, and, having previously served in the army and the diplomatic corps, naturally thought himself at least a couple of pegs higher than ordinary consuls. At first he was very good friends with the Turkish Pasha of Triantaphyl; but wishing to show that the power of a British Consul knew no limits, he demolished the windows of the Quarantine Establishment by means of a gun and constant discharges of small shot. The Pasha thereupon revolted against the Consul, and for some months a war of notes was kept up between the conac and the consulate, without marked advantage to either army.

Finding that official penmanship was too slow a way of reducing the Pasha to bondage, young Mr. English hit upon an expedient which was fortunately crowned with complete success, and which is well worthy the imitation of all other able-bodied Consuls in Turkey.

The town of Triantaphyl is fortified, and one of the standing orders of the garrison is to the effect that no person is to be allowed to walk the streets after dark without a lantern, an order which may perhaps be dictated by a feeling of humanity, the streets being infinitely more dangerous to the pedestrian by their precipices than the "Mauvais Pas" of Chamouni can have possibly been before it was cut into steps and furnished with a guiding rope; the *Zaptiehs* (police, or rather *gens d'armes*), have strict instructions to arrest any person found infringing this edict, and no exceptions are recognized.

Whilst Mr. Consul English was on amicable terms with the Pasha, he was always accompanied in his nocturnal excursions by a servant or cavass bearing a lantern, whose many mould candles gave out an infinitely brighter light than any one of the misty lighthouses erected by a foreign company on the Turkish shores of the Euxine; when war was declared he made a rule of economizing the lantern and risking his neck and his varnished boots amongst ravines of mud and stones.

One evening as he was passing a post of Zaptiehs the sentry stopped him, saying:—

"You have no lantern; come this way."

"I am the Ingeliz Consulus," replied Mr. English.

"No matter, you must come to the guard room till we see if you really are the English Consul or not."

"Go to the devil!" replied the Consul.

The sentry of course collared Mr. English, but was immediately knocked down by a well-delivered left-hander; the rest of the guard turned out to assist their comrade, and a regular fight ensued. The Consul, being armed with a stout stick, and knowing how to use it, made good his retreat towards his own house, where he was rescued by a sortie of the inhabitants, amongst them another Consul of maturer age than Mr. English, with revolver in hand. The Zaptiehs consulted the better part of valour and ran away, thus avoiding probable bloodshed.

Next morning the young Consul consulted the old Consul, and both agreed that the Zaptiehs, in the execution of their duty, had acted like highway robbers, and that the Pasha was responsible. So in a very short time the Pasha was coerced into ordering a parade of all the force of the

Zaptiehs of Triantaphyl before the British Consulate, that the chief offenders might be identified and then severely punished by order of Her Majesty's Consul. The Pasha was moreover compelled to call upon Mr. English in full uniform and offer a humble apology for the conduct of the guardians of public safety; it is needless to remark that from that time forward he was completely enslaved to Mr. English, without even a thought of breaking his fetters.

The whole affair was referred to the British Embassy, which strongly approved of Mr. English's energetic and truly consular conduct, from which approval it may be gathered that a British Consul is quite right to bully the Turkish authorities into submission, even if in the process he should be forced into a breach of the local laws, followed by a breach of the peace. Another deduction which might possibly be made is that any act committed by a British Consul in Turkey is legal, so long as it does not infringe any English law. Poor Turkey!

In justice to Mr. Consul English we must state that he is essentially a gentleman, and had he not been a Consul would certainly not have committed such acts as we have mentioned. There is, however, an inherent property of the consular rank in Turkey which inspires its members with the proud consciousness that they own no superiors but the British Embassy and the Foreign Office.

It is not our intention to remark upon the occasionally hazy grammar to be found in the Consular Reports*—more

---

* Reports received from Her Majesty's Ambassador and Consuls relating to the condition of Christians in Turkey, 1867. Presented to the House of Commons by command of Her Majesty.

especially since the Civil Service examinations are yearly assuming a higher standard, whence it is to be presumed that the next generation of Consuls will indite despatches, whose style may unite the vigour of Macaulay with the charm of De Quincey—and therefore we shall confine ourselves to criticizing the matter of these Reports, begging our readers to bear in mind one or two preliminary statements:

1st. That we are personally acquainted (and that but slightly) with only one of the gentlemen who have furnished the Reports.

2nd. That (*teste* Lord Lyons) Consuls usually hear only one side, and that invariably from Christians; even if they endeavour to get at the truth they are prevented by their interpreters—"grattez le Consul, vous trouverez le dragoman," might unfortunately be too often predicted of the consular body.

3rd. That we by no means pretend to assert that grievances, even very gross grievances, do not exist in Turkey; we contend that these grievances press upon the Mussulman always as much as, often more than, they do upon the Christian.

4th. That whilst omitting many passages which confirm our opinions as we have given them in this work, we have not to our knowledge left untouched any statement which is contrary to them, except in cases where such a statement, constantly recurring, has previously been commented upon.*

---

* As the friend who forwarded the Consular Reports to the Authors, I think it right to state that they have not received the four additional Reports of Part II. In these we find the same general complaints of the non-reception of Christian evidence; but while the report from Diarbekir

It may be as well to notice that the very title of these Reports, as printed on the cover, might be altered with advantage; if Reports upon the condition of *Christians in Turkey* were desired, why do not the British Consuls give a few particulars concerning the status of their Prussian, French, Austrian, Russian, and Greek colleagues? If the Reports are only upon the condition of Christian subjects of the Sultan in Turkey, it might have been as well to have stated it clearly.

No. I.—SIR R. DALYELL. Rustchuk.

"On a short journey I have lately made on consular business to Kustendji and Varna, I stayed at some Bulgarian houses, and thus had occasion to hear something of the principal grievances at present complained of.

"They seem to be (as I have before mentioned to your lordship):

"1. The brigandage which prevails in many parts of the Vilayet. The nature of the country renders it difficult to repress this thoroughly; but a great deal more might be done, and ought to be done, than is done.

"2. The insufficiency and, in many instances, bad and oppressive conduct of the Zaptiehs (police). Something has been done to remedy this; but a great deal is still required.

"3. The non-admission of Christian evidence. Notwithstanding repeated assurances given to me by Midhat Pasha (who may perhaps, however, if he omits to make sufficient enquiry, be himself deceived in this, as in many other matters, by his subordinates), the reception of

---

describes the situation of the Christians in the Eastern extremity of the empire as more unfavourable, Consul Holme's account of the Christians of Bosnia entirely coincides with the Authors' experience. He says of them, "They remain in the most benighted ignorance, and destitute of any qualities calculated to excite respect; and it seems to me clear that no edict of the Sultan, however well intentioned, can possibly induce the Mahometans to regard the mass of the Christians of the empire as their equals, until the latter, by advance in education, industry, and honesty, do something to raise themselves."—L.

Christian testimony when the complainant is a Rayah still meets with great obstacles in the province everywhere, I suspect, but at Rustchuk."

Brigandage is certainly an evil which is not felt by the Rayahs alone, nor, as we have stated in the chapter upon that subject, are the brigands exclusively, or even generally, recruited from amongst Mussulmans.

That the police might be better organized is an undoubted fact, but in a quotation which we shall give from Report No. 12 it will be seen that they are not always influenced by considerations of creed; we have always found that the Turks complain of them quite as much as the Rayahs.

As to the non-admission of Christian evidence, a sufficiently plausible reason has been already given * by an extract from Report No. 22, and which may be found in the first paragraph of page 61 of the official collection. Sir Robert Dalyell, with the sense of justice inherent in an English gentleman, himself neutralizes a good deal of the effect of the complaint No. 3 by a note which, like a lady's postscript, contains some of the most important matter he furnishes:

"It may be said, 'What are the Christian members of the Medjliss about?' The Tchorbadjis (head men) and Bishops are frequently mixed up in speculations with the Turkish authorities, and put their seals to anything; from long habits of subserviency they are likewise, in many instances, afraid to do otherwise. There is still a great deal too much oppression of Christians by the Turkish authorities; but it has diminished sensibly, and is every year, at least in this part of Turkey, diminishing. What does not diminish is the oppression of the poor Christians by their Tchorbadjis. Every one of my colleagues here would confirm my opinion. I saw the same state of things at Erzeroum with an Armenian population, as here with a Bulgarian. Whenever a gross case of bribery can be traced,

---

* In the Chapter upon Eastern Commerce.

some Tchorbadji will generally be found to have received two-thirds of the bribe, the Turkish authority the remainder. I could cite instances."

No. 2.—CONSUL CUMBERBATCH. Smyrna.

"Some cases of secret persecution and assault have taken place against Protestant Armenians; but the Chiefs of the Armenian Communities were found to be the instigators of them.

"With regard to the social position of the Christian population, no Christians have yet been accepted in the army; in lieu of serving they are obliged to pay a conscription tax (bedelish), which becomes even more onerous than the haratch or poll tax."

Mr. Cumberbatch does not inform us whether any Christians have as yet volunteered to serve in the army, nor does he state the amount paid as conscription tax, which must be very heavy to counterbalance the 8000 piastres which the Mussulman is forced to pay if he chooses not to serve.

"The schools are solely open to the Mussulman population."

What schools? If they are those supported by the contributions of Mussulmans, the doctrine of the Koran naturally pervades all that is taught, and Christians would be unwilling to send their children to them. As out of Constantinople there are hardly any schools for mixed creeds supported by the Government, it would be almost an equally fair reproach against the Christians to say that their schools are not open to Mussulmans.

"To conclude my observations, I must add that I consider the stipulations referred to have been carried out to a certain extent in the large towns; but that in the districts the Hatti-Scheriff and Hatti-Houmayoun have remained a dead letter."

The Turkish Government is, alas! very weak, and if it has not been able properly to carry out its undeniably good intentions, the fault is with those foreign powers who have

CHAP. XVIII.   KUSTENDJE—SALONICA.   265

paralyzed its force and degraded its influence even with its own subjects.

"I must also add, my lord, that the Turkish population is infinitely more harshly used than the Christians as regards exaction."

No. 3.—VICE-CONSUL SANKEY. Kustendje.

"A rule exists that no subject of the Sultan can be imprisoned without a masbata or sentence. This rule is respected as regards Mussulmans; but Rayahs are arrested and thrown into prison without any form of interrogatory or trial, at the caprice of the local authorities, for any period they may choose."

We regret to say that in other parts of the Vilayet this rule is not even so well observed as at Kustendje, for Turks and Rayahs are treated as only the latter are in Mr. Sankey's Vice-Consulate; the latter can, however, usually bribe their way out sooner than the former.

"The Governor gives a list of persons chosen by himself;* this list is sent the round of the district, the electors having the option of objecting to any of the persons named in the list, but not that of substituting other names; whatever their decision, makes no difference in the result. The Governor reports to his superior that certain persons have obtained a certain number of votes, and they are declared duly elected. The members of the Medjliss receive pay, and are chosen by the Governor, they therefore, without cavil or remark, append their signatures to any document presented to them; most of them are illiterate, and the fashion of seals in lieu of signatures, in general use in Turkey, renders the knowledge of reading and writing unnecessary.

"The Turks have always the majority in these councils, which consist in the Medjliss of a Governor, of three Turkish members besides the Governor, Cadi, and Mufti, and two Christians.

"In the Medjliss of a Mudir, or Deputy-Governor, there are five Turks to one Christian."

The Medjliss is one of the many defective attempts at

---

* For election to the Medjliss or Municipal Council.

organization in Turkey, but even in places where the Christian members have a numerical preponderance the ends of justice are not much furthered by the fact; and, as may be seen in Report No. 7, when these members are freely elected by the people the result is no better.

"An ordinary police sergeant, who stands cringing and trembling in the presence of a Mudir, when sent on service to a Christian village becomes a tyrannical satrap, takes up his quarters in the best house, lives at rack and manger, and levies contributions at pleasure."

Very likely, but he is not a bit less of a "satrap" amongst the Turks than amongst the Rayahs.

"In their daily relations the Rayah is made to feel the small estimation in which he is held by his masters. A Turk will not rise to receive him; he will be kept waiting for hours, although the master of the house is unoccupied."

Something of the same *de haut en bas* treatment of a supposed inferior by a fancied superior may occasionally be witnessed even in Europe.

No. 4.—CONSUL WILKINSON. Salonica.

"The clause in the Hatti-Humayoum having reference to the participation of the Christian element in the Government appointments has likewise remained a dead letter in so far, at least, as it relates to appointments to which salaries are attached, for the few Christian members of the mixed tribunals receive no emoluments. Still, had the stipulations of the Hatti-Humayoum in this respect been carried into effect, no benefit whatever would have accrued to the Christians, or to the public service in general, from the acquisition of such an element; for the Bulgarians, who constitute the great majority of the Christian population of this province, are, both in intellect and education, far below their rulers; and even the few more or less educated Greeks who live in the towns, though perhaps naturally more intelligent than their Mussulman fellow countrymen, are, as a rule, inferior to them in administrative capacity, and are, besides, so venal and addicted to intrigue that their participation in the public administration of the provinces would perhaps promote their own private interests, but would surely confer no benefit on their co-religionists. The Christians are not likewise admitted to serve in the army. Of this however they do not complain, and would rather pay double the amount of the tax to which they are now subjected for exemption from military service, than be compelled to enter that service.

"A few elementary Turkish schools have been established in this province within the last three years, into which, however, no Christians are admitted, and yet there is a very strong desire on the part of the latter to educate their children. There is scarcely a Christian village, however small, which does not possess a school entirely supported by the villagers."

If every Christian village has its own Christian school surely it is no great grievance that the Christians are not admitted into the Turkish schools; unless, indeed, the former consider that they ought to have education without paying for it, a thing not always to be obtained at the same price even in England.

"Two important lines of road have been in course of construction in this province since 1865. The works have made but very slow progress, and the system of 'corvées,' or compulsory labour, by means of which they are carried on, gives rise to many abuses, and is a source of constant complaint on the part of the rural population."

The corvée is one of the great abuses in this country, since its exercise throws almost unlimited power of abuse into the hands of the Pasha and of his subordinates, the latter, at least, seldom failing to profit by their opportunity.

The sooner this evil remnant of feudalism is abolished, the better will it be for Christian and Turkish peasants.

No. 5.—VICE-CONSUL BARKER. Prevesa.

"The Archbishop of Arta . . . at the same time observed to me that he, too, is one of the members of the Medjlisses or councils here and in Arta; but when the decrees are passed to the different members of the court for their signatures, he, the Archbishop, is not allowed to attach his signature but under that of the meanest Turk member amongst them. In the Arta Court his Eminence's name comes after that of a Turkish barber of a disreputable character."

It is hardly surprising that members of the State religion take precedence in their signatures over those of a heterodox creed, or that the conquerors should, in their own opinion at least, be entitled to rank before the conquered.

"My reply to his Eminence was that he cannot be astonished at this, since the Ministers at the Porte seem to have lost in their Turkish vocabulary a term to denominate the sect of whom his Eminence is a spiritual chief; for in an official Turkish document received here last week his Eminence is designated as 'the President of the non-Mussulman religion!'"

FUAD PASHA *to the Governor-General of Janina.*

(*Translation.*)

"We have received, inclosed in your despatch of 11 Ramazan, 1283, the copy of the proclamation respecting the counsels given for suppressing Hellenic evil-doers, executed by the President of the non-Mussulman religion; those counsels proving the fidelity and attachment of the President of the non-Mussulman religion, which are recognized.

"You are therefore invited to state our contentment, and at the same time inform him that walking in this road of policy will occasion great progress; this conduct of his has much satisfied us, for which we have written the present reply."

What Monsignor Serafim said to Mr. Barker's insinuation that he was gratuitously insulted by the Turkish Government, we have no means of learning; but even the term "non-Mussulman religion" as applied to the Greek Church is at least as complimentary as that used by Mr. Barker, who qualifies it as "a sect."

The letter of Fuad Pasha is in itself sufficiently gracious, and his Eminence will undoubtedly make greater progress by walking in the ways of loyalty to his Sovereign, than by being induced to cavil at words, or to take offence where none is meant.

The quotation which we give next is such as to make us doubt whether Monsignor Serafim does not occasionally deviate a little from this path:

> "The Christians, too, have prayers daily, in which they implore our Creator to deliver them from the children of Agar, in the belief that the Mussulmans are the descendants of the illegitimate scion of Abraham."

If prayers were put up in Roman Catholic chapels and churches of Ireland, and authorized by Archbishop Cullen, praying for deliverance from the children of Strongbow, of Queen Elizabeth, or of Cromwell, would the English Government consider that the Archbishop was likely to make "great progress" by "walking in this road of policy"?

Mr. Barker further gives an elaborate calculation of the average yearly income of the Christian peasants in his districts, and discovers it to be, after making all deductions, 1028 piastres 22 paras, or about 8*l*. 15*s*. But there is one tax which has been entirely omitted, that paid to Monsignor Serafim and the Greek Papasses; it amounts *at least* to half the amount paid to Government—say 4*l*.—and its payment leaves only a sum of 4*l*. 15*s*. per annum for the support of five persons (for of course "a peasant" must be taken as meaning a head of a family), or about three farthings each per diem. Mr. Barker does not mention how life can be supported on this.

But he adds:

> "From which (the income arrived at by Mr. Barker's calculation), after deducting expenses of labour in raising the produce and conveying it to town for his landlord, little or nothing remains for the maintenance of his family and himself; and from year to year many sell off stock to pay the debt and taxes, most of them possessing in clothes only the ragged suit they wear daily," &c. &c.

Neither Mr. Barker nor even the worst enemies of Turkey

assert that the Christian is more oppressed now than he was a few years since; how then has he amassed stock to sell in order to pay off the debt and taxes? Can it be by some such system of exchange as we have mentioned in the chapter upon brigandage, where Vassili, having been robbed of one horse, helps himself to three others to make up his loss?

No. 6.—VICE-CONSUL A. BILIOTTI. Rhodes.

"There is no restraint as regards the exercise of the Christian religion;. and I may add that the Mussulmans here could not be more tolerant in that respect.

"With respect to their ecclesiastical dues, the inhabitants of the town refused to pay a fixed revenue to the Greek Archbishop; and though he managed to obtain an annual sum of 300*l.*, I am told, from the 15,000 souls forming the population of the villages, he nevertheless exacts, at the same time, the dues which used to be paid to bishops before the establishment of this fixed annuity.

" The inhabitants of these islands (the Sporades), who are all Christians, enjoy privileges which are quite unknown not only in Turkey but in any other part of the world. They have autonomous administrations; the authority of the Porte is but nominal.

"In conclusion, it is difficult for me to say which of the different Greek populations are suffering more, whether that of Rhodes where there is a defective administration, or those of the smaller islands in which there is no government whatever."

Mr. Biliotti's statements by no means give a flourishing account of what the Greek Christians, left entirely to themselves, have been enabled to effect in the way of order and civilization.

No. VII.—VICE-CONSUL DUPUIS. Soulina.

"By the laws of Turkey, no Christian, unless a Rayah, can hold property in the soil, and it would appear that once a house is burnt down the land reverts to Government. During the time of my predecessor a row of houses in the upper part of this town, was secretly set on fire, and, as is alleged, by order of the local authorities, or with their connivance, to dispossess Greeks and others of land acquired during the Russian and Austrian occupation of Soulina. A respectable Greek inhabitant assures me that his house and ground, for which only a short time previous to the fire he paid about 280*l*. to the then Pasha, was especially marked out for destruction, in order thus fraudulently, to re-acquire the ground which by existing law could not be held by a Christian, notwithstanding the money payment which had been effected; fortunately through his own exertions, the house escaped the conflagration, and knowing by this dishonest action, the insecurity of his tenure he was compelled to bribe the Cadi or Judge to grant him Turkish title deeds or 'hoget' made out in the name of a Mussulman. As has already been stated many of the Greek and Christian inhabitants acquired their little property in houses and enclosures, during the occupation of the place by the Russians and Austrians, but no sooner did the Turks become masters of the soil than, unless a 'hoget' of ownership could be produced, they were ordered in several instances to pull them down, or to give up a portion or an enclosure appertaining to them, and if a Mussulman desired any particular locality to build upon, and the hut of a Christian stood in the way, means were always at hand to remove the latter either by fire or the hatchet."

In spite of our intention to avoid criticizing the grammar of the Consular Reports, we are obliged to relax our rule in favour of Mr. Dupuis, in consideration of the various lapses to be found in No. 7. "Fortunately through his own exertions, the house escaped the conflagration, and knowing by this dishonest action, the insecurity of his tenure he was compelled," &c.; we will make no comments upon the rather novel system of punctuation adopted throughout this Report, but content ourselves with enquiring which is supposed, according to the sentence thus quoted, to be the dishonest action—that the house escaped conflagration, or that the Greek inhabitant's own exertions saved it?

Reverting to more serious criticism, if the laws of Turkey are as Mr. Dupuis says (and they still are so in most places), what injustice can be found in their being strictly carried out? It is scarcely fair to accuse the local Government of an act of arson upon no more serious evidence than the easily used phrase "*it is alleged.*" The respectable Greek is simply a party to a legal fraud, and by no means the least guilty one. It is by no means improbable that the land possessed by Greeks and others was originally the property of Mussulmans, a supposition which is strengthened by the fact that *some* only of them were evicted; in any case the Turkish authorities acted within the strict letter of Turkish law.

"Permission was requested several years ago of the Central Government at Constantinople by the Greek and Christian subjects to rebuild their church, which had fallen into a state of dilapidation, and the Firman granting their prayer was forwarded last September, urged to do so, perhaps in consequences of disturbance in other parts of Turkey."

What was "urged to do so," was it dilapidation, the firman, or last September?

"I should be tiring your Lordship were I to enumerate the many acts of spoliation committed by the Turkish authorities on the Christians; I cannot, however, omit mentioning, that so late as last summer an order was issued from the Konak to throw down a row of shops belonging to Greeks and other Christians, which they had acquired previous to the arrival of the Turks, abutting on the river, forming the market-place; the Greek Consul remonstrated against so harsh an edict, but, as it was alleged, their removal was necessary to improve the streets; they were all, to the number of thirty, demolished by the hatchet, and up to this day, I am sorry to say, the poor proprietors have not received the' slightest remuneration for their losses."

If Greeks and other Christians, not Rayahs, occupied these houses, the authorities had an undoubted right to evict them, according to Turkish law. If they were Rayahs, what business had the Greek Consul to interfere in their behalf? If they were foreigners, why should the law (whether bad or good in itself) be over-ridden by Hellenic intervention?

"The subordinate Turkish authorities never neglect an opportunity to oppress or annoy poor Christians; a few weeks since the Greek messenger of the Telegraph station in this town was insulted by the officers of the Turkish guard ship, and on his attempting to expostulate with them was thrown into prison, and there beaten by 'cavasses;' he complained to the Mudir, but the officers having denied the charge, no further notice was taken of the matter, and he was consequently removed from his post and sent to Toultcha."

Bearing in mind Lord Lyons' already quoted remark about the complaints made by Christians to foreign agents, it would be more satisfactory to know if Mr. Dupuis has sifted this case thoroughly, or whether "it is alleged" by the Greek messenger alone; and, if "no further notice was taken of the matter," why was he (a pronoun which after some reflection we decide to mean the Greek, not the Mudir) "*consequently*" sent to Toultcha? Is *consequently* a lapsus calami for *subsequently*?

"Instances of oppression and violence were matters of daily occurrence previous to the Ionians being handed over to the Greek authorities, and I have had fewer opportunities since of observing the conduct of Turkish authorities towards Christians; nevertheless, I venture the opinion they are worse treated now that they are no longer under British protection; and if Ionians and other Christians were treated by the Turks as described in those times, and in places where Consuls reside, I submit to your Lordship whether they fare worse or not in the interior of the country, where, perhaps, no consular establishments *are* maintained."

After expressing a considerate fear of tiring Lord Stanley, it is rather cruel of Mr. Dupuis to inflict upon his Lordship the gratuitous mental labour of answering a question in the aid of whose solution nothing but allegations of the vaguest kind are given, and which is moreover expressed in the vaguest of English.

"The Government of Soulina is composed of a Legislative Council or 'Medjlis,' of which the Cadi is the President, with eight members to assist

T

him, four of whom are Christians, and the other four Mussulmans, chosen by the people, but the former dare not differ, much less oppose any resolution or proposition of the Cadi. Knowing this, they often fall asleep in their chairs, and give their decision or concurrence with the usual 'Pekie, Efendi' (Very well, Sir)."

Abstaining from comment on the again questionable grammar, we submit that it is by no means creditable to the people that they choose from amongst themselves four members of the Medjliss who have neither the head nor the heart to do anything but talk in their sleep, and (as must necessarily be supposed) place their seals to legal documents without awaking.

"I beg leave to remark in conclusion to your Lordship, that in justice to the present Mudir of Soulina, his mild character and kindness of disposition have won for him the esteem and respect of all the inhabitants of Soulina, without distinction."

The sentence by which Mr. Dupuis "concludes Lord Stanley" is either rather at variance with his preceding statements, or is consoling as regards the future : if the Governor of Soulina had not been changed between the time of the outrage on the telegraph messenger and the date of the Vice-Consul's despatch, a period of a few weeks, it seems curious that the aggrieved person in question should have departed to Toultcha with a feeling of esteem and respect for the supreme authority of his former residence; if the amiable Mudir had arrived only shortly before Mr. Dupuis wrote his Report, his good qualities must be something beyond the average to have gained so speedy an appreciation, and we may hope that during his reign Soulina will not again be the scene of "acts of cruelty and injustice, oppressions, and hardships."

No. VIII.—CONSUL SKENE. Aleppo.

As this Report contains only matter which strongly confirms our repeated statements that the Christians are not worse treated than the Mussulmans, we will make but one quotation, which shows that Mr. Skene does not thoroughly understand the question of military service, or at least that it has never struck him in its true light, that of a great boon to the Rayahs and a curse to the Turks :—

"The Christians naturally complain, but I do not perceive more reason for complaint on their part than on that of the Mussulmans, excepting as regards the tax in lieu of military service."

No. IX.—CONSUL CALVERT. Monastir.

"Latterly, churches have been built in a more becoming style and with a superior aspect, not, however, without exciting the animosity of Mahomedan fellow-villagers, which on a recent occasion at Lazjetz (three hours from Monastir) finally vented itself in the burning down of the church at that village, after it had been robbed of its valuables twice ; and, at other intervals, the windows and doors had been broken and part of the stone wall inclosure pulled down. The offence failed to be brought home to the perpetrators of this outrage for want of sufficient evidence, the Grand Medjlis of Roumeli having required ocular testimony of the act, and the case was dismissed on the presumption that the fire might have originated through neglect in the church itself on account of the Greek practice of keeping lights burning in their churches. Scarcely a fortnight ago the robbery of a village church near Perlepé has been reported. No other than Mahomedans can have committed the crime, as no Christian would ever dare to commit so gross a sacrilege ; but no one has been brought to justice for it."

The sacking of Roman Catholic chapels is a thing not unknown in England in the year 1868. We must add that unfortunately our acquaintance amongst the Greek and Bulgarian Rayahs includes many who would rob a church almost as readily as steal a horse, and the certainty that the sacrilege will be attributed to their Turkish neighbours is in itself a promise of impunity which may strongly tempt a dishonest person. In the absence of direct evidence, which does not seem to have been forthcoming, it is a little hazardous to saddle the Mussulmans with a crime which has possibly, though perhaps not probably, been committed by Christians.

The greater part of this Report, which is long, interesting, and evidently written with great conscientiousness, contains matter proving that the provincial government in his consulate is quite as defective as the average in Turkey: but no instances of oppression of Christians in particular (unless those which we have already quoted can be considered as such) are given. We quote an opinion of Mr. Calvert's which, as coming from a gentleman who does not appear to be a professed Turcophile, ought to carry some weight with it:—

"I am bound to add that a low standard of rectitude exists among the Christian races, for whilst they are most ardently and superstitiously attached to their Church, the religion they profess seems to have been incapable hitherto of inculcating on them the principles of truth and honesty. Lying and deceit are as habitual to them as eating and drinking."

No. XI.—VICE-CONSUL MALING. Cavalla.

"The use of church bells to which the Christians particularly cling is never allowed where mixed creeds congregate."

How long is it since Roman Catholic churches and Dissenting chapels in England have been permitted a peal of bells?

"The public schools and charitable foundations are without exception closed to the Christian."

These public schools and charitable foundations are supported almost entirely by the Ulema, and the doctrine of the Koran taught in them is of course only adapted for Mussulmans: it would be expecting too much from the Ulema to ask that their revenues should be charged with the support of Christian professors. How long is it since Roman Catholics were admitted at Oxford?

"It is only to honorary posts in the Administrative Councils, and in certain law tribunals that Christians are admitted on the footing of an insignificant and powerless minority."

For this state of things, Mr. Maling himself gives a pretty good reason, as follows:—

"On the one hand every well-to-do intelligent Christian, who can, obtains some foreign protection and thus makes himself ineligible for office. On the other hand, pushed by fear of persecution or by love of trade the Christian is a very migratory being. He may thus acquire wealth and eminence as a settler in another locality, but is only qualified to hold office in the particular district which gave him birth. In this state of the law a numerous class amongst the Christians is shut out from taking any share in public life; and it is worthy of remark that the classes eligible to office, the stay-at-home and less adventurous, are also the least intelligent, worst educated, and most subservient members of the community."

So it is perhaps as well that there are not too many of them entrusted with the administration of the province.

"Before the chief district Court of Criminal Jurisdiction, two Christians were, in 1864, indicted for, and convicted of, the murder of a Mussulman, Christian witnesses in disproof of the charge being rejected, while a near relation of the alleged murdered person sat as a member of the Court. The iniquitous proceedings took their course: a judicial murder was effected in respect of one of the victims, a felon's prison opened on the other, the members of the Court officiate to this day, and the chief administrative officer, who packed the Court and approved the proceedings, was shortly after promoted to a higher post in the Christian province of the Lebanon."

The above paragraph seems very like an anticipation of

certain comments upon the "judicial murders" at Manchester, which appeared in the 'Irishman' and 'Freeman' newspapers: we forget whether they formed a part of the articles upon which these journals were indicted.

"The sectarian principles by which the law's administration is guided further appear in the fact that no conviction for any grave offence has for many years been recorded against a Mussulman, and that in several notorious cases of murder by persons of that creed no proceedings have ever been set on foot."

The first part of this sentence might lead people to form a very favourable idea of Mussulman morality and freedom from crime, were it not for the sweeping condemnation of its close, for which, however, no evidence is adduced.

"The indulgence, however, which, even under prison régime, is shown to the Mussulman, but never to the Christian, marks the practical inequality of the races."

But, since "no conviction for any grave offence has for many years been recorded against a Mussulman," either the system of indulgence finds no scope for its exercise, or Turkish justice is a little more vigilant than Mr. Maling would have us believe, and Turks are imprisoned for *slight* offences.

"Centuries of subjection and estrangement from the profession of arms has (*sic*) not destroyed the Christian's liking and aptitude for that career. On the contrary shows a decided hankering after the 'pride, pomp, and circumstance of glorious war,' and it is instructive to witness on those occasions when the Christian is called out to assist the civil power against brigands with what alacrity he obeys the summons, and how favourably the raw recruit of a few days in his military bearing contrasts with the trained and veteran, but ever unsoldierlike, Turkish trooper."

This testimony is strangely at variance with that given upon the same subject by other Consuls: if the Turkish Government ever enforces military service upon the Christians it is to be hoped that besides looking twice as well, they will fight even half as well, as the "unsoldierlike" Turks. Why does Mr. Maling single out the cavalry soldier (trooper) for contempt? Does he make an exception in favour of regiments of foot?

"Taxation is supported equally by all classes in theory only. Passing over the military capitation tax, the excessive duties levied on pigs, native wines, and spirits, are burdens falling substantially on Christians only and have proved ruinous to native production."

Pigs, wine, and spirits being all articles interdicted by the law of the Koran, which is that of Turkey, a duty upon these productions, even if almost prohibitive, cannot be wondered at: if Christians throughout Turkey abstained a little more from the consumption of wine and spirits, they would soon be able to pay even a quadrupled tax upon pigs.

"The excessively high licensing system on taverns is considered by Christians a grievance peculiar to them; but it is only fair to say that Mussulmans come fairly under its operation, for they are perhaps the greatest consumers. In fact, inordinate drunkenness is fast becoming a decidedly Turkish vice. It spreads to all ranks, renders any intercourse with their public men a very unpleasant duty, and creates a new barrier to the social fusion of the races: for the Christians as a body partake of the characteristic abstemiousness of the Southern races, and disgust and contempt are now added to the other unfavourable feelings with which they regard their oppressors."

We beg most sincerely to congratulate Mr. Maling upon the fact of his residence amongst a population of warlike and sober Eastern Christians: in our provinces the Rayah has not the least hankering after war, glorious or otherwise, and drunkenness is the vice which is most prevalent amongst the Christians, whilst we have *never* seen a Turkish peasant drunk; and a Mussulman who thus disgraces himself is always spoken of by his co-religionists of the Balkan as "a bad man—one who gets tipsy."

No. XII.—VICE-CONSUL BLUNT. Adrianople.

Mr. Blunt's well written and exhaustive Report, after giving a very detailed and interesting account of the exports, produce, taxes, and general prospects of the district of Adrianople, proceeds to touch upon many of the evils caused by the want of a properly organized administration; whilst he has evidently avoided hearsay evidence, as may be seen from the manner in which he takes care to verify events before committing himself to their report, it will be noticed that he does not consider the Christians to be the only, or even the chief, sufferers by governmental mal-administration.

"The Government states the gross amount it requires from each community, leaving to the notables the method of its assessment and the responsibility of its collection. These notables, be they Turks, Christians, or Jews, are, generally speaking, very despotic, and they take care to force the poorer class to pay much more than the richer, or to exact more than the legal amount."

"The Greek Primates in this city levy a great deal more than the legal quota; the surplus falling exclusively on the poorer class. What they do with this surplus is a secret. They pretend that they employ it in support of the schools in this place. If this is true, Adrianople should have a greater number of schools and pupils than the other cities in the Vilayet, which is not the case."

"Shortly after I wrote the above, I learnt that gross defalcations had been detected in the accounts of the community, and that some of the Primates had misemployed large sums of money belonging to the public. Kibrisli Mehmed Pasha was fully determined to bring the offenders to justice, but he was soon after recalled, and his successors have not had the will or the courage to deal with the matter. The fact is, a hue and cry was raised against the local Government by the Greek Primates and their partizans for wishing to revise their accounts; and the Greek Consul, who at the time attributed to himself a large share in the direction of the affairs of the Greek community, was very incensed at the Ottoman authorities for their proceedings against the Primates, and pretended that they grossly violated the rights of the Christians, enjoyed by them, *ab antiquo*, of regulating by themselves the affairs of their community."

"When a village, Christian or Turkish, is very slow in paying the taxes, the Tchorbadjies and Muhtars call in the police to enforce the payment of the amount due, and something more besides. The police generally perform this duty with little lenity, and frequently with unjustifiable severity. This is done at the instigation and with the sanction of the Tchorbadjies or Muhtars.

"Last year, Ali Pehlivan, a Lieutenant or Captain of Police, was placed under arrest, and ultimately in irons, for having ill treated Christian and Mahomedan peasants, and during his investigation it appeared that the Mahometans suffered more from his misdeeds than the Christians."

"The Christians are not more oppressed by taxation than the Turks. Both pay the same taxes; both suffer alike by the unequal assessment of these taxes. If the condition of both elements be fairly measured, it will be found, I think, that the position of the Christians is better than that of the Turks.

"The Christians are not subjected to the military service (in lieu of it they pay the 'askeriyé' tax), while the Turks are. The sufferings constantly inflicted on the latter by the exigencies of this service are inconceivable. I have seen during my journeys in the interior, ripe corn rotting on the ground, and on inquiring the cause, was informed that the owners of it were enrolled in the Rediffs ('militia'). Villages are in the course of time stripped of their Mahomedan inhabitants by the frequent calling out of this militia, and the abandoned fields are quietly occupied by the Christians. The Mahomedans now begin to complain that they only are forced into the military service, and would wish to relieve themselves of some of its burdens by including in it other elements of the population."

"The evidence of Christians is admitted against Mahomedans in criminal and, generally, in commercial cases before these Courts; but it is not in cases chiefly regarding real and intestate property brought before the Mehkemeh, where the only law, 'Sheri-Sheri' (holy law), administered by the judge ignores the evidence of non-Mahomedans in cases in which they are the plaintiffs or defendants: it only admits this evidence in cases in which Mahomedans are not concerned."

"The Christians and Jews are not in the least molested by the Mahomedans in the exercise of their private and public religious observances, nor, I am happy to say, can I furnish any evidence that, since the Crimean war, the conduct of the Ottoman authorities towards the Christians has been marked with the stamp of religious intolerance or persecution. If there is a spirit of intolerance and persecution in the districts of this Vilayet, it will, unfortunately, be found among the different denominations of the Christians who dislike each other with all the virulence of Sectarians."

"Before the Crimean war the education of the Christian inhabitants was generally under the control and patronage of the Greek clergy. This clergy is very ignorant, and it had a great interest in trying to keep the people ignorant. They, therefore, instead of patronizing and encouraging intellectual culture, did all they could to keep it down to the lowest possible level, particularly among the Bulgarians, whose language they banished from the few schools that then existed in the country. But since then, and more especially from the time the Bulgarians, owing to the misconduct of this clergy, have broken their connection with the Greek Patriarchate, the extension of public education has, comparatively speaking, become very general throughout the provinces."

"The Ottoman authorities do nothing to arrest this educational movement; on the contrary, they endeavour to assist it."

The letter of Monsignor Kivillos, from which we give extracts below, is curious only as a specimen of Dragoman's French, and as showing the lenity of the Turkish Government in allowing subscriptions to be collected for the sufferers in the Cretan insurrection, and to be received by a Greek banker, without apparently taking any means to prevent the sums thus bestowed being devoted to the only too probable purpose of buying rifles instead of lint, and gunpowder instead of grain.

"En outre, comme le Gouvernement de Sa Hautesse de notre ville a su d'après les journaux que dans plusieurs endroits des contributions ont été faites pour subvenir aux souffrances des Crétois; de même il y aurait ici des personnes charitables pour ouvrir une contribution spontanée, en faveur de ceux de nos compatriotes qui ont souffert et souffrent des troubles extraordinaires de Candie, il a été jugé convenable que la maison du Banquier Simonatzi recevra les contributions contre des reçus qu'elle délivera."

"Le nombre et le nom des contribuants sera publié dans le journal Turc, 'Monhoir,' pour que le public en prenne connaissance."

We cannot take leave of this Report without calling attention to the clearness of Mr. Blunt's statements, the evident pains taken by him to learn the truth about any matter on which he touches (no easy task in Turkey) and the completeness of his sketch of the economical and political state of his vice-consulate, a sketch which has no rival in the Consular Reports.

No. XV.—CONSUL READE. Scutari.

"Taking therefore into consideration the difficulties in the way of the authorities, created generally by foreign interference and local peculiarities, with the exception of what I have said respecting the system of administration of justice, I cannot find that the Porte has in any way worthy of notice failed in its engagements respecting the treatment of its Christian subjects."

From this passage it will be seen that Mr. Reade recognizes (very justly) foreign interference as preventing the execution by Turkey of the promises contained in the Hatti-Humayoun.

No. XVIII.—ACTING CONSUL-GENERAL ROGERS. Beyrout.

"Christians do not serve in the army; but I doubt whether they would be willing to serve, even if the highest ranks were open to them."

"In mixed councils, Mahometans always take precedence of other sects, both in their seats and their signatures. Mahometanism being the religion of the Government and of the majority of the inhabitants, this fact can hardly be criticised."

"But on the whole, making distinct exception of those cases, and times and places in which circumstances have arisen to cause a general outburst of Mahometan fanaticism, I think that the Christian sects in Syria in their reciprocal jealousy and hatred, are more persecuted by each other than by the Mahometans, and often by Mahometans at the instigation of other Christians."

"The subordinate officers are often fanatical and generally oppressive and exacting, but they are selected from a host of place-hunters who have received little or no education and who are not actuated by right principles."

"I cannot believe that any decree of the Turkish Government can remedy the evil as it exists in Syria. Any further political change must destroy the principles of Mahometanism, and a subject of discontent amongst the larger class of Turkish subjects is raised, which sooner or later will break out in revenge upon the unfortunate recipients of a chimerical boon."

This passage is well worthy of consideration, for it shows that so-called Reforms carried to excess may cause a massacre of Christians in Asia: we have, in another chapter, already stated our fear of a similar catastrophe in European Turkey, arising from the same causes.

"In my humble opinion there can be but one effectual remedy, and this may be hoped for in the increase of liberal, sound, and secular education in the Ottoman dominions."

No. XIX.—CONSUL MOORE. Jerusalem.

Mr. Moore's laconic Report contains one observation which in general might be made everywhere in Turkey:—

"The precise nature of the stipulations referred to in the Address not being stated, I can only reply that here the Greek and other Christian subjects of the Sultan receive practically the same general treatment as their Mahometan fellow-subjects, and that there is vast room for improvement in the treatment of both."

No. XX.—VICE-CONSUL SANDWITH. Larnaca, Cyprus.

"It is to the composition of the Courts of Justice, indeed, that almost all the grievances of which the Christians have to complain may be traced, with the exception of those which they suffer in common with Mussulmans from the incapacity of the Government."

The question of the Medjliss has been so often discussed, and so many excuses, or at least palliatives, for its undeniably defective construction have been given, that it is useless to repeat more than the assertion, that the venality of the Christians themselves is one of the principal causes rendering null the benefits which might arise to the Rayahs from the system of mixed tribunals. The Rayah has also the advantage of being able to bribe higher than his Mussulman opponent. This fact Mr. Sandwith recognizes, as may be seen from the following :—

"But it must not be forgotten that all their members are open to bribery, and the rich Christian suitor is often more than a match for his poor Mussulman adversary."

No. XXI.—CONSUL STUART. Janina.

"The administration of justice is extremely defective in this country... All these Courts are characterized by the deepest corruption and venality. Judgments are sold with but little attempt at concealment, so that in suits between Ottoman subjects, and sometimes, too, when others are concerned, the verdict is commonly in favour of the party which pays best... Judgment is too often suspended for no other reason than to give time for underhand solicitations, and to see which of the litigants will bid highest for the verdict."

This being almost exactly the complaint made by Mr. Sandwith, and indeed, only too justly, by almost every Consul, we need not recapitulate our former comments.

"There are about 220,000 Christians in Epirus, and about 130,000 Mussulmans. The ordinary Government revenue may be stated at 300,000*l.*, of which 240,000*l.* is paid by the Christians, and 60,000*l.* by the Mussulmans. The latter are the chief landowners, but the former have almost the monopoly of the trade, industry, &c., of the country, the duties of which they consequently have to pay. They are moreover charged with the military exemption tax, which figures for about 26,000*l.* Nevertheless, largely as the Christians contribute to the Government revenues, they derive scarcely any benefit from the Government expenditure; while of the Mussulmans several thousand, indeed at present nearly the whole of them, are receiving Government pay."

Mr. Stuart gives a reason for the apparently large disproportion between the amount of taxes paid by Christians and Mussulmans, but there is an easy and just calculation to be made which turns the scales much in favour of the former; allowing that only one-fifth, or 26,000 of the Mussulman population are called upon to serve in the army, and that each man therefrom loses only 10*l.* per annum (which is far understating the case), they pay to Government an indirect tax of 260,000*l.* by their military service, which sum, added to the 60,000*l.*, forms a total of 320,000*l.* paid by 130,000 agricultural Mussulmans as against 240,000*l.* paid by 220,000 Christians engaged in the more lucrative occupations of trade.

It is a little startling to hear that nearly every Mussulman in the Epirus is a Government employé, or at least pensioner, and very much so when we reflect that of course the women and children (or nearly the whole of them) must be included in this long list. Speaking seriously, it is a little too bad to insinuate, that there is unjust favouritism shown to the Mussulman, and a " benefit " conferred upon him, because he receives some sort of pay in return for a burden of military service, past or present, which his Christian fellow-subject, if the privilege of a like bargain were offered to him, would refuse to touch with the tip of his finger.

No. 22.—CONSUL-GENERAL LONGWORTH. Belgrade.

On reading Mr. Longworth's Report we were almost tempted to give it *in extenso*, without further comment from ourselves, as a refutation to all the unfounded charges brought by others against the Turks; as, however, the

Consular Reports probably lie upon few library tables but those of members of either House, it is perhaps better to have given passages from them both *pro* and *con*. Whilst we regret that the space already occupied by this chapter prevents us giving such extensive extracts as we should wish, we feel that there are many passages in Report No. 22 which it would be wrong to omit, and we recommend the careful perusal of the whole to those who are really interested in the condition of the Rayah, and who are open to conviction. Mr. Longworth's reputation for knowledge of Turkey gives a value to his Report, and will not permit even those who most differ from him to regard it as unworthy of notice; as for ourselves we have been encouraged in our relation of what we know to be the truth by the conviction that should this book ever fall into the hands of Mr. Longworth, there will be at least one man who agrees with us in our estimation of the genuine Turkish peasant, and who does not believe that the Rayah is the most deserving or the most unfortunate being on the face of the earth.

"Whatever the distance left between the promises of the Hatti-Humayoum and the Porte's performances, anybody who fairly and soberly takes into account all it has to contend with, must feel far less surprise at its shortcomings than at what has been actually done by it."

"Ten years later the Rayah had begun to take his seat in the Medjlis, but his abject spirit and obsequious dependent habits, quite as much as his want of experience in affairs, made him unfit for such functions; he usually sat crouching in a corner and gave a silent vote on all occasions. As years went by his position improved; what the Christians wanted in rank and dignity they made up for by wealth and intelligence. They now claim equal representation, and, in some places, even a majority of votes in the Mixed Assemblies.

"In those of Rustchuk and Widdin, when I visited those places in 1865, I was surprised to see the independent Burgesses (Tchorbadjees) in European costume, fairly educated and freely discussing the interests of the community with the Pasha and other administrative and legal authorities. Such changes it may be supposed could not have been effected in the Rayah without a corresponding transformation of the Turk, the contrast of whose present demeanour to the Christian with that which I once remember it to have been is indeed remarkable; the only parallel I can think of, for that which it used to be, is in conduct perhaps equally unjust, unreasonable, and arrogant, which has been recently exhibited by Orthodox and Catholic Europeans to the Turks.

"The rapid transformation I have alluded to, and about which I feel little doubt, would not be fairly and satisfactorily explained were we not also to take into account the action and influence of the Consular Body. I have naturally no wish to detract from the merits of these gentlemen, but there are circumstances which must unavoidably contribute to mould their opinions and colour their reports. They have, in the first place, though aliens, been constituted into tribunes of the native Christians, indirectly, if not directly, standing between them and their Government. How is it possible that, invested with this character, they should not favour their clients, extenuate their misdeeds, or exaggerate those of their real or imagined oppressors? And who, it may be asked, are almost invariably their informers, prompters, and agents? Are they Turks or Christians? Is it fair to put any man in a position which he is so liable and under such strong temptation to abuse? For the Corps includes men of all ages, characters, and nations; from the circumspect and self-controlled veteran to the rash subaltern, self-sufficient and rarely reflecting how little things are advanced, if he have succeeded in changing, now and then, measures only, and not men, who, whether Christians or Mussulmans, are not easily changed, and with a change of functionaries even seldom improved. As a general rule, and as regards themselves, the tendency of this Consular interference is clear. We see them all at first flushed with, but soon forgetting, past achievements, all intent on future triumphs, all bearing down on the Turk with the whole of Christendom at high pressure behind them. It would be surprising indeed if the progress were not precipitate, or even if madness did not eventually fire the wheels."

"Paradoxical as it may appear, I am more than ever convinced that the too eager pursuit of justice may involve much injustice, as it does now in this country to both governed and governing classes of the Turks, but more particularly to the former, who, as all who know anything of them must likewise know, are by far the most upright and truthful of the two. And even the governing class, I should say, however depraved by the traditions of Byzantine venality and intrigue, are, from their innate respect for order and authority, better qualified to bear sway, and make even misrule more tolerable, than the Christians."

"The treatment of the Christians in Turkey with reference to the pledges of the Hatti-Humayoum opens an interminable field of inquiry; even as the document itself confers on those invested with this inquisitorial power the unlimited right of interference. At least this is the construction put upon it; and the most complete conquest ever made of a nation, that which entitles the conqueror to say 'woe to the vanquished' has never conferred a right more sweeping, vexatious, and intolerable than this. And yet Turkey I need scarcely say, was not among the vanquished. And if, as we continually hear, we and others fought her battles for her, we did so not more, it may be answered, than she ours for us."

"The Greeks, on the other hand, to whom I see the address of the House of Commons especially alludes, are a highly sensitive race, in whose minds this secular humiliation has been so deeply branded that they can far less easily afford to forget and forgive, even if a keen sense of self-interest and lust of dominion, acting as provocatives to their thirst of vengeance, would allow them. Their purpose is not to kill the Turk merely, but plunder him also if they can; there is not only the glory, but the profit of the achievement."

"The only tax borne exclusively by the Christians is that of commutation for military service, 'Bedel Askerich,' of which much has been said as harsh and invidious, confounding it with the old capitation impost, or 'Kharatch.'

"Between this, however, and military service, the free choice was given them, and as I well remember, they unanimously preferred paying the tax, and no wonder when we come to know (what might, perhaps, have forestalled much indignant criticism had it been previously ascertained), that it amounted to something less than the annual contribution of 4s. for each male adult.

"Exemption from service would, but for a sense of duty, be gladly purchased at this price, told ten times over, by the Turks; their population is being gradually exhausted by the military ballot."

"There is another sort of benevolence which displays itself in the desire of relieving them by arming to the teeth the Christians, whether they will or not; but these kind intentions are fully appreciated, and on that account are not likely to meet with much favour from the Porte.

"Other taxes, by their application to articles consumed more generally, if not entirely, by Christians, have been thought unfair to them as a body.

The pig tax, for instance, would undoubtedly be contributed to by them alone, and having been at first imposed on sucking pigs, even caused, with a view to escape it, wholesale slaughter and a great outcry in the Christian provinces. The Porte, however, subsequently fixed the liability of the pig at a reasonable age; but though it reduced the tax, it would not wholly take it off, nor do I think it could be fairly expected to do so. Sheep are taxed as well as pigs, and the consumers of pork cannot be expected to consume mutton to the same extent as those who eat no other description of animal food, to say nothing of the sacrificial purposes to which it is periodically applied by Mussulmans.

"Similar objections have been raised with reference to spirits and wine; but raki, or wine either, as I have always understood, and, indeed, can bear witness, is not entirely rejected by the Turks, who, moreover, if the inquiry be pursued exhaustively, may, by way of compensation and from their peculiar habits, be found to be larger consumers of certain taxed articles than others; if, for example, the Christians make a less stinted use of wine, the Mussulman indulges certainly more unsparingly in soap."

"On the subject, in like manner, of the claims, as allowed by the Hatti-Humayoum, of Christians to a fair participation in the employments, offices, and dignities offered by the service of the State, I have nothing in the shape of statistical information to impart. But I have every reason to believe that careers of a description for which they discover a peculiar aptitude—those, for instance, connected with the Diplomatic and Consular services, or the Medical Service of the Government, or the Finance Department, or important political functions expressly created for them in the vilayets, where they are attached to the Governor-General and transact business with the Foreign Consular Agents—I have reason to believe, I repeat, that all such careers have been liberally opened to them."

"If, in the Executive Department of the State, the Christians have hitherto been admitted but to few of the highest offices of trust and dignity, and that, too, where the population is exclusively Christian, the Porte says, and I believe truly says, that, were such absolute power confided to them, no Mussulman, as a general rule, would feel secure as to either life or property. I have myself been told by Greeks in the employment of the Porte that where the interests of the Hellenic cause are at stake, they would not hesitate a moment at promoting them to the Porte's detriment; and yet these men have bitterly complained that they were not advanced with sufficient rapidity."

"The consequence has been that, while the Christians have thriven (and their prosperity is proved by their personal appearance and their having possessed themselves of the best houses and most eligible sites in the great towns I have of late years re-visited, such as Varna, Tournova, Rustchuk, and Kustendje) the Turks seem to be gradually shrinking from public view into the obscure and unfrequented suburbs. Still, their demeanour is that of stoical endurance; poorly clad, badly housed, and indifferently fed; if they still look the masters it is merely because neither they nor the Christians can help themselves in the matter. Still it must be with a gloomy and bitter feeling that they contrast their present with their past condition; that they ask themselves or others what further hardship and humiliation fate can have in store for them. They hear no doubt what all the world is constantly repeating, that they are sick and dying out of the land, to which, indeed, they never had a just title, being merely encamped upon it. They know better than that, however; they know the price their forefathers paid for it, and that their title deeds are just as good as those of the bravest people on the face of the earth. What is worse, if driven to it, they would willingly pay the same price over again. Why, therefore, should they not once more have recourse to the means which their Maker has peculiarly gifted them with—bold hearts and strong hands. Why not revert to—'The good old plan, that those shall take who have the power, and those shall keep who can.' Would not this be better than the lingering death to which the world so confidently dooms them, or to a life even spent in unavailing efforts to unlearn the most cherished traditions of the past. Why, then, are they prevented from doing this? Simply because, as I in my conscience believe, they are not only a brave but a docile and religious people; and they have been taught to think that the honour and good faith of their Sovereign, their Padishah, is engaged to the Governments of Europe, and cost them what it may, as assuredly it has cost them much, his word must be kept to them."

No. 23.—CONSUL SANDISON. Brussa.

"Her Majesty's Government has taken a constant interest in the result on the condition of the Christian populations in the provinces, and in the general working of the edict. I am not aware that any other power has evinced the same solicitude on that head. And I regret to state that Russian protected subjects here, with the sanction of their authorities, have been enabled to profit by judicial decisions, and maintain claims of the same sort, in manifest contravention of the text and spirit of the Hatti-Sheriff, but which in one case have not been successful."

No. 24.—CONSUL PALGRAVE. Trebizond.

"In this tribunal, sufficiently impartial from its very organization, no legal difference is made between Turk and Christian, and the witness of either is equally admitted in every case.

"Indeed, whatever occasional injustices may here occur weigh, for the most, heavier on a Turk than on a Christian, because the former has, in matter of fact, no ulterior appeal, while the latter habitually interposes the authority of some Consulate, especially the Greek or the Russian.

"The free exercise of religion.—In this respect also the Christian subjects of the Sultan have no cause for complaint. A Firman is, indeed, required for the erection of a new church, but so it is also for that of a new mosque; and it is granted, perhaps, with too much facility in either case. Bells are put up and rung, crosses and pictures carried about, and ecclesiastical dresses worn everywhere and openly.

"The general bearing of Mahometans towards Christians in these parts is in a word one of absolute and unequivocal toleration.

"The only approach to a grievance, and that, too, of a strictly local character, within the last ten years, has been that of the 'Kroomleyahs,' or the inhabitants of Kroom, a village about half-way between Trebizond and Erzeroom, somewhat eastward. Here a considerable population of 2000 hearths, or 10,000 souls in all, and it would appear, of Byzantine origin, had for a long time past been Mahometans in public, and Christians in private.

"During the extension of Russian influence in these parts, which followed hard on the Crimean war, these families declared themselves altogether Christian, and many of them took besides a sort of Russian naturalization. This done, they declined to furnish any longer the customary military contingent because they were Christians, or to pay the compensatory 'Indadeeyah,' because they had been Mahometans, and for better security each man signed himself in the village registers by a double name, one of Christian signification, one Mahometan.

"The Government of Constantinople decided, with the agreement, I understand, of the European representatives then residing, that these Kroomleyahs should continue to furnish the military contingent as before, but should be in return exempt from the Indadeeyah. The reasons of this decision are obvious, and perfectly just. But the arrangement did not suit the Kroomleyahs, who, like most of their kind in the East, were not fighting men; and they attempted again and again to evade it. Considerable irregularities were the result; and sometimes, in virtue of their double names on the register, the Kroomleyahs had not only to furnish the military contingent, but to pay the Indadeeyah also. This was unfair; the local Governor or 'Mudir' of Kroom is said to have pocketed the money. Recently the matter was carried before the Pasha of Trebizond himself, and the vexation was put an end to. But the Kroomleyahs, not content with this, now demand exemption from military service, offering pecuniary compensation."

The latter part of the history of the Kroomleyahs is amusing as shewing how people may be a little too clever; it was a rather sharp thing of the Mudir to take advantage of the double registration, but the Kroomleyahs seem to have been rather sharp customers, and it was only diamond cut diamond.

"It is precisely in these same quarters (Trebizond and its environs), and among the Greek and Armenian populations, that foreign influence and intrigue are most real and active, rendering the Christians hereabouts habitually restless, and exciting the suspicions of the Mahometans. And should at any time some general manifestation of Turkish ill-will or outbreak (though of that there is at present no sign) occur, such influence and intrigue, and no other, will be the real cause.

"The complaints of the Christians, here at least, and especially of the Greeks, are unjust. They do not aim at equality, which they have got already, but at mastery."

CHAPTER XIX.

THE CAPITULATIONS.

Prejudice of foreign residents — Origin of the Capitulations — Privilege of a Greek subject — Codes of law innumerable — Justice defeated — Try Turkish tribunals.

ASK any foreigner resident in Turkey what he thinks of the Capitulations, and you will hear a sermon upon the terrible maladministration or entire absence of justice amongst the Turks and the impossibility of foreigners remaining in the country if once their palladium, consular jurisdiction, were removed or infringed upon. "As for me," he will tell you, "the day that the Zaptiehs of the infidels have the power to lay a finger upon me I shall quit Turkey, never to return"—which of course would be an immense loss to the Ottoman Empire.

This infatuation in favour of the Capitulations is one of the weak points of the foreign colonies established in Turkey, and, indeed, of all Europeans, who fancy themselves so far superior to the Turks in all points, that it would be an insult and a degradation for one of their number to be judged by a Mussulman tribunal.

Besides, the abolition of the Capitulations would be naturally displeasing to the Consuls, who would thereby not only lose a good deal of their prestige and influence, but also various perquisites and fees to which they attach a good deal of importance.*

If we view the Capitulations and their effects by another light than that which filters through the ill-glazed windows of an Eastern Consulate, an analysis based upon common sense, and not upon national prejudices, will shew the pernicious influence which they exercise over the relations between Turkey and other nations, and even upon the welfare of foreigners themselves.

Their origin is comparatively ancient; when Mahomet II. conquered Constantinople he granted an "Aman" or Capitulation to the Greeks and Genoese who inhabited his future capital, in order to induce the foreign merchants to remain in it. Soliman I. granted a Capitulation to the subjects of his ally François I., and in succeeding reigns the other great Powers obtained similar rights of independent jurisdiction over those of their subjects residing in Turkey.

In the times when these were accorded there was a logical reason for their existence, since the only laws in force in Turkey were those derived from the Koran and its appendices; for this reason, there being no civil tribunals in existence, the Christian Rayahs were permitted to settle their differences and to judge causes amongst themselves; but in our days the laws of the Prophet are no longer the only ones in Turkey, an entire code has been promulgated, and though we may admit that this code is in some points defective, and its administration not all that might be desired, yet such justice as is to be obtained in a consular court is

---

* British Consuls may be excepted from this charge, their fees having been in most instances commuted.

infinitely more faulty and more feeble in its action than that of the worst of the Turkish tribunals.

One question is, whether or no all the nations to whom Capitulations have been granted have themselves good laws and a good method of administering justice.

If the Capitulations were merely an insult to Turkey, whom they virtually, but most falsely, accuse of being a barbarous country in which justice is unknown, or if they were granted only to civilized States possessing laws compatible with justice and a sound morality, the evil would be less.

That Western Europe should enjoy such privileges is tolerable, but when Modern Greece obtains the right of judging her subjects by such laws as are in force at Athens the Capitulations become a premium to dishonesty, and a negation of all justice.

Let us suppose that his Imperial Majesty the Sultan thought fit to grant Capitulations to the Emperor of Timbuctoo or the King of Dahomey, and that the jurisdiction of these cannibal potentates thereby acquired the force of law in Turkey, what would happen? If a subject or a *protégé* of either of these Powers indulged his taste for human flesh, if Sambo or Chimbo made an African stew of a Rayah Papas, or a fat Cadi, the Turkish Government would be as powerless against them as it is against a Hellene subject. Even if the same gentlemen carried their gastronomical experiments so far as to lunch off slices of English or French missionary, all that the Consuls of the two greatest Powers in the world could do would be to commence a suit against Sambo or Chimbo in the respective Consulates of the anthropophagi; and as the laws of Timbuctoo and the Gaboon permit cannibalism, just as those of Modern Greece tolerate equivocal speculation, Sambo or Chimbo—in spite of the fact that the laws would probably be more strictly interpreted in the black Consulate than in the white—could no more be punished for the homicide committed than Aristides could be made to give up the box which he appropriated by a fraud, or Mr. M. to give up the money due to Messrs K. Brothers.

Sambo and Chimbo are fictitious; but Aristides, and Mr. M., and the Hellenes, and the manner in which we have described the administration of "justice" in Hellene tribunals, are all sad realities.*

We have already given examples of Greek commercial morality and the manner in which it is fostered by the action of the Capitulations; such instances could be multiplied almost *ad infinitum*, but we will select only one more from the number. A Mr. R., one of the most honest Hellenes in the country, makes a contract with the Varna and Rustchuk Railway Company for 15,000 sleepers; † like all the speculators of this country, he has no capital (or at least owns to none) with which to carry out the undertaking, and on the strength of his fair reputation, succeeds in getting paid in advance by the English Company; shortly afterwards he announces that 6000 sleepers are procured, and agents of the Company are sent to examine them; they arrive, and find a heap of charred and smoking wood. Strong suspicions of incendiarism are entertained, and doubts

---

* See the Chapter on Oriental Commerce; and Appendix L.

† In this case we are unable to guarantee the exactitude of the figures, although we can vouch for the accuracy of the main facts.

raised whether the 6000 sleepers ever existed, but the heap of wood is too thoroughly destroyed to allow any decision as to its original constituent parts; the Greek Consulate is referred to, but it is found advisable not to proceed in the matter, and the Company has to put up with the loss of the sum advanced.

The Capitulations granted to Greece not only ruin Turkey, by allowing 200 per cent. to be gained by Hellene merchants upon the exports, and a still greater proportion upon the taxes of the country, but give them a species of monopoly of Eastern commerce, based upon the system of administration of justice by the Greek courts and the impossibility of other nations altering their code in order to fight the Greeks with their own weapons.

Reading the Greek code, you would naturally think that it is worth twenty such as that of the Turks, but you have yet to learn the laxity of interpretation of which it is capable. A Greek cheats you, you apply to his Consulate, which declines to judge the affair, and refers you to Athens, where the case is settled on the broad and convenient principle that a Greek is never in the wrong as regards a foreigner, and you lose your suit; you appeal, and the decision is confirmed, or, if the superior court is intimidated by the remonstrances of your minister or *chargé d'affaires*, the tribunal adjourns your cause—to the Greek Kalends. Hence it follows that no conscientious lawyer will advise you to prosecute for fraud, or even for attempted assassination, any individual who claims Hellenic nationality or protection.

It would seem easy to avoid these difficulties by transacting business only with Turkish subjects or your own countrymen, but besides the impossibility of entirely keeping clear of the ubiquitous Hellene trader there is another stumbling-block, which the case of Mr. M., already alluded to under its commercial aspect, clearly exemplifies; any Russian, French, Austrian, or other subject can change his passport and become a Hellene with the same facility as did Mr. M. The Rayahs have their protectorate, and they, as well as foreigners, manage to change their nationality oftener than their shirts, and with at least equal ease.

When a French or English subject is forced to abandon any attempt at obtaining justice against a Greek, it may be imagined how little chance the Turkish subject will have in a Hellene court of law!

There is a severe quarantine against the plague, and Turkey is obliged to conform to sanitary laws; yet she is prevented from putting in force the quarantine of severe laws against the moral contagion daily imported from Greece to her shores.

It is impossible for a legitimate commerce to exist, so long as the Capitulations prevent justice being done in any case where the defendant belongs to that nationality whose subjects can do no wrong, and the administration of justice is rendered impossible by the facility with which false witness is procured and admitted in court.

Even admitting that all the nationalities which exercise the right of independent jurisdiction possess equitable laws administered by just and upright judges, how is it possible to obtain justice or to engage in business without having studied the codes of a dozen different people? Where can we find a Mezzofanti lawyer who has at his fingers' end the codes of all nations, from the hundred volumes of the Russian

Zakons to that of San Marino? This alone is a strong argument against the Capitulations, but when we recollect that it is owing to them that fraud is the basis of Oriental commerce, that they are but a "legalization" of dishonesty, that they permit the open use of false weights and measures, and that by their extension to a petty nation whose only strength lies in its absence of conscience they have rendered the trade of Turkey a Greek monopoly—it is impossible not to wonder at their existence being tolerated.

Even the action of the consular courts of the great Powers is tardy and occasionally unjust, and the well-grounded complaint is made that, whilst a foreigner is sure of obtaining justice against a Turkish subject, the Turkish subject is always in the wrong when he ventures to go to consular law with a foreigner.

The following is one of the many methods in which the Capitulations are made to obstruct the path of justice. Three years ago the Pasha of Varna wished to verify the weights and measures of the town, and as most of the traders are foreign subjects or *protégés*, he applied to the different Consuls for their consent; with one single exception (that of the British Consul) they all refused to permit such an interference with commercial privileges, and the Pasha was in consequence obliged to abandon the project entirely, as to compel the Turkish subjects to sell by the proper standard, whilst authorizing or at least ignoring the frauds practised by foreigners, would have been simply to ruin the former and still further enrich the latter.

As regards public order the Capitulations are as hurtful to the country as they are in point of their encouragement of dishonesty; we have seen a Consul thrashing the police and exacting excuses from the authorities, profiting by the position in which the Capitulations place him to break through the laws of the country with impunity;* let us take another case.

A certain Mr. B. enlisted in one of the (Christian) Cossack regiments of the Sultan, but finding military life not much to his taste, deserted, and escaped to Greece; there he married an old woman with a little money, but the discipline of matrimony proved as unpleasant as that of the Turkish army, and he ran away again, returning to Turkey, a country which, owing to foreign laws, &c., is the foster-mother of parasitism; here he contrived to live for some time, though without apparent means, but at last, meeting with some old comrades of the Cossacks, he was arrested as a deserter. His Polish nationality procured him the privilege of remaining a prisoner on parole, but this he broke, and took refuge in the Greek Consulate, which sheltered him from pursuit until means were found to ship him back to Greece.

If the Capitulations did nothing worse than encourage desertion, Turkey would not have much to complain of, for the Christian soldiers of the Sultan are few in number, nor would their loss be a serious one; but they promote the political disorders and discontent with which Europe reproaches the Ottoman Government, and they prepare the way for insurrection and revolt. A foreign Consul in Turkey who furnishes arms to the rebels at Crete, or the brigands of Thessaly, is inviolable and unapproachable by Turkish law; would a Consul (even an American Consul) who was con-

---

* See the Chapter on British Consuls and Consular Reports.

victed of giving or selling revolvers to Fenians in Ireland be allowed to go unpunished? America demands payment from England for the depredations committed by the Alabama; dare Turkey send a battalion to Greece? What foreign vessel of war would venture to do in Irish waters half what Russian ships did on the coast and even in the harbours of Crete?

An Englishman who should join the Bourbonist reaction in Southern Italy and fall into the hands of the Italian authorities, would, notwithstanding his quality of *civis Romanus*, be beyond the reach of official protection from England; in Turkey Russian agents openly preach revolt and its accompaniments of murder and pillage; the Government is well aware of this fact, but owing to the Capitulations, dare not arrest nor even impede them.

Two Servians or Wallachians (it matters little which), agents of the Revolutionary Committee of Bucharest, come to Rustchuk in an Austrian steamer; Mithat Pasha determines to arrest them, and obtains from the Austrian Consul the necessary permission for the police to board the steamer; the two persons in question resist, wound some of the passengers, and are finally shot down by the Zaptiehs, whereupon there is an outcry raised against Mithat Pasha and Turkey, and the Consul (who in behalf of justice relaxed the rigour of the Capitulations) is removed from his post.

As Turkey has granted Capitulations to Greece, why does she not accord them to Servia and Wallachia?

Europe is not yet sufficiently logical to abolish this great source of evil to Turkey, but at least she might consent to the adoption, instead of the dozen now existing, of one general and rational code of laws, such as could be easily understood by the Turks; for whatever right we may have to think and call Turkey a barbarous country, we certainly are not justified in forbidding it ever to enjoy internal peace or impartial justice. Strangely enough, those who are loudest in their vituperation of Turkish jurisdiction and administration of justice, and who impute as a crime the rejection of Rayah false witness in a Mussulman tribunal, are the very persons who protect with all their power the Capitulations, that is, the negation of all justice.

But even in this plan a local difficulty arises, in the choice of judges and juries; for although the change from a multitude of codes to a single one would be an undoubted benefit, it is to be feared that if the jury were chosen from the divers nationalities which abound in the seaport towns of Turkey, such an equivocal constitution would render justice but little less Hellenic than it is at present.

Supposing the Capitulations to be given up, the application of a general and international code by the Turkish judges becomes simple, and in the case where a foreigner considers himself wronged by an unjust sentence, he appeals to Constantinople, his Embassy takes up the matter, the cause is judged over again by public opinion, and if the Cadi is found to be in the wrong he is in his turn judged by the Turkish Government.

In the days when the Seven Isles were under British protection, an English judge at Constantinople, Sir E. H., dismissed ten Ionian witnesses out of eleven in one cause, telling them that they were all perjuring themselves; even amongst the English Levantines it would be hard to find a jury who would convict a prisoner of forgery or fraud, although on the strongest evidence; and from this fact it may be imagined what sort of justice would be administered by a jury composed for the most part of genuine Hellenes.

The only way to establish justice in the East, amongst both foreigners and natives, is to call in the aid of the justice-loving Mussulman element, and to strengthen its hands by the abolition of the Capitulations.

CHAPTER XX.

THE POLICY OF FOREIGN POWERS IN TURKEY, AND ITS EFFECTS.

Russian agents — Russian ecclesiastical intrigue — Mysteries of French policy — No-policy of England — Religious equality — Attacks on the Ulema — Save me from my friends — Colonel Bobrikoff's scientific mission — A thankless task — French civilization — French intervention — The day of retribution — Educate the Rayah — Considerations of expediency — England's true policy.

IF you have ever spent a day in a Bulgarian house when some Saint's Day or other Feast was celebrated—and according to the Greek calendar the chances are about ten thousand to one that any day you may choose will be a Feast or a Fast—you can hardly help having remarked amongst the assembled guests an individual whose costume is more that of the town than of the forest, who makes more signs of the cross than even the Bulgarians themselves, and whose dialect smacks strongly of that Slavonic in which are written the canons of the orthodox and imperial religion.*

He by no means spares the wine, crosses himself twice before and twice after each draught, boasting continually that he is "an orthodox Christian of the only orthodox and imperial Church," and when his potations have loosened his tongue, he begins to sing the praises of Russia, and to dis-

---

* In Russia the State religion is qualified as " orthodox *and imperial*," to distinguish it from the Greek at Constantinople, which is merely "orthodox."

member Turkey with the same facility with which he tears in pieces the over-boiled fowl he is eating.

This gentleman is the unaccredited Russian agent, the supplement to the still more influential Papas, and his mission is to warn the peasants that the time for raising the fiery cross of open insurrection is more or less near, and to keep them firm in the good resolutions implanted by their clergy.

In Turkey these emissaries have no need to conceal themselves, or to bridle their tongues with even the gentlest of snaffles, for there is no fear of their being meddled with by the authorities or denounced by the peasants.

The latter possibility causes them no anxiety, the influence of the friends of the Eastern Christians being so strong and so widely spread that the Rayah has learned to preserve nothing but an outward semblance of fear and respect as far as his Mussulman rulers are concerned, whilst he considers every one that is not an Eastern Christian as necessarily his enemy, and those of his own creed as his natural friends, so that even if denunciation of brigandage enters (which it by no means does) into the morals and habits of the country, any robber who entered a Rayah cottage and made the orthodox number of signs of the cross would be safe from betrayal and from pursuit.

Thanks to the action of that foreign policy of which we are about to treat, Christianity in the East is no longer merely a religion, it has degenerated into a secret society not less dangerous, and but little more scrupulous, than Fenianism.

The Christians of Turkey have this advantage over the Fenians that they are *openly* protected by foreign powers, and yet the aspirations of the Irish are certainly more legitimate than those of the Rayah, who has no history and therefore no fatherland. Englishmen as we are, we believe that Ireland, if separated from the British empire, would show something better than the abortions produced by those States which the coercive force of a "disinterested friendship" has severed from Turkey. The Servians were by far the best of the Rayahs; and yet Servia has not done much for the cause of civilization, or indeed for any cause but that of insurrection and Russia. We admire ambition in a giant, but we laugh at it in a dwarf; yet it is the ambition of the dwarf which has ruined certain little States which owe their existence to the tolerance or docility of Turkey, and which indulge in dreams of future greatness whilst they had much better be occupied with the organization of their country and their finances; it is this ambition which has upset the many weak brains which imagine themselves to be the leaders and originators of a patriotic movement, because more wily conspirators make use of them as tools.

The Russians have one weak point in common with the Chinese, that of being a little too cunning; their brain is Slavonic, that is, more fitted to imagine than to calculate, and they have in many instances injured themselves whilst fancying that they were overreaching their neighbours; of their many failures occasioned by this defect perhaps the most absurd, as it is the latest, is the "Bulgarian ecclesiastical schism."

The true Bulgarian—the peasant, not the Bulgarian in fancy dress as he is imagined in Europe—is able, though a poor arithmetician, to count up on his fingers that the Papas and the Greek clergy cost him about double what he pays to the Ottoman Government, so that when he was offered a chance of getting rid of his real oppressor by the simple method of signing (with his mark of course) a petition, and not by risking his person amongst rifle-bullets, he was only too glad to avail himself of the opportunity.

This petition was the first shot fired in the war between the Bulgarians and the Greek Patriarch of Constantinople, and the origin of this movement, like that of many others, can easily be traced to the influence of Russia, who, however, probably wished and expected a very different result from that which has taken place, and is now trying to undo all that she has done by effecting a reconciliation between the Bulgarians and the Phanar,* which is the more difficult to bring about as her agents have preached but too truly and too well against the Greek hierarchy and in favour of a religious autonomy. The logic of the peasant, whose conclusions are drawn in pounds, shillings, and pence, is too much opposed to this reconciliation for the unaccredited agents to have an easy task before them.

We will endeavour to explain the motives of Russia in trying thus to counteract a scheme which she had herself suggested: she had hoped that when the schism between the Greek Church and the Bulgarians was complete, the Turkish Government with its ordinary good nature would grant to their Christian subjects a Bulgarian, that is, an orthodox *and imperial* patriarchate. But in this expectation she was deceived, as the Porte replied that the three existing patri-

---

* The seat of the Greek patriarch; the Phanar, outside the walls of Constantinople, was the first place granted by the Sultans as an ecclesiastical residence to the patriarchs of the orthodox Church.

archs (Roman Catholic, Armenian, and Greek) were surely enough, and that the Bulgarians had perfect liberty to choose any one of the trio as their spiritual head; an answer which may probably have given rise to a report at one time circulated of an union between the Bulgarians and the Church of Rome. It is said that the Greek patriarch has offered as a *mezzo termine* to erect the Vilayet of the Danube (Bulgaria proper) into an Archiepiscopal See, dependent upon the Phanar, but of which the archbishop shall be a Bulgarian. This, however, is not what the people want, their great wish being to escape from the licensed pillage of the Greek clergy, and to avoid the imposts which the maintenance of the Greek patriarch and hierarchy annually imposes upon them.

We have thus sketched in a few lines the true history of the Bulgarian schism, one of the intrigues from which Russia hoped much and reaped nothing; but in spite of its failure she will still continue to use for her own purposes the Fenianism of Eastern Christianity—one of the most powerful levers of agitation in Turkey, since its action is but little seen outside this country, or, if seen, is attributed to the purest and most laudable motives.

Russian policy is at least comprehensible, for it has a reason for its existence, a definite end to be attained, and a coherent action; but who can understand the policy of France in Turkey? Why does she interfere in the affairs of the Sublime Porte in such a manner as always to force the Turkish Government into "Reforms" which are not only unreasonable, but dangerous to the very existence of the Ottoman empire as well as opposed to the true interests of the Rayahs?

It may be replied, that she is desirous of forming a party

amongst the Christians, but with what object? Can it be that of obtaining a certain influence over the future cabinet of "Byzantium, the capital of a Christian empire?" We can hardly believe the Tuileries to be so foolish as to build expectations upon such unstable foundations as the gratitude of the Rayah; and it seems possible to explain the action of French policy only by supposing a complete ignorance of the state of Turkey and the true character of its populations—an ignorance which must embrace the diplomatic and consular agents abroad as well as the Foreign Office at Paris.

But this uncomplimentary hypothesis does not satisfactorily account for a policy which, whilst meddling with everything, is always changing and vacillating, constant only in its deleterious effects upon the state of Turkey, political, economical, and financial: its mainspring is perhaps to be found in an ambition, but an ambition which is as yet but vaguely defined, for how otherwise can we attribute any motive to the action of France in favour of Servia and the Moldo-Wallachian Provinces; how explain the unceasing stream of Frenchmen, for the most part incapable, who are sent (not exactly officially, it is true, but with an understanding that they will be well received) from Paris to Stamboul to fill all sorts of posts and to graft the wall-fruit of French civilization upon the Turkish crab-apple? What can this motive be, and will it ever be revealed to us by the 'Livre Jaune'? We will presently describe the effects of this policy as pursued by France, and our readers will judge whether it has in any way aided the progress of Turkey or of Europe in the path of civilization.

Upon English policy in Turkey it is impossible to enlarge,

as England has *none*; and since her ambassadors at Constantinople have taken to being afraid of shadows—their own or any one else's—the influence formerly possessed by England is now hardly even a tradition. Whilst new Russian ambassadors may be found ready to put on the "Palctôt de Menchikoff," it seems as if there would be no inheritor of the mantle of Lord Stratford de Redcliffe. Lord Stratford, or a man of his stamp, would have prevented such an insurrection as that of Crete, or if he failed in preventing it, would have stopped it: a couple of gunboats would have blockaded the ports of Greece, and every Russian vessel of war would have been well watched by English ships; an Eden would not have been changed into a desert, and a whole people would not have become mendicants. Such a policy might have cost a couple of firmly-worded notes to Prince Gortchakoff, and perhaps even a British garrison at the Piræus, but it would have saved us the expenses of the second Eastern war.

Russia sows agitation and disorder in the country districts, but at present her harvest is reaped in the capital, and as it is there that France, leaving the provinces to the other speculator upon Ottoman weakness, casts her seed and cuts her grain, we will conduct our readers to Stamboul or rather to Péra, to estimate the profit made by each of the agriculturists.

The policy of France, though professedly friendly, is as we have said perhaps even more hurtful to Turkey than the hostile, almost avowedly hostile, action of Russia.

Article IX. of the Treaty of Paris begins by stipulating for liberty of conscience (a liberty which existed in Turkey long before its benefits were extended to certain countries of

Europe, *e. g.*,. Ireland, Scotland, France, &c., and which even now does not flourish everywhere (witness Poland) very vigorously), and then notifies the intention of the Sultan to ameliorate the condition of his subjects " without distinction of religion or of race."

In commenting upon this Article, Russia might have said, with her habitual sophistry, that this amelioration could be carried out only by the cession of the European provinces of Turkey to her, when both Mussulman and Christian would gain by coming under the kindly sceptre of the Czar: the Treaty of Paris fortunately guaranteed the territorial integrity of the Ottoman empire, and therefore France is obliged to differ from Russia in such an interpretation of Article IX. The way in which it is understood by her is however just as prejudicial to Turkey: for since it is acknowledged by all those who know Turkey thoroughly, that if there are subjects of the Sultan who are oppressed, they are the Mussulmans (as may be seen from the chapter upon the Military Service of the Turk), why does France drive the Porte to oppress them still further, and why does she exact reforms which must have the effect of some day causing a revolution of Mussulmans, which will not only be excusable, but necessitated, by the virtual outlawry of the Turk?

It is possible to be the friend of the Eastern Christian, but it is scarcely fair to carry this friendship to the extent of wishing to ruin an entire nation of Mussulmans, especially when the Christian's friend is a party to the Treaty of Paris, and is not Russia, but France.

In our difficult search after an explanation for French policy we are then reduced to two hypotheses, one (already mentioned) that of complete ignorance of the real state of Turkey, the other that France intends to force the Mussulman populations into a revolt against the Sultan.

The ambition of being the protector of the Eastern Christians does not afford a sufficient motive; for though Russia may well " protect " them in the hope of one day becoming their sovereign, and transforming them, if not into useful members of the working community of the world, at least into handy tools for her own projects, what could France do with all these millions of Rayahs? And if she does *not* want them, the part she plays is not only deadly to the true interests of the country, but is a flagrant absurdity.

Without speaking of the autonomies which France has obtained for Servia, for the Principalities, &c., or of the course adopted by her in the affairs of Crete, a sufficient proof of the evils arising from her counsels will be found in the part she has taken against the *Ulema*, the great bond, moral and religious, of Mahommedanism in Turkey; than which nothing can be more calculated to exasperate the Mussulmans, who look upon the proposed change as a direct attack upon one of the most cherished articles of their faith.

Let us suppose for a moment that the French ambassador in London demanded an interview with the Premier, and expressed himself after the following manner:—" You must acknowledge that these Fenian troubles are weakening the prestige if not the power of the country, and that you have vainly tried to put an end to them in various ways; now let France, as a friend, strongly advise and counsel you to adopt the only remedy which will get you out of your difficulties, namely, to secularize, or confiscate, all the remaining property of the Established Church, which will find a sufficient means of support in the contributions of its zealous members. By this means you will effectually check Fenianism, whose ranks are chiefly recruited from Roman Catholics, and England will again enjoy domestic peace, and regain her former position amongst the great powers of Europe."

Of course such language, and such advice from France to England, would be considered as an impertinence, whilst from France to Turkey it is disinterested friendship of the purest kind; yet such a proposition, *per se*, would find many supporters and approvers amongst Dissenters and even amongst nominal members of the Church of England: the present generation may perhaps even live to see a Bill to this effect brought before an ultra-Reformed House of Commons.

In Turkey, however, the case is not entirely a parallel one, for the proposal to annihilate the Ulema is most distasteful to all classes of the Turks, who are distinguished by attachment to their religion, and whose faith is not divided by such thousand-and-one schisms as agree to differ from the State religion of England.*

Confessing ourselves foiled in our endeavour to find a solution to the enigma of French policy, we will again turn to its effects in conjunction with that of Russia, in the hope of thereby aiding the mental efforts of some diplomatic Œdipus.

The action of Russian policy is to be clearly traced in

---

* In Persia there are, it is true, many Mussulmen sectaries, but in the Asiatic dominions of the Sultan there are very few, whilst in European Turkey (of which we are writing) they are utterly unknown.

continual agitations amongst the Christian populations, and in bribes to some Kurd or Karamanian Beys, which, while serving to arm and excite them against their legitimate sovereign, explain in some measure the large sum of 3,200,000*l*. which by the avowal of Prince Gortchakoff the Eastern Question costs Russia under the head of secret service money in the East.

At Constantinople the tactics of Russia consist in asking from Turkey what she knows it is impossible to grant, like a skilful fencer who endeavours to *embrouiller le jeu* of his adversary by almost impossible thrusts, profiting by the disorder into which the latter is thrown to inflict a wound deep enough to make him surrender at discretion, but not deep enough to cause death—for Russia is prevented from killing Turkey outright by the presence of the seconds and other lookers-on. France steps in as a friend, but she is, to say the least, very unskilful, and by no means shows the same cunning of fence which she has occasionally exhibited on her own account in one or two affairs of honour; she is constantly telling her principal, "Guard your head" when the chest is threatened, or "Parry in tierce" against a thrust in *carte;* sometimes she even says "Let me parry for you," and does it so adroitly that she inflicts a wound upon Turkey deeper than any from the adversary's sword.

The duel is enlivened by the attacks of two or three small cur dogs who are always to be found at the heels of Russia, and make frantic efforts to bite the legs of Turkey.

Formerly there was a big English policeman always standing by to see fair play, and occasionally his staff came down with a heavy rap upon the knuckles of Turkey's opponent, or even of the disinterested friend, whilst a kick from his heavy boot sent one of the cur dogs yelping away into a corner. Now, however, the policeman, though he is still present, is but an inactive if not an uninterested spectator, and the Turk is left to his own resources. As a professor of political small sword, one at least of the Sultan's Ministers is more than a match for any one that can be brought against him, little dogs included, but he is so encumbered by the advice and useless parries of his second that he occasionally lays himself terribly open.

The old saying, "Preserve me from my friends, I will take care of my enemies," has never had a more practical application than in the diplomatic duel which is going on in the political circles of Constantinople.

The consequences of these interventions, whether hostile or friendly, in the domestic affairs of Turkey are most deplorable, for they are the cause of the animosity existing between the Mussulman and Christian subjects of the Sultan, of the undeveloped state of the moral and material resources of the country, of the paralysis of its Government, of the ruin of its finances, in a word, of the ruin of the whole of Turkey.* Their worst effect is, however, one which will appear strange when we remember the apparently philanthropic intentions of French policy, since it is nothing less than checking civilization and hindering its taking root in this country : as we continue to study the action of French policy we shall see that this deplorable result does ensue from it.

---

* Although other causes may have contributed to this ruin, such as Eastern commerce, the idleness of the Rayah, the Capitulations, the system of taxation, &c., yet all these wounds are, if not inflicted, at least kept open by the action of this policy.

The great question, nominally at least, for which foreign powers are struggling at Constantinople is "the amelioration of the condition of the Christians;" yet but little progress is made in this direction by intrigues, avowed or unavowed, of foreign diplomacy.

The Russian policy of urging the Christian population to covert resistance, if not to open revolt, by its official notes and constant demands for new concessions in their favour (whilst good care is taken that both the demands and results shall be reported throughout the country by its secret agents or by such scientific travellers as Colonel Bobrikoff*) has at

---

* "La mission que le Gouvernement Russe a envoyée en Bulgarie est composée comme il suit : le Colonel Bobrikoff, le Capitaine Karatassoff, le Capitaine Artamonoff, le Capitaine Escalon, le Capitaine Soltikoff.

"La Sublime Porte, dont la complaisance est extrême, a attaché à cette mission trois officiers d'état major, *Haqqui* Bey, Faïg Bey, et Tefik Bey. En outre elle a donné ordre aux autorités des provinces pour faciliter les travaux de la mission russe.

"Les officiers de cette mission ont parcouru la Bulgarie, la Thrace et une partie de la Macédoine, du Danube aux Dardanelles et à Salonique, de la Mer Noire à la frontière de Serbie ; ils ont visité les gorges et les issues les moins connues du Rhodope et du Balkan ; ils ont parcouru les vallées, se sont informés des ressources de chaque localité, et n'ont pas oublié de visiter les couvents grecs.

"Il paraît qu'ils n'ont pas achevé leurs opérations, car ils ont promis de revenir. Est-ce en qualité de mission savante ou de mission militaire— plus nombreuse?"—' Courrier d'Orient,' *Jan.* 27, 1868.

In course of conversation with a Turkish official upon the subject of this mission, we were told, "Mithat Pasha n'est pas si bête, allez : l'escorte qu'il a donnée à ces Messieurs n'est tout bonnement que des espions ; " but what is the use of spies upon people who are allowed to do as they like without check or hindrance? Of what use is a report "that Colonel Bobrikoff has taken plans of all the passes of the Balkans, and that Captain Karatassoff made a regular Russian propaganda in every Bulgarian village where the mission halted," when the plans go safely to Russia, when

least no great tendency to produce good feeling between Mussulmans and Christians, the latter having been promised such great benefits from the Protectorate of Russia that they consider the Czar as their best friend, and as subjects of the Sultan feel but little devotion or attachment to their sovereign.

How then is it possible, without real tranquillity and cordial good feeling between the rulers and the ruled, for civilization to spread in Turkey?

If Vassili harbours the orthodox brigand, and if he is but a lukewarm subject of Turkey, the fault lies with the policy of Russia; but if Turkey is too weak—we will not say to chastise her children when they are disobedient or noisy or idle, but—to distribute an even-handed justice, to eradicate the fraud which is ruining and the dishonesty which is killing all legitimate enterprise and draining all the available resources of the land, or to establish a logical system of government in the country; if Turkey is too weak to do all this, and if the Ministers of the Sultan occupy their time in imagining impracticable Utopias, the fault is greatly if not exclusively with the French policy of intervention in Turkey; and this policy is direct or indirectly the cause that a whole country stagnates instead of flourishing, it is responsible for rivers of blood shed without the world's reaping any benefit from the sacrifice, it is the cause, in short, that though Sebastopol has disappeared, the Eastern Question still exists.

Captain Karatassoff is not arrested, and the seed he has been allowed to sow, is also allowed to germinate—to be reaped in good time, no doubt? 'Quem Deus vult perdere, prius dementat.'

Whilst to France herself the consequences are sufficiently sensible—ten men per thousand in every conscription being the least that the Eastern Question costs her, and the actual state of the agriculture of the corn-producing provinces of Turkey keeping the price of the French workman's bread above what he would pay if the sublime Porte were well and honestly advised, instead of receiving such counsels as are every day forced upon it by the French ambassador—Turkey suffers still greater and more serious evils.

The advice of the friend of Turkey has always tended to promote changes advantageous only to the Christians, and most unfavourable to the Mussulmans; we will allow that the agents of France act from ignorance and not from any dishonest or interested motives, but the effect is the same whatever may be the cause of the policy which produces it. Its first result is, that France appears to be entirely subservient to Russia, whose influence in the country districts she can never hope to dominate, for the Rayahs (whom we have faithfully delineated in their true colours) are sufficiently ignorant to think and say, "If France helps our friend and master the Czar, it is because he has ordered France to do so," and of course such an opinion is not likely to be weakened by the ubiquitous agents of Russia.

Secondly, these concessions are demanded for a race which is in a position more than favourable for everything but work and civilization,* and the reason we have to make these

---

* As may be seen in the Chapter upon Military Service, the Rayah, instead of paying an average exemption tax of 25 piastres which (counting one adult male in every family of five persons for the total of twelve millions) brings in sixty millions of piastres (about 540,000*l.*) should be forced to pay a sum of from 500 to 800 piastres, which would be an in-

exceptions is because the Turkish Government has rendered the life of the Rayahs too easy, and afforded them too many opportunities of indulging in their favourite luxuries of idleness and drunkenness, and because the Greek clergy, and the Greek religion as they preach and practise it, are incompatible with any degree of civilisation worthy of the name, serving merely to keep the peasantry in their present state of parasitism, and to make them the friends of Turkey's enemies as well as a germ of trouble and agitation which checks all material progress; while there is yet a worse feature of the Greek Church, its elasticity of doctrine in all matters of public morality, which is in a great measure the cause of the universal want of confidence prevailing in all transactions, mercantile or other, throughout the East.

And why should a never-ending war be waged against all the institutions of Islam? Is it because the Emperor of the French occupies the throne of the most Christian and most crusading kings of France? "Because," we shall be told, "Islamism is incompatible with the march of civilization."

---

crease to the Budget of from 1,200,000,000 (twelve hundred millions) to 1,920,000,000 (nineteen hundred and twenty millions) of piastres, or in round numbers, 11 to 17½ millions of pounds sterling.

We shall be told that the *Aman*, or Quarter, granted to the Christians, forbids the imposition of such a tax.

This we deny, but even supposing it to be so, the condition of the Turk has been so changed since that Aman was granted and his privileges have been so entirely taken from him, that if the Rayah were called upon for an annual exemption tax of a thousand piastres, he would still be in a better position than is the Mussulman.

How do Russia, Prussia, and even liberal Austria keep to the stipulations of the *Aman* by them granted to Poland?

They are, however, stronger than Turkey, and have no foreign intervention to fear.

In reply we refer our readers to previous chapters* of this book, and we say that our experience leads us to believe the Mussulman to be far more susceptible of civilization than the Christians of the East, and that as applied to Islamism it will produce results far better than the defective and warped "civilization" prevailing in those former provinces of Turkey which have been granted an autonomy, or even than that which is thinly spread over the surface of the "France of the North,"† where it chiefly consists in embroidered uniforms, képis after the latest French model, and the deepest and streakiest of mud, material and moral.‡ Such a reform as this will not, however, be lightly accepted by the snowy beards and turbans of the Ulema.

It would almost appear as if the civilization of Prefects and Sous-Prefects, of the Code Napoléon, and of what Victor Hugo calls "*la représentation du garde champêtre,*" were the only form possible in Turkey, since it is this which is so unceasingly advocated by the French Ambassador, who yet can scarcely be ignorant that at less than eleven hours' distance from Paris there lies a city called London, the capital of a country in which reigns a civilization far different from, but perhaps not inferior to, that of France.

Germany, too, is regarded as one of the civilized nations of Europe, although her civilization is no more based upon Christianity than would be that which Turkey, left to

---

* Upon the Ulema, the Turks of the Country, &c.
† A self-attributed title, upon which Russia greatly prides herself.
‡ To see both kinds of mud in a superlative degree, travel in Wallachia. *Passim* during a wild rainy winter, for the material; *passim* at any season, for the moral.

Y

herself, might, or perhaps even would, adopt with complete success.

Continuing our supposition that France is actuated by sound, though inscrutable, reasons of State policy in her anxiety to bestow upon Turkey the blessings of a civilization not *alla Franca* but *à la Française*, her manner of paving the way to this result is at least open to criticism.

She urges the Turkish Government to grant autonomies to States who avail themselves of the gift only to intrigue against the giver and to turn their own countries into a chaos of disorder and misrule; she compels concessions to a population which is neither prepared to benefit by them, nor even fit to receive them; she seeks to destroy the *Ulema* by the abolition of the *Vakouffs*, she forces the Porte to fill an unlimited number of places created, *ad hoc*, with Frenchmen who are for the most part incapable, and she says to Turkey, " You must have railroads, forest rangers, professors of logic, of chemistry, of mathematics, a French official Turkish newspaper," and a hundred other instruments of civilization; the only effect of this last piece of advice being that some scores, or even hundreds, of Frenchmen receive enormously high salaries, which are drawn from the slender budget of the country, and spent in the cafés of Péra: but the railroads are still things of the future; the roads are not traced even on paper; the forests are still cut and burned down by the Rayah, or sold by him to the Greek merchant; the mathematician, who cannot solve a quadratic equation, and has not even heard of differential calculus, has not one pupil for every hundred pounds of his salary; the chemist occupies himself in the analysis of the ingredients which form a Constantinopolitan "*Ponche à l'Anglaise;*" and the logician wonders from what premisses Turkey can have drawn the conclusion to be so yielding as she is.

We have already said that Turkey is distressed, that she is in a state of disorder almost impossible to imagine, and all this in spite of, or rather owing to, the mania which has seized upon France for urging her to "reforms" as absurd as they are ill-timed. Is the "sick man" any the better for the large doses of reform pills which he swallows with so much resignation?

A Turk arms himself with a thick stick, and administers a sound thrashing to a Rayah, or to a merchant whose primitive nationality is lost in the mists of many consulates, but who has finally obtained French protection. The story is published in the Constantinople newspapers, and the Russian Ambassador goes to the Porte; he adopts a tone a little too menacing and obtains no "redress," so he calls upon the French envoy, and with an ironical smile and a shrug of the shoulders suggests to his "*cher collègue*" a private intervention in the matter, adding "You see now what a nice set of fellows these Turks are that you are so bent upon civilizing." The French Ambassador feels that the credit of France is at stake, for he has just learnt that the Rayah is a Catholic, or the merchant an Armenian, so he hastens to the grand Vizier, says the rudest things to him in the politest manner possible, and throws in his face the old, old story of that Crimean campaign, in which England took a sufficiently prominent part, but which every Frenchman tries to prove to the world in general, and Turkey in particular, was carried on by France alone, who succeeded in beating the Russians, notwithstanding the chain tied to her feet by the presence of the British army, or rather contingent, which did nothing but impede the movements of her forces.

The result of this representation is that a Commission is sent to the spot from Constantinople with orders to punish the Turk in question, and all that is Turkish in the affair. The Turkish Minister knows that he is committing an injustice; the Commission knows beforehand that it will be forced to act without regard to law or evidence; but the repose of the Cabinet is at stake, and so the Turk goes to Widin* for seven years, and the Pasha of the district loses his place—a couple of sacrifices to French policy.

There is, however, a true version of the affair, which the Commission will not report; or if it does find courage to do so, no newspaper in Constantinople will publish it. The Turk has been robbed of his last pair of buffaloes by the Rayah, or cheated out of his poor savings by the merchant; he has complained to the Pasha, and been told that orders had come from Stamboul to treat the Rayahs with all possible lenity, and that political reasons forbid the punishment of the thief. The Turk who feels that this "policy" strips him every day of a right or a privilege, that it is abusing his nationality and attacking his religion, that it not only despoils but insults the Mussulman†—thinks he has had enough of this patriotic policy, and says to a friend, "Look here, I suppose I shall go to Widin for it, but at any rate the Giaour shall have what he deserves," and as he has failed in obtaining justice at its source he takes the law into his own hands.

---

* Widin, on the Danube, is a sort of Turkish Spike Island.

† Vide Chapters upon the Military Service of the Turk, the Real Position of the Rayah, &c. &c.

In an English police court he would probably have been sentenced to pay a fine between five shillings and five pounds; but in Turkey foreign policy interferes, and he gets seven years' penal servitude; but by those of his own faith he is regarded as a martyr.

The Rayah rejoices, and prays still more fervently for his patron the Czar; the French Ambassador is delighted at the "victory" he has gained over the Russian, who smiles the smile of Russian diplomacy as he congratulates his colleague upon his "great influence with the Sublime Porte," and is secretly perfectly contented with the real advantage which he has obtained.

Meanwhile, the Turkish Minister is not quite so well pleased, and calculates how long this state of affairs can go on, consoling himself with the reflection that he is clever enough to make it last out his time, and quoting—for he is a good French scholar, and well up in the sayings of eminent Frenchmen—

"Après moi le Déluge,"

and by the next time he meets his enemy and his "disinterested friend" at a grand dinner which he gives to the *corps diplomatique* on the anniversary of the accession of H.M. Abdul Aziz, he has quite recovered his usual equanimity, and greets both of them with the most charming cordiality.

At Stamboul the affair is finished, for the moment; in the country, however, it is not so, and the looks of the Turks are darker when they meet the Rayahs, who tremblingly hope that the day is near—that is, the day of retribution, which when it comes will be far different from that expected by the Christian.

The Turkish cup of endurance will one day overflow, and it is the Ambassador of France who will pour in the last drops, and who, perhaps unknowingly, has cast a bullet whose shrill whistle will sooner or later mingle its voice with the debates upon the Eastern Question, since it is *his* influence which is rapidly tending to drive the Mussulmans into a war of retribution, such a war as they believe to be foretold in the Koran, " When blood shall flow higher than your knees, when the infidels shall unite against you and strive to crush you ; but to every believer shall be given the strength of ten men."*

We believe that Russian diplomatists are clever enough and sufficiently well informed as to the real state of the country districts to foresee, and even to wish for such an event. Poland has steeled the nerves of Alexander II., and he would not shudder at being called upon to reign over a desert, though that desert were still reeking with Christian as well as Mussulman blood ; it is even possible that the scheme may be premeditated, for Turks who rose against their Christian oppressors could as little expect sympathy from Europe as the Turk who struck the Rayah could obtain justice from foreign intervention in his country.

As Russia numbers amongst her generals a Suvoroff and a Muravieff, it is not impossible that she should possess diplomatists who wish for nothing more than to see the road to Constantinople paved with corpses, whether Christian or

---

* This verse was quoted to us lately by a Turkish peasant, in speaking of such an eventuality as we have mentioned ; the words are given from memory, and possibly are inexact, but the sense remains the same.

Mussulman, provided that the Czar's entry into Stamboul would be facilitated thereby; but such an eventuality can hardly be contemplated in cold blood by France, who though she may blush for a Pelissier, can never boast of a Muravieff, and it is the conviction of this impossibility which throws us back upon our first hypothesis of utter ignorance as the reason of the policy pursued by the French Ambassador, which must finally result in one of two misfortunes, either an armed invasion by Russia, or a revolution of the Turks against their Government, preceded or followed by a massacre of the Christians.

Very many well-meaning people will say, that if the civilization of Turkey cannot be effected without causing a Christian massacre it would be much better to let Russia have her way, and even to assist her as much as possible; but those who may hold this opinion do not reflect that even in their alternative or *pis aller* a slaughter is involved, for Turkey will never succumb to Russia until hundreds of thousands of Turks have fallen "with their feet to the foe." It is a suggestion which may lay us open to the suspicion of being more Mussulman than Christian, but we nevertheless hazard the question, Which could the world spare best, the Rayah or the Turk?

An English navvy working on a railroad in this country once said to us, " As far as I can make out, the Turks are the only Christians here," and his experience amongst a certain class of both races had been pretty large. The Turk of the country is usually remarkable by his honesty, sobriety, and charity, three virtues which are supposed to be extensively cultivated by the genuine Christian; whilst the Rayah has only learnt from his clergy theft, drunkenness, idleness, and disloyalty to his sovereign. Which of the two, to repeat the *Bull* of the English navvy, is in reality the best *Christian?* And if such a fearful calamity as an extermination of one race or the other is to take place, which of the two will be the greater loss?

The deplorable necessity for a choice between these antagonistic peoples is, however, not like to occur, for twenty millions of Turks, backed by one hundred millions of Mussulmans, cannot be got rid of with the same facility as the remonstrances of the Burgesses of the ex-free city of Frankfort; and if the standard of Mahomet be once raised, the armies of Europe would find themselves no over-match for the myriads who would assemble under its folds.

Even European discipline, and Dreyse, Snyder, or Chassepot rifles may fail before the faith or the valour of Mahommedans who are fighting for their homes, for their religion, for their very existence as a people, and who in the 19th century have still the same strength of belief which our forefathers had in the 12th, when the chain armour of the knights of Europe was found not to be proof against the Asiatic scimetar, and when the chivalry of the West was forced to recoil before the fanaticism of the East, a fanaticism which even now is not extinct, and needs but an appeal such as the sight of the Oriflamme of Islam to awaken it into undiminished vigour.

But, thank Heaven! the signal for such a shock of arms has not yet been given, and the Turkish peasant is anxious for even a greater amount of real civilization than it would be yet expedient to bestow upon the Rayah, who for his part does not wish for it at all; and if France really desires the civilization of the East she has but to aid in curing those diseases and maladies which are now slowly consuming the vitals of Turkey.

Injustice being incompatible with civilization, let the efforts of French policy tend to restore to the Turkish Government sufficient strength, moral and material, to enable it to redress the crying wrong of the present system of exempting the Rayahs from military service, either by forcing them to serve like the Mussulman, or by making the tax they pay for exemption proportionate to the loss of time and labour sustained by the soldier.

Let France prove, clearly and officially, to the Government of the Sultan the ruinous absurdity of the present system of taxation.

In spite of Russia let the clergy, Greek or Armenian, be forced to preach a moral doctrine which shall *not* be incompatible with the existence of a civilized society or with the incontestable rights of property, which is but another name for labour capitalized; although in Turkey, thanks to the Rayah clergy, that most absurd axiom of communism "*La propriété c'est le vol*" would be almost a desideradum, since at present it is inverted, and here "*Le vol c'est la propriété.*"

Might not Turkey, with the aid of France, crush under her heel the hydra head of Eastern commerce, and even annul the Capitulations, or at least modify them in such a manner that they should not interfere with the very existence of justice?

Why not found Government schools for the Rayah—not at Constantinople, for would-be apothecaries or Dragomans to some foreign Consul, but in the country villages, for the Bulgarian peasant?

The Rayah is but a child—a naughty child it is true, but

the fault is not so much with him as with his Russian guardian and his tutor the Greek Papas; educate him, and you may yet make a man of him, not without a good deal of trouble certainly, but when he *is* a man he may contribute greatly to the welfare of the East, and the experiment is worth its cost. But his education must not be after the system of the Russian agent, who teaches him to hate the Sultan; nor after that of the Papas, who tells him that "to rob or cheat a Mussulman is no sin;"* nor even after that of the good-natured Turkish Government, which allows him to waste his time in dancing, drinking, and idleness; he must be taught by the aid of the ferule of impartial justice that the duty of man is to be honest and to labour, and that he who offends against this law is punishable by society.

If the French Ambassador would take the pains to study Turkey and to learn its real condition (not such as it is described by some hostile powers), he would find questions enough to occupy him without taking up those which are already worn out, or which Russia has appropriated to herself.

Whilst in studying the Rayah, we have, alas! got no further than the A B C of civilization, with the Turks it is far different; for amongst them civilization will find a congenial soil in which to take root and flourish, provided that the noxious foreign weeds which choke its growth be removed once and for all. To civilize Turkey it is first necessary to establish justice, and to strengthen her hands so that

---

* Fact: the Papas, if interrogated by one of his flock in such a case of conscience, almost always replies in the above words.

she may no longer fear the culprit she is called upon to judge.

Our *Standpunkt* in criticizing the action of France has hitherto been more or less that of morality: let us now descend to that of expediency, and ceasing to reiterate that it is neither just nor honourable to force upon the Porte reforms whose consequences will be the dismemberment of the Ottoman empire and a massacre of the Christians, or a war whose disastrous effects will be felt throughout the world, let us affirm that the ruin of Turkey is against the interests of all civilized nations.

Who, or what is to replace the Mussulman dominion at Constantinople, is a point upon which it is unnecessary for us to enlarge, as it has already been discussed by the Duc de Valmy in a pamphlet, which, since it succeeded in penetrating even to our cottage in the Balkans, has doubtless found many readers in England: but there is another question which by right should precede this—

Who is able to drive the Turks from Europe?

We have already said that though the Turkish Government is feeble, the Turks themselves are a warlike and determined race, and that they will die sooner than surrender the country which has belonged to them for nearly five centuries; the struggle will be a hard one, but if a man of energy, for genius is not necessary, attain during this crisis to the Vizierate, he will summon the whole of Islam to the aid of Turkey, and such a reinforcement may do more than turn the scale in favour of the Padischah. But whatever may be the final issue of the conflict, the Christians of the East will assuredly be its first victims, and in what will these changes or troubles or massacres benefit Europe?

Surely the slight political advantage of having a little more influence than one's neighbour with the Turkish Cabinet, or the petty vanity of being considered as protector or civilizer, is not such as to counterbalance the real relief of awaking for good and all from that nightmare of Europe, the Eastern Question, or the real benefit of enabling a whole country to enjoy the blessings of a well-founded and permanent peace, and to produce its proper proportion of the raw products required by the industry of Europe, and of the food necessary for her support. Yet this end could be attained with less trouble than is required for one of the innumerable little "victories" which one ambassador gains over another by taking advantage of the intestine troubles and misfortunes of Turkey.

As, however, no steps are taken for the attainment of such a result, it would almost appear as if Europe considered that the Eastern Question is a seton necessary for the general health of the *corps diplomatique*, or as if her ambassadors acted like some unworthy physicians, who retard an easy cure that they may the longer profit by the fees which they daily extract from the pocket of their patient.

Assist Turkey to reform her defective organization, to heal her economical and social wounds, to burn out the cancer of parasitism, and whilst doing so keep Russia in her proper position, without threatening, but without suffering her to threaten.

Minor ambitions are more easily checked, though one or two of them might require a couple of English battalions at the Piræus, a regiment or two of Austrians at Belgrade, and an envoy extraordinary at Bucharest. Such "intervention" would do more good to the States in question by checking brigandage in the neighbourhood of their capitals, and by the inevitable expenditure of sovereigns, napoleons, and ducats, than has been effected by any one of their numerous cabinets upon which the changes have of late been so frequently rung: and the armies of occupation on their departure would be as cordially regretted by the people as are the former garrisons of Corfu and Zante by the inhabitants of the Seven Isles.

As for the Christian subjects of the Sultan, help their Government to make them into men, undeterred by the fear that, if Russia makes a demand for new concessions in their favour to which you do not adhere, they will become your enemies; for their hostility to you exists already and cannot easily be increased.

If General Ignatieff urges upon the Porte fresh concessions to the Rayah, if Fuad Pasha communicates these demands to the Ambassadors of England and France, if the former answers that he has telegraphed orders to Gibraltar that the day on which these demands are reiterated every Russian ship of war in the Mediterranean will be taken or sunk, if the latter adds that the *corps d'armée* now at Toulon and Lyons have received instructions to hold themselves in readiness; if the Russian Ambassador then seeks an interview with his two colleagues, and insists upon the necessity for these concessions, accusing England and France of acting against the interests of civilization, might not Fuad Pasha reply in the pithy phrase of Prince Gortchakoff about Poland, "Le charbonnier est maître chez lui"?

Might not the Sultan have answered the collective note of the Four Powers relative to the insurrection in Crete, as Alexander II. replied to the notes addressed to Russia in

1863 relative to the affairs of Poland, by sending a Muravieff to desolate the island with famine, fire, and sword instead of an Ali Pasha to propose such terms as the following :—" Perpetual exemption from military service, and from the tax upon the salt and tobacco produced by the island; exemption for two years from the tax upon wine and from the tithe of produce; for the two subsequent years the tithe to be reduced from 10 to 5 per cent., and the revenue therefrom accruing to be applied to the indemnification of the losses caused by the insurrection"? And yet these terms are not considered by the island as sufficiently liberal! We would recommend some patriotic Irish Member of the House of Commons to propose an equally munificent donation as a sop to the Celtic Cerberus who, less greedy than his congener of Crete, would be only too glad to accept it.

The *action* of English policy in Turkey, of late years, cannot certainly be blamed.;

"Fiorenza mia, ben puoi esser contenta
Di questa digression che non ti tocca"—

it is its *inaction* which is culpable, and if France hurries Turkey into an abyss of misery and blood, if Retribution is allowed to take the form of Massacre, surely the conscience of England will not be silent. Had our country the same influence in the East which she formerly possessed, and which was based upon the firm carrying out of a clearsighted and equitable policy, this chapter would not have been filled with protestations against the evil influences of the enemy and the disinterested friend of Turkey. If England stands by in apathy whilst a nation is being murdered, she is surely *particeps criminis*, and it will little avail her in the judgment of posterity that she may have turned informer, and that her voice is the loudest in the outcry against her accomplices.

Let her adopt at Constantinople not the policy of non-intervention fashionable in the West, but a policy of action, such action as, while it serves Turkey, will benefit the true interests of civilization throughout the world: she herself will be no loser by the change.

CHAPTER XXI.

THE ARMY AND THE MILITARY RESOURCES OF TURKEY.

Born soldiers — Exploits in the last war — English generalship and commissariat at Balaklava — French uniforms — Onerous service of the militia — Organize volunteers — Expense of the militia — Requisites for volunteers and estimated expense — Christian non-combatant corps.

AMONGST all the mis-used or totally neglected resources of Turkey there is none greater than her military force; of her thirty-five millions of subjects at least twenty-five millions are Mussulmans, and of these fifteen millions are Turks, leaving out of consideration Egyptians and Arabs; these fifteen millions, counting the family at five persons, give the number of three million adult males, that is to say, as all who know Turkey will allow, three millions of warriors.

France with her utmost efforts has not succeeded in raising an army of more than 800,000 men from a population of thirty-five millions, but the Turk is not a Frenchman any more than France is Turkey. Even in the event of a hostile invasion of France, that country could not afford to abandon her industry, and if one adult out of ten joined the army it would be as much as could be expected, for after all a war of invasion in France would not threaten the lives of all Frenchmen, whilst in Turkey every step of the enemy would be a step towards the political and social—even towards the physical—extirpation of the Osmanli race, and the Turks, well knowing this, are resolved in such a case to conquer or to die fighting.

The conscripts of Europe, moreover, require certain military instruction before the civilian can be changed into a soldier, whilst the unweaned Turkish child is just as much a soldier as the Prussian veteran; it is only the military system at present in force which neutralizes the instincts of the Turk, blunts his courage, and does its best to turn him into a worthless soldier. If Turkey were threatened with invasion, and the Sultan preferred a serious war to a treaty of Kainardji, he would have but to raise the standard of Mahomet, and (even supposing that the whole of Islam did not flock to the banner of the faith) the three millions of Turks, from the boy of sixteen to the old man of eighty, would unanimously rise against the enemy. Allowing that of these one half were retained for garrison duty, and that only 1,500,000 strong and vigorous men formed the active army, what power in Europe could raise such a force and such soldiers?

There is the difference of weapons; but the mail-clad chivalry of Europe were often repulsed by the Turkish light troops, the Akindjis, who wore no defensive armour— courage supplied the place of weapons; yet in the 19th century an army which loses in one battle five per cent. of its number considers itself as irremediably beaten, whereas in the good old times fifty per cent. of killed was but an ordinary "butcher's bill," and the battle though lost for the day was recommenced on the next. What would become of the 800,000 soldiers of Russia if opposed to only one third of the possible army of Turkey, that is, 500,000 men, even supposing the Russians to be armed with breech-loading rifles and the Turks only with their knives? The Polish scythemen have shown the military weakness of Russia and the small value to be set upon her troops, as well as the superiority of courage over weapons; although the inaction of our forces before Sebastopol raised the damaged prestige of the Russian army, the Polish campaigns of 1863 demonstrated that the Russian's proper trade is not that of soldiering.

Unhappily for Turkey and the civilized world, there is not a Vizier who has the courage to appeal to the valour of the people; but should Russia again attempt an invasion, the Turks are resolved to act without, or in spite of, their Vizier.

As for the organization and military instruction of these *Levées en masse*, the routine so necessary to transform the peace-loving citizen of Europe into a soldier, a legalized assassin, an amateur of danger and slaughter, is but little required by the Turkish peasant, and 500 villagers of the Balkan, armed with their own quaint old rifles, are worth more than 2000 Turkish regulars with the latest invention in breech-loaders, an anomaly which is caused by the faulty system on which the Turkish army is organized. And yet this army is not to be despised; the most brilliant actions of the campaign of 1853–1854 were certainly those fought by the Turks, and the battles of Oltenitza and Kalafat, the defences of Kars, Silistria, and Eupatoria, are well worth Alma, Inkerman, Balaklava, and the indecisive siege of Sebastopol. If we recollect, too, that the Turkish soldiers fought without being led by their officers—that the heroes of Kars and Oltenitza were badly armed, unpaid, and dying of hunger—we must allow that the glory of having broken the power of Russia should be at least equally shared between the Turkish army on one side, and the united forces of the two greatest nations of Europe on the other.

Our forces landed at Varna when the strength of Russia was already weakened, even broken, and we profited by the victories of the Turks to claim the glory for ourselves; because the Turkish soldier did not complain of the misery he was suffering, we called him apathetic, and said he was incapable of energy; yet those who saw the same soldiers at Eupatoria had reason to alter their opinion.

An unpractical general abandoned in some field-works, barely traced out, four batallions of Turkish Rediff, at a distance of more than a league from the nearest assistance, and because they retired before the corps of Liprandi, 40,000 strong, we not only laughed at the Turkish soldier, we insulted him. The Ottoman Brigade encamped near the hill of Balaklava was dying of hunger; it was attached to the English army, and provisions were supplied to it—but what provisions? Barrels of salt pork. Not only were the Mussulmans thus insulted, but the affair was laughed at as " a capital joke " played upon these starving men, and everybody wondered at their " stupidity " in not eating good pork. The facetious commissariat officer who was the author of this excellent jest ought to have been hanged for murder, for his amusement cost the lives of 400 brave soldiers, who preferred death to violation of a precept of their religion.*

A couple of volumes such as this would not be enough for a detailed account of all the absurdities in the organization and military instruction and institutions of Turkey, so we shall content ourselves with studying this all-important

---

* Of this fact I was an eye witness—S. G. B. St. Clair.

question only from the political point of view of military strength, touching merely upon such details as are necessary to convey a popular idea of the latent and unemployed force of Turkey, as compared with the amount of resources utilized.

The war budget of Turkey is very small, certainly smaller than that of any power in Europe, although she is more menaced than any other country, and has more need of a large army. This budget, small as it is, is distributed in the most foolish manner, for whilst the pay of a Turkish general or colonel is far better than that of English officers of the same rank, the Turkish officers of inferior rank and the non-commissioned officers and men receive almost nothing.

The arms* and musketry instruction are very bad, but the clothing and equipment reach the climax; in 1854 they wore short jackets, which protected them neither from heat nor cold, narrow trousers of rotten cloth, *eminehs* or slippers, in which they could not walk, and which they generally carried on the points of their bayonets, and a fez; even then the whole uniform was a species of parody of those of Europe, but now it is still more ludicrous and less comfortable. The Frenchman dearly loves a disguise, and just as in Paris you may see a number of individuals dressed up as Arabs or Moors, who cannot tell the difference between an Alif and a Bé, and who have probably never even spent a night at Algiers, so some regiments were clothed in a masquerade of Eastern costume; and as this uniform was borne

---

* Within the last few weeks the Turkish Government has commenced serving out breech-loading rifles (converted) to the army.

by brave men who ennobled it on the battle-field, the fancy dress of the Zouaves came to be regarded in France and Europe as the outward sign of an *esprit de corps*. But what traditions of glory or what feelings of pride does this uniform inspire in the bosom of the Turks? For them it is a mere parody of their national dress, and that is all; yet the Turkish soldiers have been dressed in Zouave uniform—no doubt for the pleasure of French tourists in Constantinople. Fancy an Englishman copying the costume of "Lord Williams Tobi, *ein reisender Engländer*," from some German comedy played at a minor theatre of Vienna! The case is very nearly a parallel one.

When the Turkish recruit compares his own comfortable trousers of good home-spun cloth to the ill-shaped knickerbockers of the Zouave, which the latter threw off so gladly at Palestro, and resumed so unwillingly at Milan;* his *Miltan*† to the useless waistcoat; his turban, which is proof against heat and cold, and even against a sabre cut, to the theatrical red rag which replaces it; and lastly his charreks and *sarhas*‡ (the best covering in the world for the foot of a soldier, as they can be replaced whenever a horse or an ox is killed, can be made by the soldier himself in five minutes, and neither hurt the foot nor cost a farthing), to the ammunition boots which pinch him, and the gaiter which takes five minutes to put on—what does he think of the Padischah's

---

* At Palestro the Zouaves found their knickerbockers so uncomfortable for fighting that they took them off, and it was not till some weeks afterwards that they could be induced to resume them.

† A kind of doublet, in shape like that worn by the knights of the Middle Ages.

‡ Rolls of thick flannel, in which the foot and ancle are swathed.

uniform, which is delivered by contract, ready made from rotten materials which will fall to pieces in two or three months?

But even the inconvenience and discomfort of the Zouave uniform is not its greatest evil, for whatever imposing effects it may produce in the Place Vendôme or the Champs de Mars, it has none at Constantinople, and the Turkish soldier, seeing in it only a mockery of his national dress, considers it as an insult to his nationality.

Both the drill and the military instruction are foreign, and, being neither national nor suited to the nation, are worse than useless; for whilst they endeavour to form the Turk, who is born a soldier, upon the model of European troops, these two powerful levers of military organization succeed only in making of the Turkish line soldiers inferior on the field of battle to the undisciplined and uninstructed Turk of the mountains.

After the battle of Preston Pans, the English copied from the Scotch their immobility under fire, their destructive volleys and their irresistible charge, because the Scotch would never have learned the file firing à la Frederick the Great of the English army; this system has been abandoned within our time, and our army is not so good as it was fifty years ago. In Turkey they copy Europe, who was always beaten by the Turks when the respective forces were at all equal, and when money did not win the battles; what is the consequence of this imitation we have already said.

The organization of the army and its reserves is also imitated from Europe, the Rediff being merely a Turkish Landwehr, and, like all exotics transported into a climate unsuited for them, producing no good fruits. The soldier who has served five years enters the Rediff, returns to his village, marries, and farms his land, merging the soldier in the agriculturist, forgetting the intricate manœuvres which astonished the loungers, and which he learned with so much difficulty after five years of drill, and thinking only of his farm and his duty towards his family; but at the moment that his fields begin to look green, a Zaptieh arrives, and brings him the order to report himself at Shoumla and to rejoin the army.

If the Turkish soldier of the Rediff were summoned from his family when the first Muscovite cannon proclaimed that the soil of Islam was sullied by the foot of the invader, when the light of burning Turkish homesteads reminded him that before he became a father he was the son of his country, and that the Houris of Paradise have a stronger claim upon him than the caresses of his wife, he would abandon the axe and the plough for the rifle and sword, and with a heart warm with patriotic fire, dry the tears of his wife, and teach his young son to long for the day when he, too, shall be strong enough to fight against the enemies of Turkey.

But when the peasant is called from his home, his farm, from all that he loves, to be dressed up like a baboon at a fair, to execute manœuvres fatiguing in time of peace, and impossible in war, to saunter through the streets of a town where for months he is the dupe of every petty Greek shopkeeper—and all to facilitate a political combination—it is hard, and worse than hard, it is demoralizing.

The *morale* of an army is a great capital which cannot be purchased with gold; in Turkey no attention is paid to it, and it shares the common fate of all the riches of the empire, neglect. But imagine the difference of feeling between the peasant who goes to drive the invader from his native soil, and the one who is torn from his family to idle at Shoumla or Scutari.

"But," say objectors, "time is necessary for mobilization, and to remind the Rediff of its duties and habits as soldiers; was it not want of time to mobilize, equip, and arm its forces, which caused the reverses of the Germanic Confederation?" Plausible as this argument may at first sight appear, it is used only by soldiers who have no knowledge of the raw material of the Ottoman army, who belong to that school of officers whom Turkey has unwisely chosen to instruct her troops in European discipline, and whose ideas of the Turkish peasant, whom they seek to grind into a soldier in the mill of a foreign military instruction unsuited to his nature, are only such as they have picked up in the cafés of Péra.

Those who have known something of war, who have studied the Turkish peasant in his home as well as in his masquerade uniform, and have seen how he behaves under fire in spite of the imbecility or cowardice of his chiefs, can truly assert that the worthy Prussian citizen is no more to be compared to the Balkan Chelibi than the winner of a farmer's plate in some obscure country meeting to the winner of the Derby; one may get over the course by dint of hard spurring and language, but the race-horse is born a race-horse, just as the cart-horse is born and remains a cart-horse, even though he may win a cup in bad company.

With the Germans war is an acquired vice; with the Turks it is second nature.

Make the drill and manœuvres clear and simple, as is the true Art of War, and you will solve the problem of creating a great military force at little expense—but in Turkey alone.

In Prussia the Landwehr is worth more than the line, because it consists of men in the prime of their strength, but its mobilization entails enormous expense and heavy loss upon the country; in England the Volunteers are, as it were, permanently mobilized, but in spite of their original, if not eccentric uniforms, they cannot become soldiers until after some months of campaigning. Courage will probably not be wanting in their ranks, but the habits of camp life (not the camp life of Wimbledon), the confidence in a Kismet which the soldier acquires only by long familiarity with danger, and which the Turk drinks in with his mother's milk, that talent of *se fournir à lui* which the Zouave claims as his own invention, and that indescribable feeling which causes one man to kill another with as little remorse as if he were shooting a hare, will take our Volunteers some time to acquire—whilst all these qualities are innate in the Turkish peasant, and will only be extinguished with the Osmanli race.

The Volunteer system of England applied to this country would produce a vast army of soldiers, and a Turkish peasant, who had the good fortune to learn the manœuvres and musketry instruction taught to the Englishman, would be more than a match for any five of the machine-soldiers turned out by the great military organizations of continental Europe. Turkey needs but little to render her the greatest military power in the world, for she already possesses a courageous population, disciplined by nature, dressed in a costume better adapted for campaigning than any other, and who to become good soldiers need but good rifles, cartridges, a little drill to enable them to act together in masses, and good officers to lead and command them.

Two millions of rifles would cost six millions of Turkish

pounds, paid once for all; forty millions of cartridges (twenty per man) would cost ten millions of piastres, or about 90,000*l.* a year.

As the pay of the officers of the Rediff might consist in grants of land, which is now almost valueless in Turkey, it need not be taken into consideration, and we find that (counting 10 per cent. interest on the sum paid for the rifles) for seventy millions of piastres, or about 600,000*l.* per annum, Turkey might have, in addition to her standing army, a reserve of two millions of the best soldiers in the world ready to take the field at a moment's notice.

Omitting the details of such an organization, which would be interesting only to military readers, we will merely state that the plan itself is eminently practical, and would be profitable both to the country and the Government, and we will make a comparison between it and the present system of Rediff.

By the latter, if the Government wishes to mobilize 20,000 Rediffs, so many labourers are taken away from the fields, and, their pay and rations being insufficient, are forced to subsist at their own expense after having abandoned their families and their growing crops,* and consequently are not worth, in point of *morale,* half what they would be if called out only at the actual commencement of hostilities.

Here then we find both a great loss of *morale* and a great injury to the country; and tracing the system onwards, we notice other evils caused by the necessity of mobilizing at least three or four months before the outbreak of war, such as diseases incident to all large permanent assemblages of

---

* As rumours of war are more rife in spring than at any other time, it is always at that season that the Rediff soldier is obliged to leave his family.

men, and the fact that even the bravest soldiers, those who are soldiers by nature and experience, do not directly or easily feel themselves at home in a strange regiment.

It requires some months for officer and soldier to become acquainted with one another, and for masses of men to form into that homogeneous monster which is called a battalion, for the discipline and the nervous system of the men to be so developed as to establish a rapid communication between the brain and the limbs, and finally for the battalion to learn to march, to condense itself into columns, to deploy into line, and to break up into skirmishers; in short, not only is a good deal of time necessary to re-drill and discipline the troops, but means of transport as well as a medical and commissariat service have to be organized; in a word, an army has to be organized, disciplined, and equipped every time that the Rediff is called out.

These operations cannot well take less than four months, during which time the Turkish Government has to feed, pay, and clothe the soldiers, without counting their arming, or the organization of the various non-combatant branches of the service, which last form important items; the following is an approximative calculation of the cost of 20,000 Rediffs:—

	Piastres.
Pay of 20,000 soldiers for four months at 20 piastres per month	1,600,000
Pay of the officers calculated at a minimum of 3000 piastres per battalion of 1000 men, colonels and general officers not included—for twenty battalions, for four months	240,000
20,000 uniforms at 500 piastres each	10,000,000
2,400,000 rations at 4 piastres	9,600,000
Thus the Rediff (without counting other branches of the service) costs, before it is ready for a campaign, for every 20,000 men	21,440,000

Taking account of the various other expenses incident to the mobilization of troops, we shall find that it is no exaggeration to calculate every 20,000 men as costing thirty millions of piastres, and such a body forms but an insignificant *corps d'armée* in these days of large armaments, when even 100,000 soldiers is not a very imposing number. This latter number would cost Turkey 150 millions of piastres (about 1,350,000*l*.) before they were ready to take the field, and, as we have said, they would be badly equipped, demoralized, disgusted with military life from their camp experience, and decimated by sickness before they made a single strategic movement; if war does not break out after all, 150 millions of piastres have been entirely wasted.

By such a system as we advocate, 2,000,000 good soldiers could be mobilized, and 1,500,000 thrown upon the frontier, at less expense to the Government and country: such an organization, far from being novel in Turkey, is nearly the same as that which rendered her in the days of her grandeur the most formidable military power of Europe.

If instead of having recourse to the organization and other operations necessary for the formation of an army only at the moment of danger, the Turkish people were kept under a permanent military organization, the great question of military strength would be at once solved. The characters, manners, habits, customs, and costume of the Turk permit of this being done in the following manner without difficulty and at little expense: the Turk is born a soldier, and after his service in the army is hardly more of one than before, but even the bravest man requires a good weapon with which to make the most of his courage; he is submissive to authority, honest and upright by nature, but he requires discipline and good officers to transform these virtues into military obedience; he is active, and stands fatigue well, but he requires instruction in rifle shooting and to be accustomed to his weapon,* and finally he must be able to manœuvre so as to be easily handled when forming part of masses of troops, as well as have a few cartridges to make him acquainted with the capabilities of his weapon.

Thus then there are four requisites:—
1. Arms.
2. Ammunition for practice.
3. Officers.
4. A simple system of drill, and a discipline compatible with time of peace.

In our opinion the plan to be followed is this: limit the time of service in the line to four or even three years, and offer a good bounty for re-enlistment in order to keep good men in the regiment; when the soldier has served his time let him return to his home, taking with him his rifle, ammunition, and accoutrement; as for his uniform (*maimoun roubasi*, monkey's dress, as the Turks call it) make an *auto-da-fé* of it, or if you are absolutely bent upon having soldiers disguised as learned poodles, keep it for the body guard of the Sultan or even for the line, but let the reserve wear a dress fitted for campaigning. According to the conduct of the soldier let him wear upon the arm a metal plate, gilded, silvered, or of bronze; if he is a bad character, take his arms from him: these rewards and punishments would not only act as an incentive to good conduct, but create in

---

* Every one who shoots, knows how much easier it is to shoot well with a rifle or gun to which one is accustomed, than with one which is strange or new.

the breast of the soldier an attachment for his rifle like that which the artilleryman feels for his gun, and a soldier who threw away his rifle would be as much dishonoured as a field battery which abandoned its cannon—which is not now the case in the armies of Europe.

The Turkish soldier arriving with his rifle at his village reports himself to the commanding officer,* who inspects his arms, &c., and the man returns to his work. On every Friday (the Mahommedan Sabbath) and holiday, after Divine Service in the mosque, the peasant-soldier takes his arms, and musters on the village green for inspection and drill, platoon or other according to the number of men in the village, and in the season when there is not much work in the fields battalion manœuvres may be practised; the peasant-soldier should be liable to military punishment for every infraction of discipline, and a certain number told off every day to act as police and guard the village prison.

Every man should have twenty cartridges per annum served out to him, of which five are to be fired against the butts according to regulation, and fifteen given to him to be used in shooting game, no small shot being allowed to enter the village. There is no danger of the Turk selling his cartridges, he is far too much of a sportsman to do that, and as he would be allowed to buy others from the military arsenals at regulation price on the written recommendation of his commanding officer, there would be no temptation for comrades to buy from one another; besides, as his pouch will hold sixty cartridges, the reserve of forty must be always kept

---

* This presupposes an organized staff of officers, &c., of which we shall speak presently.

up and shown at every inspection, and as from it would be taken those allowed for ball practice and sporting purposes (which would be replaced by others), his ammunition would always be fresh and in good condition.*

---

* We do not here enter into such details of organization as the subdivision of the Reserve into three classes; the first from 24 to 30 years of age, who rejoin the line in time of war and fill up the cadres; the second from 30 to 50 years, forming the chief reserve and having its own organization, officers, &c.; the third from 50 to 70 years, employed in garrison and escort duty, &c. Nor do we speak of the distribution of the officers amongst the three classes in time of mobilization, nor of the drill or method of fighting; we purposely abstain from all questions either purely military or of detail, as not being likely to interest the general reader. We have merely sketched out, in as popular a manner as possible, a system of organization in order to prove that Turkey possesses all the material necessary for a *Reserve, numerically, morally, and in all ways more powerful than those of Russia and Prussia united;* and that with a good system she might *create and keep* such a force *without much increasing her budget.*

A single point will prove the latter part of this assertion; a great economy might be made in the following manner; the uniforms and boots of the soldier cost the Government at present 500 piastres a year per man at the least; now if the soldier had merely a plate of metal with his regimental number and that of his company and regiment, and 200 piastres per annum to clothe himself with (we have already said enough upon the national costume as an uniform), we shall have a saving of 300 piastres yearly per soldier, which, on the total number of 400,000 (which we believe to be the strength of the Ottoman army) gives 120,000,000 piastres. A very good breech-loading rifle can be procured for 300 piastres, so that by this saving on the uniforms alone, Government would be able to arm 400,000 men annually, or in eight years to arm the whole Reserve of three millions of soldiers. The only expense besides this would be for cartridges, but this might be borne by arming 350,000 or even 300,000 only annually; in other words, by issuing 50,000 or 100,000 rifles less annually. There are many other economies possible and even advisable, such as a reduction in the salaries of the high officials and other public functionaries, but we have said enough to show that if Turkey has the will to become a great military power, it need not be the question of expense that stops her.

Thus then we have our soldier well armed, well equipped, and a good shot; for a man who can bring down a deer or a hare with a rifle ball will seldom miss an enemy's skirmisher, and never a section of five men. Now remains the question of the officers.

At present, an officer serves twenty or thirty years, retiring on a pension of five or six pounds, on which he starves for the rest of his life unless he happen to possess private means; offer every officer, who has served five years in one rank, a house and (according to his rank) from 50 to 100 dulums of land gratis, but not free from taxes: to sergeants and other non-commissioned officers grant smaller tracts of from 10 to 30 dulums, and these attractions, besides that of commanding, will procure you as many officers as you want, and at the same time agriculture will be encouraged.

By this organization (which the Turks would not only merely *accept*, but hail as the greatest possible boon) Turkey would acquire a Reserve ready armed and equipped; for, as we have already remarked, though the costume of the European would be unpractical and even ridiculous in war, the national costume of the Turk, from the turban to the charreks, is the best uniform that could be invented, and this immense force would cost only the arms and a little of that land which is being daily given away to the Rayahs, the enemies of Turkey; the only annual expense would be the cartridges, but surely 2,000,000 of good soldiers are worth twenty millions of piastres, or 1s. 8d. each.

As there are volunteer cavalry and artillery in England, the same system might be adopted for these branches of the service in Turkey, where the material is at least equally good. Again, if the Rayah were subjected to military service equally with the Turk (as in justice he ought to be) all the non-combatant corps* would be organized, and in order to enter upon a campaign the whole Reserve would need but two days' notice, the time necessary for the women to cook fifteen days' provisions which the soldier carries in his *chanta*,† thus saving the country the expense of the four months' organization of the present system. These soldiers too, leaving their homes only in the moment of danger, would be far superior in point of *morale* to troops who had wasted months in camp and become home-sick before a shot was fired. Unencumbered with heavy packs and painful boots, the men of the new Reserve would easily march their thirty miles a day, and 50,000 or 100,000 of them might be thrown upon any frontier in a week, and at very little cost to the Government.

A medical staff would be of course necessary, and if army doctors were sent from the army into country districts (without losing their right to promotion) it would be an immense benefit to the villages, which have no other doctor than the witch, and the Rediff might take the field followed by its surgeons.

It may be thought that this permanent arming of the Mussulmans would be a danger to the Christians, and render their position even more precarious than do the insults and wrongs daily inflicted upon the Turks by the Turkish Government; the Turk, however, seeing at his side the Rayah who procures him his food, and who digs to-day the intrenchment

---

* See the Chapter on the Military Service of the Turk.

† A bag made of goat-skin or deer-skin, and used by the Turks for carrying food, &c.; it is worn slung on the back, from the shoulder to the hip.

which the soldier will defend to morrow, will cease to regard him as his enemy and that of Turkey, whilst the Christian Rediff (of volunteers) rallying with the Mussulman regiments will also produce a beneficial effect in reconciling hereditary antipathies. Politically speaking, every Rayah with the army will be a hostage for the internal peace of the country, and a guarantee against such massacres by Christian peasants of Mussulman women and children as took place during the Russian invasion.

The whole plan is, however, too logical, and, whilst very easy of execution, affords too little scope for speculation ever to be adopted by the Turkish Government—and so we leave it.

What we have endeavoured to prove is that the Governmental resolution of Sultan Mahmoud upset the military organization of Turkey to replace it only by an irrational and anti-national copy of European systems, whereas the ancient institutions, with a little necessary alteration, would have raised the military power of the country in the same manner that a little discipline would have reformed the Janissaries and avoided the massacre of one of the finest bodies of soldiers in the world: in short, that Turkey has only to *wish* in order to regain her position amongst the first Powers of Europe, and to be the mistress of the destinies of Asia. One single man of energy at the head of the Government could effect this, for the Turkish people would rise as one man to support him with heart and hand. But though the people are ready, the man is not forthcoming, for it is only amongst the villages, and not in the towns, that we can hope to find men of energy, brains, and courage.

CHAPTER XXII.

GOVERNMENT AND GOVERNMENT FUNCTIONARIES, ADMINISTRATION OF JUSTICE, &C. &C.

Authority of the Sultan — Edict of Gul Hane — The future regenerator — Temporizing policy — Palace of the Porte — Palace of a Pasha — A mixed assemblage — The Cadis and the Medjliss.

THE Turkish Government has been ever since its foundation an autocracy, the Sultan being responsible for his actions to but one person, the Moufti or Head of the Ulema; but, as this dignitary could be deposed from his functions at the will of the sovereign, his authority offered a feeble barrier to the absolute power of the master of the destinies and lives of 35,000,000 subjects. Various authors who have written upon Turkish history give widely differing figures, from 7 (Von Hammer) to 1000 (Rycaut), as the number of persons whom the Padischah might put to death in one day without other cause than his own pleasure. As, however, the Sultans were bound to submit to the civil and religious precepts of the Koran, even the most bloodthirsty amongst them were restrained in their excesses by the laws of the Prophet, and although they united in their own persons both the legislative and executive power, their edicts had not the force of law unless sanctioned by the doctrines of the Koran; these edicts of the Sultans are styled *Ourfi*, and have never been considered otherwise than as supplementary to the great laws contained in the Koran and the Sounna (the traditional sayings of Mahomet), and to the decisions and sentences of the four great Imams.

The Ottoman Government was personified as a large tent, under which the ancient Sultans distributed justice, and from the Italian translation of the "lofty portal" we derive the term Sublime Porte, by which it is now distinguished.

The Sultan governed with the aid—in the great reigns more properly through the medium—of Viziers or Ministers, of whom the Grand Vizier, or chief of the ministerial council, was formerly also Seraskier or Minister of War.

Justice was, as it still partly remains, in the hands of the Ulema, or corporation of legists and learned men, amongst whom the priests formed a comparatively insignificant proportion. The edict of Gul Hane was the first Charter granted by the sovereign, and, like the Hatti Sheriff of 1856, was not so much an address to his subjects as a sort of promise to Europe to conduct himself like a civilized ruler on condition of being treated as such by the great Powers.

Since this time the statesmen of Turkey have taken, or rather pretended to take, the new position of their country as seriously meant; hence the dangerous though often laughable hops, skips, and jumps they make on the road of civilization, and that political lofty tumbling which, without benefiting Turkey, fatally shakes such of her ancient institutions as still cement together and give a species of consistency to the State, and is not always even successful in obtaining the applause of *blasés* European spectators, who demand that each summersault shall be higher than the last.

It must not be imagined, however, that Turkish statesmen are fools, or even puppets; there are amongst them intellects which would do honour to any Cabinet of Western Europe; but even a man of the talent of Fuad Pasha has a hopeless task before him, when he finds himself in presence of that immense chaos which has resulted from destroying the old order of things before laying the foundation of a new edifice, social, political, economical, financial, and even governmental.

To create order out of such disorder is too much for an ordinary brain or an ordinary ambition; a Napoleon, a Doria, or a Selim II. might erect from this ruin a vast military power, a country enormously rich, or even the great centre of a civilization based upon the precepts of the Koran, and around which would gravitate all the peoples of Islam; a still greater genius might even unite all these, but such a genius does not exist in Turkey. A man of talent and skill may sound the abyss, calculate the latent strength, estimate the resources, and discover the means, but between appreciation and action there is a wide gulf, and this gulf must be crossed in Turkey not by talent but by genius, which alone will hazard the perilous step necessary.

The statesmen at present in power know as well as we do all the abuses and economical vices which we have pointed out in this book; for not to perceive them they must be more than short-sighted, they must be wilfully blind. The immense but undeveloped resources, the formidable but latent strength, the alluring prestige of a possible future domination over 140 millions of Mussulmans—a population equal to all the members of the Protestant and Greek Churches—no doubt appear before the eyes of men in office as a brilliant mirage; but between such a dream and its realization there is this terrible step to be dared, such a step as few men will take, especially when they are already in a position which, though precarious, does not demand either the heroic courage or indefatigable exertions which spring only from ambition or genius; they will not exchange a luxurious palace for the hard life of a camp, a court of flatterers for a crowd of enemies, a peaceable and tranquil existence for a life full of dangers. Yet such must be the choice of the man who seeks to regenerate Turkey; he must neither quail before circumstances, nor tremble before his sovereign, he must march boldly on the road he has traced out, overcome all obstacles, and crush all enemies without other support than his own force of mind, without other motive than his own belief in his mission, and without other hope of success than that inspired by the consciousness of his own strength of will.

It is the easiest course to dismiss these fair visions, to prefer the routine of temporization to such a warfare, and a skilful but vacillating policy to a menacing display of force. Such is the reason that, though Fuad Pasha is perhaps the most clever diplomatist of Europe, Turkey is gliding slowly, but surely, into the gulf of a blood-stained future, whose result is uncertain; even this terrible eventuality causes less fear than the prospect of the struggle by which it might be avoided, and this feeling explains all the anomalies which strike any one who studies even the minor questions of Turkey, for the general policy of this country may be resolved into one word, temporization.

There is not a statesman in Turkey who seriously intends the reforms he proclaims, not one who sincerely desires progress or the welfare of the Christians; these are but the keys of the great political organ upon which the Minister plays, and hence the reforms are in direct proportion to the wind which originates them. A little whitewash for the walls of a town, a road or two traced out but never made, a railway which does not open up the country, but whose shares quoted in European newspapers produce a general effect of civilization, a few attempts at florid domestic architecture—all these cost but little, are dangerous neither to the country nor to the Ministry, whilst they have the desired result in Europe, and so they are now all the fashion.

But if a Minister accidentally touches, even with the tips of the fingers, one of those grave and vital questions which affect the very existence of his country, he recoils in dismay from the electric shock. Who then will dare to raise the question of the military service of the Turk? The Ministry of Constantinople are well aware that the Mussulman is crushed by this burden; but they know that he is faithful and loyal to his sovereign, so they do not hesitate to continue the oppression, since to distribute even-handed justice would make the Rayah complain, and draw down lightning from the surcharged clouds of the North.

To reform the army practically would be unpleasant to those foreign officers officially attached to it, and ruinous to the contractors; to put a stop to the frauds of Eastern commerce would extirpate half a million of robbers, but it would awaken the wrath of half a hundred Consuls; to change the tenure of landed property and the system of taxation would give prosperity to the country, but it would aggrieve the Rayahs and offend the tax-farmers. Better to give up all idea of improving the finances of Turkey, better to obtain a new loan at a sacrifice of 80 per cent., than to bring this nest of wasps about ministerial ears!

Thus all vital questions are shelved, and if Europe speaks, she is answered by a touch of paint given to some superannuated institution, by a new concession to the Christians, or a patent organization which looks well in a despatch, but in reality is worth nothing or less than nothing.

The Cabinet of Stamboul well knows that in Turkey there is but one element susceptible of immediate civilization, but not one of its members dare contradict the received opinion that the Turk is a barbarian incapable of all progress; it repeats without ceasing that the Ministers have to struggle against the prejudices of the Mussulman population, and are as yet unable to communicate to their country the civilization they have themselves acquired, on account of this semi-savage people.*

This comedy, with its scenery of whitewashed towns, costumes almost European, even the uniforms of the army being a ridiculous and expensive flattery of France, may be played to the approbation of the audience in the boxes, but behind the scenes you see the bareness and superficiality of everything, and that the rouge on the actors' cheeks does not conceal their pallor, whilst there are piles of weapons thrown away into a corner, and heaps of gold covered by heaps of dust, the actors having neither the courage to seize the one nor to use the other. Sooner or later this comedy will change to a sanguinary drama.

---

* See the communication from Fuad Pasha enclosed in the Despatch of H. E. Lord Lyons to Lord Stanley, dated May 6, 1867 (Appendix M).

We have now said enough upon Turkish civilization and organization, and have sketched in truthful colours the cause of the existing monomania for embellishing the towns; we have seen Turkish politicians struggling against the current of progress, hoodwinking or deceiving European diplomatists, and throwing whole sackfuls of gilded dust in the eyes of the public opinion of the West; we will then pass from generals to particulars, and having found out the motive principle of the great governmental engine, we will proceed to examine its works.

Perhaps some of our readers may have found themselves in contact with the Turkish Government in its bodily shape, and know as well as we do the interior of that supremely ugly yellow building in which the Sublime Porte deigns to reside, the great *Salle des Pas Perdus*, in which swarm throngs of petitioners, from the officer to the Jewish pedlar, whilst amongst the motley crowd circulate the *karchjis* with their trays of tiny coffee cups, or mendicant dervishes whose proud eyes and stern features seem to proclaim them the emperors of poverty, and the long, matted corridors, along which the humbler natives glide in their stockinged feet as silently as shadows, whilst the Embassy Attaché or privileged Frank makes his boots creak as if in disdain of the Mussulman, and seems at each step to be giving a kick to the poor wretches condemned to dance attendance upon the Sublime Porte.

From these corridors open numerous doors, each covered with a hanging carpet, behind which are divans occupied by cross-legged and bearded employés, all fat and apparently bloated with a self-consciousness of importance, smoking and counting the amber beads of their rosaries; then the offices, filled with big scarlet-bound books littered about on the floor, and the shelves in a thoroughly Turkish disorder; and finally the inner sanctuaries where the great official personages give you a cup of coffee, a chibouque, and an evasive answer.

Seeing all this, it is difficult to help being astonished when one recollects that this Tower of Babel is the centre of a Government which numbers 35,000,000 subjects, or not to fancy that one such office as this would be enough to drive the rest of the world demented; yet it is really in these offices filled with loungers, and in these *sancta sanctorum* where his Highness converses with so much wit, politeness, and tact, that the destiny of Turkey is settled.

At the Seraskierat* things are still worse, for it is a very pandemonium of employés; in the English War Office and Horse-Guards there are three clerks too many in every four; at the Seraskierat forty-nine too many in every fifty, who form a regular army, unfortunately dangerous to the Ottoman troops only. Thanks to, or in spite of, the English superfluity, the British soldier receives his pay regularly and is clothed in good stout materials; but thanks to the flood of Turkish employés, the Turkish soldier seldom gets more than a fleeting glimpse of part of the money which he ought to have received two years before, and is dressed in fantastical rags and tatters.†

The Turkish Admiralty is a little, though but very little, better managed; the only office (if we may so call it), where there reigns a kind of order and imposing gravity, being

---

* Ministry of War.
† See the Chapter on the Military Resources of Turkey.

that of the Grand Moufti, who presides over matters having reference to religion and canonical law; in everything connected with the Ulema there is something which compels veneration and respect, and you no longer seem to be in the booths of a fair, but may almost fancy yourself in presence of the white-bearded Patriarchs of the Bible.

The Conacs of the provinces are only smaller and less crowded copies of the great foci of Government at Constantinople, and to describe one of them is to describe all.

Below is the usual Salle des Pas Perdus on which (space being more restricted than in the capital) open the doors of the various bureaux, but if you have come to see the Pasha you must go upstairs, official dignity in Turkey being measured by the number of stairs mounted to arrive in its presence; if there were here houses with fourteen stories as in Edinburgh, it would be on the fourteenth flat that His Excellency would grant audience. As such monumental structures as these are not to be found in the country, you are ushered into a little room on the first or second floor, scantily furnished with a divan, a stove, a few chairs, and an arm-chair for the Pasha. It is generally the dragoman or interpreter of the Conac who receives you, and does the honours until his master's arrival; he is invariably a Greek or Armenian, and has a friendly habit of calling you "mon cher" after the first two minutes of a conversation which will probably be on politics, and in which he lays down the law as if he were an embodiment of the Sultan and Mr. John Stuart Mill; he is sometimes intelligent, but always shallow, and ten minutes' talk will get him well out of his depth.

When the Pasha arrives, you mutually bow, shake hands, and begin another conversation which, whatever may be your knowledge of Turkish, is usually carried on through the medium of the dragoman, out of politeness to this functionary, who, in spite of the oath he has taken to interpret faithfully, will (if he thinks that you are ignorant of Turkish) enliven the tedium of his duty by twisting and turning your phrases into something that you never meant them to mean, and that he knows they never could mean. Sometimes, however, the Pasha has a knowledge of French or German, and ventures boldly into the intricacies of one of these languages, dismissing the dragoman with a majestic wave of the hand. Talk of shooting, Paris, Constantinople —any indifferent subject you please—and the Pasha will answer you frankly and pleasantly, taking his full share in the interchange of ideas; but if you hazard a word concerning the internal government or state of Turkey, his face sets into official fixity, and he either contradicts you flatly or is altogether silent. If you come on business, address yourself to some subordinate, and bribe him well; if you wish to speak of the country, never cross the threshold of the Conac.

During your visit (unless it is a private audience) many different personages pass in and out of the room; that man with a cunning face, Greek trousers, and a Rayah fez, who sits upon a square inch of his straw chair near the door, who rises every time that the Pasha opens his lips, and who receives from the attendants only a cup of coffee, and neither chibouque (which is the greatest honour) nor cigarettes, is the Chorbaji, or mayor of the town, and farmer of the taxes of the district; he robs the Government, and cheats the peasant without scruple or remorse, but he bows to the ground before the Pasha.

The old grey-bearded Turk, seated by your side on the divan, who is telling the beads of his rosary and smoking his chibouque with such sublime indifference to all passing around him, is the Cadi, or Judge.

The gentleman who has just entered, attired in the latest Parisian fashion of 1840, with a convex waistcoat, and the riband of the Green Tiger of Teufelschwanz (8th class) in his button hole, is Mr. Frenkel, Vice-Consul of Monaco, buyer and seller of stolen cattle, agent for the famous manufacturers of chemical matches, A. M. Pollak of Vienna, and head of the Post-office of the Messageries Grand-ducales of Modena; he has come to obtain a concession for building a new landing-place in the harbour, and he will succeed in getting it, or diplomatic relations will be interrupted between his Excellency the Pasha and the Government of Monaco.

With another bow, and another shake of the hands, you withdraw, and as you go downstairs you notice a Cherkess in rags, but armed with a dagger which would fetch fifty pounds in a curiosity shop, and seemingly as proud in his poverty as other people are of their wealth; he has come to get a Tapou for some land he is clearing, but not being able to pay his way into the Registration-office, he is forced to wait, evidentally much to his disgust; but he looks, despite his rags, more like a king about to grant an audience than a humble petitioner.

Meanwhile a being with bare and unwashed feet has sneaked into the bureau of the Tapouji, and backs humbly out of it almost on all fours: it is a Bulgarian who has obtained the Tapou for the land of the Circassian, whom he accidentally touches in passing, and to whom he pours forth a flood of abject excuses.

There stands a group of Turkish peasants discussing the justice of a sentence given against their village, and in favour of the Beylikji;* these the Rayah carefully avoids as he makes his way to the door.

There is a knot of Greeks and Jews concocting some little scheme of cheatery, and deep in the endeavour to divide the anticipated spoil so that each man shall have the satisfaction of outwitting his accomplices by pocketing the largest share.

Moving amongst these various groups is a *Deli* (madman) begging his daily bread, a Jew gives him ten paras (a half-penny), and he passes on, the Cherkess gives him the last piastre he can spare, and the Deli offers him in return ten piastres, saying, "You want this more than I do, take it for your land; as for me I require nothing but a few leaves of cabbage, to keep me from dying of starvation; I am a philosopher, or what the world calls a madman, and the philosopher needs nothing but the strictly necessary." The Cherkess replies, "Others are poorer than I am: give your money to the crippled, not to the strong man, I have yet my two arms to work with." The Deli puts the money in his pocket, and, as he goes out into the street, gives it to a Christian beggar woman with three children.†

A few words about the distribution of justice in Turkey. A poor fellow said to us one day, "My law-suit will be judged by the Medjliss, so it is lost; for I am very poor. Ah! if it had pleased God that it should be tried before the Cadi, I should have had some chance of justice!"

The venality of the mixed tribunals is proverbial; the Cadis are sometimes, though not often, corruptible, but their

---

* Tax-farmer.   † This scene is not imaginary.

misdeeds are as nothing compared with those committed by the Medjliss and the Tijarret (Tribune of Commerce), and more especially by those Rayah tribunals presided over by Rayah ecclesiastics. The Cadis often judge rather summarily, but in their slightly Solomonic decisions there is a basis of justice; they may occasionally be venal, but are usually upright and inflexible as a bar of iron; besides, in the nature of the Turk there is a deep rooted natural sense of right and wrong, and the Cadi is sometimes obliged to yield, even against his will, to the expressed convictions of the bystanders in the Court.

This is not the case with the mixed tribunals: it does not always happen that in these the Mussulman element is numerically superior, and even when it is so the Rayahs are the richer and consequently more influential members of the Council; in a trivial affair they will not even take the trouble to vote, putting their seals to any decision whatever; but if the business has any importance for themselves, or if they are bribed accordingly, they leave no stone unturned to have it settled as they wish; false witnesses amongst the Rayahs are almost a drug in the market, and though the Cadi may refuse them the Medjliss will admit their testimony.

Whenever a Rayah bears witness in a Turkish Court, justice is in danger: Consul-General Longworth proves this assertion in a passage already quoted from the Consular Reports.

CHAPTER XXIII.

TURKISH REFORMS AND REFORMERS.

Races unfit for liberty — Denationalizing reforms — Despatch of Fuad Pasha — 'The tax of blood' — Mussulman troops and Christian officers — Extreme concessions — A village Medjliss or council — The Vilayets.

A SOCIAL and liberal revolution effected by an absolute Government can bear no fruits, for the good and simple reason that it is generally "against the grain" of the people, that Reforms the most liberal in appearance, and from which the happiest results are hoped for—being without a reason for their existence, and neither wished for nor comprehended by the country—can serve no useful purpose, and not being appreciated by the people are put to uses far different from those for which they were intended.

Liberty in the abstract is beautiful and desirable, but in order that liberty may be valued and valuable, it must have been won by a people who have felt the need of it, and whose struggles in its attainment have taught them its worth, and prepared them to use, and not abuse, it; to give liberty and civil rights to those who are ready neither for the one nor the other, is to throw pearls before swine.

An absolute and powerful Government, or a vigorous aristocracy, are the schoolmasters of an infant people; stern masters sometimes, and yet it is in their schools that the greatest nations of the civilized world have been educated.

Grant to the Russian Mougick all that he asks, and see what he will do with it; look at the state of Russia since the enfranchisement of the peasants; compare the exports of grain from Wallachia before and after the *coup d'état* of Prince Couza. The reason is simple; the Russian or Wallachian peasant, ignorant of the value of liberty, and not understanding the advantages of becoming a landowner, hating work above all things, and having seen, as he imagined, his master profit by his rights of property only to do nothing—for he is not aware that capital represents the result of dormant labour coined into money or transmuted into land—says to himself, "When I am free, and a landowner, I will do like the masters, I will do nothing but enjoy myself."

The idea has never presented itself to him, that land without labour is entirely unproductive, and when he has found out this truth by experience, and his money is spent, he sells his property instead of working, and sinks back into proletarianism: the whole country suffers, and the peasant has gained nothing.

We are very far from asserting that the despotism of a Government, or of a class, is a good or desirable state of things, but we maintain that liberty, when it is neither won nor deserved, degenerates into licence, and can produce only disorder and stagnation; give the peasant such an education as will make him a *man*, and then bestow on him all civil rights.

Suppose that entire liberty were granted to children, what use would they make of it?

Happily, in civilized Europe there are no such peasantry as those of whom we have been speaking, and our argument will perhaps be little understood for that reason; but if, ceasing to generalize, we glance at the state of Turkey, it will become more easily comprehensible.

The edict or Hatti Sheriff of Gul Hane grants to the Rayahs a species of Charter: that the life, liberty, and honour of every subject of the Sultan should be ensured and guaranteed is but just, but the spoliation of one race for the benefit of the other is unjust, and especially when the favoured people has no real right to the favours it has obtained. The Government has performed what it promised, but it has forgotten to do so " without distinction of religion or of race."

Turkish reformers have acted in precisely the same manner as the official Liberals of Russia, they have granted the widest concessions to a class which did not feel the want of them, and which has not yet even the hope of a future, and they have stripped another class whose tendencies are towards civilization, and who are not without elements of progress; the Russian nobles, and the Turks, are despoiled for the benefit of the peasants and the Rayahs. Russia, where civilization had already gained a footing and industry was beginning to spring up, is ruined, and Turkey is in a state of chaos almost irremediable.

Such is the first cause and origin of the disastrous anomalies from which Turkey suffers, and which render her the theatre of civil and political disorder; it is owing to this governmental revolution that property is no longer property, that everywhere you see immense *Chifliks* * lying waste and uncultivated, that agriculture is the ruin instead of the

---

* Farms.

wealth of the country, that industry does not exist, that the Turk is forced to spend half his time in sauntering along the streets of a garrison town dressed up like a gipsy's ape, and that the Rayah wastes his capital of labour, and the resources of the land bestowed on him by the Government, in idleness and drunkenness.

Such is the great sin of commission of the reformers, by whom public disorder and misery have been sown broadcast; and as we have stigmatized the social and economical crime of which they are guilty, we will now follow them in their operations and examine the unskilful and sometimes laughable palliatives to which they have recourse.

The Ottoman Government is well aware that there is something radically wrong in the administration and even in the organism of the country; but it does not know where— "on entend sonner, mais on ne sait pas dans quelle église" —and would give a good deal to be enlightened on the point. Such knowledge is not very difficult to arrive at, and if the Sultan were to call up any Balkan Chelibi and ask him what the country really needs, he would learn more than from all the political economists of Europe and Turkey, or any *conseil d'état* present or future. The Balkan Chelibi knows the wants of Turkey, because he feels them himself, and its anomalies, because he suffers from them; and the remedies he would propose are logical, because they would be national. In Turkey it is necessary to base institutions upon one nationality alone, since it is impossible to satisfy all of them, and those who imagine themselves capable of doing so would do well previously to call to mind the fable of the old man, his son, and his ass; we have already said that there is but one nationality fitted to serve as a basis for sensible reforms, and even if any other were chosen the attempt would be in vain, for what would the Greeks and Armenians say if the Bulgarians were thus selected?

Unfortunately the Balkan Chelibi has not yet been summoned to the councils of his Majesty; and we have only to occupy ourselves with the reformers at present in fashion.

Undeniably the reforms of the day have no national or even popular foundation; everything is copied from foreign models, and it is fancied that by closely imitating a great foreign nation in its laws, institutions, and customs, a people equally great will be created in Turkey; but the Turkish Government forgets that the Frenchman is a Frenchman before he is a Republican or an Imperialist, and that those who have ventured to place party before nationality, and to be Royalists before they are Frenchmen, have abdicated their civil rights, and are no longer anything but a class without influence and without action in that great society of France which, whatever else may be said of it, is, to begin with, based upon nationality.

If Turkey can imitate so closely everything French, from a *café chantant* to a *conseil d'état*, how is it that she has overlooked or neglected the principle of French nationality?

The greatest and most essential want of the country is justice, justice everywhere; the Turks cry aloud for it, and the Rayah speechifies about it, although he knows too well what impartial justice would do for him to be really anxious about seeing it introduced.

Such justice would be difficult to establish, for the Government which made the attempt would find itself impeded by foreign residents, it would have to alter or

modify the Capitulations, to make war against robbery and
swindling, that is against the Eastern commerce which has
taken a lease of Turkey on a pepper-corn rent; it would
have to reform the method of conscription and to re-establish
the rights of property, both of which changes would be
most distasteful to the Rayah. Supposing this want to have
been supplied, the second requirement of Turkey is strength;
military strength to repel those who might endeavour to
prevent the country from forming itself, political strength
to be able to introduce order, and strength of internal
organization in order to execute justice and repress evil.
The Balkan Chelibi would thus have defined the wants of
his country, but it is hardly necessary to say that this is not
the view taken by Turkish reformers.

A curious and very significant document,* which may be
considered as the programme of the Turkish reformers, is to
be found appended to the English Consular Reports on
Turkey; it is a species of Memoir presented to Lord Lyons
by Fuad Pasha, in which that diplomatist explains the
progress achieved and the progress yet remaining to be
achieved, and the efforts made and yet to be made to satisfy,
as the Memoir says, the conditions imposed upon Turkey
before admitting her into the political family of the nations
of Europe, and confidently asserts that his country has
behaved well, and will still continue to do so, in spite of the
Turks!

This document proves most convincingly that the Turkish
authorities have done all in their power to ameliorate the
physical, if not the moral condition of the Christians, but

---

* See Appendix M.

not a word is said upon the subject of the Mussulmans, if we except a passage which is worth quotation, as it shews the manner in which even Turkish Ministers express themselves upon those questions which concern the Mussulmans.*

"L'admission en fait des sujets non-Musulmans dans l'armée Ottomane a rencontré des obstacles dérivant presque exclusivement de la répugnance qu'inspire aux sujets non-Musulmans le service militaire. Mais le Gouvernement, loin de renoncer à l'exécution de cette mesure, qui est tout à l'avantage des Musulmans, qui actuellement supportent seuls l'impôt du sang, recherche les moyens d'introduire l'élément non-Musulman dans l'armée, soit par voie d'engagement volontaire, soit dans d'autres conditions propres à écarter des susceptibilités ou des répugnances encore persistantes. Il existe au surplus dans l'armée Ottomane deux régiments de Cosaques mixtes, c'est à dire, composés de Musulmans et de Chrétiens."—*Consular Reports*, page 82, paragraph 17.

And what are the effects of these " répugnances " and these " susceptibilités " which render military service little to the taste of the Rayahs, and of that dislike to Ottoman rule which

---

* We would strongly recommend those of our readers who may refer to Fuad Pasha's letter to read it in the original French, as the English translation is weak and incorrect throughout, and occasionally even alters and perverts the meaning of the Turkish Minister; can the following, for instance, be called a translation?

"'Telle institution nouvelle que l'on trouve à peine ébauchée, après plusieurs années de luttes et d'efforts consciencieux, atteste plus victorieusement le progrès que telle autre reforme entièrement accomplie dont l'introduction n'a heurté ni les sentiments ni les préjugés des populations."

" A fresh institution, at first roughly sketched out, after several years of struggles and conscientious efforts, whose introduction has wounded neither the feelings nor prejudices of the population, affords a better proof of progress than any other reform entirely carried out."

This English version is mere nonsense: what a pity that the traditional schoolboy did not happen to be spending his holidays at the Embassy; with the aid of a French dictionary he would easily have produced something better than this.

prompts them to desire a "separation," and is the cause of those troubles which force the unhappy Turkish peasant to leave his home and join the army?

The sorrow and tears of the abandoned women and children, the muttered oath of the Turk as he leaves his cottage, the cry of his sick child still ringing in his ears and mingled with the discordant sound of the gaida or some Bulgarian revelry, as, heavy-hearted and sad, he passes at night by a non-Mussulman village where all is dancing, feasting, and drunkenness, and contrasts this merriment with the grief which reigns in that other village behind the distant hills—all this suffering, all this injustice, is lightly passed over by Fuad Pasha, with the vague penny-a-liner's phrase, "the tax of blood," a phrase which means nothing at all.

The Frenchman pays his "tax of blood" when, with ribands streaming from his cap, he sets out laughing and singing, with "the field-marshal's *bâton*" in his knapsack, to join a fine regiment, whose eagles glitter in a brilliant sun, which the crowd applauds, and which is accompanied by patriotic cheers; a glorious career is open to him, his comrades are gay as himself, and till the day of battle he is well fed, well clothed, well lodged, respected by all and envied by not a few; and when the bullets whistle around him, ambition, the thirst for glory, and patriotism, combine to urge him forward, and he fights with the assurance that he is serving his country and that he will be the conqueror in the battle, and not (like the poor Turks) vanquished in spite of victory. If the attractive, gay, and brilliant picnic of French military life is called "the tax of blood," what name shall we give to the life of misery and privation, to the lingering death of the Turk? What phrase shall we find for the hardship of the Turkish Rediff's being snatched from his home at a moment's notice? Perhaps the "tax of tears and of blood" would not be inappropriate.

Fuad Pasha at Constantinople has never witnessed the distressing scenes at which we, who live amongst the peoples of the Balkans, have but too often been present; he has never seen, as we have, men weep—and the heart must bleed before a tear moistens the eye of a Turk of the mountains—or he would understand that the tears of a brave man are more menacing than words.

Perhaps this very phrase "the tax of blood" with which the question of military service, so far as it regards the Turks, is dismissed, may yet prove to be a terrible though involuntary prophecy, for we know that prophets may be such unknown to themselves, and utter words which are dictated to them, but of which they are far from understanding the full meaning.

But if in paragraph 17 of the Ministerial Memoir the Turks are disposed of in a couple of words, this is not the case with the Rayahs, or, to adopt the periphrasis in fashion, the "non-Mussulman subjects of the Sultan;" the grievance is all on their side, for they are denied the exciting chances of distinguishing themselves in the ranks of an army which ought to be national in order that they may find in it a support for their "legitimate national ambition." Fuad Pasha apologizes for being unable to create such an army just at present, and adds, that it is almost entirely owing to the "répugnance qu'inspire aux sujets non-Musulmans le service militaire" that their praiseworthy aspirations have not yet been gratified, but "le Gouvernement, loin de renoncer à l'exécution de cette mesure, recherche les moyens d'introduire l'élément non-Musulman dans l'armée," &c. &c.

It is very evident that the "tax of blood" has not been reduced into figures or into days of labour by the Ottoman Ministry.

A *mezzo termine* was possible which would have suited the ambition of the non-Mussulman youth of Turkey, namely, to throw open to them the military colleges, and offer them all the highest ranks in the army, without forcing them to carry the rifle and knapsack; there are plenty of non-Mussulman Pashas in the most lucrative civil posts, and the most distinguished positions in the Civil Service and the administration of the country are open to them, so why should the military service form an exception? Paragraph 9 of the same Memoir offers an apology;* we will hope that it is from a sense of justice that "certaines réserves ont été apportées dans l'admission des élèves non-Musulmans" into the military colleges, and not from a fear of seeing the beardless non-Mussulman captain lifted from the ground, not by the arms, but by the feet of his company of veteran Mussulmans. Perhaps the Turkish War Office may yet adopt our plan of substituting *charreks* for the regulation boots of rotten leather, in order to be no longer compelled to " limiter le nombre des officiers Chrétiens appelés à y exercer des commandements," a change which would certainly render the position of the non-Mussulman officer more bearable.

---

* " Les officiers sortant de cette école étant appelés à former les cadres d'une armée composée exclusivement de soldats Musulmans, il était nécessaire de limiter le nombre des officiers Chrétiens appelés à y exercer des commandements."

We see by this sketch of a single point in the Memoir in what manner vital questions are solved, or rather eluded, and we limit ourselves to this one specimen, as the reader can, if he chooses, continue the criticism by comparing the document in question (although, indeed, it carries its own criticism with it) with this book.

We must, however, notice slightly the organization of the Vilayets, "cette récente institution qui embrasse les plus larges et les plus importantes réformes," "fruit de longues études," &c. &c. Before doing so, however, we must render justice to the skilful author of the document in question, and admit that although the Memoir does not, in a Turkish point of view, solve a single important question, it is as regards Europe the most ample and complete, the most honest and true apology for the Turkish Government that could possibly be made. Reading this letter, which in no way exaggerates the favours bestowed upon the Christians, it is impossible to deny that all that could be done, and a great deal more than ought to have been done, has been done for them by the Ottoman Government, to the detriment of the Osmanli people, against all interests but those of the favoured race, and even to the prejudice of the Government itself.

If Europe were enlightened as to the state of this country by able, honest, and impartial agents, this document would be no longer an apology, but the bitterest and most sarcastic criticism on European influence in Turkey; for to those who know the country it says, "See, Europe, what we have done to gratify your unreasonable and ill-founded sympathies; the country, the State itself, has been turned upside down that your *protégés* may be able to come to the surface; we have given them unbounded licence in everything, from their religion to their pettiest wishes; the Giaour of fifty years ago, the oppressed Rayah without civil or political rights, has become the non-Mussulman subject, he alone possesses rights, and he oppresses in his turn; we have made the Turk the Rayah of him who was formerly the Giaour. The non-Mussulman subject governs himself as he pleases and after his own fashion, and he even governs the Turk; not one of his least wishes have we left ungratified, except, perhaps, that of becoming commander-in-chief of the Ottoman armies, but even this denial is for his own good, so long as the Turkish soldiers wear boots and not *charreks;* the day on which the non-Mussulman subject prefers the bivouac of the camp to that in front of the Tukhan, the intoxication of glory to that of wine and spirits, long marches to a *dolce far niente,* and death by the sabre or the bullet to death by delirium tremens—on that very day his wish shall be satisfied. The non-Mussulman subject has but to say the word and he is appointed a civil Pasha; for him we reform, for him we organize. Look around, Europe, behold your work, and be content, for the Russians themselves could not have done more in Turkey than we have done to please you!"

Compare Fuad Pasha's letter, not only with this book, for we have no pretensions to be the only persons who dare to speak the truth, but with the Report of Consul-General Longworth, or even with the majority of the Consular Reports, and this satirical form will be easily appreciable.

The organization by Vilayets, of which the Government is so proud, and which it only succeeded in evolving after such "longues études," is neither more nor less than a copy of

French organization; for Vilayet read Province, for Sanjak, Préfecture, for Caza, Sous-préfecture, and you have the Vilayet system before you. There are elective "Conseils Communaux" presided over by a Maire, who is styled Kuoi Chorbaji in the Rayah villages, *Mukhtiar* amongst the Mussulmans; there are "Conseils Municipaux," also elective, and a "Conseil d'état" is in process of formation; probably before long the country will be blessed with a Sénat and a Corps Législatif, and then the resemblance to France will be complete—in all points.

A very interesting and edifying spectacle is a debate of the village *Medjliss*, or Rayah "Conseil Communal;" the "Mairie" is the Tukhan or public-house, and "M. le Maire" is a being remarkable by the dirt with which he is thickly encrusted, and who is, moreover, three-quarters tipsy; he is as uneducated as the rest of his colleagues, who differ from him in physical appearance only by being a little more or less unwashed, and a little more or less inebriated.

The whole council is seated on the ground *alla Turca*, or lying about in any attitude they find convenient; smoking and drinking go on uninterruptedly, for a Bulgarian Medjliss is always thirsty, and the Bakal steps over the bodies of prostrate honourable members to fill their glasses and give his opinion on the subject in question.

The case undergoing discussion is as follows: An honest Turk has caught a horse-thief *in flagrante delicto*, and as the horse belongs to the village of Derekuoi he has delivered up thief and stolen property to the "authorities" of the village; the culprit is seated in a corner of the Tukhan, drinking his mastica, and occasionally joining in the debate, as do also the village witch and various other women whom the gravity of the occurrence has attracted to the door of the public-house.*

"What were we talking about?" says M. le Maire, who has taken off his old sheepskin cap, and is engaged in a minute investigation of its recesses.

"Kto snaje?" (who knows?) answers Vassili, pausing for a moment in his occupation of washing his feet with a penknife.

"You're an idiot, Vassili!" cries Nikolaki, his political opponent, an advanced Liberal who detests the old-fashioned Conservatism of Vassili.

Vassili replies by some strictly unparliamentary language, and Nicolaki continues—

"An idiot and nothing else! We were talking about the horse, and you are too great a fool to recollect even that!"

Hereupon ensues a free fight; but, as everybody has been drinking too freely to be able to hit out, not much damage is done, except that a few pipes and one of the Bakal's two glasses are broken; finally, order and harmony are restored, and M. le Maire, who has effected an exchange of caps during the scuffle, recovers the thread of his discourse and resumes—

"Yes, we were talking about the horse and what we are to do in this case——"

But what they did, or rather what they did not do, is related in the Chapter on Brigandage, where the reader will find the sequel of the story.

The Medjlisses of the Cazas (sous-préfectures), and even of the Sanjaks (préfectures), though better composed, and

---

* This scene is related as it really occurred.

not enlivened by wine or mastica, are but little more expeditious in their deliberations, owing in a great measure to that chronic somnambulism of the Christian members which Mr. Dupuis, their chief friend amongst the English Consular Corps, has depicted with so much pathos and clearness.*

The mixed tribunals, and a new code of law, criminal, civil, and commercial, are also institutions depending on the new organization; but in spite of them goods are bought and sold openly by false weights and measures, and brigandage is not yet extinct in the Balkan.†

The whole of the Vilayet system consists in the establishment of a new administrative sub-division and of various elective councils or tribunals, in which the non-Mussulman element enters largely.

This organization would be a real boon to the country if the people were ready and fitted to profit by it, if non-Mussulman evidence were not too often false, if non-Mussulman members could keep awake when other interests than their own are at stake, and above all if Mithat Pasha had been left a little longer at Rustchuk to correct its faults by his energy, and to venture upon reforms which are really needed by the country, and which his reputation would have enabled him to attempt. As yet, in spite of the Vilayet system, not one of the important questions which form the titles of many of our chapters has been solved, or even raised, and the new organization is still nothing but a name;

---

* See Consular Reports, No. VII.

† The energy of Mithat Pasha has greatly diminished brigandage, but the Capitulations prevented him putting a stop to fraud.

on the appreciation of its principles depends the salvation of the empire, but if it is carried out, as seems to be intended, it is merely the ass's kick given to the Turkish people.

Having thus described the Vilayet system, we cannot pass over in silence its originator, or rather introducer, and we shall therefore devote a chapter to Mithat Pasha.

CHAPTER XXIV.

MITHAT PASHA.

Mithat Pasha's attempted reforms — Suppression of brigandage — Secularization of education — Inspection of weights and measures — The Agio — Lending banks — Orphanages — Recovery from Philorayahism.

MITHAT PASHA, the late Governor of the Vilayet, or Province, of the Danube, is an honest and upright man, and possesses a quality even more valuable than these, for he is energetic in times when energy seems to have deserted the governing classes of Turkey to take refuge amongst the governed. Had Mithat Pasha been allowed to prosecute his scheme of reform a little longer, he might have succeeded, in spite of Constantinople, in bringing about some definite result by means of experiments which he alone could venture to make; but the present Government of Turkey imagine that perfection has been reached, and so the analytical chemist is ordered to turn apothecary's boy, and to serve out drugs which he has neither examined nor rectified.

To men in power the organization of the Vilayets is the *ne plus ultra* of progress, and if the friends of the Eastern Christian are not contented with it, it is because they are insatiable; but now the great chemist has departed, his box of chemicals, carefully locked up and minus the key, is given to another, and the new professor has only the right to amuse himself by looking at the outside; the Vilayet of the Danube has ceased to be a centre of creation for reforms.

We have said that the education of the civilized Turk is very incomplete, and to give it that European finish which is natural to the European brain is very difficult if not impossible; thus, when a Turk wishes to cease to be a Mussulman and Osmanli, and to look at things with European eyes, he finds himself in a very embarrassing position; for, owing to his entirely theoretical education, he is irresistibly impelled to mistake cause for effect, and effect for cause; Mithat Pasha, though unable to avoid falling into this error, struggled gallantly against it, and seemed to be on the eve of victory when he was suddenly called upon to preside over the future *Conseil d'État* * at the very moment when he was beginning his work of re-organization in earnest.

Mithat Pasha has done much for the Vilayet of the Danube, and would have done more; for he possessed both the energy to venture innovations, and a reputation which permitted him to do so unchecked by official ignorance or timidity.

He began his career by a serious attack upon brigandage, and even ventured to hang a few brigands and to send some robbers to Widin; these repressive measures were rendered necessary by the establishment of agricultural banks, which

---

* This is a rather complicated mechanical toy, which, having been much admired in Paris, has lately been sent as a present to Constantinople; the packers, however, either forgot to put in the works, or these were lost on the journey, so the clever little Turkish boys have not been able to play with it yet; however, all the grandest clock-makers have been ordered to make a new set of works, very strong, and adapted to the climate; these are not yet ready, but it is hoped they will soon be finished, and great expectations are formed of the Conseil d'État when it is once in working order.

naturally led to the establishment of bands of thieves. He actually dared to treat political brigands coming to Turkey from other countries as common brigands, and nothing more, and even administered a slap to the Capitulations, a very gentle one, it is true, and quite within the limits of the law, but in time he might have learned to hit harder and straighter. He has dared to place himself in the path sacred to Eastern commerce, by creating Government agricultural banks, very petty banks, very foolishly contrived, and not very useful, but they have had the effect of ruining a few small bankers (every Rayah who owns a capital, stolen or borrowed, of ten shillings, is a banker, and lends money, and of this class were the victims of the agricultural banks), a trifling result certainly; but in time Mithat Pasha might have succeeded in cutting off the other heads of the hydra. Mithat Pasha ventured to put obstacles in the way of Agio, and would one day have abolished it; he even conceived the bold idea of educating the Rayahs, and wished to establish schools in which something else would have been taught than the precepts of the "Tserkierne,"* and which would have inculcated honesty and morality; and one day he would have dared to enforce the one and the other, and perhaps even to do justice to the Turks. But Mithat Pasha is dead and buried in the Conseil d'État. *Requiescat in pace!*

As we have pronounced the funeral oration of his Excellency Mithat Pasha, we will now enter a little more into the details of some of the institutions traced out by him. First in point of importance comes the question of Bulgarian

---

* Russian 'Church Books.'

education, which, as our readers will perhaps have noticed, has been rather neglected.

Since the schism, the Bulgarians have established a few schools which they call National, and in which an individual strongly perfumed with garlic gives lessons to a dozen of the village children; but what does he teach them? To read what are called the Bulgarian characters, a strange medley of Russian lay and ecclesiastical type, to know the figures of the Russian ecclesiastical arithmetic, which are letters, and finally to repeat the orthodox and imperial catechism prepared for the Bulgarian nation in books printed for this special purpose: this catechism teaches one great truth to the infant Bulgarians, that above the Sultan is God, and above God is the Czar. Such is the primary school: what do more pretentious schools teach? What results do they produce but troubles, and what morality that can be expressed otherwise than by a high figure with a minus before it? Mithat Pasha knew this perfectly well, and wished to secularize the schools—to secularize is the right word, for the education given in them is, though not religious, entirely ecclesiastical—but the Bulgarians refused, in spite of the very advantageous offers made to them; had Mithat Pasha remained at his post he would have carried out this scheme in spite of their opposition.

Once upon a time Mithat Pasha went so far as to order a verification of weights and measures by the police; but here he was stopped by the Capitulations, the great protector of all abuses committed by foreigners; the Consuls cried out with one voice, "This is an attack upon our rights, we *only* can judge or interfere in any way with our respective subjects: to allow the Turkish police to enter the shop of a foreigner is to open the door to Turkish peculation and corruption." In the face of this refusal nothing could be done, and consequently false weights and measures flourish as they always did and always will do in Turkey.

To abolish false weights and measures, or a fraudulent Agio, the prohibition and penalties must apply equally to all; had Mithat Pasha punished those Turkish subjects who infringed the law, whilst foreigners were outside or rather above the law, he would but have granted a new monopoly. As a natural consequence that article of the Turkish Penal Code which punishes this species of cheating is a mere dead letter.

The fraudulent Agio which exists in this country also attracted the attention of Mithat Pasha. An Agio on foreign coin exists everywhere, but in all other countries it is insignificant,* and more or less justly regulated: in Turkey, on the contrary, it is enormous, and varies largely according to the interest of speculators, a fact which greatly injures the Ottoman finances.

This is bad enough, but in what other country will you find an Agio upon the coin issued by Government?

The English and French bronze coins are only counters representing a nominal value, but who would dare to ask fifteen pence for a shilling, or twenty-five sous for a franc? This, however, is what is done in Turkey: the gold pound (lira) is worth 100 piastres, 110 or 115 are asked for it in copper, and the Turkish copper has a far greater intrinsic value than the English or French bronze; the silver Medjidie

---

* We do not here allude to bank notes or other paper, but to current coin.

is worth twenty piastres, and twenty-two are asked for it; besides this, there is an Agio between gold and silver; but this is not all, you buy the lira at 110, but you sell it at 105! This Agio forms the means of existence of a swarm of petty parasites who style themselves Serafs or bankers.

Oriental commerce has of course seized upon this Agio which it has invented for its own speculations; thus, when the peasants sell their corn, the lira is at 110 or 115, and is paid to them for their grain at this rate; but when the peasants come to buy, the lira has suddenly fallen to 102 or 104! The peasant, too, is obliged to pay his taxes in gold or silver, and the Government will receive the lira only at 100; not that the Government profits by this, as it gives out the lira at the same price that it takes it; and as the emission of silver is at the same rate, it in reality loses.

Mithat Pasha wished to put a stop to these evils; but to prevent the existence of Agio by decreeing that gold, silver, and copper should each have only their proper value, could be done only by the central Government, for if this were the case in one Vilayet alone, that province would have been robbed by the others of the percentage on the Agio, and speedily drained of all gold coin; he took then a *mezzo termine*, and prohibited the circulation of copper; but Eastern commerce was too clever for him, and peculated as much as ever by inventing an Agio on silver! So Mithat Pasha had to leave the Agio alone.

The agricultural banks were originated in order to remedy another evil, usury, which was, and is, terrible and excessive.

In this country the peasant, that is, the one person who can offer a security which is worth anything, cannot raise money under 60 per cent., and often pays double that interest. Mithat Pasha created agricultural banks to check this, but he set about their formation in a very original manner; he ordered every village to sow so much grain, and when the corn was sold,* employed the proceeds to form the capital of the rural bank. These banks are bound to lend to the peasant at 10 or 12 per cent., but it seems somewhat unreasonable to say to the people "Pay us your money, and we will lend it you again at 10 or 12 per cent."

It will give some idea of the country, and of Eastern commerce, when we say that even such an absurdity as these banks would have been a great benefit to the country, had not Greeks and Rayahs contrived to slip in as clerks, &c. As soon as this pernicious element seized upon the agricultural banks they changed their nature and became mere counting-houses of a commerce carried on after the Greek fashion. The clerks speculate on the Agio, in grain, and in usury, all with the money of the peasants; if one of the latter comes to ask for a loan, he is refused—"There is no money, it has all been lent," and so the peasant goes sadly away. "Wait a bit, my friend," says a private *employé*

---

* In other Vilayets every peasant is taxed two bushels of corn per pair of oxen or buffaloes per annum, but though he may have paid for years, he cannot borrow money if he is poor; even if he can, what does he really pay for it? The peasant if he requires money, usually needs about 5*l.* or 500 piastres, for this he pays, at 10 per cent., 50 piastres, but as since the three years that these banks have been established he has paid yearly two bushels of corn of the value of 50 piastres, he really gives 200 piastres to borrow 500 for a year!

In justice, as the capital of the bank comes out of the peasants' own pocket, he ought to be able to borrow at 1 per cent., or indeed without paying any interest whatever.

of the official clerk of the agricultural bank, "if you want five pounds, I can let you have them if you will pay me *seven* at harvest time."

The peasant needs the money, and accepts; "But," says the usurer, "we will do it on the bank paper; I will lend seven pounds to the bank, and you will sign a bill, for the bank to keep, of seven pounds payable in three months: come along." The peasant goes upstairs, signs the bill, and receives five pounds for his promise to pay seven, whilst the unaccredited clerk hands over to the accredited clerk seven pounds which in reality belong to the peasant, who, by-the-bye, is very lucky if he is paid in gold, and not in copper.

This is what the Rayahs have made of the benevolent agricultural institutions of Mithat Pasha. Until there is a severe justice executed in the country, and the Capitulations cease to protect robbers of all nations, the admittance of a Rayah or an Eastern Christian into any undertaking, in any capacity, is the admittance of fraud and theft, and, still worse, is the ruin, physical and moral, of the undertaking, if it be intended as an honest one.

Mithat Pasha, in his solicitude for the welfare of the provinces he ruled, and in his anxiety to copy everything good that he had seen in Europe, actually built an orphan asylum.

The house was ready, the *employés* at their places, and the revenue assured by a hotel* built out of his Excellency's private purse, of which the profits were to be spent in keeping up this charitable establishment; but there wasn't an

---

* The *Isla Khane* at Rustchuk.

orphan to be found in all the country! And for the simple reason that every Turkish house is a ready-made orphan's home, as the poorest Turk will adopt any child left at his door.

However, as the asylum existed, it was necessary to give a reason for its existence by the presence of one or two children, but no foundlings were to be found; at last a zealous *employé* promised to procure a real orphan, and kept his word, so the asylum at last boasted of an inmate, who was brought up as a Christian, as he declared himself to be so. The philanthropic Pasha was delighted, but alas! one day an individual presented himself, and claimed the child as being his relation. Great was the consternation, and many the discussions as to whether the orphan should be surrendered or no, but it was found that the Turkish laws required that he should be given up to his affectionate uncle, which was accordingly done amidst the tears of the whole establishment. But this was not quite the end; the relative who had given up the orphan to the zealous *employé* brought a claim against the Pasha for the loss of his nephew's services as an apprentice shoemaker—and the Pasha had to pay!

We must not laugh at this rather Quixotic undertaking of Mithat Pasha, for he intended to benefit the country, and there are not many Pashas of whom the same can be said.

Cheated and deceived whenever he had anything to do with the Rayahs, Mithat Pasha was beginning to understand them, and to see the falsity of that fundamental principle of the Vilayets which prescribes (in Article V., if we are not mistaken), "that all the tribunals, offices, appointments, &c., shall be equally divided between Turks and Rayahs.'"

Mithat Pasha saw that by abolishing the Chorbajis who held their office for life, and replacing them by Chorbajis who were elected for a year only, he had but increased the disorder without extirpating robbery or preventing the ruin of the Rayah villages, that ruin whose throne is the *Tukhan*; he was recovering from the dangerous fever of Philorayahism,* and was already sufficiently convalescent to commence scouring the country, attended only by one or two Zaptiehs, and executing a summary and much-needed justice, when he was suddenly snatched away from his Vilayet by the inexorable *Conseil d'État*. Mithat Pasha is dead and buried—Resurgetne?

---

* Mithat Pasha had two nicknames, Gueuzluklu (spectacled) Pasha and Giaour Pasha, the latter being gained by the favour which he at first showed to the Rayahs; latterly, however, the second name has a good deal fallen into disuse.

CHAPTER XXV.

THE POLITICAL PARTIES OF TURKEY.

Bulgarian politicians — The project of independence — The project of autonomy — Young Turkey — Old Turkey.

THERE is perhaps no country and no capital in the world where there are so many political parties (many of them, it is true, only styled so by themselves) as in Turkey and Constantinople; every nationality and every shade or phantom of a nationality constitutes itself a party, and is divided according to the most approved European principles into various sections differing in their opinions, and distinguished by colours, black, blue, green, or yellow. But, from the party of the Armenians to that of the Bulgarians, they are agreed upon no single point except the one which, thanks to their conscientious agitation, is so constantly repeated in Europe, that Turkey has no future before her, and can hope for nothing save from their magnanimous toleration and assistance.

These little revolutionary parties of the divers nationalities under the rule of Turkey have no real force but that which consists in the total ignorance of Europe upon the real state of the country, and the misrepresentations by which Eastern Christianity has obtained an ill-deserved sympathy from that of the West; and if the eyes of Europe were once opened to the true condition and character of the subjects of Turkey, and the action and influence of Eastern Christianity made widely known, the proceedings of such committees as those of Belgrade and Bucharest would be merely laughable, because they would have nothing to expect from the public opinion of Europe, whilst at present they are painful from their effects, and revolting from the audacious falsehood of their statements.

It is curious and amusing to hear two gentlemen in Péra doing all they can to make their language incomprehensible to one another by torturing Russian into all sorts of impossible forms, and making the bystanders believe that they are talking Bulgarian. Both of them understand Russian thoroughly; but this comedy is not without design, and produces the desired effect, for the wonder-struck Pérotes repeat, and the newspapers publish, that "yesterday, at such and such a place, two of the most eminent Bulgarian politicians (or literary men) had an interview which in the present crisis is not without its signification." What neither the Pérotes nor the journalists know is, that the two eminent Bulgarians are in reality two Russian Vice-Consuls of two tumble-down little towns somewhere in Bulgaria.

Rich Bulgarians there certainly are, remarkable by the glossiness of their clothes, by ear-rings, and by half-a-dozen rings on each finger, but perhaps the most eminent literary man of the nationality is a Choban of our acquaintance who has composed and set to music (to the gaida, of course) a threnodia on the death of one of his herd of pigs; as for politicians, they may be judged by their works, which chiefly consist in magniloquent incendiary proclamations written at Péra and printed at Bucharest.

These Bulgarian proclamations form a good example, by

their respective effects in this country and in Europe, of the difference between the true state of affairs as it exists in Turkey, and the false ideas conveyed to foreign nations; all these inflated pamphlets and terrible threats excite Europe, affect even the Funds, and are the cause of various sapient diplomatic notes from the great Powers to the Porte, who orders the mobilization of the Reserve, at great expense to the exchequer and still greater loss to agriculture and the poor Turkish peasant, and grants a new concession to the Christians in addition to the previous 750. But Bulgaria does not share this alarm, and the Turk, confident in his own courage and the cowardice of the Rayah, goes to his work in the fields humming an "Aman;" the Rayah drinks his wine and mastic as usual, listens with many signs of the cross (to prove that he is a Christian) to the emissary who reads the proclamation of the representatives of the oppressed, but in his heart he thinks, "not if I know it."

A Bulgarian revolution, or even serious agitation, is impossible without the consent, and even aid, of the Turkish Government, and the presence of a large Russian army in these provinces; not, as certain newspapers affirm, because the Rayahs are devoted to the Sultan, but because they are cowards. A Bulgarian, even when drunk, will never dare to lift his hand against a Turk unless the latter is disarmed and wounded, and even then only if there are a dozen Russians ready to back him; and if those who have formerly seen the Rayahs commit nameless atrocities under the protection of a foreign invasion hope the same results from the present agitation, they are, thank Heaven! mistaken; the Bulgarians will never renew the scenes of 1827, and the eyes of their disinterested friends will never again be gladdened by the pleasing spectacle of old men, women, and children burnt alive,* so long as Russia remains a peaceable spectator on the other side of the Pruth, for the Rayah's valour only appears when it is rendered perfectly unnecessary by the presence of powerful allies.

The Armenians, the Greeks, and the Servians, have a history, the Bulgarians have none,† but does the possession of a history constitute a nation or a people? One example is sufficient; Europe took up the cause of the modern and (Eastern) Christian Greeks on account of their very doubtful descent from the ancient and pagan Greeks; the result is—Modern Greece; but not content with the triumphant success of this experiment, she hit upon the brilliant idea of autonomy, and created Servia and the Moldo-Wallachian Provinces!

There is now some talk of conferring this latter benefit upon Bulgaria, but it never will be conferred, for the Turkish people have had enough of hostile autonomies and will tolerate no extension of the system; as, however, this is one of the questions in which Europe is interested at the present moment, it may be worth while to examine it.

The Bulgarian agitators are divided into two parties, both tending to one common object, the spoliation of Turkey; of these, one, hatched under the wings of the Russian eagle, sees no chance of salvation for the Slavonic Rayah save in revolu-

---

* In 1827 more than 2000 old men, women, and children (Turks) were burned alive in the village of Akdere alone by the Bulgarians, whilst a Russian corps d'armée looked on.

† The Bulgarian Rayahs are the descendants of the serfs of the old Bulgarian nobility, which was exterminated by the Turks.

tion and a separation, by force of arms, of the Balkan and the plains between that chain and the Danube from Turkish rule. This party talks loudly of war, massacre, and revenge for centuries of oppression, but it will do no more than threaten unless Russia risks a war against the Porte; we say "*risks* a war" because in Russia there exists a hostile element widely different from the subjected races of Turkey, a nationality which has proved its rights by courage and by martyrdom, and a national spirit which, unaided from without, lately shook the foundations of Russian rule during nearly three years, and forced the victor to revenge himself. If a child strikes a strong man, he does not "revenge himself," except perhaps in some such manner as would suffice for the vengeance of Turkey upon her naughty children in Bulgaria, and which need not exceed a wholesome use of the birch rod; but Russia has thought it necessary to ruin a whole people, and to redden her scaffolds and her dungeons with Polish blood to avenge herself for the insurrection of Poland.

If, then, in the case of Turkey being attacked by Russia, the Sultan, unaided by those so-called friends whose assistance has generally done nothing more than envenom the question at issue, appealed to his people, and, following the example set by his enemy, availed himself of an unfriendly nationality in the midst of Russia to permit the white eagle of Poland to accompany the crescent, what chance would Russia have if an army of only 100,000 Turks seconded an insurrection such as that of 1863?

These questions of nationality are like double-edged tools, dangerous to play with, and resemble the proverbial stick "with two ends."

If Russia is wise, she will leave Turkey alone, for there

may not always be found traitors amongst the Pashas nor heroes amongst the Bulgarians, whilst there will always be Poles in Poland and Turks in Turkey.

The other Bulgarian party takes the hint given by the Eastern policy of France, which consists in advocating national autonomies, demanding unlimited concessions from the central Government, and strongly recommending liberty and equality; acting upon this system, the second party proclaims loudly and constantly, through its organ, a newspaper printed at Constantinople in French, the unalterable loyalty of the Bulgarians to the Sultan, and endeavours to prove to Europe at large that it is owing to the efforts of its members that the great Bulgarian nation perseveres in its fidelity to Turkey, and that to this fidelity the Ottoman empire is indebted for its present existence. As a recompense for so much devotion, it demands merely a Bulgarian autonomy, declaring that "Bulgaria, free and independent, but owning H.I.M. the Sultan as its suzerain, will always be faithful to him, and like Roumania (!) will repel Muscovite influence," &c. Such, neither more nor less, is its programme.

The slight difficulty caused by the presence of some millions of Mussulmans in Bulgaria seems to be as completely ignored by the authors of this ingenious plan as it is by Europe in general; but, nevertheless, this obstacle is sufficient to render the success of the project impossible, as it is hardly likely that the Turks will consent to a wholesale migration, and, although unrepresented at Constantinople, they have sufficient strength in their own provinces to prevent Bulgaria ever becoming a second Servia; for this reason the party of which we are speaking would infallibly collapse if the "friends" of Turkey would leave that empire to itself, or even if they really desired the welfare of all its inhabitants "without distinction of religion or of race."

The Christian subjects of the Sultan have already obtained all that, and even more than, they can in justice demand; now the Mussulmans begin to ask that some attention should be paid to *their* claims, and hence has arisen the gradual formation, amongst the Turks themselves, of various parties of reform which, however (with the exception of that of "Old Turkey"), have as yet, unfortunately, neither settled convictions nor a definitive plan of action, and are consequently powerless for the present, although the day is approaching when the destinies of Turkey will be in their hands.

These parties are numerous, and agree only in the well-founded conviction that Turkey, ill-governed, and on the high road to ruin, must effect sensible and radical reforms if she wishes to avert her entire destruction ; but what is to be reformed, or how the necessary reforms are to be carried out, is still a blank in their programmes.

There are of course the two parties to be found in all organized States, the "ins" and the "outs," both of whom the Sultan has criticized in the words "they promise, and that is all;" what they promise is civilization and progress. The Ministers, addressing themselves to Europe, say "We are doing all in our power to civilize;" the opposition say, "But *we* could do better," and the end of either party is merely the retention of or attainment to power.

Besides these, there is another party whose head-quarters are not in Turkey; this consists of Turkish political exiles who, adopting the system in favour with refugees from European States, can find no better weapon than personalities with which to attack the Government, and no other political programme than such vague Utopias as are in fashion amongst the unhappy class to which they belong, whose members regenerate Europe and decide the destiny of a country between a couple of cigarettes in a Leicester Square *café*; by means of a newspaper printed in London on rose-tinted paper, and largely, though privately, circulated at Constantinople, this party has, it is said, excited the anger of the Sultan against a Minister of great talent on whom they have made a virulent personal attack, but who has cleared himself most successfully from their accusations. These persons cannot have the least chance of doing any good to Turkey, since they err in the same manner as those they accuse, and are equally ignorant of the real grievances of the country as of the remedies to be applied; we do not deny their patriotism any more than that of the present Ministry, but we are constrained to admit that the ideas of the one party are as powerless as the efforts of the other to open a new and prosperous era for Turkey.

The above parties take the generic name of "Young Turkey," and their policy may be compared to that of the Liberals in England; whilst "Old Turkey" represents the extinct English Tories.

Having said enough upon the action of Young Turkey, we will sketch its principles; these, like the ideas of the present Ministry, consist in advocating a copy of French institutions, varying, it is true, from absolutism to absolute democracy, but always keeping to a French model; mistaking effect for cause, they imagine that by building seven-storied houses of pretentious architecture, and dressing the army as Zouaves, or by proclaiming the principle of universal suffrage and the civil rights of the citizen, they will at once change Turkey into France and Turks into Frenchmen.

The one party forgets that civilization, arising from the requirements of a people, cannot be established by a decree, like a new street or a new uniform; the other, that the Turks have neither the same aspirations nor the same class of ideas as the peoples of Europe, and least of all as the French; quote to a Turk of the country Prudhon's well-known maxim, "*La propriété c'est le vol*," and he will tell you that it is just by the application of this principle that the foreign trader grows rich, and that the Rayah holds lands which belonged to his (the Turk's) ancestors.

In Europe certain social questions exist which are entirely unknown in Turkey, but nevertheless everybody seems to think that they *ought* to exist, takes their existence for granted, and agitates accordingly.

The youth of Turkey educated in France (we do not here allude to the vast majority whose only study is fashionable vice, but to the few who have endeavoured to make the most of their opportunities and talents) having merely gone through a course of study unsupplemented by the practical appreciation of the life of a citizen in a civilized country, know nothing of France except as represented by the student world, and import into Turkey ideas in vogue in the *Quartier Latin* but impossible in practice, ideas emanating from young brains and hearts filled with good and noble feelings but unpractical as the principles they profess. Arrived at Constantinople, these young men struggle, or fancy they struggle, against the current for a time, then, yielding to it, accept some Government appointment.

Young Turkey preaching a Parliamentary system of unlimited liberty, the Government decreeing civilization *alla Franca* and progress according to law; each party preaching or acting against the two principles most sacred to the Turkish people, the religion of Mahomet, and Ottoman nationality—what wonder that the one is not more listened to than the other is obeyed!

The letter of Prince Moustapha Fazyl Pasha to the Sultan, in spite of the laconic criticism of his Majesty ("deli," "a madman") contained by chance a vital and important question, that of military service. This letter has been read, and has produced a certain effect amongst the Turks of the country, but if you ask them what they think of the plan proposed by the Prince for the regeneration of Turkey, all, from the Bey or Hodja to the Choban, will answer in the words of the Sultan, "the man is mad."

Young Turkey is powerless because it falls back upon the democracy of the *Quartier Latin* and seeks no assistance from the strong arms and stout hearts of the Osmanli people.

Old Turkey, of which the majority of the members belong to the Ulema, and which unfortunately numbers a few fanatics amongst its ranks, is in reality the only party with which the Ministry, backed though it be by all the embassies, must needs come to an account; for though the Sultan's voyage to Europe was hardly in accordance with the wish of the Grand Mufti, his Majesty was at least obliged to obtain from him a Fetva in toleration if not in approval of the journey. Through this party only is there a chance for

Turkey, but unhappily it is more than conservative, it is retrogressive, and though the old state of things may have been in some respects better than the new, it is impossible to return to it. The Beys, Timars, and Ziamets are ruined, and their fiefs destroyed beyond the possibility of reconstruction; the Turkey of Mahomet II. is fallen, never again to rise to the same pinnacle of power; new laws, good or bad, are in force, and must remain so, but Old Turkey is still able to better the condition of the country, to save it from total destruction and to revive some species of justice in the land, if this party make a proper use of its influence and position.

Might not the Mufti say, "Padischah! you have despoiled the Ulema, create order amongst the Greek Clergy; you have ruined the Turks, tax the Rayahs as well; robbery is contrary to the law of God and the Prophet, abolish Eastern commerce; the whole world will be against you, but the Prophet has said 'When the world is in arms against you, on that day shall you fight and conquer in the name of God and of the law.'"

The gravest questions might thus be submitted to the Sultan, who is not only a just but a brave man, and if this were done Turkey might with reason hope something from the Tories of Turkey; and such bold champions of their country's cause would have nothing to fear, for there is not a heart amongst the brave Turkish people, or even amongst the European lovers of justice, which would not go with them in the great work of doing that justice which is one of the attributes of God himself.

CHAPTER XXVI.

COMPARISON BETWEEN THE BULGARIAN RAYAH AND THE TURK.

The cause of humanity — Sham civilization — Bad material in the Rayah — Good material in the Turk of the country — Constantinople a school of vice — Discipline for the Rayah — Self-defence.

HAVING already depicted both Turk and Rayah conscientiously and truly, though in very different colours from those used for the purpose in Europe, we ask permission to glance at the Eastern Question as it is seen by attentive observers who have studied it in its birthplace, and lived with and amongst the two races whose cause is being now judged by the tribunals of the West, and who have not formed any opinions but such as are based upon and supported by facts of which they have a personal knowledge.

This question presents itself under three distinct phases:—

1. As a pretext for aggression leading to territorial aggrandisement; this is the view taken by Russia.

2. As a political expedient, Turkey in her disorganized state being used as a counter to incline the balance in favour of him who can make the best use of her weakness; this is the view taken by certain Powers calling themselves the friends of Turkey.

3. As a serious question affecting the cause of humanity, of civilization, and of progress; this is the view taken by

public opinion as represented by honest men of all nations, and is also the political *thema* upon which temporizing or aggressive statesmen execute their most brilliant variations, profiting by the general ignorance of the true state of things and the perversion of public opinion, which has formed its conclusions on falsehoods which by dint of continual repetition have attained the dignity of axioms.

In other chapters we have touched upon the first two phases, and shall now occupy ourselves only with the third, which, as it is now handled by the skilful artificers who are engaged upon its manufacture for the foreign market, is in reality more dangerous to—we will not repeat that hackneyed phrase, "the dignity of the Ottoman empire," but—the cause of civilization, humanity, and progress throughout the whole world, than the Russian bayonet, or even the mania for reforms and innovations fashionable amongst the statesmen of the present day, inasmuch as on it depends the verdict of the civilized world upon this question.

We have been asked, what would become of the fragments of Turkey if once the Ottoman empire ceased to exist; but we have never heard the infinitely more important question, what would become of the chances of civilizing the East if the Turkish element ceased to exist, or even if it were modified by the vague ideas of vague reformers?

To these questions we reply Socratically.

Is civilization based upon the material progress of a country? Certainly not, for it is but the outward sign of the strong vivacity and powerful constitution of society.

In what then does civilization consist, and what is its indispensable principle?

In our opinion it is this powerful organization and tenacious vivacity which form the only fruitful germ of real progress; all civilization grafted upon a society of which the foundations are unstable, or which is corrupt at heart, and unguided by a healthy and practical public morality, can be but superficial, and will produce no results tending to the advance of the human race towards that goal which is marked out for it, and which is general amelioration or progress.

When it is once admitted (and it is difficult to deny) that where no strongly organized society and no practical public morality exist, and where the population is brutish and idle, no civilization useful to humanity can spring up—the Eastern Question is at once solved, as far as its third phase is concerned.

Even the mere tourist who has passed through Russia, whirled along by a locomotive manufactured in one of the great centres of European industry, has surely not been able to help observing that the civilization he sees around him is exotic and assimilates ill with the country itself; the Mougick in a railway carriage is an anomaly. The gold laced uniforms of Wallachia or the brilliant toilettes of the ladies of St. Petersburg are equally out of place, and we wonder at the presence of the French képi or the Parisian salon so many hundred miles from France.

Those who know Russia with the experience of years can easily account for the new institutions which seem to be destined always to remain foreign to the true nature of the country, and it is not necessary to remember the old muddy roads nor the *perekladnyje*, the Post Britschkas which travelled along them, to know that the railroad is there not in answer to the wants of the country, but by virtue of an ukase.

If we examine the populations which inhabit Turkey, and submit them to such a powerful test as the question of their respective adaptability to civilization, it is difficult to avoid giving a verdict very different from that which has hitherto been pronounced in Europe upon false testimony or none at all.

Taking the Bulgarian Rayah as we have painted him from the life, brutish, obstinate, idle, superstitious, dirty, *sans foi ni loi*—in short, the degraded being amongst whom we have dwelt so long, and for the accuracy of whose picture we hold ourselves responsible—can any one say that he is capable of being civilized without a long and difficult course of preparation?

If we take the well-to-do classes, we fall into the gulf of Oriental commerce, and if the civilization which these gentlemen are supposed to call for so loudly were suddenly to appear amongst them followed by a figure bearing a balance and a sword, many of them would be compelled to exchange their counting-houses and their *cafés* for the less luxurious abode of a prison.

Not knowing much of the mass of the Armenian people, and not having studied them in their own country, we can pronounce no opinion upon them; for their own sakes we trust they are better than the other Christians of the East; as for the Greek Rayah, he is, unfortunately even worse than the Bulgarian.

If the Rayah be as we have described him, how is it possible to plant any genuine civilization in such a soil, and what element can we find fitted to receive it?

Such an element is to be found amongst the Turks alone; not the kid-gloved loungers in official ante-rooms, but the

Turkish peasantry, who not only believe in the doctrines but practise the precepts of their creed, whose word is ten thousand times more valuable than the bond of the Rayah. The Turks of the country possess all the force, vitality, and uprightness of character necessary to form a basis for a national civilization; for Turkey can boast of an element which is entirely wanting in Russia and in those nationalities which have been detached from the parent stem of the Ottoman empire, a vigorous and honest people who would be always ready and able to aid the right and to punish any violation of the principles of true justice. Western Europe, after long years of struggle, has obtained a public morality such as is innate in the Turkish peasantry, and she has been obliged to create an organized force to protect the first basis of society, property and family; the police has been formed in Europe, it exists ready made amongst the Turks of the country.*

Granting that the "civilized Turks" are incapable of civilization, the "uncivilized Turks" are already in a great measure civilized by nature, by instinct, and even by taste. But to civilize Turkey this element must be used as an aid, and no attempt made to destroy it; the Turkish peasants ask for nothing better than to have civilization introduced among them, but they have the right to demand that the new system shall be opposed neither to their religion, their habits, nor their customs, and they will not be induced to co-operate in the great work if they find that insults are lavished upon all these three.

---

* See, for instance, the history of Kara Kostia in the Chapter on Brigandage.

How is it possible for the village Turk to think well of a civilization under whose auspices Greek and Rayah traders buy and sell with false weights and measures unpunished, and false witness is admitted in the mixed tribunals of the towns?

Another serious question now arises, whether or no Islamism is compatible with civilization.

This point has been often discussed, and even Fuad Pasha appears inclined to think that the two *are* compatible; as for us, we are of opinion that a religion which produces such fruits as that of Mahomet is quite as fit to serve as the basis of civilization as that faith which condemned the discoverer of the earth's rotation.*

The Hodja will not deny an astronomical truth, nor would he have condemned the disciple of Copernicus, but he will certainly stigmatize the ingenious inventor of a corn measure with a sliding bottom.

See with what eagerness the Turkish villagers, from the Hodja to the Choban, will flock round you as you speak of the great conquests of science over the realms of space, or that bold calculation by which Leverrier, armed with the single weapon of reasoning, wrested a planet from the void of the unknown; you would almost think that they were listening to the history of Amurath II., or Sultan Selim the Gentleman, and you feel that your audience have almost as much interest in science as love for their country; unfortunately the weapons necessary to enable them to benefit either are wanting.

---

* Of course no comparison is intended between Islamism and Christianity proper, but between Islamism and such spurious Christianity as alone is practically taught in the East, and therefore alone comes in question.

If at the colleges of Constantinople something better were taught than depravity of conduct and a contempt for their own religion and all others, how many Turks would be anxious to drink at the pure springs of learning! As it is the surrounding mud keeps them away.

Some days since, a friend said to us, "I shall send my son to England, to study in London." (The son he alluded to is an intelligent, bright little fellow of eleven years old, who can already read and write eleven different Turkish writings).

"Why not to Constantinople?"

"Because there he would learn to despise his religion and his country."

"But are you not afraid that in England he might be converted to Christianity?"

"Listen, Dostum (my friend); I would rather see my son a *really good* Christian and an honest man, than a Constantinople Turk *alla Franca* and a Pasha."

It is a great misfortune that the Turkish reformers do not seek the aid of this honest and upright element, and perhaps a still greater that it does not assert its rights; its present silence is, however, caused by a consciousness of its own strength, and if the lion once puts forth his power he will do so to some purpose: to the chain of a national civilization he will submit willingly, any other he will break through as easily as if it were a spider's web.

With this element, then, civilization of the East is not only possible but easy, for with an Osmanli police force it will be possible to civilize even the Rayah; change his clergy, make severe laws which will teach him that robbery is a crime, and prove practically that crime is punished, which last may be done by the assistance of the Turkish people, and civilization will spring up and grow without the necessity of forcing it in the *alla Franca* hotbeds of Constantinople whose foundation is—that of most hotbeds.

But here intervenes another question, that of the *force* necessary to do this; an honest man will never be able to do honest good to Turkey until two millions of Turkish bayonets are ready to support the just cause of infant civilization from the enemies, and even from the friends, of the Sultan; for until a Prime Vizier can answer a Russian Bombastes Furioso or Menchikoff by a million of rifle balls, or a Western Doctor Sangrado by a statement of the forces of his Imperial Majesty the Sultan, civilization will never develope itself nor even germinate in Turkey, and statesmen will go on reforming and deforming without any effect but that of producing a sanguinary intestine conflict.

For the good of Turkey, and the world, let Europe study this country, and then judge it, but *not* on the evidence of Philhellenic tourists or newspapers.

APPENDIX.

APPENDIX A.

On the first Sunday after Easter (1868) there was a betrothal in this village, celebrated as usual by unlimited dancing and drinking; about midnight some young men, by no means sober, commenced firing loaded guns and pistols, an ordinary accompaniment of any festivity in the East. One of them, in drawing a pistol from his belt, accidentally touched the trigger, and the charge of buck-shot was lodged in the thigh of a youth standing about three paces from him. Next morning we were asked to come and cure the wounded man, but, having none of the necessary surgical implements, we declined to interfere in so serious a case, and strongly recommended the removal of the patient to the hospital at Varna: we were told, however, that the Medjliss or Council of the village had assembled, and decided that he was not to be taken to Varna, whereupon we made an appeal to the feelings of his mother, representing that her son's life was in danger; her answer was that "whether he lived or died he should not go out of the village." An hour or two later another messenger came to inform us that a "Hekim" (doctor) had passed through the village, and promised to effect a cure if we would come and watch his proceedings: on enquiry we found that this "doctor" was a mere peasant, who had already commenced his treatment by bleeding the patient in the thigh and in the mouth! Of course we declined to give the sanction of our presence to this kind of surgery, for which we had no power of substituting a proper system. At this date (May 7th) the wounded man is still under the care of the "Hekim" (whose fee is 5l.), but as none of the buck-shot have been extracted, and the hot weather seems to have set in definitively, gangrene may very possibly intervene and carry off the poor fellow.

We learned afterwards that the reason of the interference of the Medjliss was that they feared an official enquiry into the affair at Varna, which might result in the arrest of the man who fired the pistol, and even a general confiscation of the fire-arms of the village, as Turkish subjects have (nominally) no right to possess arms without a Government license.

For the sake of the young man, we had the affair represented to the authorities at Varna, urging the necessity of his being sent to the hospital there, but as yet no notice has been taken of the occurrence, and it is very doubtful whether the Conac will act in the matter, although it involves a breach of Turkish law.

APPENDIX B.

The real origin of the Bulgarian "sins" is probably pagan, although the people say "It is the custom: the Papas says so;" but at any rate, since they must be confessed to the priest, the clergy cannot be ignorant of them, and even if they have not originated they at least sanction and tolerate these superstitions.

APPENDIX C.

BALLAD OF DELI MARKO AND PHILIP JUNAK, IN BULGARIAN.

[*This poem is given in Polish characters, as those assigned by Russia to the very scanty and altogether modern literature of Bulgaria would probably be difficult to procure in England.*]

FILIP JUNAK I DELI MARKO.

Pochwalił sia Filip Junak
        Hej Kulada moj Kulada!
Po siedanki na pred mumita,
        Hej Kulada moj Kulada!
Po bielanki na pred bulkite,
        Hej Kulada moj Kulada!
Na Tukanie pred mumey,
        Hej Kulada moj Kulada!
Swierdzyl try Zmieje.
        Hej Kulada, &c.
Gdie go zaczyt Deli Marko,
        Hej Kulada, &c.
To je go zatresi * . . . .
        Hej Kulada, &c.

---

* Here there seems to be a word missing.

Po siedanki na pred mumita,
    Hej Kulada, &c.
Po bielanki na pred bulkite,
    Hej Kulada, &c.
Na Tukanie pred mumcy.
    Hej Kulada, &c.
Czy mu kaza mumcy.
    Hej Kulada, &c.
"Gdie siede Filip Junak?"
    Hej Kulada, &c.
"Toj siede tam na gore
    Hej Kulada, &c.
Zrysrty słońca
    Hej Kulada, &c.
Žymžyr porty."
    Hej Kulada, &c.
Czy sty utidie Deli Marko.
    Hej Kulada, &c.
I Filip Junaka Konacy
    Hej Kulada, &c.
Deli Marko namiery,
    Hej Kulada, &c.
Kak go namiery j powika
    Hej Kulada, &c.
Deli Marko powika i za Lopota
    Hej Kulada, &c.
Filip Junak žymžyr porty nie otory;
    Hej Kulada, &c.
Czy siergnał Deli Marko.
    Hej Kulada, &c.
Filip Junaka žymžyr porty,
    Hej Kulada, &c.
Czy się ryknął Demir porty,
    Hej Kulada, &c.
Czy się freknął na sine niebo,
    Hej Kulada, &c.
Kak to gie ryknął Deli Marko,
    Hej Kulada, &c.
Czy się w lazi Deli Marko
    Hej Kulada, &c.
Na Filipowy Konacy.
    Hej Kulada, &c.
Filip Junak nie izlezi,
    Hej Kulada, &c.

Filipica izlezi.
      Hej Kulada, &c.
Szyszty Deli Marko zlezi.
      Hej Kulada, &c.
Na stronia z ima kita,
      Hej Kulada, &c.
Czy je zie Deli Marko.
      Hej Kulada, &c.
Tuga się zlezi Filip Junak,
      Hej Kulada, &c.
Czy plesnął vecy do Sobora
      Hej Kulada, &c.
Ulowili sia da se bora
      Hej Kulada, &c.
Z Deli Marko Filip Junak.
      Hej Kulada, &c.
Czy go ulowr Deli Marko,
      Hej Kulada, &c.
Filip Junaka ulowi.
      Hej Kulada, &c.
Czy go swerdzi reca na zad,
      Hej Kulada, &c.
Deli Marko—Czy go powiedi
      Hej Kulada, &c.
Po siedanki pred mumita,
      Hej Kulada, &c.
"Ty to Filip Junak die to sofali,
      Hej Kulada, &c.
" Pred mumity na siedanki,
      Hej Kulada, &c.
" Gdie ty swierdil try Zmieje?"
      Hej Kulada, &c.
Tam go zie czy go zawiedie
      Hej Kulada, &c.
Na bielanki pred bulki,
      Hej Kulada, &c.
Czy go pyta "Tyśli, Filip Junak,
      Hej Kulada, &c.
" Gdie to zachwali
      Hej Kulada, &c.
" Czy swardow dór try Zmieje?"
      Hej Kulada, &c.
I od tam go zie Deli Marko,
      Hej Kulada, &c.

Czy go zawło na Tukany,
    Hej Kułada, &c.
Na Tukany pred mumityty
    Hej Kułada, &c.
Czy go pyta Deli Marko,
    Hej Kułada, &c.
"Toś li, Filip Junak,
    Hej Kułada, &c.
" Die to się zachali po Tukan
    Hej Kułada, &c.
" Aż się zwierdził dór try zmieje?"
    Hej Kułada, &c.
Filip Junak se moli, na Deli Marko,
    Hej Kułada, &c.
" Pusti mnie, Deli Marko!"
    Hej Kułada, &c.
Deli Marko ni pusti Filip Junak
    Hej Kułada, &c.
Nie pustił. Obwiesił.
    Hej Kułada moj Kułada.

APPENDIX D.

This same monk, Padre D., a most excellent man and true Christian, whose life is spent in deeds of self-abnegation and charity, said to us: "I have lived many years in the East, and I assure you that I have seen the Christian name so uniformly profaned by its professors that when I hear any one in the street say of me 'That is a Christian,' old man and Cappucino monk as I am, I feel inclined to go up and hit him with my stick."

APPENDIX E.

MONSIGNOR BENEDICTOS.

(" *Correspondance particulière du ' Courrier d'Orient.'*")

"MONASTIR, 25 *décembre.*

" Nos affaires avec M. Bénédictos s'embrouillent de plus en plus, et son renvoi d'ici est maintenant tout au moins problématique. On lui reproche des actes qui méritent l'interdiction de toutes fonctions ecclésiastiques, mais il a de l'argent.

" D'abord son affaire allait assez mal, non parce qu'on avait mauvaise opinion de lui, mais parce qu'il est d'une extrême avarice et qu'il ne reconnaissait pas dignement les services rendus. A ce propos je puis dire que si Mgr. Bénédictos a été chiche envers . . . il n'a pas été généreux envers les pauvres d'ici.

" Le voilà installé ici depuis quinze ou seize ans. De l'aveu de personnes en état de connaître ce que rapportent l'*affermage* des monastères et des paroisses, les permis de mariages et de divorces, l'*odzek* ou impôt sur les familles, etc., etc., Sa Grandeur ne ramasse annuellement pas moins de 700,000 piastres : supposez maintenant qu'il dépense chaque année 200 mille piastres, il ne lui reste pas moins de 500 mille piastres par an, soit 8 millions pour les 16 années. Et pourtant, chose cruelle à dire ! malgré la misère qui nous entoure en ville et la pauvreté qui règne dans les villages, on ne l'a jamais vu donner cinq paras à un pauvre.

" Son affaire allait donc mal, même très mal, s'il faut en croire le rapport de nos premiers délégués, et cela non pas qu'aux yeux du patriarcat ce fut un archevêque peu honorable, mais parce qu'il gardait trop pour lui. Toutefois, menacé d'être honteusement renvoyé d'ici, lui qui avait brigué le patriarcat, il voulut en savoir la cause ; il lui fut, m'assure-t-on, répondu ou insinué, qu'un seul parti lui restait : celui d'ouvrir sa bourse.

" D'ailleurs, lui aurait-on fait observer, les dépenses occasionnées par l'envoi d'exarques doivent être supportées par ceux qui perdront. Voyez donc s'il ne vaut pas mieux donner pour gagner votre cause ce que vous donneriez en la perdant.

" L'avis était bon, et Mgr. Bénédictos passe, à tort ou à raison, pour l'avoir suivi. Effectivement qu'en est-il résulté ? D'abord que, pendant l'examen juridique de son administration par les exarques, Sa Grandeur devait aller au monastère de Saint Naoum sur le lac d'Ochrida, puis seulement au monastère de Pirlepé, puis à celui de Serfidjé. Finalement Sa Grandeur a obtenu de rester ici.

" Ajoutez qu'au lieu de jouer à Monastir un rôle impartial, les deux exarques ont préalablement à tout examen pris fait et cause pour Mgr. Bénédictos. En effet, le dimanche qui suivit leur arrivée, l'évêque de Caroveria monta en chaire, et s'adressant au peuple l'exhorta à pardonner à Mgr. Bénédictos toutes les offenses qu'il pouvait en avoir reçues.

"' D'ailleurs,' ajouta l'exarque orateur, vers la fin de son discours, ' Mgr. Bénédictos est le meilleur évêque que la Grande Église puisse vous donner. Si vous en attendez un plus digne, plus capable et connaissant mieux vos besoins, vous êtes dans l'erreur. Le mieux pour vous est donc un pardon complet et une réconciliation sincère avec un aussi bon et si digne pasteur.'

"Et maintenant ai-je besoin de le dire, l'attitude des exarques et la révocation par le patriarcat de l'ordre donné à Mgr. Bénédictos d'aller à St. Naoum ou tout au moins à Pirlepé, sont à nos yeux la preuve tout ensemble et le résultat de la venalité.

"Quant aux exarques, une chose va se présenter. Leur évidente partialité envers Mgr. Bénédictos rend complètement superflu leur envoi ici et par conséquent inutiles tous les sacrifices que nous nous imposons.

"Or, les sacrifices déjà considérables vont l'être chaque jour d'avantage, car notez ceci : outre leurs frais de voyage, aller et retour, et le loyer de la maison où ils habitent, on leur paye trois livres par jour. Dimanche passé on a fait à l'église une quête pour eux et l'on a ramassé environ deux mille piastres. Mais qu'est-ce que deux mille piastres? Les dépenses d'une semaine.

"Supposez maintenant qu'il faille renouveler cette quête tous les dimanches pendant six mois ou un an. Supposez aussi que les exarques mettent leur suffrage à prix et qu'il faille enchérir Mgr. Bénédictos, à quelle somme ne monteront pas nos dépenses ? Le plus sage était donc pour nos députés à Constantinople de repousser l'offre d'exarques."

In spite of the very indifferent French of the 'Courrier d'Orient's' Special Correspondent, it is easy to see from the above quotation that the orthodox Church *ne lave pas son linge sale en famille*, and that reforms might be advantageously introduced amongst its hierarchy. The dispute between Monsignor Benedictos and his affectionate flock is not yet (May, 1868) by any means terminated ; the last accounts we have seen report that each party had sent three new representatives to Constantinople, and that those of the people had succeeded in making the other trio very drunk, and in this state they were presented to plead the Archbishop's cause before the Patriarch, who is said to have been highly amused by the scene. How greatly such disputes and such manœuvres tend *ad majorem Dei et ecclesiæ gloriam!* and how much they must edify the infidel Mussulmans!

APPENDIX F.

The present value (May, 1868) of two sheniks of corn at Varna is 38 piastres. As a proof that our calculation of the Papas's income is by no means exaggerated, we may mention that the pastor of Dereknoi (who has also another parish, and is not resident here) took away with him sixty skins of lambs, and at least ten okes of meat: the average value of the skins (to sell) is 8 piastres each, and of the meat 5 piastres per oke, making a total of 530 piastres, or nearly 9 piastres from each house, for the "voluntary contributions" collected in one day.

APPENDIX G.

Before the Bulgarian ecclesiastical schism, the tax paid to the Wladyka by the villages in this neighbourhood was 28 piastres; to keep possession of his flock the Wladyka offered to reduce this sum to 16 piastres, a proposition which was accepted or rejected according to the preponderance of Greek or Bulgarian blood amongst the different villages.

APPENDIX H.

In the neighbouring Vilayet of Adrianople, near Cape Eminch, there are now two bands of brigands, amounting to thirty in number: they are said to be from the Greek village of Akdere, whose inhabitants have for many years borne an infamous reputation as robbers and wreckers: one of the Authors was fired at a few days since whilst returning from that part of the country, probably by one of these gentlemen; but as Hassan, who killed Kara Kostia, has set out on their track, and the Turks have the intention, if the robbers are not captured by the police, of making a grand *battue* of the woods they frequent, it is likely that they will soon be exterminated.

APPENDIX I.

PAY OF THE TURKISH ARMY.

The same for all branches of the Service.

No. of Rations allowed.	Monthly pay in Piastres.	Rank in Turkish.	Corresponding rank in English.
Virtually un- limited	14,000	Ferik Pasha.	General of Division.
	7,000	Liva Pasha.	General of Brigade.
16	4,500	Mirialai.	Colonel.
12	4,000	Kaimakam.	Lieut.-Colonel.
8	1,800	Binbaschi.	Major.
5	700	Colassi.	Captain.
4	400	Yuzbaschi.	Lieutenant.
2	250	Mulazim.	Ensign.

Non-commissioned Officers.

	80	Basch Chiaousch.	Serjeant Major.
	60	Sera Chiaousch.	Serjeant.
	50	Beulikeminch.	Pay-sergeant.
	40	Onbaschi.	Corporal.
1	25	Nefer.	Private.
	60	Harmandar.	The *Fourrier* of the French Army.
	80	Demirji.	Armourer.
	80	Marangos.	Wheelwright.
	60	Nalbant.	Farrier.
	40	Sakka.	Water-carrier.

The Talimji baschi (in French, Adjutant Major) receives 1700 piastres monthly.

RATIONS. (Taïn.)

(*Roughly, 10 drams may be counted as equal to 1 oz. avoirdupois.*)

Bread	300 drams	} per diem.
Meat	30 ,,	
Fat	12½ ,,	
Rice	15 ,,	
Soap	30 ,,	} per mensem.
Candle	20 ,,	

A new uniform, shirt, boots, &c., are served out every two years.

The Turkish private soldier has to spend (owing to the bad quality of his uniform and the long time that Government supposes it to last) at least 400 piastres per annum, out of his own pocket, for clothes. In addition to this, if he is receiving pay and rations he must spend 60 paras (1½ piastre) per diem in food, tobacco, &c., making 547 piastres annually, in addition ; if he receives neither, as is frequently the case, he must keep himself, which he can do upon 3 piastres per diem or 1095 piastres per annum.

Thus we see that the pay and rations of the Turkish soldier being both insufficient to keep him, he is obliged whilst serving in the army to possess private means amounting (at least) from 947 to 1495 piastres per annum.[*]

APPENDIX K.

The following statistics, which we know to be correct, will show the difference between the produce of grain by Christian and Mussulman villages, and consequently the comparative poverty imposed upon the latter by the amount of labour confiscated by military service. All the villages mentioned, with the single exception of Akindji, may be taken as fairly representing the mass of those in this part of Bulgaria, being neither richer nor poorer than the average of those inhabited by Turk and Rayah. It must be recollected that the "tithe" was raised last year from 10 to 15 per cent. :—

---

[*] These latter calculations are taken from information supplied by soldiers.

1867.

Name of Village.	No. of houses.	No. of kilés of grain paid as tax.
Sindel (Mussulman)	40	600
Evrein (Mixed)	100	2400
Derekuoi (Christian)	60	2400
Testiji (Mixed)	60	2000
Akindji (Mussulman)	30	170

After paying the tax, there remained per house :—

To Sindel	85	kilós.
,, Evrein	136	,,
,, Derekuoi	226	,,
,, Testiji	188	,,
,, Akindji	33	,,

The small amount raised by the last named village is explained by the fact that of its inhabitants no less than fifteen are at present serving with the army, and of this number seven are heads of families which by their absence are entirely prevented from growing corn, and are dependent chiefly on the charity of their neighbours.

APPENDIX L.

A miller at Devna, a Rayah claiming Greek protection, employed a Bulgarian servant: one day the master used very harsh language to the man, who thereupon said that he would not remain to be abused in that manner, and that he should seek another service; the miller said in that case he should not pay him his wages; these the Bulgarian preferred to sacrifice rather than to stay in his place, and went to work in another mill. The miller went to the Greek Consulate, related the affair, and further accused his late servant of having threatened to kill him, an allegation of which he could bring *no proofs whatever;* however, the servant was arrested, and is now in prison in Varna.

APPENDIX M.

EXTRACTS FROM THE MEMORANDUM OF FUAD PASHA.

"A une époque encore peu éloignée, c'est à dire, avant la proclamation du Tanzimat, que l'on peut appeler la charte de l'égalité, les sujets du Sultan se divisaient en deux classes, séparées l'une de l'autre par un préjugé en apparence invincible; une classe dominante représentée par les Musulmans, et une classe inférieure entièrement soumise à l'autorité de la première et représentée par la population non-Musulmane. Cette inégalité qui avait alors toute la force d'un dogme politique sans en avoir la légitimité, a été supprimée par l'acte de Gulhané, qui a proclamé l'égalité absolue de tous les sujets du Sultan, sans distinction de race et de religion. Mais cette grande réforme sociale n'était à l'origine que la consécration d'un droit qui pouvait rester stérile et à l'État de lettre morte. Il s'agissait de la convertir en fait, c'est à dire, de l'introduire dans les mœurs comme on venait de l'introduire dans les institutions. C'est à cette œuvre ardue que le Gouvernement a consacré tous ses soins, et aujourd'hui la seconde partie de sa tâche est accomplie. L'égalité est admise; et non-seulement le principe n'en est plus contesté, mais il a déjà pénétré et pénètre chaque jour davantage dans les mœurs de la nation.

"Essaiera-t-on d'atténuer l'importance de cette conquête morale en rappelant que le principe d'égalité n'est point accepté et mis en pratique au même degré dans toutes les parties de l'Empire? Mais les exemples qu'on en pourrait citer ne témoigneront jamais que d'une chose qu'il n'est point dans la pensée du Gouvernement de contester, c'est qu'en Turquie, non plus que dans tout autre pays si avancé qu'il soit dans la civilisation, on ne saurait improviser la réforme des mœurs. Si donc chez certains individus et dans certaines localités les plus éloignées du centre administratif les convictions ne se sont point encore modifiées au profit des idées nouvelles, ce fait n'a rien d'alarmant, rien surtout qui puisse permettre de nier la réalité ou de diminuer l'importance de la victoire obtenue par le Gouvernement Impérial. La preuve la plus éclatante qu'on en puisse fournir, c'est qu'aujourd'hui il serait impossible aux conseillers de la Turquie de demander et à la Sublime Porte d'adopter une réforme nouvelle, quelle qu'en fût l'objet, sans que les bienfaits s'en étendissent immédiatement à toutes les classes de la population, tellement assimilées entre elles par l'égalité de condition que ce qui serait fait au profit de l'une proliterait aux autres au même titre et au même degré.

"Les propriétés ecclésiastiques sont placées sous la sauvegarde du droit commun, et d'ailleurs entièrement assimilées, quant aux privilèges dont elles sont entourées, aux propriétés qui ont le même caractère ou la même affectation chez les Musulmans.

"Les unes et les autres, en tant que fondations pieuses, sont affranchies des taxes qui pèsent sur les autres immeubles. Cette égalité de condition est telle que les objets qui sont destinés à l'exercice des cultes non-Musulmans sont exemptes des droits de douane au même titre que les objets consacrés au culte des Musulmans.

"Aucune entrave n'a jamais été apportée à la construction de nouvelles églises, ou à la réparation des anciennes. Loin d'y mettre obstacle, le Souverain et le Gouvernement viennent souvent en aide à ces fondations pieuses, soit par des concessions gratuites de terrains soit par des subventions pécuniaires.

"Enfin l'on peut proclamer hautement que dans aucun pays les cultes ne s'exercent avec plus de liberté, plus de tolérance, et d'une manière plus ostensible et publique qu'en Turquie. C'est là une vérité dont témoigneront tous ceux qui ont habité ou visité le pays.

"Les mesures prises pour interdire l'emploi de toute dénomination injurieuse tirée des différences de religion et de race ont leur plein et entier effet; et ces appellations irritantes sont exclues aussi bien du langage ordinaire dans les rapports d'individu à individu que des pièces et actes officiels. Au surplus le Code Pénal, plus récemment promulgué, a édicté des peines sévères contre ceux qui enfreindraient ces prohibitions.

"Le principe de l'admissibilité des sujets du Sultan sans distinction de religion, à tous les emplois publics, solennellement proclamé par le Gouvernement Impérial, a été depuis lors mis en pratique. C'est aujourd'hui un fait accompli. Beaucoup d'emplois importants sont déjà confiés à des Chrétiens, tant dans les administrations de la capitale que dans les provinces et dans les légations à l'étranger; et si l'on considère le nombre des Chrétiens admis depuis quelques années aux fonctions publiques, on restera convaincu que le Gouvernement Impérial désire faire l'appel le plus loyal et le plus sérieux au concours de ses sujets non-Musulmans et donner au principe d'égalité tout le développement qu'il comporte.

"C'est au même titre et dans la même pensée que les écoles civiles du Gouvernement, telles que l'école de médicine, l'école des mines, des ponts et chaussées, l'école administrative, etc., s'ouvrent également devant les élèves Musulmans et non-Musulmans.

"La loi sur les Vilayets réalise et au-delà le vœu exprimé dans le Firman de 1856 au sujet de la présence dans les conseils de l'Empire d'un certain nombre de délégués des populations non-Musulmanes. Aux termes de cette loi les Conseils Provinciaux doivent être composés de membres Musulmans et non-Musulmans, librement élus par les populations, suivant un système approprié à l'état des mœurs dans les provinces de l'Empire.

"Dans le Grand Conseil de Justice, qui est le premier corps de l'État, siégent au même titre que leurs collégues Musulmans, des membres Chrétiens, non pas seulement, comme le promettait le Firman de 1856, avec des pouvoirs purement momentaires, mais d'une manière normale et à titre permanent.

THE END.

LONDON: PRINTED BY WILLIAM CLOWES AND SONS, DUKE STREET, STAMFORD STREET, AND CHARING CROSS.

ALBEMARLE STREET, LONDON,
September, 1868.

MR. MURRAY'S

GENERAL LIST OF WORKS.

ALBERT'S (PRINCE) SPEECHES AND ADDRESSES ON
PUBLIC OCCASIONS; with an Introduction giving some Outlines
of his Character. Portrait. 8vo. 10s. 6d.; or *Popular Edition*. Portrait.
Fcap. 8vo. 1s.

ABBOTT'S (REV. J.) Philip Musgrave; or, Memoirs of a Church of
England Missionary in the North American Colonies. Post 8vo. 2s.

ABERCROMBIE'S (JOHN) Enquiries concerning the Intellectual
Powers and the Investigation of Truth. Fcap. 8vo. 6s. 6d.

—————— Philosophy of the Moral Feelings. Fcap.
8vo. 4s.

ACLAND'S (REV. CHARLES) Popular Account of the Manners and
Customs of India. Post 8vo. 2s.

ÆSOP'S FABLES. A New Translation. With Historical
Preface. By Rev. THOMAS JAMES. With 100 Woodcuts, by TENNIEL
and WOLF. 50th Thousand. Post 8vo. 2s. 6d.

AGRICULTURAL (THE ROYAL) SOCIETY'S JOURNAL. 8vo.
Published half-yearly.

AIDS TO FAITH: a Series of Theological Essays. By various
Writers. Edited by WILLIAM THOMSON, D.D., Archbishop of York.
8vo. 9s.

AMBER-WITCH (THE). A most interesting Trial for Witchcraft. Translated from the German by LADY DUFF GORDON. Post
8vo. 2s.

ARMY LIST (THE). *Published Monthly by Authority.* 18mo. 1s. 6d.

ARTHUR'S (LITTLE) History of England. By LADY CALLCOTT.
New Edition, continued to 1862. Woodcuts. Fcap. 8vo. 2s. 6d.

ATKINSON'S (MRS.) Recollections of Tartar Steppes and their
Inhabitants. Illustrations. Post 8vo. 12s.

AUNT IDA'S Walks and Talks; a Story Book for Children. By
a LADY. Woodcuts. 16mo. 5s.

AUSTIN'S (JOHN) LECTURES ON JURISPRUDENCE; or, the Philosophy
of Positive Law. *New and Cheaper Edition.* 2 Vols. 8vo.

—————— (SARAH) Fragments from German Prose Writers.
With Biographical Notes. Post 8vo. 10s.

B

LIST OF WORKS

ADMIRALTY PUBLICATIONS; Issued by direction of the Lords Commissioners of the Admiralty:—

A MANUAL OF SCIENTIFIC ENQUIRY, for the Use of Travellers. Edited by Sir JOHN F. HERSCHEL, and Rev. ROBERT MAIN, M.A. Third Edition. Woodcuts. Post 8vo. 9s.

AIRY'S ASTRONOMICAL OBSERVATIONS MADE AT GREENWICH. 1836 to 1847. Royal 4to. 50s. each.

——— ASTRONOMICAL RESULTS. 1848 to 1858. 4to. 8s. each.

——— APPENDICES TO THE ASTRONOMICAL OBSERVATIONS.

1836.—I. Bessel's Refraction Tables.
II. Tables for converting Errors of R.A. and N.P.D. into Errors of Longitude and Ecliptic P.D. } 8s.
1837.—I. Logarithms of Sines and Cosines to every Ten Seconds of Time.
II. Table for converting Sidereal into Mean Solar Time. } 8s.
1842.—Catalogue of 1439 Stars. 8s.
1845.—Longitude of Valentia. 8s.
1847.—Twelve Years' Catalogue of Stars. 14s.
1851.—Maskelyne's Ledger of Stars. 6s.
1852.—I. Description of the Transit Circle. 5s.
II. Regulations of the Royal Observatory. 2s.
1853.—Bessel's Refraction Tables. 3s.
1854.—I. Description of the Zenith Tube. 3s.
II. Six Years' Catalogue of Stars. 10s.
1856.—Description of the Galvanic Apparatus at Greenwich Observatory. 8s.
1862.—I. Seven Years' Catalogue of Stars. 10s.
II. Plan of the Building and Ground of the Royal Observatory, Greenwich.
III. Longitude of Valentia. } 3s.

——— MAGNETICAL AND METEOROLOGICAL OBSERVATIONS. 1840 to 1847. Royal 4to. 50s. each.

——— ASTRONOMICAL, MAGNETICAL, AND METEOROLOGICAL OBSERVATIONS, 1848 to 1864. Royal 4to. 50s. each.

——— ASTRONOMICAL RESULTS. 1848 to 1864. 4to.

——— MAGNETICAL AND METEOROLOGICAL RESULTS. 1848 to 1864. 4to. 8s. each.

——— REDUCTION OF THE OBSERVATIONS OF PLANETS. 1750 to 1830. Royal 4to. 50s.

——— ——— LUNAR OBSERVATIONS. 1750 to 1830. 2 Vols. Royal 4to. 50s. each.

——— 1831 to 1851. 4to. 20s.

BERNOULLI'S SEXCENTENARY TABLE. London, 1779. 4to.

BESSEL'S AUXILIARY TABLES FOR HIS METHOD OF CLEARING LUNAR DISTANCES. 8vo.

— — FUNDAMENTA ASTRONOMIÆ: Regiomontii, 1818. Folio. 60s.

BIRD'S METHOD OF CONSTRUCTING MURAL QUADRANTS. London, 1768. 4to. 2s. 6d.

——— METHOD OF DIVIDING ASTRONOMICAL INSTRUMENTS. London, 1767. 4to. 2s. 6d.

COOK, KING, AND BAYLY'S ASTRONOMICAL OBSERVATIONS. London, 1782. 4to. 21s.

ENCKE'S BERLINER JAHRBUCH, for 1830. Berlin, 1828. 8vo. 9s.

GROOMBRIDGE'S CATALOGUE OF CIRCUMPOLAR STARS. 4to. 10s.

HANSEN'S TABLES DE LA LUNE. 4to. 20s.

ADMIRALTY PUBLICATIONS—*continued*.
HARRISON'S PRINCIPLES OF HIS TIME-KEEPER. PLATES. 1797. 4to. 5s.
HUTTON'S TABLES OF THE PRODUCTS AND POWERS OF NUMBERS. 1781. Folio. 7s. 6d.
LAX'S TABLES FOR FINDING THE LATITUDE AND LONGITUDE. 1821. 8vo. 10s.
LUNAR OBSERVATIONS at GREENWICH. 1783 to 1819. Compared with the Tables, 1821. 4to. 7s. 6d.
MASKELYNE'S ACCOUNT OF THE GOING OF HARRISON'S WATCH. 1767. 4to. 2s. 6d.
MAYER'S DISTANCES of the MOON'S CENTRE from the PLANETS. 1822, 3s.; 1823, 4s. 6d. 1824 to 1835, 8vo. 4s. each.
————— THEORIA LUNÆ JUXTA SYSTEMA NEWTONIANUM. 4to. 2s. 6d.
————— TABULÆ MOTUUM SOLIS ET LUNÆ. 1770. 4to. 5s.
————— ASTRONOMICAL OBSERVATIONS MADE AT GOTTINGEN, from 1756 to 1761. 1826. Folio. 7s. 6d.
NAUTICAL ALMANACS, from 1767 to 1871. 8vo. 2s. 6d. each.
————— SELECTIONS FROM THE ADDITIONS up to 1812. 8vo. 5s. 1834-54. 8vo. 5s.
————— SUPPLEMENTS, 1828 to 1833, 1837 and 1838 8vo. 2s. each.
————— TABLE requisite to be used with the N.A. 1781. 8vo. 5s.
POND'S ASTRONOMICAL OBSERVATIONS. 1811 to 1835. 4to. 21s. each.
RAMSDEN'S ENGINE for DIVIDING MATHEMATICAL INSTRUMENTS. 4to. 5s.
————— ENGINE for DIVIDING STRAIGHT LINES. 4to. 5s.
SABINE'S PENDULUM EXPERIMENTS to DETERMINE THE FIGURE OF THE EARTH. 1825. 4to. 40s.
SHEPHERD'S TABLES for CORRECTING LUNAR DISTANCES. 1772. Royal 4to. 21s.
————— TABLES, GENERAL, of the MOON'S DISTANCE from the SUN, and 10 STARS. 1787. Folio. 5s. 6d.
TAYLOR'S SEXAGESIMAL TABLE. 1780. 4to. 15s.
————— TABLES OF LOGARITHMS. 4to. 3l.
TIARK'S ASTRONOMICAL OBSERVATIONS for the LONGITUDE of MADEIRA. 1822. 4to. 5s.
————— CHRONOMETRICAL OBSERVATIONS for DIFFERENCES of LONGITUDE between DOVER, PORTSMOUTH, and FALMOUTH. 1823. 4to. 5s.
VENUS and JUPITER: OBSERVATIONS of, compared with the TABLES. London, 1822. 4to. 2s.
WALES' AND BAYLY'S ASTRONOMICAL OBSERVATIONS. 1777. 4to. 21s.
WALES' REDUCTION OF ASTRONOMICAL OBSERVATIONS MADE IN THE SOUTHERN HEMISPHERE. 1764—1771. 1788. 4to. 10s. 6d.

LIST OF WORKS

BARBAULD'S (Mrs.) Hymns in Prose for Children. With 112 Original Designs. Small 4to. 5s.; or *Fine Paper*, 7s. 6d.

BARROW'S (Sir John) Autobiographical Memoir. From Early Life to Advanced Age. Portrait. 8vo. 16s.

——— (John) Life, Exploits, and Voyages of Sir Francis Drake. With numerous Original Letters. Post 8vo. 2s.

BARRY'S (Sir Charles) Life. By Alfred Barry, D.D. With Portrait, and Illustrations. Medium 8vo. 24s.

BATES' (H. W.) Records of a Naturalist on the River Amazons during eleven years of Adventure and Travel. *Second Edition*. Illustrations. Post 8vo. 12s.

BEAUCLERK'S (Lady Di) Summer and Winter in Norway. *Second Edition*. With Illustrations. Small 8vo. 6s.

BEES AND FLOWERS. Two Essays. By Rev. Thomas James. Reprinted from the "Quarterly Review." Fcap. 8vo. 1s. each.

BERTHA'S Journal during a Visit to her Uncle in England. Containing a Variety of Interesting and Instructive Information. *Seventh Edition*. Woodcuts. 12mo. 7s. 6d.

BERTRAM'S (Jas. G.) Harvest of the Sea: a Contribution to the Natural and Economic History of British Food Fishes. *Second and Cheaper Edition*. With 50 Illustrations. 8vo.

BICKMORE'S (Albert S., M.A.) Travels in the East Indian Archipelago. With Maps and Illustrations. 8vo. (*In preparation*.)

BIRCH'S (Samuel) History of Ancient Pottery and Porcelain: Egyptian, Assyrian, Greek, Roman, and Etruscan. With 200 Illustrations. 2 Vols. Medium 8vo. 42s.

BISSET'S (Andrew) History of the Commonwealth of England, from the Death of Charles I. to the Expulsion of the Long Parliament by Cromwell. Chiefly from the MSS. in the State Paper Office. 2 vols. 8vo. 30s.

BLAKISTON'S (Capt.) Narrative of the Expedition sent to explore the Upper Waters of the Yang-Tsze. Illustrations. 8vo. 18s.

BLOMFIELD'S (Bishop) Memoir, with Selections from his Correspondence. By his Son. *Second Edition*. Portrait, post 8vo. 12s.

BLUNT'S (Rev. J. J.) Undesigned Coincidences in the Writings of the Old and New Testament, an Argument of their Veracity: containing the Books of Moses, Historical and Prophetical Scriptures, and the Gospels and Acts. *Ninth Edition*. Post 8vo. 6s.

——— History of the Church in the First Three Centuries. *Third Edition*. Post 8vo. 7s. 6d.

——— Parish Priest; His Duties, Acquirements and Obligations. *Fourth Edition*. Post 8vo. 7s. 6d.

——— Lectures on the Right Use of the Early Fathers. *Second Edition*. 8vo. 15s.

——— Plain Sermons Preached to a Country Congregation. *Fifth and Cheaper Edition*. 2 Vols. Post 8vo.

——— Essays on various subjects. 8vo. 12s.

BOOK OF COMMON PRAYER. Illustrated with Coloured Borders, Initial Letters, and Woodcuts. A new edition. 8vo. 18s. cloth; 31s. 6d. calf; 36s. morocco.

BORROW'S (GEORGE) Bible in Spain; or the Journeys, Adventures, and Imprisonments of an Englishman in an Attempt to circulate the Scriptures in the Peninsula. 3 Vols. Post 8vo. 27s.; or *Popular Edition*, 16mo, 3s. 6d.

—— —— Zincali, or the Gipsies of Spain; their Manners, Customs, Religion, and Language. 2 Vols. Post 8vo. 18s.; or *Popular Edition*, 16mo, 3s. 6d.

—— —— Wild Wales: its People, Language, and Scenery. Third Edition. With Introductory Remarks. Post 8vo. 6s.

—— —— Lavengro; The Scholar—The Gipsy—and the Priest. Portrait. 3 Vols. Post 8vo. 30s.

—— —— Romany Rye; a Sequel to Lavengro. *Second Edition*. 2 Vols. Post 8vo. 21s.

BOSWELL'S (JAMES) Life of Samuel Johnson, LL.D. Including the Tour to the Hebrides. Edited by Mr. CROKER. Portraits. Royal 8vo. 10s.

BRACE'S (C. L.) History of the Races of the Old World. Post 8vo. 9s.

BRAY'S (MRS.) Life of Thomas Stothard, R.A. With Personal Reminiscences. Illustrated with Portrait and 60 Woodcuts of his chief works. 4to. 21s.

BREWSTER'S (SIR DAVID) Martyrs of Science; or, Lives of Galileo, Tycho Brahe, and Kepler. *Fourth Edition*. Fcap. 8vo. 4s. 6d.

—————— More Worlds than One. The Creed of the Philosopher and the Hope of the Christian. *Eighth Edition*. Post 8vo. 6s.

—————— Stereoscope: its History, Theory, Construction, and Application to the Arts and to Education. Woodcuts. 12mo. 5s. 6d.

—————— Kaleidoscope: its History, Theory, and Construction, with its application to the Fine and Useful Arts. *Second Edition*. Woodcuts. Post 8vo. 5s. 6d.

BRITISH ASSOCIATION REPORTS. 8vo.

York and Oxford, 1831-32, 13s. 6d.
Cambridge, 1833, 12s.
Edinburgh, 1834, 15s.
Dublin, 1835, 13s. 6d.
Bristol, 1836, 12s.
Liverpool, 1837, 16s. 6d.
Newcastle, 1838, 15s.
Birmingham, 1839, 13s. 6d.
Glasgow, 1840, 15s.
Plymouth, 1841, 13s. 6d.
Manchester, 1842, 10s. 6d.
Cork, 1843, 12s.
York, 1844, 20s.
Cambridge, 1845, 12s.
Southampton, 1846, 15s.
Oxford, 1847, 18s.
Swansea, 1848, 9s.
Birmingham, 1849, 10s.

Edinburgh, 1850, 15s.
Ipswich, 1851, 16s. 6d.
Belfast, 1852, 15s.
Hull, 1853, 10s. 6d.
Liverpool, 1854, 18s.
Glasgow, 1855, 15s.
Cheltenham, 1856, 18s.
Dublin, 1857, 15s.
Leeds, 1858, 20s.
Aberdeen, 1859, 15s.
Oxford, 1860, 25s.
Manchester, 1861, 15s.
Cambridge, 1862, 20s.
Newcastle, 1863, 25s.
Bath, 1864, 18s.
Birmingham, 1865, 25s.
Nottingham, 1866, 24s.
Dundee, 1867, 26s.

BROUGHTON'S (LORD) Journey through Albania and other Provinces of Turkey in Europe and Asia, to Constantinople, 1809—10. *Third Edition.* Illustrations. 2 Vols. 8vo. 30s.

———— Visits to Italy. *3rd Edition.* 2 Vols. Post 8vo. 18s.

BROWNLOW'S (LADY) Reminiscences of a Septuagenarian. From the year 1802 to 1815. *Third Edition.* Post 8vo. 7s. 6d.

BUBBLES FROM THE BRUNNEN OF NASSAU. By Sir FRANCIS B. HEAD, Bart. *7th Edition,* with Illustrations.' Post 8vo. 7s. 6d.

BUNYAN (JOHN) and Oliver Cromwell. Select Biographies. By ROBERT SOUTHEY. Post 8vo. 2s.

BURGON'S (REV. J. W.) Christian Gentleman; or, Memoir of Patrick Fraser Tytler. *Second Edition.* Post 8vo. 9s.

———— Letters from Rome. Post 8vo. 12s.

BURN'S (COL.) Dictionary of Naval and Military Technical Terms, English and French—French and English. *Fourth Edition.* Crown 8vo. 15s.

BUXTON'S (CHARLES) Memoirs of Sir Thomas Fowell Buxton, Bart. With Selections from his Correspondence. By his Son. Portrait. 8vo. 16s. Or *Popular Edition.* Fcap. 8vo. 2s. 6d.

———— IDEAS OF THE DAY ON POLICY, ANALYSED AND ARRANGED. *Third Edition.* 8vo. 6s.

BYRON'S (LORD) Life, Letters, and Journals. By THOMAS MOORE. Plates. 6 Vols. Fcap. 8vo. 18s.

———— Life, Letters, and Journals. By THOMAS MOORE. Portraits. Royal 8vo. 9s.

———— Poetical Works. *Library Edition.* Portrait. 6 Vols. 8vo. 45s.

———— Poetical Works. Plates. 10 Vols. Fcap. 8vo. 30s.

———— Poetical Works. 8 Vols. 24mo. 20s.

———— Poetical Works. Plates. Royal 8vo. 9s.

———— Poetical Works. (PEARL EDITION.) Crown 8vo. 2s. 6d.

———— Childe Harold. With 80 Engravings. Crown 8vo.

———— Childe Harold. Vignettes. 16mo. 1s.

———— Childe Harold. Portrait. 16mo. 6d.

———— Childe Harold. 16mo. 2s. 6d.

———— Tales and Poems. 24mo. 2s. 6d.

———— Miscellaneous. 2 Vols. 24mo. 5s.

———— Dramas and Plays. 2 Vols. 24mo. 5s.

———— Don Juan and Beppo. 2 Vols. 24mo. 5s.

———— Beauties. Portrait. Fcap. 8vo. 3s. 6d.

BURR'S (G. D.) Instructions in Practical Surveying, Topographical Plan Drawing, and on sketching ground without Instruments. *Fourth Edition.* Woodcuts. Post 8vo. 6s.

BUTTMAN'S LEXILOGUS; a Critical Examination of the Meaning of numerous Greek Words, chiefly in Homer and Hesiod. Translated by Rev. J. R. FISHLAKE. *Fifth Edition.* 8vo. 12s.

—— —— CATALOGUE OF IRREGULAR GREEK VERBS. With all the Tenses extant—their Formation, Meaning, and Usage, accompanied by an Index. Translated, with Notes, by Rev. J. R. FISHLAKE. *Fifth Edition.* Revised by Rev. E. VENABLES. Post 8vo. 6s.

CALLCOTT'S (LADY) Little Arthur's History of England. *New Edition, brought down to 1832.* With Woodcuts. Fcap. 8vo. 2s. 6d.

CAMPBELL'S (LORD) Lives of the Lord Chancellors and Keepers of the Great Seal of England. From the Earliest Times to the Death of Lord Eldon in 1838. *Fourth Edition.* 10 Vols. Crown 8vo. 6s. each.

—————— Lives of the Chief Justices of England. From the Norman Conquest to the Death of Lord Tenterden. *Second Edition.* 3 Vols. 8vo. 42s.

—————— Shakspeare's Legal Acquirements Considered. 8vo. 5s. 6d.

—————— Life of Lord Chancellor Bacon. Fcap. 8vo. 2s. 6d.

—————— (GEORGE) Modern India. A Sketch of the System of Civil Government. With some Account of the Natives and Native Institutions. *Second Edition.* 8vo. 16s.

—————— India as it may be. An Outline of a proposed Government and Policy. 8vo. 12s.

—————— (THOS.) Short Lives of the British Poets. With an Essay on English Poetry. Post 8vo. 3s. 6d.

CARNARVON'S (LORD) Portugal, Gallicia, and the Basque Provinces. From Notes made during a Journey to those Countries. *Third Edition.* Post 8vo. 3s. 6d.

—————— Recollections of the Druses of Lebanon. With Notes on their Religion. *Third Edition.* Post 8vo. 5s. 6d.

CASTLEREAGH (THE) DESPATCHES, from the commencement of the official career of the late Viscount Castlereagh to the close of his life. Edited by the MARQUIS OF LONDONDERRY. 12 Vols. 8vo. 14s. each.

CATHCART'S (SIR GEORGE) Commentaries on the War in Russia and Germany, 1812-13. Plans. 8vo. 14s.

CAVALCASELLE AND CROWE'S History of Painting in Italy, from the Second to the Sixteenth Century, from recent researches, as well as from personal inspection of the Works of Art in that Country. With 100 Illustrations. 3 Vols. 8vo. 63s.

—————— —— History of Painting in North Italy, including Venice, Lombardy, Padua, Vicenza, Verona, Parma, Friuli, Ferrara, and Bologna. With Illustrations. 2 Vols. 8vo. (*In preparation.*)

—————— Notices of the Lives and Works of the Early Flemish Painters. Woodcuts. Post 8vo. 12s.

CHILD (G. CHAPLIN, M.D.) Benedicite; or, Song of the Three Children; being Illustrations of the Power, Wisdom, and Goodness of the Creator. *New and Cheaper Edition.* Post 8vo.

CHURTON'S (ARCHDEACON) Gongora. An Historical Essay on the Age of Philip III. and IV. of Spain. With Translations. Portrait. 2 Vols. Small 8vo. 15s.

CICERO'S LIFE AND TIMES. With his Character viewed as a Statesman, Orator, and Friend, and a Selection from his Correspondence and Orations. By WILLIAM FORSYTH, Q.C. *New Edition.* With Illustrations. 8vo. 16s.

CLIVE'S (LORD) Life. By REV. G. R. GLEIG, M.A. Post 8vo. 3s. 6d.

COLCHESTER (THE) PAPERS. The Diary and Correspondence of Charles Abbott, Lord Colchester, Speaker of the House of Commons, 1802-1817. Portrait. 3 Vols. 8vo. 42s.

COLERIDGE'S (SAMUEL TAYLOR) Table-Talk. *New Edition.* Portrait. Fcap. 8vo. 6s.

COLLINGWOOD'S (CUTHBERT) Rambles of a Naturalist on the Shores and Waters of the China Sea. Being Observations in Natural History during a Voyage to China, Formosa, Borneo, Singapore, &c., during 1866—67. With Illustrations. 8vo. 16s.

COLONIAL LIBRARY. [See Home and Colonial Library.]

COOK'S (Canon) Sermons Preached at Lincoln's Inn Chapel, and on Special Occasions. 8vo. 9s.

COOKERY (MODERN DOMESTIC). Founded on Principles of Economy and Practical Knowledge, and adapted for Private Families. By a Lady. *New Edition.* Woodcuts. Fcap. 8vo. 5s.

CORNWALLIS (THE) Papers and Correspondence during the American War,—Administrations in India,—Union with Ireland, and Peace of Amiens. *Second Edition.* 3 Vols. 8vo. 63s.

COWPER'S (MARY, COUNTESS) Diary while Lady of the Bedchamber to Caroline Princess of Wales, 1714-20. Edited by Hon. SPENCER COWPER. *Second Edition.* Portrait. 8vo. 10s. 6d.

CRABBE'S (REV. GEORGE) Life and Poetical Works. Plates. 8 vols. Fcap. 8vo. 24s.; or Complete in 1 Vol. Plates. Royal 8vo. 7s.

CREE'S (E. D.) Portrait of the Primitive Church. Fcap. 8vo. 1s.

CROKER'S (J. W.) Progressive Geography for Children. *Fifth Edition.* 18mo. 1s. 6d.

———— Stories for Children, Selected from the History of England. *Fifteenth Edition.* Woodcuts. 16mo. 2s. 6d.

———— Boswell's Life of Johnson. Including the Tour to the Hebrides. Portraits. Royal 8vo. 10s.

———— Essays on the Early Period of the French Revolution. 8vo. 15s.

———— Historical Essay on the Guillotine. Fcap. 8vo. 1s.

CROMWELL (OLIVER) and John Bunyan. By ROBERT SOUTHEY. Post 8vo. 2s.

CROWE'S AND CAVALCASELLE'S Notices of the Early Flemish Painters. Woodcuts. Post 8vo. 12s.

——— History of Painting in Italy, from 2nd to 16th Century. Derived from Historical Researches as well as Inspection of the Works of Art in that Country. With 100 Illustrations. 3 Vols. 8vo. 21s. each.

——— North Italy, including Venice, Lombardy, Padua, Vicenza, Verona, Parma, Friuli, Ferrara, and Bologna. With Illustrations. 2 Vols. 8vo. (*In preparation.*)

CUMMING'S (R. GORDON) Five Years of a Hunter's Life in the Far Interior of South Africa; with Anecdotes of the Chace, and Notices of the Native Tribes. *New Edition.* Woodcuts. Post 8vo. 5s.

CUNNINGHAM'S (ALLAN) Poems and Songs. Now first collected and arranged, with Biographical Notice. 24mo. 2s. 6d.

CURTIUS' (PROFESSOR) Student's Greek Grammar, for Colleges and the Upper Forms. Edited by DR. WM. SMITH. *Third Edition.* Post 8vo. 6s.

——— Smaller Greek Grammar for the Middle and Lower Forms. 12mo. 3s. 6d.

CURZON'S (HON. ROBERT) ARMENIA AND ERZEROUM. A Year on the Frontiers of Russia, Turkey, and Persia. *Third Edition.* Woodcuts. Post 8vo. 7s. 6d.

——— Visits to the Monasteries of the Levant. *Fifth Edition.* Illustrations. Post 8vo. 7s. 6d.

CUST'S (GENERAL) Warriors of the 17th Century—The Thirty Years' War—and the Civil Wars of France and England. 4 Vols. Post 8vo. 6s. each.

——— Annals of the Wars—18th & 19th Century, 1700—1815. Compiled from the most Authentic Sources. With Maps. 9 Vols. Post 8vo. 5s. each.

DARWIN'S (CHARLES) Journal of Researches into the Natural History of the Countries visited during a Voyage round the World. Post 8vo. 9s.

——— Origin of Species by Means of Natural Selection; or, the Preservation of Favoured Races in the Struggle for Life. *Fourth Edition, revised.* Post 8vo. 15s.

——— Fertilization of Orchids through Insect Agency, and as to the good of Intercrossing. Woodcuts. Post 8vo. 9s.

——— Variation of Animals and Plants under Domestication. With Illustrations. 2 Vols. 8vo. 28s.

——— Fact and Argument for. By FRITZ MULLER. With numerous Illustrations and Additions by the Author. Translated from the German by W. S. DALLAS. 8vo. (*Nearly ready.*)

DAVIS'S (NATHAN) Visit to the Ruined Cities of Numidia and Carthaginia. Illustrations. 8vo. 16s.

——— (SIR J. F.) Chinese Miscellanies: a Collection of Essays and Notes. Post 8vo. 6s.

DAVY'S (SIR HUMPHRY) Consolations in Travel; or, Last Days of a Philosopher. *Fifth Edition.* Woodcuts. Fcap. 8vo. 6s.

——— Salmonia; or, Days of Fly Fishing. *Fourth Edition.* Woodcuts. Fcap. 8vo. 6s.

DELEPIERRE'S (OCTAVE) History of Flemish Literature. From the Twelfth Century. 8vo. 9s.

——————— - Historical Difficulties and Contested Events. Being Notes on some Doubtful Points of History. Post 8vo. 6s.

DENISON'S (E. B.) Life of Bishop Lonsdale, D.D. With Selections from his Writings. With Portrait. Crown 8vo. 10s. 6d.

DERBY'S (EARL OF) Translation of the Iliad of Homer into English Blank Verse. *Fifth Library Edition*. 2 vols. 8vo. 24s.; or *Seventh Edition*, with Translations from the Poets, Ancient and Modern. 2 Vols. Post 8vo. 10s.

*** Translations from the Poets, may be had separately. 8vo. 3s. 6d.

DE ROS'S (LORD) Memorials of the Tower of London. *Second Edition*. With Illustrations. Crown 8vo. 12s.

——————— Young Officer's Companion; or, Essays on Military Duties and Qualities: with Examples and Illustrations from History. *New Edition*. Post 8vo.

DIXON'S (W. HEPWORTH) Story of the Life of Lord Bacon. *Second Edition*. Portrait. Fcap. 8vo. 7s. 6d.

DOG-BREAKING; the Most Expeditious, Certain, and Easy Method, whether great excellence or only mediocrity be required. With a Few Hints for those who Love the Dog and the Gun. By LIEUT.-GEN. HUTCHINSON. *Fourth Edition*. With 40 Woodcuts. Crown 8vo. 15s.

DOMESTIC MODERN COOKERY. Founded on Principles of Economy and Practical Knowledge, and adapted for Private Families. *New Edition*. Woodcuts. Fcap. 8vo. 5s.

DOUGLAS'S (SIR HOWARD) Life and Adventures. By S. W. FULLOM. Portrait. 8vo. 15s.

——————— Theory and Practice of Gunnery. *Fifth Edition*. Plates. 8vo. 21s.

——————— Military Bridges. *Third Edition*. Plates. 8vo. 21s.

——————— Naval Warfare with Steam. 8vo. 8s. 6d.

——————— Modern Systems of Fortification. Plans. 8vo. 12s.

DRAKE'S (SIR FRANCIS) Life, Voyages, and Exploits, by Sea and Land. By JOHN BARROW. *Third Edition*. Post 8vo. 2s.

DRINKWATER'S (JOHN) History of the Siege of Gibraltar, 1779-1783. With a Description and Account of that Garrison from the Earliest Periods. Post 8vo. 2s.

DU CHAILLU'S (PAUL B.) EQUATORIAL AFRICA, with Accounts of the Gorilla, the Nest-building Ape, Chimpanzee, Crocodile, &c. Illustrations. 8vo. 21s.

——————— Journey to Ashango Land; and Further Penetration into Equatorial Africa. Illustrations. 8vo. 21s.

DUFFERIN'S (LORD) Letters from High Latitudes; an Account of a Yacht Voyage to Iceland, Jan Mayen, and Spitzbergen. *Fifth Edition*. Woodcuts. Post 8vo. 7s. 6d.

DYER'S (THOS. H.) History of Modern Europe, from the taking of Constantinople by the Turks to the close of the War in the Crimea. 4 Vols. 8vo.

EASTLAKE'S (SIR CHARLES) Italian Schools of Painting. From the German of KUGLER. Edited, with Notes. *Third Edition*. Illustrated from the Old Masters. 2 Vols. Post 8vo. 30s.

EDWARDS' (W. H.) Voyage up the River Amazon, including a Visit to Para. Post 8vo. 2s.

ELDON'S (LORD) Public and Private Life, with Selections from his Correspondence and Diaries. By HORACE TWISS. Third Edition. Portrait. 2 Vols. Post 8vo. 21s.

ELLESMERE'S (LORD) Two Sieges of Vienna by the Turks. Translated from the German. Post 8vo. 2s.

ELLIS'S (W.) Visits to Madagascar, including a Journey to the Capital, with notices of Natural History, and Present Civilisation of the People. *Fifth Thousand.* Map and Woodcuts. 8vo. 16s.

—— —— Madagascar Revisited. Setting forth the Persecutions and Heroic Sufferings of the Native Christians. Illustrations. 8vo. 16s.

—— (MRS.) Education of Character, with Hints on Moral Training. Post 8vo. 7s. 6d.

ELPHINSTONE'S (HON. MOUNTSTUART) History of India—the Hindoo and Mahomedan Periods. *Fifth Edition.* Map. 8vo. 18s.

ENGEL'S (CARL) Music of the Most Ancient Nations; particularly of the Assyrians, Egyptians, and Hebrews; with Special Reference to the Discoveries in Western Asia and in Egypt. With 100 Illustrations. 8vo. 16s.

ENGLAND (HISTORY OF) from the Peace of Utrecht to the Peace of Versailles, 1713—83. By LORD MAHON (now Earl Stanhope). *Library Edition,* 7 Vols. 8vo. 93s.; or *Popular Edition,* 7 Vols. Post 8vo. 35s.

—————— From the First Invasion by the Romans. By MRS. MARKHAM. *New and Cheaper Edition, continued to* 1863. Woodcuts. 12mo. 4s.

—— —— From the Invasion of Julius Cæsar to the Revolution of 1688. By DAVID HUME. Corrected and continued to 1858. Edited by WM. SMITH, LL.D. Woodcuts. Post 8vo. 7s. 6d.

—— —— (Smaller History of). By WM. SMITH, LL.D. *New Edition, continued to* 1865. Woodcuts. 18mo. 3s. 6d.

—————— Little Arthur's. By LADY CALLCOTT. *New Edition, continued to* 1862. Woodcuts. 18mo. 2s. 6d.

ENGLISHWOMAN IN AMERICA. Post 8vo. 10s. 6d.

ESKIMAUX and English Vocabulary, for Travellers in the Arctic Regions. 16mo. 3s. 6d.

ESSAYS FROM "THE TIMES." Being a Selection from the LITERARY PAPERS which have appeared in that Journal. 2 vols. Fcap. 8vo. 8s.

ETHNOLOGICAL SOCIETY'S TRANSACTIONS. New Series. Vols. I. to VI. 8vo. 10s. 6d. each.

EXETER'S (BISHOP OF) Letters to Charles Butler, on his Book of the Roman Catholic Church. *New Edition.* Post 8vo. 6s.

FAMILY RECEIPT-BOOK. A Collection of a Thousand Valuable and Useful Receipts. Fcap. 8vo. 5s. 6d.

LIST OF WORKS

FARRAR'S (A. S.) Critical History of Free Thought in reference to the Christian Religion. Being the Bampton Lectures, 1832. 8vo. 16s.

—— (F. W.) Origin of Language, based on Modern Researches. Fcap. 8vo. 5s.

FERGUSSON'S (JAMES) Palaces of Nineveh and Persepolis Restored. Woodcuts. 8vo. 16s.

—— History of Architecture in all Countries: from the Earliest Times to the Present Day. With 1200 Illustrations and an Index. Vols. I. and II. 8vo. 42s. each.

—— History of Architecture. Vol. III.—The Modern Styles. With 312 Illustrations, and an Index. 8vo. 31s. 6d.

—— Holy Sepulchre and the Temple at Jerusalem; being the Substance of Two Lectures delivered at the Royal Institution, 1862 and '65. Woodcuts. 8vo. 7s. 6d.

FISHER'S (REV. GEORGE) Elements of Geometry, for the Use of Schools. *Fifth Edition*. 18mo. 1s. 6d.

—— First Principles of Algebra, for the Use of Schools. *Fifth Edition*. 18mo. 1s. 6d.

FLEMING (WM.) Student's Manual of Moral Philosophy. Post 8vo. 7s. 6d.

FLOWER GARDEN (THE). By REV. THOS. JAMES. Fcap. 8vo. 1s.

FONNEREAU'S (T. G.) Diary of a Dutiful Son. Fcap. 8vo. 4s. 6d.

FORBES' (C. S.) Iceland; its Volcanoes, Geysers, and Glaciers. Illustrations. Post 8vo. 14s.

FORSTER'S (JOHN) Arrest of the Five Members by Charles the First. A Chapter of English History re-written. Post 8vo.

—— Grand Remonstrance, 1641. With an Essay on English freedom under the Plantagenet and Tudor Sovereigns. *Second Edition*. Post 8vo. 12s.

—— Sir John Eliot: a Biography, 1590—1632. With Portraits. 2 Vols. Crown 8vo. 30s.

—— Biographies of Oliver Cromwell, Daniel De Foe, Sir Richard Steele, Charles Churchill, Samuel Foote. *Third Edition*. Post 8vo. 12s.

FORD'S (RICHARD) Gatherings from Spain. Post 8vo. 3s. 6d.

FORSYTH'S (WILLIAM) Life and Times of Cicero. With Selections from his Correspondence and Orations. *New Edition*. Illustrations. 8vo. 10s.

FORTUNE'S (ROBERT) Narrative of Two Visits to the Tea Countries of China, 1843-52. *Third Edition*. Woodcuts. 2 Vols. Post 8vo. 18s.

—— Third Visit to China. 1853-6. Woodcuts. 8vo. 16s.

—— Yedo and Peking. With Notices of the Agriculture and Trade of China, during a Fourth Visit to that Country. Illustrations. 8vo. 16s.

FOSS' (Edward) Judges of England. With Sketches of their Lives, and Notices of the Courts at Westminster, from the Conquest to the Present Time. 9 Vols. 8vo. 126s.

———— Tabulæ Curiales; or, Tables of the Superior Courts of Westminster Hall. Showing the Judges who sat in them from 1066 to 1864; with the Attorney and Solicitor Generals of each reign. To which is prefixed an Alphabetical List of all the Judges during the same period. 8vo. 10s. 6d.

FRANCE (History of). From the Conquest by the Gauls. By Mrs. Markham. New and Cheaper Edition, continued to 1856. Woodcuts. 12mo. 4s.

———— From the Earliest Times to the Establishment of the Second Empire, 1852. By W. H. Pearson. Edited by Wm. Smith, LL.D. Woodcuts. Post 8vo. 7s. 6d.

FRENCH (The) in Algiers; The Soldier of the Foreign Legion— and the Prisoners of Abd-el-Kadir. Translated by Lady Duff Gordon. Post 8vo. 2s.

FRERE'S (M.) Old Deccan Days; or, Hindoo Fairy Legends Current in Southern India. Collected from Oral Tradition. Illustrated by C. F. Frere. With an Introduction and Notes, by Sir Bartle Frere. Crown 8vo. 12s.

GALTON'S (Francis) Art of Travel; or, Hints on the Shifts and Contrivances available in Wild Countries. *Fourth Edition.* Woodcuts. Post 8vo. 7s. 6d.

GEOGRAPHY (Ancient). By Rev. W. L. Bevan. Woodcuts. Post 8vo. 7s. 6d.

———— (Modern). By Rev. W. L. Bevan. Woodcuts. Post 8vo. *In the Press.*

———— Journal of the Royal Geographical Society of London. 8vo.

GERMANY (History of). From the Invasion by Marius, to Recent times. By Mrs. Markham. *New and Cheaper Edition.* Woodcuts. 12mo. 4s.

GIBBON'S (Edward) History of the Decline and Fall of the Roman Empire. *A New Edition.* Preceded by his Autobiography. And Edited, with Notes, by Dr. Wm. Smith. Maps. 8 Vols. 8vo. 60s.

———— (The Student's Gibbon); Being an Epitome of the above work, incorporating the Researches of Recent Commentators. By Dr. Wm. Smith. Woodcuts. Post 8vo. 7s. 6d.

GIFFARD'S (Edward) Deeds of Naval Daring; or, Anecdotes of the British Navy. Fcap. 8vo. 3s. 6d.

GLADSTONE'S (W. E.) Financial Statements of 1853, 60, 63, and 64; with Speeches on Tax-Bills and Charities. *Second Edition.* 8vo. 12s.

———— Speeches on Parliamentary Reform. *Third Edition.* Post 8vo. 5s.

GLEIG'S (G. R.) Campaigns of the British Army at Washington and New Orleans. Post 8vo. 2s.

———— Story of the Battle of Waterloo. Post 8vo. 3s. 6d.

———— Narrative of Sale's Brigade in Affghanistan. Post 8vo. 2s.

———— Life of Robert Lord Clive. Post 8vo. 3s. 6d.

———— Sir Thomas Munro. Post 8vo. 3s. 6d.

GOLDSMITH'S (OLIVER) Works. A New Edition. Edited with
Notes by PETER CUNNINGHAM. Vignettes. 4 Vols. 8vo. 30s.

GONGORA; An Historical Essay on the Times of Philip III. and
IV. of Spain. With Illustrations. By ARCHDEACON CHURTON. Portrait. 2 vols. Post 8vo. 15s.

GORDON'S (SIR ALEX. DUFF) Sketches of German Life, and Scenes
from the War of Liberation. From the German. Post 8vo. 3s. 6d.

——— (LADY DUFF) Amber-Witch: A Trial for Witchcraft. From the German. Post 8vo. 2s.

——— French in Algiers. 1. The Soldier of the Foreign
Legion. 2. The Prisoners of Abd-el-Kadir. From the French.
Post 8vo. 2s.

GOUGER'S (HENRY) Personal Narrative of Two Years' Imprisonment in Burmah. *Second Edition.* Woodcuts. Post 8vo. 12s.

GRAMMARS (LATIN and GREEK). See CURTIUS; SMITH; KING
EDWARD VITH., &c. &c.

GREECE (HISTORY OF). From the Earliest Times to the Roman
Conquest. By WM. SMITH, LL.D. Woodcuts. Post 8vo. 7s. 6d.

——— (SMALLER HISTORY OF). By WM. SMITH, LL.D. Woodcuts. 16mo. 3s. 6d.

GRENVILLE (THE) PAPERS. Being the Public and Private
Correspondence of George Grenville, including his PRIVATE DIARY.
Edited by W. J. SMITH. 4 Vols. 8vo. 16s. each.

GREY'S (EARL) Correspondence with King William IVth. and
Sir Herbert Taylor, from November, 1830, to the Passing of the Reform
Act in 1832. 2 Vols. 8vo. 30s.

——— Parliamentary Government and Reform; with
Suggestions for the Improvement of our Representative System.
Second Edition. 8vo. 9s.

——— (SIR GEORGE) Polynesian Mythology, and Ancient
Traditional History of the New Zealand Race. Woodcuts. Post
8vo. 10s. 6d.

GRUNER'S (LEWIS) Terra-Cotta Architecture of North Italy,
From careful Drawings and Restorations. With Illustrations, engraved
and printed in Colours. Small folio. 5l. 5s.

GROTE'S (GEORGE) History of Greece. From the Earliest Times
to the close of the generation contemporary with the death of Alexander
the Great. *Fourth Edition.* Maps. 8 Vols. 8vo. 112s.

——— PLATO, and the other Companions of Socrates.
Second Edition. 3 Vols. 8vo. 45s.

——— (MRS.) Memoir of Ary Scheffer. Post 8vo. 8s. 6d.

GUIZOT'S (M.) Meditations on Christianity, and on the Religious
Questions of the Day. Part I. The Essence. Part II. The Present
State. 2 Vols. Post 8vo. 20s.

——— Meditations on Christianity. Part III. Its Relation
to the State of Society and Progress of the Human Mind. Post 8vo.
(*Nearly Ready.*)

HALLAM'S (HENRY) Constitutional History of England, from the Accession of Henry the Seventh to the Death of George the Second. *Seventh Edition.* 3 Vols. 8vo. 30s.

———— History of Europe during the Middle Ages. *Tenth Edition.* 3 Vols. 8vo. 30s.

—— The Student's Hallam. An Epitome of the History of Europe during the Middle Ages. With Additional Notes and Illustrations. By WM. SMITH, LL.D. Post 8vo. Uniform with the "Student's Hume." (*In Preparation.*)

———— Literary History of Europe, during the 15th, 16th and 17th Centuries. *Fourth Edition.* 3 Vols. 8vo. 36s.

——— Historical Works. Containing History of England, —Middle Ages of Europe,—Literary History of Europe. 10 Vols. Post 8vo. 6s. each.

———— (ARTHUR) Remains; in Verse and Prose. With Preface, Memoir, and Portrait. Fcap. 8vo. 7s. 6d.

HAMILTON'S (JAMES) Wanderings in North Africa. With Illustrations. Post 8vo. 12s.

HANNAH'S (REV. DR.) Bampton Lectures for 1863; the Divine and Human Elements in Holy Scripture. 8vo. 10s. 6d.

HART'S ARMY LIST. (*Quarterly and Annually.*) 8vo.

HAY'S (J. H. DRUMMOND) Western Barbary, its Wild Tribes and Savage Animals. Post 8vo. 2s.

HEAD'S (SIR FRANCIS) Horse and his Rider. Woodcuts. Post 8vo. 5s.

———— Rapid Journeys across the Pampas. Post 8vo. 2s.

———— Bubbles from the Brunnen of Nassau. Illustrations. Post 8vo. 7s. 6d.

———— Emigrant. Fcap. 8vo. 2s. 6d.

———— Stokers and Pokers; or, the London and North Western Railway. Post 8vo. 2s.

———— (SIR EDMUND) Shall and Will; or, Future Auxiliary Verbs. Fcap. 8vo. 4s.

HEBER'S (BISHOP) Journey through the Upper Provinces of India, from Calcutta to Bombay, with an Account of a Journey to Madras and the Southern Provinces. *Twelfth Edition.* 2 Vols. Post 8vo. 7s.

———— Poetical Works, including Palestine, Europe, The Red Sea, Hymns, &c. *Sixth Edition.* Portrait. Fcap. 8vo. 6s.

———— Hymns adapted to the Weekly Church Service of the Year. 16mo. 1s. 6d.

HERODOTUS. A New English Version. Edited, with Notes and Essays, historical, ethnographical, and geographical, by Rev. G. RAWLINSON, assisted by SIR HENRY RAWLINSON and SIR J. G. WILKINSON. *Second Edition.* Maps and Woodcuts. 4 Vols. 8vo. 48s.

FOREIGN HANDBOOKS.

HAND-BOOK—TRAVEL-TALK. English, French, German, and Italian. 18mo. 3s. 6d.

——— NORTH GERMANY,—HOLLAND, BELGIUM, PRUSSIA, and the Rhine from Holland to Switzerland. Map. Post 8vo. 10s.

——— SOUTH GERMANY, Bavaria, Austria, Styria, Salzberg, the Austrian and Bavarian Alps, the Tyrol, Hungary, and the Danube, from Ulm to the Black Sea. Map. Post 8vo. 10s.

——— KNAPSACK GUIDE TO THE TYROL. Post 8vo. 6s.

——— PAINTING. German, Flemish, and Dutch Schools. Woodcuts. 2 Vols. Post 8vo. 24s.

——— LIVES OF THE EARLY FLEMISH PAINTERS. By CROWE and CAVALCASELLE. Illustrations. Post 8vo. 12s.

——— SWITZERLAND, Alps of Savoy, and Piedmont. Maps. Post 8vo. 10s.

——— KNAPSACK GUIDE TO SWITZERLAND. Post 8vo. 5s.

——— FRANCE, Normandy, Brittany, the French Alps, the Rivers Loire, Seine, Rhone, and Garonne, Dauphiné, Provence, and the Pyrenees. Maps. Post 8vo. 12s.

——— CORSICA and SARDINIA. Maps. Post 8vo. 4s.

——— PARIS, and its Environs. Map and Plans. Post 8vo. 3s. 6d.

*** MURRAY'S PLAN OF PARIS, mounted on canvas. 3s 6d.

——— SPAIN, Andalusia, Ronda, Granada, Valencia, Catalonia, Gallicia, Arragon, and Navarre. Maps. Post 8vo. (In the Press.)

——— PORTUGAL, LISBON, &c. Map. Post 8vo. 9s.

——— NORTH ITALY, Piedmont, Liguria, Venetia, Lombardy, Parma, Modena, and Romagna. Map. Post 8vo. 12s.

——— CENTRAL ITALY, Lucca, Tuscany, Florence, The Marches, Umbria, and the Patrimony of St. Peter's. Map. Post 8vo. 10s.

——— ROME AND ITS ENVIRONS. Map. Post 8vo. 9s.

——— SOUTH ITALY, Two Sicilies, Naples, Pompeii, Herculaneum, and Vesuvius. Map. Post 8vo. 10s.

——— KNAPSACK GUIDE TO ITALY. Post 8vo. 6s.

——— SICILY, Palermo, Messina, Catania, Syracuse, Etna, and the Ruins of the Greek Temples. Map. Post 8vo. 12s.

——— PAINTING. The Italian Schools. Edited by Sir CHARLES EASTLAKE, R.A. Woodcuts. 2 Vols. Post 8vo. 30s.

——— LIVES OF ITALIAN PAINTERS, FROM CIMABUE to BASSANO. By Mrs. JAMESON. Portraits. Post 8vo. 10s. 6d.

——— DENMARK, SWEDEN, and NORWAY. *New Edition.* Maps. Post 8vo. (*In Preparation.*)

PUBLISHED BY MR. MURRAY. 17

HAND-BOOK—KNAPSACK GUIDE TO NORWAY. Map.
Post 8vo. 5s.
———— — GREECE, the Ionian Islands, Albania, Thessaly,
and Macedonia. Maps. Post 8vo. (*In preparation.*)
———— — TURKEY, Malta, Asia Minor, Constantinople,
Armenia, Mesopotamia, &c. Maps. Post 8vo. (*In preparation.*)
———— EGYPT, Thebes, the Nile, Alexandria, Cairo, the
Pyramids, Mount Sinai, &c. Map. Post 8vo. 15s.
———— HOLY LAND—Syria and Palestine, Peninsula
of Sinai, Edom, and Syrian Desert. Maps. 2 Vols. Post 8vo. 24s.
———— INDIA. — Bombay and Madras. Map. 2 Vols.
Post. 8vo. 24s.
———— RUSSIA, St. Petersburgh, Moscow, Poland, and
Finland. Maps. Post 8vo. 15s.

ENGLISH HANDBOOKS.

HAND-BOOK—MODERN LONDON. Map. 16mo. 3s. 6d.
———— WESTMINSTER ABBEY. Woodcuts. 16mo. 1s.
———— KENT AND SUSSEX, Canterbury, Dover, Ramsgate, Sheerness, Rochester, Chatham, Woolwich, Brighton, Chichester, Worthing, Hastings, Lewes, Arundel, &c. Map. Post 8vo. 10s.
———— SURREY AND HANTS, Kingston, Croydon, Reigate, Guildford, Winchester, Southampton, Portsmouth, and Isle of Wight. Maps. Post 8vo. 10s.
———— WILTS, DORSET, AND SOMERSET, Salisbury, Chippenham, Weymouth, Sherborne, Wells, Bath, Bristol, Taunton, &c. Map. Post 8vo.
———— DEVON AND CORNWALL, Exeter, Ilfracombe, Linton, Sidmouth, Dawlish, Teignmouth, Plymouth, Devonport, Torquay, Launceston, Truro, Penzance, Falmouth, &c. Maps. Post 8vo. 10s.
———— BERKS, BUCKS, AND OXON, Windsor, Eton, Reading, Aylesbury, Uxbridge, Wycombe, Henley, the City and University of Oxford, and the Descent of the Thames. Map. Post 8vo. 7s. 6d.
———— GLOUCESTER, HEREFORD, and WORCESTER, Cirencester, Cheltenham, Stroud, Tewkesbury, Leominster, Ross, Malvern, Kidderminster, Dudley, Bromsgrove, Evesham, Map. Post 8vo. 6s. 6d.
———— CATHEDRALS OF GLOUCESTER, HEREFORD and Worcester. Illustrations. 2s. 6d. each, or in 1 Vol., Post 8vo. 8s. 6d.
———— NORTH AND SOUTH WALES, Bangor, Carnarvon, Beaumaris, Snowdon, Conway, Menai Straits, Carmarthen, Pembroke, Tenby, Swansea, The Wye, &c. Maps. 2 Vols. Post 8vo. 12s.
———— DERBY, NOTTS, LEICESTER, AND STAFFORD, Matlock, Bakewell, Chatsworth, The Peak, Buxton, Hardwick, Dove Dale, Ashborne, Southwell, Mansfield, Retford, Burton, Belvoir, Melton Mowbray, Wolverhampton, Lichfield, Walsall, Tamworth. Map. Post 8vo. 7s. 6d.
———— YORKSHIRE, Doncaster, Hull, Selby, Beverley, Scarborough, Whitby, Harrogate, Ripon, Leeds, Wakefield, Bradford, Halifax, Huddersfield, Sheffield. Map and Plans. Post 8vo. 12s.

c

HAND-BOOK—DURHAM AND NORTHUMBERLAND, Newcastle, Darlington, Gateshead, Bishop Auckland, Stockton, Hartlepool, Sunderland, Shields, Berwick-on-Tweed, Morpeth, Tynemouth, Coldstream, Alnwick, &c. Map. Post 8vo. 9s.

———— WESTMORLAND AND CUMBERLAND—Lancaster, Furness Abbey, Ambleside, Kendal, Windermere, Coniston, Keswick, Grasmere, Carlisle, Cockermouth, Penrith, Appleby. Map. Post 8vo. 6s.

*** MURRAY'S MAP OF THE LAKES, on canvas. 3s. 6d.

———— EASTERN COUNTIES, Essex, Suffolk, Norfolk, and Cambridge. Map. Post 8vo. (In the Press.)

———— SCOTLAND, Edinburgh, Melrose, Kelso, Glasgow, Dumfries, Ayr, Stirling, Arran, The Clyde, Oban, Inverary, Loch Lomond, Loch Katrine and Trossachs, Caledonian Canal, Inverness, Perth, Dundee, Aberdeen, Braemar, Skye, Caithness, Ross, Sutherland, &c. Maps and Plans. Post 8vo. 9s.

———— IRELAND, Dublin, Belfast, Donegal, Galway, Wexford, Cork, Limerick, Waterford, the Lakes of Killarney, Coast of Munster, &c. Maps. Post 8vo. 12s.

———— EASTERN CATHEDRALS, Oxford, Peterborough, Norwich, Ely, and Lincoln. With 90 Illustrations. Crown 8vo. 18s.

———— SOUTHERN CATHEDRALS, Winchester, Salisbury, Exeter, Wells, Chichester, Rochester, Canterbury. With 110 Illustrations. 2 Vols. Crown 8vo. 24s.

————WESTERN CATHEDRALS, Bristol, Gloucester, Hereford, Worcester, and Lichfield. With 50 Illustrations. Crown 8vo. 16s.

———— NORTHERN CATHEDRALS, York, Ripon, Durham, Carlisle, Chester, and Manchester. With Illustrations. Crown 8vo. (In preparation.)

HAND-BOOK OF FAMILIAR QUOTATIONS. From English Authors. Third Edition. Fcap. 8vo. 5s.

HESSEY (REV. DR.). Sunday—Its Origin, History, and Present Obligations. Being the Bampton Lectures for 1860. Second Edition. 8vo. 16s. Or Popular Edition. Post 8vo. 9s.

HICKMAN'S (WM.) Treatise on the Law and Practice of Naval Courts-Martial. 8vo. 10s. 6d.

HOLLWAY'S (J. G.) Month in Norway. Fcap. 8vo. 2s.

HONEY BEE (THE). An Essay. By REV. THOMAS JAMES. Reprinted from the "Quarterly Review." Fcap. 8vo. 1s.

HOOK'S (DEAN) Church Dictionary. Ninth Edition. 8vo. 16s.

———— (THEODORE) Life. By J. G. LOCKHART. Fcap. 8vo. 1s.

HOPE'S (A. J. B.) English Cathedral of the Nineteenth Century. With Illustrations. 8vo. 12s.

HOPE'S (T. C.) ARCHITECTURE OF AHMEDABAD, with Historical Sketch and Architectural Notes by T. C. HOPE, and JAMES FERGUSSON, F.R.S. With 2 Maps, 120 Photographs, and 22 Woodcuts. 4to. 5l. 5s.

———— BEJAPOOR, with Historical Sketch and Architectural Essay by Col. MEADOWS TAYLOR and JAS. FERGUSSON. With 2 Maps, 78 Photographs, and 13 Woodcuts. Folio. 10l. 10s.

———— DHARWAR and MYSORE. With Historical Sketch and Architectural Essay by Col. MEADOWS TAYLOR and JAS. FERGUSSON. With 2 Maps, 100 Photographs, and numerous Woodcuts. Folio. 12l. 12s.

HOME AND COLONIAL LIBRARY. A Series of Works adapted for all circles and classes of Readers, having been selected for their acknowledged interest and ability of the Authors. Post 8vo. Published at 2s. and 3s. 6d. each, and arranged under two distinctive heads as follows:—

CLASS A.
HISTORY, BIOGRAPHY, AND HISTORIC TALES.

1. SIEGE OF GIBRALTAR. By JOHN DRINKWATER. 2s.
2. THE AMBER-WITCH. By LADY DUFF GORDON. 2s.
3. CROMWELL AND BUNYAN. By ROBERT SOUTHEY. 2s.
4. LIFE OF SIR FRANCIS DRAKE. By JOHN BARROW. 2s.
5. CAMPAIGNS AT WASHINGTON. By REV. G. R. GLEIG. 2s.
6. THE FRENCH IN ALGIERS. By LADY DUFF GORDON. 2s.
7. THE FALL OF THE JESUITS. 2s.
8. LIVONIAN TALES. 2s.
9. LIFE OF CONDE. By LORD MAHON. 3s. 6d.
10. SALE'S BRIGADE. By REV. G. R. GLEIG. 2s.
11. THE SIEGES OF VIENNA. By LORD ELLESMERE. 2s.
12. THE WAYSIDE CROSS. By CAPT. MILMAN. 2s.
13. SKETCHES OF GERMAN LIFE. By SIR A. GORDON. 3s. 6d.
14. THE BATTLE OF WATERLOO. By REV. G. R. GLEIG. 3s. 6d.
15. AUTOBIOGRAPHY OF STEFFENS. 2s.
16. THE BRITISH POETS. By THOMAS CAMPBELL. 3s. 6d.
17. HISTORICAL ESSAYS. By LORD MAHON. 3s. 6d.
18. LIFE OF LORD CLIVE. By REV. G. R. GLEIG. 3s. 6d.
19. NORTH-WESTERN RAILWAY. By SIR F. B. HEAD. 2s.
20. LIFE OF MUNRO. By REV. G. R. GLEIG. 3s. 6d.

CLASS B.
VOYAGES, TRAVELS, AND ADVENTURES.

1. BIBLE IN SPAIN. By GEORGE BORROW. 3s. 6d.
2. GIPSIES OF SPAIN. By GEORGE BORROW. 3s. 6d.
3 & 4. JOURNALS IN INDIA. By BISHOP HEBER. 2 Vols. 7s.
5. TRAVELS IN THE HOLY LAND. By IRBY and MANGLES. 2s.
6. MOROCCO AND THE MOORS. By J. DRUMMOND HAY. 2s.
7. LETTERS FROM THE BALTIC. By a LADY. 2s.
8. NEW SOUTH WALES. By MRS. MEREDITH. 2s.
9. THE WEST INDIES. By M. G. LEWIS. 2s.
10. SKETCHES OF PERSIA. By SIR JOHN MALCOLM. 3s. 6d.
11. MEMOIRS OF FATHER RIPA. 2s.
12. 13. TYPEE AND OMOO. By HERMANN MELVILLE. 2 Vols. 7s.
14. MISSIONARY LIFE IN CANADA. By REV. J. ABBOTT. 2s.
15. LETTERS FROM MADRAS. By a LADY. 2s.
16. HIGHLAND SPORTS. By CHARLES ST. JOHN. 3s. 6d.
17. PAMPAS JOURNEYS. By SIR F. B. HEAD. 2s.
18. GATHERINGS FROM SPAIN. By RICHARD FORD. 3s. 6d.
19. THE RIVER AMAZON. By W. H. EDWARDS. 2s.
20. MANNERS & CUSTOMS OF INDIA. By REV. C. ACLAND. 2s.
21. ADVENTURES IN MEXICO. By G. F. RUXTON. 3s. 6d.
22. PORTUGAL AND GALLICIA. By LORD CARNARVON. 3s. 6d.
23. BUSH LIFE IN AUSTRALIA. By Rev. H. W. HAYGARTH. 2s.
24. THE LIBYAN DESERT. By BAYLE ST. JOHN. 2s.
25. SIERRA LEONE. By a LADY. 3s. 6d.

_{*} Each work may be had separately.

HORACE (WORKS OF.) Edited by DEAN MILMAN. With 100 Woodcuts. Crown 8vo. 7s. 6d.
—————— (Life of). By DEAN MILMAN. Woodcuts, and coloured Borders. 8vo. 9s.
HOUGHTON'S (LORD) Poetical Works. Fcap. 8vo. 6s.
HUME (THE STUDENT'S) A History of England, from the Invasion of Julius Cæsar to the Revolution of 1688. Corrected and continued to 1858. Edited by DR. WM. SMITH. Woodcuts. Post 8vo. 7s. 6d.
HUTCHINSON (GEN.) on the most expeditious, certain, and easy Method of Dog-Breaking. *Fourth Edition.* Enlarged and revised, with 40 Illustrations. Crown 8vo. 15s.
HUTTON'S (H. E.) Principia Græca; an Introduction to the Study of Greek. Comprehending Grammar, Delectus, and Exercise-book, with Vocabularies. *Sixth Edition.* 12mo. 3s. 6d.
IRBY AND MANGLES' Travels in Egypt, Nubia, Syria, and the Holy Land. Post 8vo. 2s.
JAMES' (REV. THOMAS) Fables of Æsop. A New Translation, with Historical Preface. With 100 Woodcuts by TENNIEL and WOLF. *Fiftieth Thousand.* Post 8vo. 2s. 6d.
JAMESON'S (MRS.) Lives of the Early Italian Painters— and the Progress of Painting in Italy—Cimabue to Bassano. *New Edition.* With 50 Portraits. Post 8vo. 10s. 6d.
JENNINGS' (L. J.) Eighty Years of Republican Government in the United States. Post 8vo. 10s. 6d.
JESSE'S (EDWARD) Gleanings in Natural History. *Eighth Edition.* Fcp. 8vo. 6s.
JOHNS' (REV. B. G.) Blind People; their Works and Ways. With Sketches of the Lives of some famous Blind Men. With Illustrations. Post 8vo. 7s. 6d.
• JOHNSON'S (DR. SAMUEL) Life. By James Boswell. Including the Tour to the Hebrides. Edited by MR. CROKER. Portraits. Royal 8vo. 10s.
—————— Lives of the English Poets. Edited by PETER CUNNINGHAM. 3 vols. 8vo. 22s. 6d.
KEN'S (BISHOP) Life. By a LAYMAN. Portrait. 2 Vols. 8vo. 18s.
—————— Exposition of the Apostles' Creed. Fcap. 1s. 6d.
—————— Approach to the Holy Altar. Fcap. 8vo. 1s. 6d.
KENNEDY'S (GENERAL) Notes on the Battle of Waterloo. With a Memoir of his Life and Services, and a Plan for the Defence of Canada. With Map and Plans. 8vo. 7s. 6d.
KERR'S (ROBERT) GENTLEMAN'S HOUSE; OR, HOW TO PLAN ENGLISH RESIDENCES, FROM THE PARSONAGE TO THE PALACE. With Tables and Cost. Views and Plans. *Second Edition.* 8vo. 24s.
—————— Ancient Lights; a Book for Architects, Surveyors, Lawyers, and Landlords. 8vo. 5s. 6d.
—————— (R. MALCOLM) Student's Blackstone. A Systematic Abridgment of the entire Commentaries, adapted to the present state of the law. Post 8vo. 7s. 6d.
KING'S (REV. C. W.) Antique Gems; their Origin, Use, and Value, as Interpreters of Ancient History, and as illustrative of Ancient Art. *Second Edition.* Illustrations. 8vo. 21s.
KING EDWARD VITH's Latin Grammar; or, an Introduction to the Latin Tongue. *Seventeenth Edition.* 12mo. 3s. 6d.
—————— First Latin Book; or, the Accidence, Syntax, and Prosody, with an English Translation. *Fifth Edition.* 12mo. 2s. 6d.

KING GEORGE THE THIRD'S CORRESPONDENCE WITH
LORD NORTH, 1769-82. Edited, with Notes and Introduction, by
W. BODHAM DONNE. 2 vols. 8vo. 32s.

KIRK'S (J. FOSTER) History of Charles the Bold, Duke of Burgundy. Portrait. 3 Vols. 8vo. 45s.

KUGLER'S Italian Schools of Painting. Edited, with Notes, by SIR CHARLES EASTLAKE. *Third Edition.* Woodcuts. 2 Vols. Post 8vo. 30s.

——— German, Dutch, and Flemish Schools of Painting. Edited, with Notes, by DR. WAAGEN. *Second Edition.* Woodcuts. 2 Vols. Post 8vo. 24s.

LAYARD'S (A. H.) Nineveh and its Remains. Being a Narrative of Researches and Discoveries amidst the Ruins of Assyria. With an Account of the Chaldean Christians of Kurdistan; the Yezedis, or Devil-worshippers; and an Enquiry into the Manners and Arts of the Ancient Assyrians. *Sixth Edition.* Plates and Woodcuts. 2 Vols. 8vo. 36s.

* A POPULAR EDITION. With Illustrations. Post 8vo. 7s. 6d.

——— Nineveh and Babylon; being the Narrative of a Second Expedition to Assyria. Plates. 8vo. 21s.

* A POPULAR EDITION. With Illustrations. Post 8vo. 7s. 6d.

LEATHES' (STANLEY) Short Practical Hebrew Grammar. With an Appendix, containing the Hebrew Text of Genesis i.—vi., and Psalms i.—vi. Grammatical Analysis and Vocabulary. Post 8vo. 7s. 6d.

LENNEP'S (REV. H. J. VAN) Missionary Travels in Asia Minor. With Illustrations. 2 Vols. Post 8vo. (*In preparation.*)

LESLIE'S (C. R.) Handbook for Young Painters. With Illustrations. Post 8vo. 10s. 6d.

——— Autobiographical Recollections, with Selections from his Correspondence. Edited by TOM TAYLOR. Portrait. 2 Vols. Post 8vo. 19s.

——— Life and Works of Sir Joshua Reynolds. Portraits and Illustrations. 2 Vols. 8vo. 42s.

LETTERS FROM THE BALTIC. By a LADY. Post 8vo. 2s.

——— MADRAS. By a LADY. Post 8vo. 2s.

——— SIERRA LEONE. By a LADY. Post 8vo. 3s. 6d.

LEVI'S (LEONE) Wages and Earnings of the Working Classes. With some Facts Illustrative of their Economic Condition. 8vo. 6s.

LEWIS (SIR G. C.) On the Government of Dependencies. 8vo. 12s.

——— Glossary of Provincial Words used in Herefordshire, &c. 12mo. 4s. 6d.

——— (M. G.) Journal of a Residence among the Negroes in the West Indies. Post 8vo. 2s.

LIDDELL'S (DEAN) History of Rome. From the Earliest Times to the Establishment of the Empire. With the History of Literature and Art. 2 Vols. 8vo. 28s.

——— Student's History of Rome, abridged from the above Work. With Woodcuts. Post 8vo. 7s. 6d.

LINDSAY'S (LORD) Lives of the Lindsays; or, a Memoir of the Houses of Crawfurd and Balcarres. With Extracts from Official Papers and Personal Narratives. *Second Edition.* 3 Vols. 8vo. 24s.

LISPINGS from LOW LATITUDES; or, the Journal of the Hon. Impulsia Gushington. Edited by LORD DUFFERIN. With 24 Plates. 4to. 21s.

LITTLE ARTHUR'S HISTORY OF ENGLAND. By LADY
CALLCOTT. New Edition, continued to 1862. With 20 Woodcuts.
Fcap. 8vo. 2s. 6d.
LIVINGSTONE'S (DR.) Popular Account of his Missionary
Travels in South Africa. Illustrations. Post 8vo. 6s.
——————— Narrative of an Expedition to the Zambezi and
its Tributaries; and of the Discovery of Lakes Shirwa and Nyassa.
1858-64. Map and Illustrations. 8vo. 21s.
LIVONIAN TALES. By the Author of "Letters from the
Baltic." Post 8vo. 2s.
LOCKHART'S (J. G.) Ancient Spanish Ballads. Historical and
Romantic. Translated, with Notes. New Edition. Post 8vo. 2s. 6d.
——————— Life of Theodore Hook. Fcap. 8vo. 1s.
LONDON (OLD). A series of Essays on its Archæology and
Antiquities, by DEAN STANLEY; A. J. BERESFORD HOPE, M.P.; G. G.
SCOTT, R.A.; R. WESTMACOTT, R.A.; E. FOSS, F.S.A.; G. T. CLARK;
JOSEPH BURTT; REV. J. R GREEN; and G. SCHARF, F.S.A. 8vo. 12s.
LONDON'S (BISHOP OF) Dangers and Safeguards of Modern
Theology. Containing Suggestions to the Theological Student under
present difficulties. Second Edition. 8vo. 9s.
LONSDALE'S (BISHOP) Life. With Selections from his Writings.
By E. B. DENISON, Q.C. With Portrait. Crown 8vo. 10s. 6d.
LOUDON'S (MRS.) Instructions in Gardening. With Directions
and Calendar of Operations for Every Month. Eighth Edition. Wood-
cuts. Fcap. 8vo. 5s.
LUCAS' (SAMUEL) Secularia; or, Surveys on the Main Stream of
History. 8vo. 12s.
LUCKNOW: a Lady's Diary of the Siege. Fcap. 8vo. 4s. 6d.
LYELL'S (SIR CHARLES) Elements of Geology; or, the Ancient
Changes of the Earth and its Inhabitants as illustrated by Geological
Monuments. Sixth Edition. Woodcuts. 8vo. 18s.
——————— Principles of Geology; or, the Modern Changes
of the Earth and its Inhabitants considered as illustrative of Geology.
Tenth Edition. With Illustrations. 2 Vols. 8vo. 32s.
——————— Geological Evidences of the Antiquity of Man.
Third Edition. Illustrations. 8vo. 14s.
LYTTELTON'S (LORD) Ephemera. Post 8vo. 10s. 6d.
LYTTON'S (LORD) Poems. New Edition. Post 8vo. 10s. 6d.
——————— Lost Tales of Miletus. Second Edition. Post 8vo. 7s. 6d.
MACPHERSON'S (MAJOR S. C.) Memorials of Service in India,
while Political Agent at Gwalior during the Mutiny. With Portrait
and Illustrations. 8vo. 12s.
MAHON'S (LORD) Works. See STANHOPE (Earl of).
M°CLINTOCK'S (SIR L.) Narrative of the Discovery of the
Fate of Sir John Franklin and his Companions in the Arctic Seas.
Twelfth Thousand. Illustrations. 8vo. 16s.
M°CULLOCH'S (J. R.) Collected Edition of RICARDO's Political
Works. With Notes and Memoir. 8vo. 16s.
MACDOUGALL'S (COL.) Modern Warfare as Influenced by Modern
Artillery. With Plans. Post 8vo. 12s.
MAINE (H. SUMNER) On Ancient Law: its Connection with the
Early History of Society, and its Relation to Modern Ideas. 8vo. 12s.

MALCOLM'S (Sir John) Sketches of Persia. Post 8vo. 3s. 6d.
MANSEL (Canon) Limits of Religious Thought Examined. Being the Bampton Lectures for 1858. Post 8vo. 8s. 6d.
MANSFIELD (Sir William) On a Gold Currency for India. 8vo. 3s. 6d.
MANTELL'S (Gideon A.) Thoughts on Animalcules; or, the Invisible World, as revealed by the Microscope. Plates. 16mo. 6s.
MANUAL OF SCIENTIFIC ENQUIRY. For the Use of Travellers. Edited by Sir J. F. Herschel and Rev. R. Main. Maps. Post 8vo. 9s. (Published by order of the Lords of the Admiralty.)
MARKHAM'S (Mrs.) History of England. From the First Invasion by the Romans, down to Recent Times. New Edition, continued to 1863. Woodcuts. 12mo. 4s.
——— History of France. From the Conquest by the Gauls, to Recent Times. New Edition, continued to 1856. Woodcuts. 12mo. 4s.
——— History of Germany. From the Invasion by Marius, to Recent Times. New Edition. Woodcuts. 12mo. 4s.
——— (Clements R.) Travels in Peru and India. Maps and Illustrations. 8vo. 16s.
MARRYAT'S (Joseph) History of Modern and Mediæval Pottery and Porcelain. With a Description of the Manufacture. Third and revised and enlarged Edition. Plates and Woodcuts. 8vo. (Nearly Ready.)
——— (Horace) Jutland, the Danish Isles, and Copenhagen. Illustrations. 2 Vols. Post 8vo. 24s.
——— Sweden and Isle of Gothland. Illustrations. 2 Vols. Post 8vo. 28s.
MARSH'S (G. P.) Student's Manual of the English Language. Post 8vo. 7s. 6d.
MAUREL'S (Jules) Essay on the Character, Actions, and Writings of the Duke of Wellington. Second Edition. Fcap. 8vo. 1s. 6d.
MAYNE'S (Capt.) Four Years in British Columbia and Vancouver Island. Its Forests, Rivers, Coasts, and Gold Fields, and Resources for Colonisation. Illustrations. 8vo. 16s.
MELVILLE'S (Hermann) Typee and Omoo; or, Adventures amongst the Marquesas and South Sea Islands. 2 Vols. Post 8vo. 7s.
MILLS' (Rev. John) Three Months' Residence at Nablus, with an Account of the Modern Samaritans. Illustrations. Post 8vo. 10s. 6d.
MILMAN'S (Dean) Historical Works. Containing: 1. History of the Jews, 3 Vols. 2. History of Early Christianity, 3 Vols. 3. History of Latin Christianity, 9 Vols. Post 8vo. 6s. each.
——— Annals of St. Paul's Cathedral. Portrait and Illustrations. 8vo. (In preparation.)
——— Character and Conduct of the Apostles considered as an Evidence of Christianity. 8vo. 10s. 6d.
——— Translations from the Agamemnon of Æschylus and Bacchanals of Euripides. With Illustrations. Crown 8vo. 12s.
——— Works of Horace. With 100 woodcuts. Small 8vo. 7s. 6d.
——— Life of Horace. Woodcuts. 8vo. 9s.
——— Poetical Works. Plates. 3 Vols. Fcap. 8vo. 18s.
——— Fall of Jerusalem. Fcap. 8vo. 1s.
——— (Capt. E. A.) Wayside Cross. A Tale of the Carlist War. Post 8vo. 2s.

MEREDITH'S (MRS. CHARLES) Notes and Sketches of New South Wales. Post 8vo. 2s.

MESSIAH (THE): A Narrative of the Life, Travels, Death, Resurrection, and Ascension of our Blessed Lord. By the Author of "Life of Bishop Ken." Map. 8vo. 18s.

MICHIE'S (ALEXANDER) Siberian Overland Route from Peking to Petersburg, through the Deserts and Steppes of Mongolia, Tartary, &c. Maps and Illustrations. 8vo. 16s.

MODERN DOMESTIC COOKERY. Founded on Principles of Economy and Practical Knowledge and adapted for Private Families. New Edition. Woodcuts. Fcap. 8vo. 5s.

MOORE'S (THOMAS) Life and Letters of Lord Byron. Plates. 6 Vols. Fcap. 8vo. 18s.; or 1 Vol. Portraits. Royal 8vo. 9s.

MOTLEY'S (J. L.) History of the United Netherlands: from the Death of William the Silent to the Twelve Years' Truce, 1609. Embracing the English-Dutch struggle against Spain; and a detailed Account of the Spanish Armada. Portraits. 4 Vols. 8vo. 60s. Or Popular Edition. 4 Vols. Post 8vo. 6s. each.

MOUHOT'S (HENRI) Siam, Cambojia, and Lao; a Narrative of Travels and Discoveries. Illustrations. 2 vols. 8vo. 32s.

MOZLEY'S (REV. J. B.) Treatise on Predestination. 8vo. 14s.

———— Primitive Doctrine of Baptismal Regeneration. 8vo. 7s. 6d.

MUNDY'S (GENERAL) Pen and Pencil Sketches in India. Third Edition. Plates. Post 8vo. 7s. 6d.

MUNRO'S (GENERAL SIR THOMAS) Life and Letters. By the REV. G. R. GLEIG. Post 8vo. 3s. 6d.

MURCHISON'S (SIR RODERICK) Russia in Europe and the Ural Mountains. With Coloured Maps, Plates, Sections, &c. 2 Vols. Royal 4to. 5l. 5s.

———— Siluria; or, a History of the Oldest Rocks containing Organic Remains. Fourth Edition. Map and Plates. 8vo. 30s.

MURRAY'S RAILWAY READING. Containing:—

WELLINGTON. By LORD ELLESMERE. 6d.	HALLAM'S LITERARY ESSAYS. 2s.
NIMROD ON THE CHASE. 1s.	MAHON'S JOAN OF ARC. 1s.
ESSAYS FROM "THE TIMES." 2 Vols. 8s.	HEAD'S EMIGRANT. 2s. 6d.
MUSIC AND DRESS. 1s.	NIMROD ON THE ROAD. 1s.
LAYARD'S ACCOUNT OF NINEVEH. 5s.	CROKER ON THE GUILLOTINE. 1s.
MILMAN'S FALL OF JERUSALEM. 1s.	HOLLWAY'S NORWAY. 2s.
MAHON'S "FORTY-FIVE." 3s.	MAUREL'S WELLINGTON. 1s. 6d.
LIFE OF THEODORE HOOK. 1s.	CAMPBELL'S LIFE OF BACON. 2s. 6d.
DEEDS OF NAVAL DARING. 3s. 6d.	THE FLOWER GARDEN. 1s.
THE HONEY BEE. 1s.	LOCKHART'S SPANISH BALLADS. 2s. 6d.
JAMES' ÆSOP'S FABLES. 2s. 6d.	TAYLOR'S NOTES FROM LIFE. 2s.
NIMROD ON THE TURF. 1s. 6d.	REJECTED ADDRESSES. 1s.
ART OF DINING. 1s. 6d.	PENN'S HINTS ON ANGLING. 1s.

MUSIC AND DRESS. By a LADY. Reprinted from the "Quarterly Review." Fcap. 8vo. 1s.

NAPIER'S (SIR CHAS.) Life; chiefly derived from his Journals and Letters. By SIR W. NAPIER. Second Edition. Portraits. 4 Vols. Post 8vo. 48s.

———— (SIR WM.) Life and Letters. Edited by H. A. BRUCE, M.P. Portraits. 2 Vols. Crown 8vo. 28s.

———— English Battles and Sieges of the Peninsular War. Fourth Edition. Portrait. Post 8vo. 9s.

NAUTICAL (The) ALMANACK. Royal 8vo. 2s. 6d. (By Authority.)

NAVY LIST (The). (Published Quarterly, by Authority.) 16mo. 2s. 6d.

NEW TESTAMENT (Illustrated). With Explanatory Commentary. Edited by Archdeacon Churton, M.A., and Basil Jones, M.A. With 110 authentic Views of Places, from Sketches and Photographs taken on the spot. 2 Vols. Crown 8vo. 30s. cloth; 52s. 6d. calf; 63s. morocco.

NICHOLLS' (Sir George) History of the English, Irish and Scotch Poor Laws. 4 Vols. 8vo.

——— (Rev. H. G.) Historical Account of the Forest of Dean. Woodcuts, &c. Post 8vo. 10s. 6d.

NICOLAS' (Sir Harris) Historic Peerage of England. Exhibiting the Origin, Descent, and Present State of every Title of Peerage which has existed in this Country since the Conquest. By William Courthope. 8vo. 30s.

NIMROD On the Chace—The Turf—and The Road. Woodcuts. Fcap. 8vo. 3s. 6d.

OLD LONDON ; Papers read at the London Congress of the Archæological Institute, July, 1866. By A. J. B. Beresford Hope, M.P.; Dean Stanley, D.D.; G. T. Clark, Esq ; G. Gilbert Scott, R.A.; Professor Westmacott, R.A.; Edward Foss, F.S.A.; Joseph Burtt, Esq.; Rev. J. R. Green; George Scharf, F.S.A. With Illustrations. 8vo. 12s.

OXENHAM'S (Rev. W.) English Notes for Latin Elegiacs ; designed for early Proficients in the Art of Latin Versification, with Prefatory Rules of Composition in Elegiac Metre. Fourth Edition. 12mo. 3s. 6d.

OXFORD'S (Bishop of) Popular Life of William Wilberforce. Portrait. Post 8vo. 10s. 6d.

PARIS' (Dr.) Philosophy in Sport made Science in Earnest; or, the First Principles of Natural Philosophy inculcated by aid of the Toys and Sports of Youth. Ninth Edition. Woodcuts. Post 8vo. 7s. 6d.

PARKYNS' (Mansfield) Life in Abyssinia : During a Three Years' Residence and Travels in that Country. New Edition, with Map and 30 Illustrations. Post 8vo. 7s. 6d.

PEEL'S (Sir Robert) Memoirs. Edited by Earl Stanhope and Mr. Cardwell. 2 Vols. Post 8vo. 7s. 6d. each.

PENN'S (Richard) Maxims and Hints for an Angler and Chessplayer. New Edition. Woodcuts. Fcap. 8vo. 1s.

PENROSE'S (F. C.) Principles of Athenian Architecture, and the Optical Refinements exhibited in the Construction of the Ancient Buildings at Athens, from a Survey. With 40 Plates. Folio. 5l. 5s.

PERCY'S (John, M.D.) Metallurgy of Fuel, Coal, Fire-Clays, Copper, Zinc, Brass, &c. Illustrations. 8vo. 21s.

——— Metallurgy of Iron and Steel. Illustrations. 8vo. 42s.

——— Metallurgy of Lead, Silver, Gold, Platinum, Nickel, Cobalt, Antimony, Bismuth, Arsenic, &c. Illustrations. 8vo. (In the Press.)

PHILLIPP (C. S. M.) On Jurisprudence. 8vo. 12s.

PHILLIPS' (John) Memoirs of William Smith, (the Father of Geology). Portrait. 8vo. 7s. 6d.

——— Geology of Yorkshire, The Coast, and Limestone District. Plates. 4to. Part I., 20s.—Part II., 30s.

——— Rivers, Mountains, and Sea Coast of Yorkshire. With Essays on the Climate, Scenery, and Ancient Inhabitants. Second Edition, Plates. 8vo. 15s.

PHILPOTTS' (BISHOP) Letters to the late Charles Butler, on his " Book of the Roman Catholic Church." *New Edition.* Post 8vo. 6s.

POPE'S (ALEXANDER) Life and Works. *A New Edition.* Containing nearly 500 unpublished Letters. Edited, with a NEW LIFE, Introductions and Notes, by REV. WHITWELL ELWIN. Portraits 8vo. (*In the Press.*)

PORTER'S (REV. J. L.) Five Years in Damascus. With Travels to Palmyra, Lebanon and other Scripture Sites. Map and Woodcuts. 2 Vols. Post 8vo. 21s.

——— Handbook for Syria and Palestine: including an Account of the Geography, History, Antiquities, and Inhabitants of these Countries, the Peninsula of Sinai, Edom, and the Syrian Desert. Maps. 2 Vols. Post 8vo. 24s.

PRAYER-BOOK (ILLUSTRATED), with Borders, Initials, Vignettes, &c. Edited, with Notes, by REV. THOS. JAMES. Medium 8vo. 18s. cloth; 31s. 6d. calf; 36s. morocco.

PUSS IN BOOTS. With 12 Illustrations. By OTTO SPECKTER. 16mo. 1s. 6d. or Coloured, 2s. 6d.

QUARTERLY REVIEW (THE). 8vo. 6s.

RAMBLES among the Turkomans and Bedaweens of the Syrian Deserts. Post 8vo. 10s. 6d.

RANKE'S (LEOPOLD) History of the Popes of Rome during the 16th and 17th Centuries. Translated from the German by SARAH AUSTIN. 3 Vols. 8vo. 30s.

RAWLINSON'S (REV. GEORGE) Herodotus. A New English Version. Edited with Notes and Essays. Assisted by SIR HENRY RAWLINSON and SIR J. G. WILKINSON. *Second Edition.* Maps and Woodcut. 4 Vols. 8vo. 48s.

——— Five Great Monarchies of the Ancient World, Chaldæa, Assyria, Media, Babylonia, and Persia. With Maps and 650 Illustrations. 4 Vols. 8vo. 16s. each.

——— Historical Evidences of the truth of the Scripture Records stated anew. *Second Edition.* 8vo. 14s.

REED'S (E. J.) Practical Treatise on Shipbuilding in Iron and Steel. With 250 Illustrations. 8vo. (*In the Press.*)

REJECTED ADDRESSES (THE). By JAMES AND HORACE SMITH. Fcap. 8vo. 1s.

RENNIE'S (D. F.) British Arms in Peking, 1860; Kagosima, 1862. Post 8vo. 12s.

——————— Peking and the Pekingese: Being a Narrative of the First Year of the British Embassy in China. Illustrations. 2 Vols. Post 8vo. 24s.

——————— Story of Bhotan and the Dooar War; including Sketches of a Residence in the Himalayas and Visit to Bhotan in 1865. Map and Woodcut. Post 8vo. 12s.

REYNOLDS' (SIR JOSHUA) Life and Times. Commenced by C. R. LESLIE, R.A., continued and concluded by TOM TAYLOR. Portraits and Illustrations. 2 Vols. 8vo. 42s.

——— Descriptive Catalogue of his Works. With Notices of their present owners and localities. By TOM TAYLOR and CHARLES W. FRANKS. With Illustrations. Fcap. 4to. (*In the Press.*)

RICARDO'S (DAVID) Political Works. With a Notice of his Life and Writings. By J. R. M'CULLOCH. *New Edition.* 8vo. 16s.

RIPA'S (FATHER) Memoirs during Thirteen Years' Residence at the Court of Peking. From the Italian. Post 8vo. 2s.

ROBERTSON'S (CANON) History of the Christian Church, from the Apostolic Age to the Death of Boniface VIII., A.D. 1122—1304. 3 Vols. 8vo.

ROBINSON'S (REV. DR.) Biblical Researches in Palestine and the Adjacent Regions; a Journal of Travels in 1838 and 1852. *Third Edition.* Maps. 3 Vols. 8vo. 42s.

———— Physical Geography of the Holy Land. Post 8vo. 10s. 6d.

ROME (STUDENT'S HISTORY OF). FROM THE EARLIEST TIMES TO THE ESTABLISHMENT OF THE EMPIRE. By DEAN LIDDELL. Woodcuts. Post 8vo. 7s. 6d.

———— (SMALLER HISTORY OF). By WM. SMITH, LL.D. Woodcuts. 16mo. 3s. 6d.

ROWLAND'S (DAVID) Manual of the English Constitution; Its Rise, Growth, and Present State. Post 8vo. 10s. 6d.

———— Laws of Nature the Foundation of Morals. Post 8vo. 6s.

RUNDELL'S (MRS.) Domestic Cookery, adapted for Private Families. *New Edition.* Woodcuts. Fcap. 8vo. 5s.

RUSSELL'S (RUTHERFURD) History of the Heroes of Medicine. Portraits. 8vo. 14s.

RUXTON'S (GEORGE F.) Travels in Mexico; with Adventures among the Wild Tribes and Animals of the Prairies and Rocky Mountains. Post 8vo. 3s. 6d.

SALE'S (SIR ROBERT) Brigade in Affghanistan. With an Account of the Defence of Jellalabad. By REV. G. R. GLEIG. Post 8vo. 2s.

SALLESBURY'S (EDWARD) "Children of the Lake." A Poem. Fcap. 8vo. 4s. 6d.

SANDWITH'S (HUMPHRY) Siege of Kars. Post 8vo. 3s. 6d.

SCOTT'S (G. GILBERT) Secular and Domestic Architecture, Present and Future. 8vo. 9s.

———— (Master of Baliol) University Sermons. Post 8vo. 8s. 6d.

SCROPE'S (G. P.) Geology and Extinct Volcanoes of Central France. Illustrations. Medium 8vo. 30s.

SHAW'S (T. B.) Manual of English Literature. Edited, with Notes and Illustrations, by DR. WM. SMITH. Post 8vo. 7s. 6d.

———— Specimens of English Literature. Selected from the Chief Writers. Edited by WM. SMITH, LL.D. Post 8vo. 7s. 6d.

SHIRLEY (EVELYN P.) on Deer and Deer Parks, or some Account of English Parks, with Notes on the Management of Deer. Illustrations. 4to. 21s.

SIERRA LEONE; Described in Letters to Friends at Home. By A LADY. Post 8vo. 3s. 6d.

SIMMONS (CAPT. T. F.) on the Constitution and Practice of Courts-Martial; with a Summary of the Law of Evidence. *Sixth and Revised Edition.* 8vo. (*In the Press.*)

SMITH'S (REV. A. C.) Attractions of the Nile and its Banks. A Journal of Travels in Egypt and Nubia. Woodcuts. 2 Vols. Post 8vo.

SOUTH'S (JOHN F.) Household Surgery; or, Hints on Emergencies. *Seventeenth Thousand.* Woodcuts. Fcp. 8vo. 4s. 6d.

SMILES' (SAMUEL) Lives of British Engineers; from the Earliest Period to the Present Time, with an account of their Principal Works; including a History of the Invention and Introduction of the Steam Engine. With 9 Portraits and 400 Illustrations. 4 Vols. 8vo. 21s. each.

—— Lives of George and Robert Stephenson. With Portraits and Illustrations. Medium 8vo. 21s. Or *Popular Edition*, with Woodcuts. Post 8vo. 6s.

—— Lives of Boulton and Watt. With Portraits and Illustrations. Medium 8vo. 21s.

—— Lives of Brindley and the Early Engineers. With Portrait and 50 Woodcuts. Post 8vo. 6s.

—— Life of Telford. With a History of Roads and Travelling in England. Woodcuts. Post 8vo. 6s.

—— Self-Help. With Illustrations of Character and Conduct. Post 8vo. 6s. Or in French. 5s.

—— Industrial Biography: Iron-Workers and Tool Makers. A sequel to "Self-Help." Post 8vo. 6s.

—— Huguenots in England and Ireland: their Settlements, Churches and Industries. *Third Thousand*. 8vo. 10s.

—— Workmen's Earnings—Savings—and Strikes. Fcap. 8vo. 1s. 6d.

SOMERVILLE'S (MARY) Physical Geography. *Fifth Edition*. Portrait. Post 8vo. 9s.

—— Connexion of the Physical Sciences. *Ninth Edition*. Woodcuts. Post 8vo. 9s.

—— Molecular and Microscopic Science. Illustrations. 2 Vols. Post 8vo. (*In the Press*.)

SOUTHEY'S (ROBERT) Book of the Church. *Seventh Edition*. Post 8vo. 7s. 6d.

—— Lives of Bunyan and Cromwell. Post 8vo. 2s.

SPECKTER'S (OTTO) Puss in Boots. With 12 Woodcuts. Square 12mo. 1s. 6d. plain, or 2s. 6d. coloured.

STANLEY'S (DEAN) Sinai and Palestine. Map. 8vo. 14s.

—— Bible in the Holy Land; being Extracts from the above Work. Woodcuts, Fcap. 8vo, 2s. 6d.

—— St. Paul's Epistles to the Corinthians. With Dissertations and Notes. 8vo. 18s.

—— History of the Eastern Church. Plans. 8vo. 12s.

—— Jewish Church. 2 Vols. 8vo. 16s. each.

—— Historical Memorials of Canterbury. Woodcuts. Post 8vo. 7s. 6d.

—— Memorials of Westminster Abbey. Illustrations. 8vo. 18s.

—— Sermons in the East, 8vo. 9s.

—— on Evangelical and Apostolical Teaching. Post 8vo. 7s. 6d.

—— ADDRESSES AND CHARGES OF BISHOP STANLEY. With Memoir. 8vo. 10s. 6d.

SMITH'S (Dr. Wm.) Dictionary of the Bible; its Antiquities, Biography, Geography, and Natural History. Illustrations. 3 Vols. 8vo. 105s.
——— Concise Bible Dictionary, for Families and Students. Illustrations. Medium 8vo. 21s.
——— Smaller Bible Dictionary, for Schools and Young Persons. Illustrations. Post 8vo. 7s. 6l.
——— Dictionary of Christian Antiquities : from the Times of the Apostles to the Age of Charlemagne. Illustrations. Medium. 8vo. (In preparation.)
——— Biblical Atlas. Folio. (In preparation.)
——— Greek and Roman Antiquities. Woodcuts. 8vo. 42s.
——— Greek and Roman Biography and Mythology. Woodcuts. 3 Vols. 8vo. 5l. 15s. 6d.
——— Greek and Roman Geography. Woodcuts. 2 Vols. 8vo. 80s.
——— Classical Atlas. Folio. (In preparation.)
——— Classical Dictionary, for the Higher Forms. With 750 Woodcuts. 8vo. 18s.
——— Smaller Classical Dictionary. With 200 Woodcuts. Crown 8vo. 7s. 6d.
——— Smaller Dictionary of Greek and Roman Antiquities. With 200 Woodcuts. Crown 8vo. 7s. 6d.
——— Copious and Critical English-Latin Dictionary. 8vo and 12mo. (Nearly Ready.)
——— Complete Latin English Dictionary. With Tables of the Roman Calendar, Measures, Weights, and Money. 8vo. 21s.
——— Smaller Latin-English Dictionary. 12mo. 7s. 6d.
——— Latin-English Vocabulary; for Phædrus, Cornelius Nepos, and Cæsar. 12mo. 3s. 6d.
——— Principia Latina—Part I. A Grammar, Delectus, and Exercise Book, with Vocabularies. Sixth Edition. 12mo. 3s. 6d.
——————— Part II. A Reading-book of Mythology, Geography, Roman Antiquities, and History. With Notes and Dictionary. Third Edition. 12mo. 3s. 6d.
——————— Part III. A Latin Poetry Book. Hexameters and Pentameters; Eclog. Ovidianæ; Latin Prosody, &c. Second Edition. 12mo. 3s. 6l.
——————— Part IV. Latin Prose Composition. Rules of Syntax, with Examples, Explanations of Synonyms, and Exercises on the Syntax. Second Edition. 12mo. 3s. 6d.
——————— Part V. Short Tales and Anecdotes for Translation into Latin. 12mo. 3s.
——— Student's Latin Grammar for the Higher Forms. Post 8vo. 6s.
——— Smaller Latin Grammar, for the Middle and Lower Forms. 12mo. 3s. 6d.
——— Initia Græca, Part I. An Introduction to Greek; comprehending Grammar, Delectus, and Exercise-book. With Vocabularies. 12mo. 3s. 6d.
——— Initia Græca, Part II. A Reading Book. Containing Short Stories, Anecdotes, Fables, Mythology, and Grecian History. Arranged in a systematic Progression, with a Lexicon. 12mo. 3s. 6d.
——— Initia Græca, Part III. Greek Prose Composition. Containing the Rules of Syntax, with copious Examples and Exercises. 12mo. (In preparation.)

SMITH'S (Dr. Wm.) Student's Greek Grammar for the Higher Forms. By Professor Curtius. Post 8vo. 6s.
———— Smaller Greek Grammar for the Middle and Lower Forms. 12mo. 3s. 6d.
———— Smaller History of England. With Illustrations. 16mo. 3s. 6d.
———— History of Greece. With Illustrations. 16mo. 3s. 6d.
———— History of Rome. With Illustrations. 16mo. 3s. 6d.
———— Classical Mythology. With Translations from the Ancient Poets. Illustrations. 12mo. 3s. 6d.
———— Scripture History. With Woodcuts. 16mo. (In preparation.)
STUDENT'S HUME. A History of England from the Invasion of Julius Cæsar to the Revolution of 1688. By David Hume. Corrected and continued to 1858. Woodcuts. Post 8vo. 7s. 6d.
*** Questions on the above Work, 12mo. 2s.
———— HISTORY OF FRANCE; from the Earliest Times to the Establishment of the Second Empire, 1852. By W. H. Pearson, M.A. Woodcuts. Post 8vo. 7s. 6d.
———— HISTORY OF GREECE; from the Earliest Times to the Roman Conquest. With the History of Literature and Art. By Wm. Smith, LL.D. Woodcuts. Crown 8vo. 7s. 6d.
*** Questions on the above Work, 12mo. 2s.
———— HISTORY OF ROME; from the Earliest Times to the Establishment of the Empire. With the History of Literature and Art. By Dean Liddell. Woodcuts. Crown 8vo. 7s. 6d.
———— GIBBON; an Epitome of the Decline and Fall of the Roman Empire. Incorporating the Researches of Recent Commentators. Woodcuts. Post 8vo. 7s. 6d.
———— OLD TESTAMENT HISTORY; from the Creation to the Return of the Jews from Captivity. Maps and Woodcuts. Post 8vo. 7s. 6d.
———— NEW TESTAMENT HISTORY. With an Introduction connecting the History of the Old and New Testaments. Maps and Woodcuts. Post 8vo. 7s. 6d.
———— BLACKSTONE: a Systematic Abridgment of the Entire Commentaries. By R. Malcolm Kerr, LL.D. Post 8vo. 7s. 6d.
———— MANUAL OF ANCIENT GEOGRAPHY. By Rev. W. L. Bevan, M.A. Woodcuts. Post 8vo. 7s. 6d.
———— MODERN GEOGRAPHY. By Rev. W. L. Bevan. Woodcuts. Post 8vo. (In the Press.)
———— ECCLESIASTICAL HISTORY. Containing the History of the Christian Church from the Close of the New Testament Canon to the Reformation. Post 8vo. (In preparation.)
———— MORAL PHILOSOPHY. With Quotations and References. By William Fleming, D.D. Post 8vo. 7s.6d.
———— ENGLISH LANGUAGE. By Geo. P. Marsh. Post 8vo. 7s. 6d.
———— ENGLISH LITERATURE. By T. B. Shaw, M.A. Post 8vo. 7s. 6d.
———— SPECIMENS OF ENGLISH LITERATURE. Selected from the Chief Writers. By Thomas B. Shaw, M.A. Post 8vo. 7s. 6d.

STANHOPE'S (EARL) History of England, from the Peace of
Utrecht to the Peace of Versailles, 1713-81. *Library Edition.* 7 vols.
8vo. 93s. Or *Popular Edition.* 7 Vols. Post 8vo. 5s. each.
——————— British India, from its Origin till the Peace of
1783. Post 8vo. 3s. 6d.
——————— "Forty-Five;" a Narrative of the Rebellion in
Scotland. Post 8vo. 3s.
——————— Spain under Charles the Second. Post 8vo. 6s. 6d.
——————— Historical and Critical Essays. Post 8vo. 3s. 6d.
——————— Life of Belisarius. Post 8vo. 10s. 6d.
——————— Condé. Post 8vo. 3s. 6d.
——————— William Pitt. With Extracts from his MS.
Papers. Portraits. 4 Vols. Post 8vo. 24s.
——————— Miscellanies. Post 8vo. 5s. 6d.
——————— Story of Joan of Arc. Fcap. 8vo. 1s.
ST. JOHN'S (CHARLES) Wild Sports and Natural History of the
Highlands. Post 8vo. 3s. 6d.
——————— (BAYLE) Adventures in the Libyan Desert and the
Oasis of Jupiter Ammon. Woodcuts. Post 8vo. 2s.
STEPHENSONS' (GEORGE and ROBERT) Lives. By SAMUEL
SMILES. With Portraits and 70 Illustrations. Medium 8vo. 21s.
Or *Popular Edition* with Woodcuts. Post 8vo. 6s.
STOTHARD'S (THOS.) Life. With Personal Reminiscences.
By Mrs. BRAY. With Portrait and 60 Woodcuts. 4to. 21s.
STREET'S (G. E.) Gothic Architecture in Spain. From Personal
Observations during several journeys through that country. Illustrations. Medium 8vo. 50s.
SULLIVAN'S (SIR EDWARD) Princes, Warriors, and Statesmen
of India; an Historical Narrative of the most Important Events, from the Invasion of Mahmoud of Ghizni to that of Nadir Shah. 8vo. 12s.
SUMNER (GEORGE HENRY), M.A. Principles at Stake, being
Essays on the Church Questions of the day. By various Writers. 8vo.
(*In the Press.*)
SWIFT'S (JONATHAN) Life, Letters, Journals, and Works. By
JOHN FORSTER. 8vo. (*In Preparation.*)
SYBEL'S (VON) History of Europe during the French Revolution,
1789—1795. Translated from the German. By WALTER C. PERRY.
Vols. 1 & 2. 8vo. 24s.
SYME'S (PROFESSOR) Principles of Surgery. *5th Edition.* 8vo. 12s.
TAIT'S (BISHOP) Dangers and Safeguards of Modern Theology,
containing Suggestions to the Theological Student under Present Difficulties. 8vo. 9s.
TAYLOR'S (HENRY) Notes from Life—on Money, Humility and
Independence, Wisdom, Choice in Marriage, Children, and Life Poetic. Fcap. 8vo. 2s.
THOMSON'S (ARCHBISHOP) Sermons, Preached at Lincoln's Inn.
8vo. 10s. 6d.
——————— Life in the Light of God's Word. Post 8vo. 6s.
THREE-LEAVED MANUAL OF FAMILY PRAYER; arranged
so as to save the trouble of turning the Pages backwards and forwards.
Royal 8vo. 2s.
TREMENHEERE (H. S.); The Franchise a Privilege and not a Right,
proved by the Political Experience of the Ancients. Fcap. 8vo. 2s. 6d.
TRISTRAM'S (H. B.) Great Sahara, or Wanderings South of the
Atlas Mountains. Map and Illustrations. Post 8vo. 15s.

32 LIST OF WORKS PUBLISHED BY MR. MURRAY.

TWISS' (HORACE) Life of Lord Chancellor Eldon, with Selections from his Correspondence. Portrait. *Third Edition.* 2 Vols. Post 8vo. 21s.

TYTLER'S (PATRICK FRASER) Memoirs. By REV. J. W. BURGON, M.A. 8vo. 9s.

VAMBERY'S (ARMINIUS) Travels in Central Asia, from Teheran across the Turkoman Desert on the Eastern Shore of the Caspian to Khiva, Bokhara, and Samarcand in 1863. Map and Illustrations. 8vo. 21s.

VAN LENNEP (HENRY J.) Missionary Travels in Little Known Parts of Asia Minor. With Map and Illustrations. 2 Vols. Post 8vo. *(In preparation.)*

VAUGHAN'S (REV. DR.) Sermons preached in Harrow School. 8vo. 10s. 6d.

WAAGEN'S (DR.) Treasures of Art in Great Britain. Being an Account of the Chief Collections of Paintings, Sculpture, Manuscripts, Miniatures, &c. &c., in this Country. Obtained from Personal Inspection during Visits to England. 4 Vols. 8vo.

WELLINGTON'S (THE DUKE OF) Despatches during his various Campaigns. 8 Vols. 8vo. 21s. each.

————— Supplementary Despatches. Vols. I. to XII. 8vo. 20s. each.

————— Civil and Political Correspondence. Vols. I. to III. 8vo. 20s. each.

————— Selections from Despatches and General Orders. 8vo. 18s.

————— Speeches in Parliament. 2 Vols. 8vo. 42s.

WHITE'S (HENRY) Massacre of St. Bartholomew. Preceded by a History of the Religious Wars in the Reign of Charles IX. Based on a Personal Examination of Documents in the Archives of France. With Illustrations. 8vo. 16s.

WHYMPER'S (FREDERICK) Travels and Adventures in Alaska and on the River Yukon, the Russian Territory, now ceded to the United States, and Visits to other parts of the North Pacific. With Illustrations. 8vo. *(In preparation.)*

WILKINSON'S (SIR J. G.) Popular Account of the Private Life, Manners, and Customs of the Ancient Egyptians. With 500 Woodcuts. 2 Vols. Post 8vo. 12s.

WILSON'S (BISHOP DANIEL) Life, Letters, and Journals. By Rev. JOSIAH BATEMAN. *Second Edition.* Illustrations. Post 8vo. 9s.

————— (GEN^{L.} SIR ROBERT) Secret History of the French Invasion of Russia, and Retreat of the French Army, 1812. *Second Edition.* 8vo. 15s.

————— Private Diary of Travels, Personal Services, and Public Events, during Missions and Employments in Spain, Sicily, Turkey, Russia, Poland, Germany, &c. 1812-14. 2 Vols. 8vo. 26s.

————— Autobiographical Memoirs. Containing an Account of his Early Life down to the Peace of Tilsit. Portrait. 2 Vols. 8vo. 26s.

WOOD (SIR W. P.) On the Continuity of Scripture, as Declared by the Testimony of Our Lord and of the Evangelists and Apostles. *Second Edition.* Post 8vo. 6s.

WORDSWORTH'S (ARCHDEACON) Journal of a Tour in Athens and Attica. *Third Edition.* Plates. Post 8vo. 8s. 6d.

————— Pictorial, Descriptive, and Historical Account of Greece. *New and Cheaper Edition.* With 600 Woodcuts. Royal 8vo.

BRADBURY, EVANS, AND CO., PRINTERS, WHITEFRIARS.

www.ingramcontent.com/pod-product-compliance
Lightning Source LLC
Chambersburg PA
CBHW051859300426
44117CB00006B/459